DISCARDED

T3-BUL-889

Exiles, Allies, Rebels

Exiles, Allies, Rebels

Brazil's Indianist Movement, Indigenist Politics, and the Imperial Nation-State

David Treece

Contributions in Latin American Studies, Number 16

GREENWOOD PRESS
Westport, Connecticut • London

Library of Congress Cataloging-in-Publication Data

Treece, Dave.
    Exiles, allies, rebels : Brazil's indianist movement, indigenist politics, and the imperial
nation-state / by David Treece.
        p. cm.—(Contributions in Latin American studies, ISSN 1054–6790 ; no. 16)
    Includes bibliographical references and index.
    ISBN 0–313–31125–0 (alk. paper)
        1. Indians of South America—Brazil—Politics and government.   2. Indians of South
America—Brazil—Government relations.   3. Indians of South America—Cultural
assimilation—Brazil.   4. Social movements—Brazil—History.   5. Indianists—Brazil.
    6. Brazil—Politics and government.   7. Brazil—Race relations.   8. Brazil—Social
policy.   I. Title.   II.   Series.
F2519.3.P58 T73   2000
981′.00498—dc21   99–049049

British Library Cataloguing in Publication Data is available.

Copyright © 2000 by David Treece

All rights reserved. No portion of this book may be
reproduced, by any process or technique, without the
express written consent of the publisher.

Library of Congress Catalog Card Number: 99–049049
ISBN: 0–313–31125–0
ISSN: 1054–6790

First published in 2000

Greenwood Press, 88 Post Road West, Westport, CT 06881
An imprint of Greenwood Publishing Group, Inc.
www.greenwood.com

Printed in the United States of America

The paper used in this book complies with the
Permanent Paper Standard issued by the National
Information Standards Organization (Z39.48–1984).

10 9 8 7 6 5 4 3 2 1

For Angela

Contents

Acknowledgments

I am indebted to many people, without whose help and support this book could not have been completed: to Plínio Doyle, John Hemming, Carlos Moreira de Araújo Neto, and Berta Ribeiro for invaluable bibliographical suggestions and assistance; to Elmar Pereira de Mello, Hilda White Rössle, Nicolau Sevcenko, and Cristina Carletti, for their interest, encouragement, and hospitality during successive stays in Brazil since 1984; to the British Academy, for the granting of a doctoral studentship to enable me to complete my initial research on this theme; to Glenys Dawkins, for her unfailing solidarity and companionship throughout the years of my doctoral research; to my friend, colleague, and former doctoral supervisor, John Gledson, for teaching me so many things and for his comments on the final draft of this book; to the staff of the International Secretariat of Survival International, London, for enabling me to gain some understanding of the struggles that tribal peoples continue to face today; to those students of King's College London whose participation in courses I have been fortunate enough to teach has stimulated me regularly to reflect on, and reassess, my own views on the subject of this book; and to Angela Dierks, for seeing me through the final stages of this project.

Translations of textual quotations are my own. For the sake of economy the original Portuguese has been retained only in the case of poetry or where matters of linguistic or stylistic importance require it. The Portuguese orthography follows that of the editions cited.

Introduction

INVENTING A TRADITION?

The argument of this book rests on a paradox. During the four centuries between Brazil's conquest in 1500 and the beginning of republican rule, the indigenous tribal population of the territory suffered a destructive process of genocidal proportions, falling from some 5 million or more to 100,000 by the turn of the twentieth century.[1] This fact, however, stands in stark contradiction to the Indians' place within the nationalist tradition of thinking in Brazil, whose integrationist mythology has repeatedly invoked their assimilation into the dominant society as the touchstone for a history of bloodless political, social, and economic integration. The concepts of "racial democracy" and "luso-tropicalism," the neocolonialist ideologies of Getúlio Vargas's "March to the West" and of the fascist Integralist movement, indeed, the entire notion of a uniquely Brazilian political culture of "conciliation,"[2] have all drawn heavily on the myth of an assimilated indigenous identity as the ethnic cornerstone of Brazil's cultural self-image, the symbolic cement of a process of cordial social and racial collaboration in the building of the nation.

As the latest phase in the integration of territories, markets, and labor was unleashed in Amazonia by Brazil's post-1964 military regime, the Indians' pivotal role in legitimating this process was reasserted by the state indigenist agency, FUNAI, whose second president, Costa Cavalcanti, announced in 1969: "We do not want a marginalized Indian, what we want is a producing Indian, one integrated into the process of national development."[3] Indeed, it was precisely on the assumption of a convergence of interests, Indian and non-Indian, in Brazil's history of national integration, that in 1970 the United Nations Educational, Scientific, and Cultural Organization (UNESCO) commissioned anthropologist Darcy Ribeiro to write a celebratory account of the incorporation of the indigenous communities into the wider society. However, the result of Ribeiro's studies, *Os Índios e a civilização* (The Indians and Civilization), turned his and his sponsors' expectations upside down, exposing the mythology of integration as a mask for social and cultural disintegration, the shattering of the collective identity of the tribal communities, and the dissolution of alienated individuals into the anonymity of the dominant society:

In fact, we can say of all the indigenous groups about which we obtained reliable information that they were not assimilated into the national society as an indistinguishable part of it. Contrary to that expectation, the majority of them have been exterminated and those who have survived remain Indian: no longer in their habits and customs, but in their self-identification as peoples distinct from the Brazilian people and victims of the latter's domination. . . . Our study, despite referring only to the twentieth century, leads to another interpretation, according to which there was no assimilation of ethnic groups, but the absorption of stray individuals, while those ethnic groups disappeared or transformed themselves in order to survive.[4]

Despite a new Constitution affirming the indigenous peoples' right to cultural diversity and recognizing their land claims as "original," predating the existence of the Brazilian state, the return to civilian rule from 1985 did not, in practice, diminish the assaults on those rights from private and state interests, which remained intent on sacrificing the Indians' territorial security and self-determination to the developmentalist demands of a geo-politics of regional integration.[5] After 500 years, indigenous cultures, identities, and lives are compelled to go on and on struggling for their survival or are shattered and dispersed forever, an awful reminder that nation-states are not born spontaneously of willing parents but must be continually and savagely bludgeoned into existence.

It is all the more remarkable, then, that during the crucial years of the Brazilian nation-state's emergence and consolidation, from the late 1700s to the last quarter of the nineteenth century, its writers, artists, and intellectuals should have celebrated the history and traditions of the Indian peoples in the country's most coherent, durable, and influential movement of cultural nationalism before Modernism. After a first wave of interest in the theme in the late eighteenth century, which produced three epic poems, Indianism went on to become the dominant expression of Romanticism in Brazil following independence. Two leading Romantics, the poet Gonçalves Dias and the novelist José de Alencar, established their reputations with Indianist works, which were among the first Brazilian literary publications to enjoy any significant commercial success. Many of the century's other important writers contributed in some way to the movement, from the "father" of Brazilian Romanticism, Gonçalves de Magalhães, to the country's greatest novelist, Machado de Assis.

More than this, under the direct patronage of the Emperor, Pedro II, Indianism was a major pillar of the Empire's project of state-building, the single most important object of artistic and political reflection to exercise the minds of its intellectual elite for more than half a century. Such was the persistence of the Romantic image of the Indian into the bourgeois culture of the Belle Époque, even as late as the second decade of the twentieth century, that progressive intellectuals and Modernist poets seeking to break with tradition felt it necessary to declare war, metaphorically at least, on the most famous imaginary hero of all, the Guarani Indian Peri.[6] The Indianist literature of the eighteenth and nineteenth centuries stands as a monument to a compelling irony: as the heroic protagonist of scores of novels, poems, plays, paintings, and ethnographic studies, mourned or celebrated, as exile, ally, or rebel, the Indian became the embodiment of the very nationalism that was engaged in his own annihilation.

Far from being lost on the Indianist writers themselves, as I shall argue, that irony was, in fact, central to the variety of reflections they generated on the legacy of colonial rule for the postindependence dispensation of the Brazilian nation-state, not least as it affected the disfranchised, nonwhite sectors of society: the indigenous communities themselves, the black slaves, and the racially diverse, propertyless free population. The hitherto neglected fact that Indianism was simultaneously an arena of sociopolitical debate as well as a purely artistic movement is also a reminder of how mistaken it would be to consider culture and politics as discrete spheres of activity in nineteenth-century Brazil, when the notion of a professionalized and autonomous community of artist-intellectuals was still a problematic one. Still less can one take for granted the homogeneous character of the literary community as a simple expression of the mentality of the Imperial elite when, as we shall see, Indianist writing reveals a diverse and often contradictory spectrum of ideological perspectives reflecting a range of social backgrounds and relationships to the Imperial state.

The hypothesis upon which this book's investigation of the Indianist movement rests is that these three phenomena—the history of official indigenist policy, the contradictory sociopolitical identity of the Brazilian nation-state, and the construction of a fictional Indian in the national imaginary—are intimately bound up with one another and that they share a common core: the preoccupation with integration. This obviously calls for a methodological approach adequate to the cultural-historical field within which the phenomenon of Indianism was constructed. With one or two exceptions, previous work on the subject has tended to adopt an exclusively "literary" focus, as if the historical location and meaning of literary works derived primarily from their reference to each other as part of an autonomous, discursive tradition or system of circulating texts and mythologies.

In the 1970s, following some early surveys of the literature offering little in the way of analytical insights, Affonso Romano de Sant'Anna and Regina Zilberman applied structuralist approaches to Alencar's fiction, typically the chief or exclusive focus of most subsequent work.[7] In the following decade, David Haberly's *Three Sad Races: Racial Identity and National Consciousness in Brazilian Literature* (1983) included chapters on Gonçalves Dias and Alencar, with a shift of emphasis toward the contribution of Indianism to the cultural imaginary and mythology of national identity. Haberly's central themes, applied in a somewhat reductionist fashion to his material, were the notion of a perennial Brazilian search for the Lost Eden and the concept of "whitening": a central plank of Brazil's particular brand of racist ideology since the second half of the nineteenth century. As thoroughly examined in Thomas Skidmore's *Black into*

White: Race and Nationality in Brazilian Thought (1974), "whitening" signifies the denial of African and indigenous ethnicity, both through individual aspirations to lighter skin color, and through official, eugenicist immigration policies aimed at Europeanizing the nation's complexion. David Brookshaw's *Paradise Betrayed: Brazilian Literature of the Indian* (1988), as the title suggests, adopted a similar mythical typology to Haberly's and is also concerned with the literature as an evolving discourse on issues of race and identity but is a rather more nuanced and detailed analysis of the Indianist tradition as a whole. Apart from my own doctoral thesis ("The Indian in Brazilian literature and ideas [1500-1945]," University of Liverpool, 1987), it was also the only attempt hitherto at a global study of this kind, including a number of little-known regionalist texts as well as the contemporary literature on the theme.

From the end of the decade, a number of studies took the analysis of myth in a new direction: exploring the sexual politics of *Iracema* and *O Guarani*, Regina Zilberman, Ria Lemaire, and Doris Sommer all deconstructed the Indianist representation of women and male-female relations in order to reveal a profoundly gendered discourse on the processes of colonization and nation-building.[8] Sommer's *Foundational Fictions* was alone, however, in contextualizing Alencar's literary project within the contemporary cultural and political worlds of nineteenth-century Brazil; indeed, she includes a brief discussion of the Imperial politics of Conciliation that, in an essay of 1986, I had cited as one example of how Romantic Indianism might be historicized and periodized as a cultural-literary movement, rather than treated as a homogeneous and autonomous discursive tradition.[9] What this rather exceptional instance in Sommer's essay highlights, though, is how rarely the critical literature on Brazilian Indianism, especially outside Brazil, has contemplated its subject as a living, historical intervention in the social milieu that its writers inhabited, how easily it has ignored the active symbiosis between intellectual and political life that, as Sommer's Introduction underscores, so characterized nineteenth-century Latin America. The ease with which the text has been abstracted from the context into a realm of pure, self-referring discourse is matched by the unanimity with which (excepting Brookshaw's study) the critical literature has stubbornly limited its analysis of "Indianism" to a single author, taking it for granted that Alencar can be considered adequately representative of a movement that extended over half a century and produced at least twenty writers.

The aim of this book, then, is to offer, unapologetically, a different contribution to the understanding of the Indianist phenomenon that both treats it as a cultural and intellectual movement in dialogue with itself and with the wider political and ideological currents of its time and seeks to rehistoricize it, to recognize in it the multiple and often contradictory voices of a collective discourse as well as of individual authors consciously intervening in the social process. In arriving at this critical standpoint, I have been encouraged by a number of shorter, individual studies on Indianism from within Brazil, in particular, Antonio Candido's essays on *O Uraguay* and *Caramuru* in *Literatura e sociedade* and *Vários Escritos*, Nelson Werneck Sodré's "As razões do indianismo; O indianismo e a sociedade brasileira" from his *História da literatura brasileira*,

Silviano Santiago's essays, "Roteiro para uma Leitura Intertextual de *Ubira-jara*" and "Liderança e Hierarquia em Alencar," and Walnice Nogueira Gal-vão's "Indianismo Revisitado," vital, above all, because it recommends a re-evaluation of Romantic Indianism as part of a complete study of the literature on Indians, including the most recent developments.

The historicist approach adopted here should not be confused, however, with a mechanical or reductionist attitude to the text; I do not propose to undertake a purely "sociological" reading of the textual material as if it were a documentary reflection of given social realities that are taken for granted a priori. Rather, in the spirit of Antonio Candido's critical method, I aim to question the dichotomy between the social and the aesthetic, the "external" and "internal" dimensions of the literary process, avoiding the treatment of the work of art as a mere epiphe-nomenon of the social world. The social is, instead, best examined as a "factor of artistic construction itself," as a structuring principle internalized in the "very immanence of literary meaning."[10] Accordingly, the reader will find here an ex-pressed concern to integrate the analysis of literary texts with an understanding of the intellectual and social environment in which they were produced and, in particular, with the political and social debates of the period, not least those concerning indigenist policy.

This of itself necessarily leads to a questioning of traditional explanations of Brazil's Indianist movement, which have tended to assume implicitly its isola-tion from political or social realities, as if a simple line could be drawn between the fictional Indian of the Romantic imagination and those tribal communities upon which the Empire declared war repeatedly from its inception. Instead, such explanations have preferred to define Indianism as somehow inauthentic, an invented or imported substitute for a national cultural tradition denied to the country by colonialism. European Romanticism had turned to a medieval golden age or to exotic overseas worlds in the search for national origins or for a conti-nuity with "ancient" cultural values. By analogy, it is argued, the first generation of self-consciously Brazilian artists found a mythological basis for their inde-pendent literature in the colonial or precolonial universe of the Indians. This view of Romantic Indianism as the "invention of a tradition" for the newly liber-ated nation-state was set out by José Guilherme Merquior as follows:

This period of national affirmation required, at the level of the culture of the elites, a mythological complex capable of celebrating the originality of the young fatherland in the face of Europe and the ex-metropolis. At this stage, two factors come into play: Ro-mantic exoticism, encouraged by the Americanism of Chateaubriand and Fenimore Coo-per, and a taste for the remote past; for Amerindian tribal society prior to Discovery was, in fact, our "Middle Ages." The Brazilian Romantics thus discover in Indianism their mythical nourishment reclaimed by Imperial civilization in the adolescence of the Brazil-nation.[11]

Likewise, for Antonio Candido, "Indianism served not only as a mystical and legendary past (in the manner of the folkloric tradition of the Germans, Celts or Scandinavians), but as a historical past, in the manner of the Middle Ages."[12] The Romantics' Indians, it is argued, were essentially Brazilian reincarnations of the European medieval knights, transplanted to the New World complete with all the trappings of the Chivalresque code of comportment and morality.

This interpretation certainly appears to be confirmed by the best-known novel of the movement, Alencar's *O Guarani* (The Guarani Indian), in which the Portuguese colonist Dom Antônio de Mariz describes the Indian hero Peri as "a Portuguese knight in the body of a savage." In Chapter 3, however, I argue that the chivalric worldview defended by Dom Antônio is, in fact, symptomatic of his obsolescence, his incapacity to adapt to the New World. For Alencar, the consolidation of a postcolonial Brazilian culture could be achieved only if the isolationist, medieval mentality of the Portuguese colonist were supplanted or superseded by the "modern" union of Indian and European. Nevertheless, the parallels and similarities with Americanist or Indianist developments within European and North American Romanticism cannot be denied. Alencar himself was obliged to answer accusations that he was a mere imitator of Chateaubriand, the author of *Atala, René*, and *Les Natchez,* or Fenimore Cooper, the creator of *The Last of the Mohicans*:

Brazil, like the United States and any other peoples of America, has a period of conquest, in which the invading race destroys the indigenous race. That struggle presents an analogous character, because of the similarity of the aborigines. Only in Peru and Mexico does it differ.

Thus the Brazilian novelist who seeks the subject of his drama in this period of invasion cannot escape the point of contact with the American writer. But this approximation arises out of history, it is inevitable and is not the result of imitation.[13]

This argument about the status of Brazilian Indianism—whether it was a local copy of a model imported from the dominant metropolitan literature or an original response to analogous historical and cultural circumstances—is thus a long-standing one. It is also part of a wider debate about the question of cultural dependency, which has received a powerful injection of fresh analysis in recent years, in particular from the work of Roberto Schwarz. Schwarz's study of the origins of the Brazilian novel, *Ao vencedor as batatas*, opens with a theoretical essay whose title—"Misplaced Ideas"—has defined the conceptual parameters of much subsequent cultural criticism. Its central feature is the location of a fundamental ideological contradiction that explains the peculiar mentality of the dominant classes in nineteenth-century Brazil: the glaring disparity between the values and principles of postrevolutionary European liberalism as adopted by the Brazilian elite, and the social realities of Imperial Brazil—slavery and patronage—on which their prosperity and well-being depended.[14]

There can be no questioning the influence of European Romanticism and liberal ideology in stimulating Brazilian interest in the Indianist theme. Chapter 2 of this study examines the role of the European philosophical tradition and of a number of key French intellectuals in the emergence of the Indianist movement from the 1830s onward. However, Brazil's postcolonial dependence on external cultural and ideological models for the invention of its national tradition is a woefully inadequate explanation for the peculiar character of Brazilian

Indianism. Other factors are needed to account for the centrality and persistence of such a tradition through sixty years of the Imperial monarchy, and for the variety of texts that shaped its evolution.

By comparison, the Spanish American republics produced relatively few Romantic Indianist texts, although one might have expected that indigenous history and culture would have offered obvious sources for the consolidation of national identity immediately following independence, as in Brazil. But interest in the theme in the Spanish American novel appears to have been sporadic until very late in the century, and Indianism does not occupy an especially privileged place within the republics' tradition of "foundational romances." Isolated examples from the middle of the nineteenth century, such as Gertrudis de Avellanada's *Guatemocín* (1846) and Eligio Ancona's *La cruz y la espada* (1864) and *Los mártires de Anáhuac* (1870), were followed by the better-known cases of Manuel de Jesús Galván's *Enriquillo* (1882) and Clorinda Matto de Turner's *Aves sin nido* (1889), but a consistent body of writing on the theme in Spanish did not appear until the twentieth century, and then in the context of social reformism and revolutionary anti-imperialism.[15]

Doris Sommer has drawn attention to the interest of nineteenth-century Latin Americans, in particular, the Argentine writer and president Domingos Sarmiento, in the work of Fenimore Cooper as a model of New World writing. For Sarmiento, the author of *Facundo: Civilización y barbarie* (1845), Cooper's originality lay in "removing the scene of the events he described from the settled portion of the country to the border land between civilized life and that of the savage, the theater of war for the possession of the soil waged against each other, by the native tribes and the Saxon race."[16] However, in Sarmiento's positivistic vision of Latin American progress there was no room for the racially unfit figure of the rural marginal: "That is why the Land's unproductive consorts, Indians and gauchos so indolently at peace in unredeemed nature, had to be erased from the national project."[17]

Where opposition to Sarmiento's anti-Indian policy of dislocation and extermination did occur, as in the case of Lucio Mansilla, it was partial, exceptional, and ambivalent. The letters collected under the title *Una excursión a los indios ranqueles* and originally published in 1870, following Mansilla's journey into Indian territory, brushed with a kind of cultural relativism that questioned Sarmiento's rigid dichotomy of barbarism and civilization. They also defended an Argentine identity located in the gauchos, Indians, and countrydwellers, yet, according to Nicolas Shumway, Julio Ramos, and others, Mansilla's identification with the Europeanized liberalism of the Buenos Aires upper class prevented him from ever seeing the Indians and gauchos as anything but an Other whose destiny must be one of assimilation and exploitation. Thus, "he ultimately recommends nothing to replace Sarmiento's program of forced assimilation, displacement and annihilation. Mansilla's best alternative is 'to civilize [the gauchos and Indians], make them Christians, and use their muscle for industry, work, and the common defense.'"[18] The other important challenge, meanwhile, to the vision of Sarmiento's *Facundo* during this period, José Hernández's *El gaucho Martín Fierro* (1872), takes the Indian wars as no more than a backdrop to its central concern, the defense of the frontier gaucho, and so reinvigorated a tradition that from early in the century had emerged as the cornerstone of Argentine literary nationalism—the gauchesque genre.[19]

The absence of a self-conscious Romantic Indianist movement as such in postindependence Spanish America may be instructive, especially when placed alongside certain other major political and social factors distinguishing the two halves of the continent. In the first place, Brazil, unlike Spain's former colonies, did not sever its links with the metropolitan power through a sustained military campaign; indeed, it retained a centralized monarchy at the head of the independent nation-state and thereby preserved important dynastic ties with the Portuguese royal family. Second, whereas the Spanish possessions evolved into a number of separate states, perhaps as a legacy of the regional system of colonial administration, the Brazilian state remained a single political entity over 3 million square miles in size and uniting regions of a remarkable ethnic, cultural, geographical, and economic diversity. Lastly, by contrast with the very large Indian populations of, for example, the Andean and Central American republics, with cultural traditions rooted in a rich material civilization, agricultural economy, and complex urban social organization, Brazil's indigenous population was fragmented into relatively small tribal communities adapted to a forest environment and dependent on a nomadic or semi-nomadic hunter-gatherer and horticultural economy. As such, they remained overwhelmingly marginalized from the dominant society, since assimilation could occur only through the piecemeal conquest of individual tribes and the disintegration of their communal subsistence culture.

These combined factors suggest that Indianism may be linked in some way to the unique political and social character of the Brazilian nation-state within postcolonial Latin America and that the roots of the movement's durability and appeal may lie within the structures of Imperial society rather than in a simple desire to emulate the cultural models of European civilization. Nelson Werneck Sodré took an initial step in the direction of an ideological explanation for the phenomenon when he related it to the historical victory of the conservative, slave-owning planter class in the Second Reign of the Empire, following the upheavals of the Regency period:

Indianism represents, in the historical process of Brazilian literature, one of its most characteristic stages, then. It is far from false, as it appears to superficial investigators. It is the manifestation of a society of landlords, with a regime of slave labor, in which there are only the merest outlines of an intermediate class. In this sense, it corresponds fully to the essential features of that society. It is its specific creation. Using old ideas and age-old concepts, it conveys, in nineteenth-century terms and in literary language, all that is most characteristic about the Brazilian milieu.[20]

Unfortunately, while this is an extremely suggestive and valuable starting point, Sodré goes no further in defining the precise nature of the relationship between Indianism and the worldview of the ruling planter and slave-owning class in Imperial Brazil. While his general description is useful in making sense of the

central phase of the movement, with its celebration of Brazil's historical com-
pleteness, its vision of social and racial harmony, it fails to account for the dissident writing of liberals and republicans such as Gonçalves Dias and Bernardo
Guimarães, which marks the beginning and end of Pedro II's Second Reign.

In order to move toward an analysis that can do justice to the dynamic and
complex character of Indianism, one must acknowledge that in Brazil, as in
Europe, Romanticism embraced a variety of contradictory responses to the political and economic upheavals announced by the French and American Revolutions and by their echoes in the rest of the colonial world. On one hand, there
was the complacent Romanticism of Gonçalves de Magalhães and Alencar, pil-
lars of the conservative establishment; their interpretation of Empire as the culmination and completion of the colonial project helped legitimate the post-
ponement of the abolition of slavery and the permanence of the plantation oligarchies as the dominant class, emerging as a victorious, agrarian bourgeoisie
following independence. On the other hand, there were those intellectuals and
artists whose marginalization from the political and economic centers of Imperial life led them to identify with the most oppressed sectors of society, such as
the Indians and the African slaves, and with a bucolic, Rousseauian Romanticism that stood both for the principles of natural freedom and equality and for a
rejection of the narrowly materialist mentality of the new bourgeois order.

Thus, the language of liberalism not only supplied the ruling elite with an
imported rhetoric of civilization and progress, allowing it the illusion of membership of a modern, international bourgeoisie while it presided over an archaic
political and social order that remained essentially that of the ancien régime. It
was also, in many cases, the authentic expression of the preoccupations and aspirations of a dissident, if not revolutionary, current within middle-class Brazilian society and an ideological response to the real conditions suffered by the
majority of the population, that is, political disfranchisement, dispossession, and
marginalization.[21]

The effort to reclaim the ideological authenticity of the liberal Romantic tradition for at least an area of nineteenth-century Brazilian culture has received an
important contribution in the form of Leonardo Fróes's biography of the poet
and minor Indianist Fagundes Varella. For Fróes, Varella's bucolic, often mystical writing, his unconventional, bohemian lifestyle, and his frequent retreats into
the rural isolation of Rio de Janeiro's interior were characteristic of an entire
generation of artists, the "peasant" or "rustic" Romantics, whose provincial,
lower-middle-class origins often set them at odds with the prevailing values of
the Romantic establishment:

With its flights of evasion, the saga of idealized Indians and a more than picturesque
exoticism, this "backwoods" [*caipira*] Romanticism corresponds very, very closely to
the merely literary stimuli absorbed from Europe. But it is likely that it also corresponds
to genuine inclinations, because these are men from the interior, from the countryside,
with well defined rural experiences, that make them what they are. In all of them [in-
cluding the Indianists Gonçalves Dias and Bernardo Guimarães], from one moment to
the next, there is reflected the presence of their common origins. All of them, imbued in
childhood by their direct experience of, their attachment to, and interaction with the

beauty of life, are partners in the credo that nature is holy, harmonious, transcendent, and they form with their lyrics and the examples of their lives, as well as with their individual torments, a kind of sensibility opposed to the sheer extractivist greed of the associates of profit. . . . The bucolic outpourings of backwoods Romanticism are therefore not a hollow poetry counterposed to the pleasure of listening to the exotic songbirds [of literary convention]. There is an ideological basis, generally attenuated or proscribed from the official history of culture, that extends from their bucolicism as a mere refuge to their outright denial of the unpoetic, materialist, filthy, unjust and false life that bourgeois society was imposing on the country.[22]

IMAGES OF EMPIRE

We are now better placed to offer a comprehensive historical account of Brazilian Indianism, no longer simply as the construction of a national cultural tradition based on imported Romantic and liberal models and uniformly defined by the stereotypical figure of the Indian "knight." Rather, the movement presents a complex, evolving series of images that served to conceptualize the actual and possible forms of the Brazilian nation-state from its inception to the end of the nineteenth century. Such an account will have to confront the hitherto unacknowledged fact that the contemporary condition of the Indian was a significant political issue throughout the period, involving historians, statesmen, and writers, including many Indianists, in protracted and often passionate debate. The development of literary Indianism was intimately bound up with the evolution of that debate about the direction of official indigenist policy. At the heart of both processes was a series of ideological and political contradictions that underpinned the construction and consolidation of the Imperial order and its eventual collapse.

The first of those contradictions, identified by Schwarz, among others,[23] was the difficulty of sustaining the modern, civilized values of individual liberty, equality and fraternity in a society economically and politically dominated by a tiny planter elite, a society whose productive relations, even after independence, were based on slavery. This was a society, too, in which the free, unpropertied white and *mestiço* population had no real access to power, no independence of action outside the patronage of the elite, and in which the radical defenders of popular democracy, republicanism, and liberalism were repeatedly crushed or systematically marginalized from the political process.

Second, independence brought with it the centralization of power in the Imperial capital, Rio de Janeiro, against the expectations of the provinces, whose adherence to the anticolonial cause had expressed their hopes of regional autonomy, previously denied by the government in Lisbon. The denial of these regionalist aspirations was only ultimately achieved through the violent repression of the uprisings that marked the 1830s and 1840s, during and immediately after the Regency.

Third, this geographical centralization was matched by the concentration of political power in the hands of the Emperor himself. Although nominally assigned the functions of a "moderating power" in the mold of the British monarchy, adjudicating between the conflicting parliamentary interests of the Liberal and Conservative Parties, Pedro II's exercise of this role was increasingly viewed as arbitrary and authoritarian. As long as the profitability of the agricultural export trade guaranteed the security of the traditional landowning class and marginalized the more progressive, entrepreneurial ambitions of the liberal bourgeoisie, opposition to the Imperial regime remained weak. The 1870s, however, saw a growing impatience with the rigid, archaic structures of the plantation economy, whose dependence on an increasingly expensive and scarce supply of slaves was viewed as an obstacle to Brazil's development along modern, capitalist lines. This impatience was manifested in the reemergence and eventual victory of the abolitionist cause in 1888 and in the overthrow of the monarchy in the following year by the military wing of the republican movement.

The large and varied body of Indianist writing that accompanied these developments, far from representing simply an exotic escape or the search for a national tradition in some lost American paradise, constituted a dramatic, imaginative arena in which those contradictions could be played out. The exclusion of large sectors of Brazilian society from access to economic and political power could be identified with the historical and contemporary marginalization of the tribal communities from the national society. On the other hand, the depiction of imagined alliances with the Indians and their successful integration into white society could provide fictional models for a harmonious nation-state where the conflicts of race, class, and ideology could be absorbed, and the antagonisms between the center of power and the periphery, government and opposition, master and slave, could be held in perfect balance. Indianism carried within it the same ideological contradictions that the intellectual community was forced to swallow and contain in order to accommodate itself within the essentially nonreformist structure of the Empire but that were bound to be thrown up again sooner or later when other pressures began to impinge on the regime. The Indianist "stage," then, can be considered analogous to the "theater of shadows," that "complex play between reality and fiction," the "dialectic of ambiguity" that for José Murilo de Carvalho characterized the dynamic of relations between the political actors under the Empire: the theatrical pretense of the pact between the Emperor and the "barões do café," the fiction of the constitutional regime, of the Crown as the moderating power, of political representation, liberalism and of a "civilized" Brazil.[24]

Chapter 1 of this study examines the precedents for the Indianist movement in the literary epics of the late eighteenth century. Here already one can witness the tensions between the libertarian ideas of Enlightenment philosophy, that were themselves informed by the positive reappraisal of the "natural" societies of the Amerindian world, and the concern with the integrity of Empire, at this stage still the Portuguese colonial empire. However, this first chapter also seeks to correct the misconception that the eighteenth-century epics amounted to a cryptonationalist precursor of Romantic Indianism. Instead, it argues that they were the expression of specific historical circumstances, namely, the struggle of the colonial regime to offset the crisis that arose out of the decline of the mining export economy. In order to launch its protocapitalist agricultural development strategy for Amazonia, the regime had to confront two obstacles to the integration of the indigenous population into the wage-labor market: Indian slavery and the ideological and political power of the Jesuit missions, which had monopolized the administration of indigenous affairs since the sixteenth century. The Indianist epics of the late 1700s expressed different responses to the specific solutions that were applied to these problems, namely, the radical reform of official Indian policy and the expulsion of the Jesuits, as well as to the broader historical conflict between the Imperial state, the church, and the colony.

Chapter 2 is concerned with the years from 1835 to 1850, which saw the consolidation of Brazil's independence from Portugal, followed by a prolonged period of open civil conflict and instability as the liberal wing of the nationalist movement struggled, unsuccessfully, to turn the "republican experiment" of the Regency into a reality. A whole series of violent provincial uprisings during the years following the abdication of Pedro I pressed for a range of reforms, including the decentralization of power and a federation. All these demands were effectively frustrated by harsh military repression, by the famous "conservative reaction," in which many parliamentary deputies shifted their party allegiances, and by the majority of Pedro II. The Indian populations, which did not remain indifferent to, or isolated from, those regional rebellions, were subject for much of the same period to a general policy of indiscriminate extermination, a continuation of that promoted before independence during the reign of João VI.

The tragic and morally outraged writing of the early Romantic Indianists emerged out of the liberal upsurge of the Regency and allowed them to link the colonial and more recent atrocities against the Indians to the injustices and inequalities that characterized colonial and contemporary Brazilian society as a whole, such as slavery. This literature recorded the destruction of an ideal, natural society by the modern, colonial civilization of Europe and thereby relegated the Indian to a mythical past, surviving into the present only as an epic tradition in a fictive folk memory. Sexual relations between Indians and between Indian and white were doomed to failure, tragically marred by the historical weight of Conquest and offering no hope of offspring for the future. Individual freedom, the bulwark of liberal and Romantic ideology and of the language of independence, found a perfect representative in the figure of the nomadic hunter and forest dweller. As such, the Indian protagonist raised serious implications for the legitimacy of an economy based on African slave labor.

However, even at this stage the contradictory nature of liberal thinking in nineteenth-century Brazil was apparent. As the work of Gonçalves Dias shows, integration, whether of the Indian or of the other marginalized sectors of Brazilian society, was already being invoked as an alternative to the geographical and political *disintegration* of Empire, as a defense against the unleashing of the dangerous monster of radical reform and regionalism. Although nominally liberal, the Regency governments of Feijó, Evaristo da Veiga, and Bernardo de Vasconcelos, in fact, strongly resisted the two chief demands of the liberals: decentralization of power and the institution of a single governing chamber. They displayed more loyalty to the ideas of national unity and authority than to the principles of liberalism, imposing a politics of nationalist "solidarity" that brought moderates and radicals together under the banner of the Society for the Defense of Liberty and National Independence.[25]

The first phase of the Indianist movement reached a kind of crisis point in about 1850, which can be related to two important debates, one political and the other literary, both of them connected with the majority of Pedro II and the particular character of the Second Reign. The first of these was conducted principally through the journal *Guanabara*, which was edited by three well-established writers, two of them Indianists. Pedro's accession to the throne completed an important shift in indigenist policy, roughly speaking, from one of extermination to integration. Articles supporting this approach had already been published elsewhere, in the journal of the Brazilian Historical and Geographical Institute, for instance.

However, when *Guanabara* published the historian Varnhagen's "Organic Petition" in 1851, it ignited a controversy that continued to smolder and erupt repeatedly over the next fifteen years. Against the tide of concessions to liberal reformism, such as that which brought about the abolition of the slave trade from Africa, Varnhagen advocated a ruthless use of force, the reintroduction of the colonial *bandeiras* or pioneer slaving expeditions, in order to subject the Indian to white control and free his lands for exploitation by Brazilian and immigrant settlers. The article promptly polarized opinion on government indigenist policy and led a number of prominent literary figures to contribute to the debate, expressing in the main their opposition to Varnhagen's views.

If, for many writers, the contemporary relevance of the Indianist theme had thus been reaffirmed, the portrayal of the Indian simply as a symbol of national independence perhaps seemed by now to have outlasted its usefulness. The political climate had shifted from one of nationalist euphoria and radical ideological and civil conflict to an atmosphere of repressive stability based on a politics of unprincipled consensus, what the contemporary observer Justiniano José da Rocha referred to as "transação," with its connotations of corrupt, unsavory compromise. Historian Raymundo Faoro sums it up as follows: "The conservative out of office becomes a revolutionary: the liberal in power forgets his inflammatory gunpowder."[26] If, as Emilia Viotti da Costa puts it, liberalism had a revolutionary function during the First Reign of Empire, as an ideological weapon for the elites in their struggle against royal absolutism and as a tool in the demolition of the remaining colonial institutions, once in power those same elites abandoned their revolutionary rhetoric and assumed a more conservative position:

The dissenters of the earlier period disappeared from the political scene, some swept away by foreign competition, others co-opted by the system. The career of Torres Homem, an important political figure of the empire, is typical: in his youth he was an active member of the opposition and author of the radical pamphlet *Libelo do Povo*, but later he became a member of the Council of State, a senator, and a minister of the empire. Very similar were the political careers of Antônio Carlos de Andrade e Silva, Bernardo de Vasconcelos, Diogo Feijó, and others who moved from liberal to conservative positions.[27]

As we shall see, this pattern of co-optation and accommodation embraced many who were directly involved in the indigenous question or the Indianist movement: the reformist politician and entrepreneur Teófilo Ottoni, for example, whose liberal pro-Indianist sympathies were put to the test when his transport and colonization project invaded tribal lands; and the novelist Alencar, who turned his back on his family's liberal traditions to become a Conservative congressional candidate and government minister.

From 1853 the new mood, reflecting the historical victory of the landowning and slave-owning class, was institutionalized by the politics of Conciliation, in which the idea of democratic liberalism now paradoxically served to legitimate semifeudal power. By the same token, the apparently progressive, liberal indigenist policy of the Second Reign, with its repeal of João VI's brutal extermination charters, in reality furthered only the interests of the planter elite. Integration signified the incorporation of Indian labor and land into the latifundist structure of the rural economy. With the formal institution of a government of Conciliation and the suppression of any genuine liberal influence over the political process, the original significance of the Indianist aesthetic had become meaningless and was submitted to critical reappraisal by a new generation.

One of the contributors to the *Guanabara* debate, Gonçalves de Magalhães, was instrumental in bringing about this reassessment when, in 1856, he published his Indianist epic, *A Confederação dos Tamoios* (The Confederation of the Tamoio Indians). The poem was immediately subjected to a detailed critique by the young novelist José de Alencar, who thus effectively challenged Magalhães's hitherto unquestioned authority and polarized old and new attitudes to the Indianist theme. *The Confederation of the Tamoio Indians* celebrated certain values—independence, patriotism, liberty, and religious faith—that were no longer sufficient to sustain a literature that had long since proved its nationalist credentials.

In accordance with the new, conciliatory politics of integration, the second phase of Romantic Indianism, discussed in Chapter 3, attempted instead to identify a set of common cultural and historical experiences that would define a unique sense of "Brazilianness," transcending the very real cultural, racial, and class differences that divided and opposed individual Brazilians—the most important of these divisions being, of course, slavery. One of the most striking and perhaps telling features of nineteenth-century Indianism is the very absence of explicit references to the issue of black slavery, at a time when it was a matter of urgent public debate. Nevertheless, Indian slavery is a central theme in the literature of this period; while the stereotypes of the freedom-loving Indian and the naturally servile African remain prominent, a number of key texts depict the tribal warrior as the willing slave to the female representative of the colonial order, the white mistress, or as the loyal servant and guardian angel of the patriarchal landowner. In both cases there is an implicit contrast between the humiliation and oppression of forced enslavement with its affront to Romantic liberal values and the voluntary servility of the Indian, who recognizes the legitimacy of the dominant social and political order and is prepared to sacrifice his personal freedom and identity in its defense. This new figure, the Ideal

Slave, epitomized by Alencar's Guarani hero Peri, suggests that the Indianism of this period was bound up ideologically with the needs of the dominant class in Imperial Brazil to perpetuate and rationalize its extremely illiberal exploitation of African labor. Indeed, as we shall see, there are striking parallels between these representations of Indian self-sacrifice and voluntary servility and Alencar's own explicit reflections on the contemporary slave-master relationship in his writing for the stage during the same years.

Linked to this myth is the other great theme of the Indianist literature associated with Alencar: miscegenation. Just as the Indian's freedom could be voluntarily sacrificed for the greater good, the *mestiço* marriage of Indian and white offered a historical model and foundation for the harmonious integration of races, classes, and cultures. If, in the Indianism of the first phase, insurmountable social and cultural barriers always prevented the sexual union of Indian and white, the protagonists of Alencar's *The Guarani Indian* and *Iracema* come together to offer the possibility of a new generation of *mestiço* offspring. The Indian is no longer destroyed on encountering the colonial invader, to sink back into a mythical, historical past but instead survives into the future as a democratizing, moderating force within the social and psychological being of the modern Brazil.

The period from 1870 to 1888, considered in Chapter 4, saw a further shift in the evolution of the Indianist movement, in response to new challenges to the social order on which the Empire was based: abolitionism, republicanism and immigration. Liberal abolitionists such as Joaquim Nabuco saw in the free labor market and the encouragement of immigrant settlement guarantees of economic progress. Such an attitude also implied an important change in perceptions of Brazilian culture and nationality. The movement toward abolition meant that the Africans were finally to be admitted as a significant element in the national physiognomy, although their servile status had until now denied them a place in the official literary image of Brazilian identity. By the end of the Second Reign well over half the population was colored, while the influx of European immigrants that had begun at midcentury was now growing.

The Indianists' old myth of a miscegenation involving just two races, the Portuguese and Indian, was no longer sustainable. Nabuco's criticisms of Alencar's fiction therefore reflected at first sight the point of view of a realist. But they had deeper roots in a "universalist" cultural perspective that really signified a rejection of the traditional, indigenous, and rural emphasis of colonial and Imperial history in favor of modern, European models of civilization and economic development. It was a perspective that, perhaps surprisingly in the light of Nabuco's abolitionist credentials, had its parallels with a return to the repressive Indian policies advocated earlier in the century by Varnhagen.

Indianist writing during the last two decades of Empire was of two kinds. One group, exemplified by the work of Bernardo Guimarães, responded to the new materialist reflections on Brazil's changing ethnic and social character by moving away from the mythical idealism of the Romantics toward a more sensationalist depiction of the contemporary *caboclo*, or detribalized Indian, in which the themes of sex and violence were expressive of a new kind of "savage" defiance of traditional notions of social order. A second group of writers, including Machado de Assis and the republican Sousândrade, drew fresh parallels between the "savage hierarchy" of tribal society and its colonial disruption, and the ethnic and class antagonisms that were resurfacing as the Brazilian nation-state confronted a fresh crisis of identity.

NOTES

1. John Hemming, *Red Gold: The Conquest of the Brazilian Indians* (London: Macmillan, 1978), pp. 487-501.

2. Carlos Guilherme Mota, *Ideologia da cultura brasileira (1933-1974): (Pontos de partida para uma revisão histórica)* (São Paulo: Ática, 1978), pp. 53-74; Renato Ortiz, *Cultura brasileira e identidade nacional* (São Paulo: Brasiliense, 1986), "Da raça à cultura: a mestiçagem e o nacional," pp. 36-44; José Honório Rodrigues, *Conciliação e reforma no Brasil: um desafio histórico-culltural* (Rio de Janeiro: Nova Fronteira, 1982), Chapter 1: "A política de conciliação: história cruenta e incruenta," pp. 29-120; Emília Viotti da Costa, *The Brazilian Empire: Myths and Histories* (Chicago and London: University of Chicago Press, 1985), Chapter 9: "The Myth of Racial Democracy: A Legacy of the Empire," pp. 234-46.

3. Luiz Beltrão, *O Índio, um Mito Brasileiro* (Rio de Janeiro: Vozes, 1977), p. 26.

4. Darcy Ribeiro, *Os Índios e a Civilização* (Petrópolis: Vozes, 1982), pp. 8, 424.

5. David Treece, "Indigenous Peoples in Brazilian Amazonia and the Expansion of the Economic Frontier," in David Goodman and Anthony Hall (eds.), *The Future of Amazonia: Destruction or Sustainable Development?* (London: Macmillan, 1990), pp. 282-83.

6. See, for example, José Bento Monteiro Lobato, "Urupês," *Obras Completas* (São Paulo: Brasiliense, 1956), vol. 1; Paulo Menotti del Picchia, "Matemos Peri!," *Jornal do Comércio* (January 1921), cited in Mário da Silva Brito, *História do Modernismo brasileiro: 1—Antecedentes da Semana de Arte Moderna* (Rio de Janeiro: Civilização Brasileira, 1978), p. 193.

7. David Miller Driver, *The Indian in Brazilian Literature* (New York: Hispanic Institute in the United States, 1942); Maria da Conceição Osório Dias Gonçalves, "O índio do Brasil na literatura portuguesa dos séculos XVI, XVII e XVIII," *Brasília* 11 (1961), pp. 97-209; Affonso Romano de Sant'Anna, "O Guarani," *Análise Estrutural de Romances Brasileiros* (Petrópolis: Vozes, 1973), pp. 54-83; Regina Zilberman, *Do Mito ao Romance: tipologia da ficção brasileira contemporânea* (Porto Alegre: Universidade do Rio Grande do Sul, 1977).

8. Regina Zilberman, "Myth and Brazilian Literature," Fernando Poyatos (ed.), *Literary Anthropology: A New Interdisciplinary Approach to People, Signs and Literature* (Amsterdam: John Benjamins, 1988), pp. 141-59, and "Natureza e Mulher—uma visão do Brasil no romance romântico," *Modern Language Studies* 19, no. 2 (1989), pp. 50-64; Ria Lemaire, "Re-Reading *Iracema*: The Problem of the Representation of Women in the Construction of a National Brazilian Identity," *Luso-Brazilian Review* 26, no. 2 (1989), pp. 59-75; Doris Sommer, *Foundational Fictions: The National Romances of Latin America* (Berkeley: University of California Press, 1993). See also Luis Filipe Ribeiro, *Mulheres de Papel: um estudo do imaginário em José de Alencar e Machado de Assis* (Rio de Janeiro: EDUFF, 1996).

9. David H. Treece, "Victims, Allies, Rebels: Towards a New History of Nineteenth-Century Indianism in Brazil," *Portuguese Studies* 1 (1985-86), pp. 56-98; Sommer, *Foundational Fictions*, p. 167.

10. José Guilherme Merquior, "O texto como resultado (notas sobre a teoria da crítica em Antonio Candido)," in Afonso Arinos et al., *Esboço de figura: homenagem a Antonio Candido* (São Paulo: Duas Cidades, 1979), pp. 122-23.

11. José Guilherme Merquior, *De Anchieta a Euclides: breve história da literatura brasileira - 1* (Rio de Janeiro: José Olympio, 1977), p. 55.

12. Antonio Candido, *Formação da Literatura Brasileira (Momentos decisivos)* (São Paulo: Martins, 1962), vol. 2, p. 20.

13. José de Alencar, "Como e porque sou romancista," *Obra Completa* (Rio de Janeiro: Aguilar, 1965), p. 117.

14. Roberto Schwarz, "As idéias fora do lugar," *Ao vencedor as batatas: forma literária e processo social nos inícios do romance brasileiro* (São Paulo: Duas Cidades, 1981), pp. 13-28. For the English translation, see Roberto Schwarz, "Misplaced Ideas: Literature and Society in Late-Nineteenth-Century Brazil," *Misplaced Ideas: Essays on Brazilian Culture* (London: Verso, 1992), pp. 19-32.

15. See Sommer, *Foundational Fictions*, Chapter 1; Antonio Cornejo Polar, *La novela indigenista* (Lima: Editorial Lasontay, 1980); Concha Meléndez, *La Novela indianista en Hispanoamérica (1832-1889)* (Rio Piedras: Universidad de Puerto Rico, 1961).

16. Domingo Faustino Sarmiento, *Life in the Argentine Republic in the Days of the Tyrants; or Civilization and Barbarism,* translation of *Facundo: Civilización y barbarie* (New York: Hurd and Houghton, 1868), pp. 24-25, cited in Sommer, *Foundational Fictions*, pp. 55-56.

17. Sommer, *Foundational Fictions*, p. 61.

18. Nicolas Shumway, *The Invention of Argentina* (Berkeley, Calif.; Oxford: University of Carolina Press, 1991), p. 260.

19. See Josefina Ludmer, *El género gauchesco: un tratado sobre la patria* (Buenos Aires: Sudamericana, 1988).

20. Nelson Werneck Sodré, *História da Literatura Brasileira: Seus Fundamentos Econômicos* (Rio de Janeiro: Civilização Brasileira, 1969), p. 269.

21. On the uses of liberalism under the Empire, see Viotti da Costa, *The Brazilian Empire*, Chapter 3.

22. Leonardo Fróes, *Um outro. Varella* (Rio de Janeiro: Rocco, 1990), pp. 96, 100.

23. Schwarz, "As idéias fora do lugar," pp. 14-19, and "Misplaced Ideas," pp. 19-25.

24. José Murilo de Carvalho, *Teatro de sombras: a política imperial* (São Paulo: Vértice, 1988), pp. 162-70.

25. Raymundo Faoro, *Os Donos do Poder: Formação do Patronato Político Brasileiro* (Porto Alegre: Globo, 1979) vol. 1, pp. 299-304.

26. Ibid, p. 335.

27. Viotti da Costa, *The Brazilian Empire*, pp. xx-xxi.

1

The Fall of the Jesuits and the Crisis of the Colonialist Project

TUPI OR TAPUIA? FROM THE INDIGENOUS "BLANK SLATE" TO THE SECOND FALL

In 1755 the marquis of Pombal, the "Enlightened Despot" who ruled the Portuguese Empire in the name of the monarchy for the next twenty-two years, issued two pieces of legislation that marked a watershed in the history of indigenist policy in Brazil. The first of these edicts stripped the Jesuit missionaries of their spiritual and political powers in the colony, beginning the process that led to the confiscation of their property and their eventual expulsion from Portugal and its dominions in 1759. The second set of edicts, the so-called Laws of Liberty, freed the Indians from the slavery legislation that had been in force since the 1680s and from the regime of the Jesuit missions, whose administration was passed into the hands of lay directors.

At a stroke, the Jesuits' political function, as mediators between the indigenous communities and the imperial state, and their cultural role in reshaping the indigenous consciousness and identity were abolished. For 200 years the figure of the missionary had accompanied the Indian like a shadow, as he would do again in the nineteenth and twentieth centuries, this time with the name of Capuchin or Salesian. His image was an ambivalent one, like that of some black-robed guardian angel: for some a protector against the cruelty and exploitation of the white colonist, and for others a savior leading the Indians out of their barbaric, heretical darkness into the light of the Christian community. Still others have recognized in him an Angel of Death, the insidious vanguard of the colonizing process, shattering the Indians' cosmology, social structure, and collectivist culture so as to prepare them for a class- and market-based economy.[1]

For two centuries up to its expulsion from Brazil and the rest of the Portuguese Empire, the Society of Jesus directed and regulated the tribal communities' incorporation into colonial society. The political and economic access of the church to the colony's indigenous population was guaranteed from its inception; on 7 June 1494, Pope Alexander VI signed the Treaty of Tordesillas, which, as well as dividing up the territories of South America between the Spanish and Portuguese Crowns, also imposed upon them the task of converting the land's native inhabitants to the Catholic faith. The founding of the militant Society of Jesus in 1539 was the other major step in the papacy's project to extend internationally its defenses against the encroachment of the Protestant Reformation.

It is not by chance, then, that the first two centuries of writing on the Indian in Brazil are almost exclusively the work of the Jesuits. This is a fact of inestimable importance to the development of an Indianist literature in the eighteenth and nineteenth centuries, since the Jesuits' detailed accounts of Indian culture and colonial relations were the chief sources for these writers, rather than contemporary ethnographic texts. The myths and stereotypes of the eighteenth-century Indianist epics and Romantic Indianist literature, although overlaid with Enlightenment and liberal ideology, were, to a large degree, inherited from this early Jesuit tradition. Moreover, it was itself a hybrid tradition, formed out of the mythological and theological preconceptions and expectations of a medieval Europe about to step into the New World and out of the missionaries' own increasingly embittered experience of the colonial reality, as they found their dream of mass conversion continually threatened and frustrated. Indeed, if the texts of the colonial period do reveal any development, it is this rapid shift from the euphoric optimism of Discovery, when the hospitable Indian appeared ripe for incorporation into the spiritual and secular kingdoms of Christian Europe, to skeptical disillusionment, as the Jesuits' project of evangelization was met with military and cultural resistance. In a kind of second Fall, the naked, Edenic innocent was transformed into a bestial, satanic monster.

This moment of disillusionment and the consequent reappraisal of the Jesuit strategy of evangelization (with the introduction of the mission system of villagization) were to supply Romantic Indianism with a crucial paradigmatic conception of indigenous identity based on a dual stereotype. On one hand, uncompromising resistance came to be associated with the figure of the Tapuia, the intractable savage whose defense of cultural and political autonomy represented the boundaries to the construction of an integrated colonial and postcolonial society. For some writers, such as Gonçalves Dias, the radical alterity of this face of indigenous identity, the internal cohesion and cosmic harmony of the tribal universe, constituted an imaginary, ideal alternative to the social fragmentation and disunity of contemporary, Imperial Brazil. On the other hand, the partial success of the missionary project, symbolized by the acculturated Tupi, kept alive the dream of incorporating this ethnic and social Other into the dominant community as the symbolic cornerstone of national integration. Paradoxically, the precondition for imagining this possibility, the negation of indigenous identity, rested on the Jesuits' earliest perceptions of the Indian as the inhabitant of an Edenic paradise, precultural by implication and therefore predisposed to receive the imprint of Christian civilization. Half a century before the arrival of the Jesuits themselves, this notion of the Indian as a culturally void "blank slate" was articulated in the first text of Brazil's colonial history, Pero Vaz de Caminha's *Letter* of 1500 to King Manuel of Portugal.

Whether or not Pedro Álvares Cabral's "discovery" of the Brazilian coast in April 1500 was accidental,[2] the impulse to explore and colonize tropical South America was nonetheless fueled by a whole complex of medieval myths and expectations of both theological and secular origin.[3] Nostalgia for a golden age of economic and spiritual plenitude is a characteristic response to moments of major political and social change, whether as an expression of conservative re-action or as a means of legitimating new, progressive systems of thought and behavior. Portugal, with its rising mercantile class and redundant, land-hungry aristocracy, its commercial expansion to Africa and the East, and its Counter-Reformation, was experiencing just such a moment in common with the rest of Europe. As the limits of the known world rapidly expanded, the golden age ac-quired an international dimension, becoming fused with legends of paradisiacal lands or Christian kingdoms overseas. The wishful thinking of medieval Chris-tendom, in its desire to uncover a universal ecumenical community, had pre-served since the second century A.D. the legend of a non-Christian people living in Asia whose way of life was essentially, though unconsciously, Christian. From the twelfth century, the country of Prester John perpetuated for the Portu-guese this myth of a wealthy Christian kingdom overseas[4]; the belief that Prester John's kingdom lay somewhere south of the North African Arab territories was one of the justifications for the Portuguese voyages initiated by Henry the Navi-gator.

Drawing on an extensive repertoire of such ideas, biblical, classical, and pa-gan sources converged to construct a geographical image of lost innocence, the infancy of Man before the Fall of Adam or Satan. The myth had important theological implications, for if a people was discovered on Earth in a state of innocence, the entire doctrine of original sin and universal corruption would be put into question. Medieval scholars determined that the Terrestrial Paradise would be situated in a temperate region—"non ibi frigi, non aestus"—beyond the barrier of a "torrid" zone, identified as the equatorial belt, and in the East.[5] It would be a land of eternal spring, perfect health, and infinite natural resources, of God-given fruits that could be enjoyed without the need for toil and drudgery. This central Edenic myth was embroidered with a variety of additional legends of fantastic, anthropomorphic fauna, of the "isle femelle" with its warrior popu-lation of misanthropic Amazons and, of course, of gold. The possibility of direct access to the gold supplies of the Sudan had motivated repeated efforts by the Iberian kingdoms to gain a foothold in North Africa and eventually to approach the region from the rear, by sailing down the coast. A faith in the material and even spiritual powers of this metal was one of the strongest motivations for Co-lumbus's voyage of discovery: "el oro es excelentísimo: del oro se hace tesoro y con él, quien lo tiene, hace cuanto quiere en el mundo, y llega a que echa las almas al paraíso" (gold is most excellent: out of gold one can make treasure and with it, whoever possesses it, does whatever he wishes in the world, and may even send souls to paradise).[6]

The South American continent, especially the tropical and sub-tropical coast of Brazil, could not have offered a fuller realization of the expectations raised by the myth of the Terrestrial Paradise. If the search for mineral wealth in the Portuguese colony was protracted and eclipsed by the spectacular conquests of the Spanish in their Andean and Mesoamerican territories, Brazil provided other compensations: its Edenic climate, its prodigious variety of flora and fauna, and its people. Chroniclers continued until well into the seventeenth century to elaborate treatises asserting that Brazil was the site of the biblical Eden.[7] As late as 1744, Pedro de Rates Honequim was executed for this heretical claim, arguing that Brazil had been saved from the Flood, that its four major rivers were those of the Garden of Eden, and that its native inhabitants were descended from the lost tribes of Israel. Later writers, such as Afonso Celso in his *Porque me ufano de meu país* (Why I Take Pride in My Country) (1901), found the myth of the Brazilian paradise equally useful to their theories of chauvinistic nationalism.

Some of the earliest descriptions of the New World and its people enjoyed an enormous popularity in Europe and exercised a great influence on the subsequent evolution of philosophical and political ideas. Amerigo Vespucci's "Mundus Novus" letter of 1503, in particular, was quickly published in numerous editions and several languages and provided the first images of the "natural state" that can be traced through Erasmus's *The Praise of Folly* (1508) and More's *Utopia* (1516) to Montaigne's "Des Cannibales" (1579) and Rousseau's *Discours sur l'origine et les fondements de l'inégalité parmi les hommes* (1753).[8] However, although the Brazilian Indian was the inspiration for much of this European tradition of radical thought, Portuguese writing played little or no role in its development. Montaigne's essay, for instance, relied for its account of Tupinambá tribespeople on the texts of the French Franciscan and Protestant friars André Thevet and Jean de Léry. Conversely, the Portuguese tradition of Indianist writing remained remarkably isolated from the literature in other languages, preferring to consult its own colonial and Jesuit texts; even the nineteenth-century Indianists seem to have absorbed their image of "natural man" via Rousseau and the European Romantics rather than directly from the original Spanish and French sources used by the latter, while for their historical and descriptive detail they returned to the colonial chroniclers Ambrôsio Fernandes Brandão, Fernão Cardim, and Simão de Vasconcellos.

This isolation from other European perceptions of the Indian and, as we shall see, from the crucial theological debate concerning the status of the Indian in Spanish America gave the Jesuit literature of Portuguese America a distinctive character that reflects the nature of the missionaries' relationship to the indigenous population. The "startle reflex" that Stephen Greenblatt sees as characterizing the Europeans' emotional and intellectual response in the presence of radical difference in the century following Columbus's voyage[9] is curiously muted in the case of Portuguese writing (itself conspicuous by its absence from Greenblatt's account). For Sérgio Buarque de Holanda, the Portuguese travel literature of the sixteenth century demonstrated a greater sense of realism, a greater resistance to fantastic invention than that of the Spanish explorers. This realism arose out of a persistently medieval worldview that was based on an acceptance of the world as it was, in expectation of a better afterlife, in contrast to the imaginative attempts of Renaissance culture to liberate humanity through fantasy, magic, and experiment. Paradoxically, the Portuguese abroad adopted an "illusory realism" or credulity in relation to the marvelous and the impossible, which were acceptable providing they did not enter the empirical sphere, whereas the natural wonders of the real world were perceived and recorded unsensationally.[10]

This was partly due to the existing half century of Portuguese experience of tropical and equatorial landscapes in Africa, but it also had to do, in the case of the Jesuits, with the more immediate experience of the missions. The Fathers' task—to bring the entire indigenous population under their economic and psychological control and thereby integrate them into the process of colonization and into the Portuguese Catholic Empire—faced an immense obstacle: the Indians' cultural bonds, their beliefs, their nomadic, collectivist economy, in short, their sense of tribal identity. The dramatic shift in the representation of the Indians and their culture that can be discerned in the Jesuit literature of the colony reflects the battle to overcome that obstacle in all its bitterness and brutality.

Against this background of the subsequent two centuries of Jesuit administration of the Indians, Pero Vaz de Caminha's *Letter* to King Manuel recorded an exceptional moment in the history of relations between the two communities. Caminha was the chronicler accompanying Pedro Álvares Cabral's fleet of thirteen ships on its way to India via the Cape of Good Hope. The expedition was blown westward across the Atlantic and touched the Brazilian coast at what is today Porto Seguro, Bahia, on 22 April 1500. Caminha's report of the few weeks' contact with the local population revealed, on one hand, the Europeans' earliest perceptions of the Atlantic Amerindian tribal peoples[11] as they were molded by the evangelical project assigned to Conquest and by the optimistic expectations that the mythology of the Terrestrial Paradise had generated. On the other hand, the chronicler's remarkable lack of sensationalism and the apparently neutral, objective register of his colonial inventory, yet his rather self-conscious deliberation over the language employed to communicate his impressions to the Portuguese monarch are suggestive of a struggle to objectify a radically unfamiliar physical and human landscape and to demonstrate its exploitable potential for Portugal's expansionist enterprise.

This underlying rhetorical purpose, which concludes Caminha's report by recommending the initiation of informal settlement and missionary activity in the territory, takes as its starting point the one observable fact that most obviously resisted secular or theological codification—the Indians' unembarrassed nakedness. Indeed, one is quickly struck by the contrast between Caminha's routine documentation of the material accouterments borne by the twenty or so individuals who first appear on the shoreline in welcome—bows, arrows and feather headgear—and his insistent scrutinization of, and speculations regarding, their physiological condition and state of undress: "Eram pardos, todos nus, sem coisa alguma que lhes cobrisse suas vergonhas."[12] (They were brown, all naked, with nothing to cover their shames.) This first instance of the peculiar, contemporary euphemism "vergonhas," or "shames," for the genitals and female breasts is soon followed by further, increasingly complex, and even ironic reflections on the moral implications of the same term. On the second direct encounter, when two young male Indians are brought on board ship, this "shameless" display of nakedness seems to mirror their failure to recognize or defer to the hierarchical rank of the expedition's commander, who waits unacknowledged seated before them in his finery, while they stretch themselves out on their backs to sleep on the rug laid at his feet:

A feição deles é serem pardos, maneira de avermelhados, de bons rostos e bons narizes, bem feitos. Andam nus, sem cobertura alguma. Não fazem o menor caso de en-cobrir ou de mostrar suas vergonhas; e nisso têm tanta inocência como em mostrar o rosto. . . . (p. 204)

O Capitão, quando eles vieram, estava sentado em uma cadeira, bem vestido, com um colar de ouro mui grande ao pescoço, e aos pés uma alcatifa por estrado. . . . Entraram. Mas não fizeram sinal de cortesia, nem de falar ao Capitão nem a ninguém. (pp. 205-6)

(Their appearance is brown, kind of reddish, with fine faces and fine noses, well formed. They walk about naked, without any covering. They give not the slightest regard to con-cealing or displaying their shames; and in this they have as much innocence as in show-ing their faces. . . ./ The Captain, when they came, was seated in a chair, well dressed, with a very large gold necklace about his neck, and at his feet a rug for a dais. . . . They entered. But they made no sign of courtesy, nor of speaking to the Captain or to anyone.)

These two aspects of the Indians' behavior signify to Caminha the absence of a certain kind of knowledge of the self and of the other, an innocent ignorance as to one's moral and political relationship to other social beings, who, it is as-sumed, must be governed by the same universal codes.

Note that, as today in Western culture, it is precisely and exclusively the ab-sence of any covering for the sexual parts that defines the Indians as "naked." The body-paint, feather headdresses and lip-plugs whose detailed description follows, however unfamiliar to European eyes, are nevertheless somehow rec-ognizable as having an aesthetic function or value that might be approximated to comparable aspects of European dress, deserving of comments such as: "the head-dress was very round, thick and even and needed no extra care to keep it up" (p. 205). The much-remarked-upon vigor of the Indians' physique, too, and their bronze skin color (noted in implicit comparison, perhaps, to the darker complexion of the West Africans already encountered by the Portuguese) are similarly aestheticized, prompting reiterated expressions of admiration, rather as one might appreciate fine zoological specimens—an analogy Caminha will take up again later on.

The sexual significance of the Indians' nakedness for the European observer, however, prevents it initially from being treated in the same way, from being unproblematically appropriated by the chronicler's gaze, for it is clearly per-ceived not simply as custom or habit but as the definitive sign of their alterity as distinct moral beings. Up to this point, then, the chronicler's ability to survey and thereby appropriate the objects of his gaze is checked by a disturbing para-dox: the Indian is not shamed by that which should be shameful—the display of his or her sexuality. Only by endlessly rehearsing and working through this paradox linguistically, deliberately exploiting the ambiguities of the expression "vergonha" in a series of tortuous puns, is Caminha finally able, as he says, "to look very closely at" these people, to neutralize the disturbing power of this display of sexuality, and to render them into the aesthetic objects of his attention. So he writes enthusiastically of one young woman: "era tão bem feita e tão redonda, e sua vergonha (que ela não tinha) tão graciosa, que a muitas mulheres da nossa terra, vendo-lhe tais feições, fizera vergonha, por não terem a sua como ela" (pp. 211-12). (she was so well-formed and rounded, and her shame (that she did not have) so fine, that many women of our country, seeing such features, would be ashamed not to have such as hers.) The following comment, meanwhile, already seems to suggest how the "innocence" of unembarrassed nakedness might extend to the beholder himself: "e suas vergonhas tão nuas e com tanta inocência descobertas, que nisso não havia vergonha alguma" (p. 219). (and their shames [were] so naked and so innocently exposed, that there was no shame in it at all.)

Elsewhere, that implication is brought to the surface of the text, and here its paradoxical formulation invites two possible interpretations: the first, accepting it at face value, would generously argue that the spectator's gaze is somehow rendered guiltless by the innocent demeanor of the one being observed in her nakedness (given the likely state of arousal of an all-male crew at sea for many weeks, this must have offered the royal addressee of Caminha's letter a reassuringly proper, if improbable, official version of events); the second interpretation would propose that the Indians' apparent lack of sexual inhibition, translated as "innocence," served to rationalize and legitimate the European's voyeuristic contemplation of the naked female Indian body, exempting him from the moral condemnation of a distant Catholic Church:

Ali andavam entre eles três ou quatro moças, bem moças e bem gentis, com cabelos muito pretos e compridos pelas espáduas, e suas vergonhas tão altas, tão cerradinhas e tão limpas das cabeleiras que, de as muito bem olharmos, não tínhamos nenhuma vergonha. (p. 210)

(Wandering amongst them were three or four girls, really young and pretty, with very dark, long hair down their backs, and their shames so upstanding and firm and free of hair that we were not ashamed to look very closely at them.)

Whichever is the preferred reading, the effect in either case is to render the shamelessly naked, autonomous Indian fully available to the unrestricted, appropriating gaze of the European observer, to realize that transition from nakedness to nudity that John Berger describes in his discussion of the Western tradition of painting:

To be naked is to be oneself.

To be nude is to be seen naked by others and yet not recognized for oneself. A naked body has to be seen as an object in order to become a nude. (The sight of it as an object stimulates the use of it as an object.) Nakedness reveals itself. Nudity is placed on display.

To be naked is to be without disguise.

To be on display is to have the surface of one's own skin, the hairs of one's own body, turned into a disguise which, in that situation, can never be discarded. The nude is condemned to never being naked. Nudity is a form of dress.

In the average European oil painting of the nude the principal protagonist is never painted. He is the spectator in front of the picture and he is presumed to be a man. Everything is addressed to him. Everything must appear to be the result of his being there. It is for him that the figures have assumed their nudity. But he, by definition, is a stranger—with his clothes still on.[13]

Note that, for Caminha, the transition from nakedness to nudity is further facilitated by the absence of hair from the Indian women's sexual parts. Again this brings to mind the European convention of excluding body hair from the representation of the female nude, thus diminishing the association of sexual power, of passion, with the naked woman. As Berger puts it, "The woman's sexual power needs to be minimized so that the spectator may feel that he has the monopoly of such passion."[14] If the absence of body hair serves to disempower the naked sexuality of the Indian in the eyes of the onlooker, it also reinforces the theological implication toward which Caminha is leading his reader: exercising no sexual self-awareness in their nakedness, these almost prepubescent innocents appear to lack the fundamental knowledge common to all other human beings—they are without Sin. This implicit discovery, that these might be the hoped-for Edenic people who had escaped the Fall, is suggested in the closing paragraphs of the letter, where Caminha writes: "Assim, Senhor, a inocência desta gente é tal, que a de Adão não seria maior, quanto a vergonha" (pp. 238-39) (Thus, Lord, the innocence of these people is such that Adam's would not be greater, in this matter of shame). One has only to be reminded of the language of Genesis, Chapter 2, verse 25, which speaks of Adam and Eve in the Garden of Eden—"And they were both naked, the man and his wife, and were not ashamed"—and of Chapter 3, verse 7, after they have eaten from the Tree of Knowledge of Good and Evil: "And the eyes of them both were opened, and they knew that they were naked; and they sewed fig leaves together, and made themselves aprons."

Moral identity and cultural identity are indivisible in Caminha's interpretation of the Indians' radical otherness, and both depend on a principle of negativity that is extended across all aspects of their existence as he perceives them. The lack of "vergonha," shame, of Sin and therefore of Knowledge becomes generalized to embrace everything that might be constitutive of culture, even where observable evidence ought to have suggested otherwise. Thus, although several members of the crew would soon visit an Indian village and see constructed dwellings, hammocks, and delicately woven fabrics, such signs of civilization are presumed to be alien to a people whose innocence, timidity, and physical cleanliness are comparable to the natural state of wild animals and birds:

E naquilo me parece ainda mais que são como aves ou alimárias montesas, às quais faz o ar melhor pena e melhor cabelo que às mansas, porque os corpos seus são tão limpos, tão gordos e formosos, que não pode mais ser.

Isto me faz presumir que não têm casas nem moradas a que se acolham, e o ar, a que se criam, os faz tais. (p. 223)

(And in that respect they seem to me even more like wild birds or beasts, whose feathers and hair are made better by the air than those of tame birds and beasts, for their bodies are as clean, as plump and beautiful as can be./ This makes me assume that they have no houses or dwellings to shelter in, and the air in which they are raised makes them thus.)

The failure to recognize any material domestic artifacts is matched by the assumption that the Indians possess no *cultura* (meaning both "culture" and "cultivation" in the sense of agriculture, in Portuguese) as such while, as we have already seen, their unfamiliarity with the significance of European ceremonial dress is interpreted as an ignorance of any notion of political hierarchy or authority. Last, but perhaps most crucial of all to the optimism of the evangelical enterprise that was to follow, the Indians are assumed to lack any belief system or cosmology of their own, an assumption reinforced by their capacity for mimicry and their fascination with ritual, which led them to participate enthusiastically in the mass on the final day of the landing, kneeling and standing in imitation of the Portuguese Christians and kissing the crucifixes that were hung about their necks. Here we can witness the crystallization of the great dream of mass conversion, that faith in the infinite malleability of the indigenous consciousness that depended not so much on Greenblatt's "sense of wonder" at the alterity of New World's inhabitants but on the denial of their very identity as cultural beings. Unpossessed of any religious, political, or economic system, physically and morally naked, divested even of their sexuality and without the essential Knowledge of Sin, Caminha's Edenic, precivilized Indians are defined as culturally void, empty vessels or blank slates awaiting, passively, the imprint of any ideology or creed the colonizer chose to stamp upon them. Their illusory predisposition to the process of evangelization seemed to confirm the historical role that the Church had appointed to itself in the colonial enterprise:

Parece-me gente de tal inocência que, se homem os entendesse e eles a nós, seriam logo cristãos, porque eles, segundo parece, não têm, nem entendem em nenhuma crença.
. . . E imprimir-se-á ligeiramente neles qualquer cunho, que lhes quiserem dar. E pois Nosso Senhor, que lhes deu bons corpos e bons rostos, como a bons homens, por aqui nos trouxe, creio que não foi sem causa. (p. 233)

(They seem to me to be people of such innocence that, if one could understand them and they us, they would soon be Christians, because they apparently neither have, nor understand any creed./ . . . And any stamp that one wishes to give them will be easily imprinted on them. And since Our Lord, who gave them fine bodies and fine faces, as He would give fine men, brought us here, I believe it was not without reason.)

The discovery of the Terrestrial Paradise, with its attendant notions of infinite exploitability and untapped potential, brought with it a curious paradox, however, in which a land already flowing with milk and honey nevertheless still required the intervention of the colonial power and its *cultura* in order to yield up a harvest. Although devoid of Sin, the Edenic, prelapsarian and precultural Indians must still acquire that Knowledge familiar to all the other descendants of

Adam and Eve, in order that they, too, might be saved: "Porém o melhor fruto, que dela se pode tirar me parece que será salvar esta gente. E esta deve ser a principal semente que Vossa Alteza em ela deve lançar" (p. 240) (But the best fruit that can be extracted from it, it seems to me, will be to save these people. And this must be the principal seed that Your Highness must sow in it). The inscription of evangelical doctrine on the blank slate of indigenous conscious-ness, like the transformation of the Indians' autonomous, self-possessed naked-ness into an objectified nudity available to the European gaze, constituted a naming of that which was unnamed, the condition of its appropriation and in-corporation into the moral and political economy of the colonial system: "E bem creio que, se Vossa Alteza aqui mandar quem entre eles mais devagar ande, que todos serão tornados ao desejo de Vossa Alteza" (p. 238). (And I firmly believe that, if Your Highness sends here someone who will wander amongst them at greater leisure, they will all be turned to Your Highness's desire.)

Caminha's letter thus articulates a momentous act of interpretation, whereby the initially incomprehensible, radical otherness of Indian identity is emptied of its force and rendered infinitely disposable to the sovereign power of the Portu-guese Crown. As we have seen, this formulation of the concept of the tabula rasa emerges piecemeal, tentatively even, during the course of the text; its role in stimulating the fervor of the Jesuit mission of evangelization half a century later could not have been anticipated. The act of interpretation takes on a rather more explicit, self-conscious form, meanwhile, when it is driven by the prospect of an immediate and spectacular economic conquest, the dream of precious metals supplied in abundance by the Indians. On the third day after the landing, the Indians' curiosity about these unfamiliar materials was already being translated as a revelation of untold wealth:

Porém um deles pôs olho no colar do Capitão, e começou de acenar com a mão para a terra e depois para o colar, como que nos dizendo que ali havia ouro. Também olhou para um castiçal de prata e assim mesmo acenava para a terra e novamente para o castiçal como se lá também houvesse prata. (p. 206)

(But one of them set his eyes on the Captain's necklace, and began to point towards land and then at the necklace, as if to tell us that there was gold there. He also looked at a silver candlestick and likewise pointed towards land and again at the candlestick as if there was also silver there.)

The power of Caminha's wishful thinking in deciphering the Indians' gestures is especially striking when one considers that there is no evidence to suggest that gold or silver or the technology to exploit them was a feature of their tribal cul-ture or economy; indeed, by the end of the letter he is candidly less certain of the presence of any metal in the territory. But it is only a short step to reading such gestures as a promise of commercial exchange, the trade of local gold for the captain's necklace and a rosary: "como dizendo que dariam ouro por aquilo" (p. 207) (as if to say that they would give gold for them). At this point, though, the Europeans' reluctance to concede any control over the transaction obliges

Caminha to admit to the ambiguity of the signs being witnessed and the arbitrary interpretation assigned to them:

Isto tomávamos nós assim por assim o desejarmos. Mas se ele queria dizer que levaria as contas e mais o colar, isto não o queríamos nós entender, porque não lho havíamos de dar. (p. 207)

(We took it this way because that is how we wished it. But if he meant that he would take away the beads and the necklace, we would not understand this, for we were not about to give them to him.)

The assumption of European sovereignty is the imperative governing both transactions, the translation of symbolic signs and the exchange of goods. It is a far cry from the picture of mutual trust painted by Caminha elsewhere in the letter, where the tentative appearances of Indians in their twos or threes give way to crowds of 200, 300, and even 400, and food and music are shared, and weapons gradually laid down or exchanged for gifts of shirts, rosary beads, and bells:

E mal desembarcáramos, alguns dos nossos passaram logo o rio, e meteram-se entre eles. Alguns aguardavam; outros afastavam-se. Era, porém, a coisa de maneira que todos andavam misturados. Eles se ofereciam desses arcos com suas setas por sombreiros e carapuças de linho ou por qualquer coisa que lhes davam. (p. 218)

(And we had hardly disembarked, when some of our men went straight across the river and went among them. Some waited: others moved off. But it happened in such a way that they all mingled together. They offered their bows and arrows in exchange for hats and linen caps or for anything they would give them.)

Buried as it is in the description of the bustle and merrymaking, it is easy to miss the subtle shift that was on the verge of taking place even during such a short encounter between the two communities, as the Indians' goodwill was appropriated in the interest of European sovereign possession, and the blank slate of exploitability began to be employed in the service of the colonial enterprise. Barely noticeable, it is nevertheless there, in the unmistakable image of the Indians' loading up a shipment of the first profitable export commodity to leave the country, the product that was to give the colony its name—*pau-brasil*, or brazilwood, a timber valued for its red dye:

Andavam todos tão dispostos, tão bem feitos e galantes com suas tinturas, que pareciam bem. Acarretavam dessa lenha, quanta podiam, com mui boa vontade, e levavam-na aos batéis. (pp. 231-32)

(They were all so well disposed, so well built and comely with their paint, that they looked fine. They conveyed that timber, as much of it as they could, with very good will, and took it to the boats.)

By 1583, however, the first generation of Jesuit missionaries had seen the illusion of the indigenous blank slate melt before their eyes and had returned to their task with a realism whose zeal and ruthlessness matched only the bitterness of their disappointment.

Before the arrival of the Jesuits, the indigenous populations of the Atlantic coast experienced nearly fifty years of contact with secular white society, in the form of deported criminals, sailors, and a few early traders and settlers. The first official expeditions of the 1530s encountered patriarchal colonies already established under the control of legendary figures such as João Ramalho, the Bacharel of Cananéia, and Diogo Álvares Caramuru. Shipwrecked or marooned, these solitary white strangers managed, through their impressive use of European technology, their military skill, or simply their mythical prestige as non-Indians, to impose their will on the local tribal communities, take Indian wives, and set up self-styled kingdoms founded on the first generation of *mamelucos*, or Indian/white *mestiços*. Only two centuries later did the literary possibilities of such stories, which became symbolic foundation myths of racial integration and evangelistic enterprise, begin to be exploited.[15] Meanwhile these patriarchs performed an important political role as mediators in the subsequent history of the colony; in addition, they were the first owners and traders of Indian slaves.

The first ships to export salable cargoes of brazilwood from the colony also took young Indian men and women, persuaded that they were going to a promised land but in reality exhibited around the European courts as exotic curiosities. Soon, the tribal communities on the coast became saturated with the metal tools and axes that they had received in return for their labor and that were the single most important instrument in their integration into the surrounding society. French competition intensified demand for the red timber, but the Indians, who traditionally worked only to the extent that their subsistence economy required it, became less and less prepared to supply the Portuguese need for manpower. Meanwhile, following Martim Afonso de Sousa's two-year expedition of 1530 and the division of the colony into administrative captaincies, the growing population of colonists discovered a more lucrative, labor-intensive industry: sugar mills began to appear in all the centers of settlement. The royal decision to create the *capitanias*, fourteen huge feudal *latifúndios* awarded to loyal members of the Portuguese aristocracy, also temporarily resolved the labor problem, for these hereditary lords, or *donatários*, enjoyed considerable juridical and economic rights over their territories, including the acquisition and sale of Indian slaves. To begin with, slaves were the "rescued" prisoners of enemy tribes, bought with the justification that they were being saved from death by cannibalism—a fate arguably more attractive than the slow torture of work in the sugar mills. As the demand for slaves increased, the Portuguese incited intertribal wars in order to obtain more prisoners, before moving on to undisguised, forced enslavement.[16]

One focus for such activities and an important sugar-producing center was Salvador da Bahia, the future colonial capital and the major port of entry for slaves from Africa. It was no coincidence that accompanying the first governor of Brazil, Tomé de Souza, on his arrival in Salvador in 1549 was the first party of six Jesuit missionaries. Souza's instructions were to identify the hostile sector of the local Tupinambá, killing or enslaving them, and then to subject the rest to a feudal regime of tribute. Ironically, though, the pretext for the enterprise was the evangelical mission to convert the same Indians to the Catholic faith. After a period of open and brutal confrontation under the administration of Duarte da Costa, the third governor, Mem de Sá, resumed Tomé de Souza's more systematic dual policy of military and missionary action, dividing the indigenous population between those determined to resist (the so-called Tapuias) and those who agreed to abandon their tribal customs and submit to the regime of the Jesuit settlements. Thus, while the inhabitants of hundreds of Tupinambá and Caeté villages were slaughtered in intertribal incidents and official campaigns supported by the Fathers, hundreds more chose arguably the lesser of two evils, sacrificing their lives to the prosperity of the colony. By 1610 Bahia boasted 8,000 mission Indians and 7,000 Indian and African slaves on the plantations, in comparison to 2,000 whites. Indeed, by the end of the sixteenth century, just 128 Jesuits controlled almost all the Indians under Portuguese rule in Brazil.

Perhaps the single most important campaign in which the Jesuits played a central role, important apart from anything else because it provided material for a Jesuit drama and numerous other Indianist works in the nineteenth century, was the war against the Tamoio confederation that led to the founding of Rio de Janeiro. The Tamoios, a Tupinambá tribe renowned for their music and dancing, were allied to the French, who, under the leadership of Nicholas de Villegaignon, had established the colony of Antarctic France on an island in the Bay of Guanabara. The Tamoios occupied lands between Cabo Frio, to the east of modern Rio de Janeiro, and Piratininga, to the west, the first mission village to be created by the Jesuit leader Manuel da Nóbrega, in 1553, and the future site of the city of São Paulo. Despite a heavy defeat in 1560 at the hands of Mem de Sá, the Tamoios remained an unsubdued and serious threat to the Portuguese, especially after the collapse of the latter's own alliance with the Tupinikin of Espírito Santo.

Nóbrega and a younger Jesuit colleague, José de Anchieta, were among the most militant advocates of an intensified campaign against the Tamoios, not least because of their passionate desire to see the expulsion of the Protestant French. A punitive raid headed by Anchieta against the Tupinikin rebels in 1561 led to a combined counterattack uniting Tupinikins and Tamoios, ending in a siege that split families in two, pitting sons, fathers, and brothers against one another.

In 1563 Nóbrega and Anchieta risked their lives by going directly to the Tamoio settlements of Iperoig, ostensibly on a diplomatic mission of peace but with the added purpose of spying out the tribe's military resources. While Anchieta remained there for three months as a hostage, a truce was arranged between the Tamoios and those Tupinikins who had remained loyal to the Portuguese, leaving the way open for an attack on the Tamoio-French alliance, which was occupying Rio de Janeiro. A protracted and bitter two-year war from 1565 to 1567 finally achieved the Jesuits' ambition to build a college and mission village in Rio. By the time the subjugation of the Tamoios was completed in 1575, tens of thousands had been killed, enslaved, or dispersed—the Tamoios were effectively annihilated.

The Jesuit Fathers were indisputably a key element in the divisive military strategy of the Portuguese against tribes that obstructed or threatened the plan of colonial settlement. Nevertheless, for those Indians who survived or escaped such massacres by entering the mission *aldeias*, or villages, the Jesuits appeared as their welcome and sympathetic saviors from the even more brutal exploitation that would have occurred under an unregulated labor system. In the first few years following their arrival the Jesuits, too, shared Caminha's enthusiasm and optimism regarding the Indians' spiritual potential. The correspondence that Nóbrega sent to his superior during the months of 1549 contains much that is familiar from Caminha's letter of fifty years previously: the erroneous conviction that the Indians had no beliefs of their own—"They are a people which has no knowledge of God, or of idols"; their capacity and affinity for assimilating Christian culture—"They wonder greatly at the fact that we can read and write, which they are most envious of, and wish to learn, and be Christians like us"; the notion of the Indian consciousness as a *tábua rasa* waiting for the Word to be imprinted on it—"Few letters are sufficient here, for this is all blank paper and one need only write freely"; even the Edenic image of the Indian as a child of Nature—"And in many things they keep the natural law."[17] He condemned the colonists' slaving attacks and spoke of Indian violence as a response to provocation. Mass conversions, baptisms, and marriages, rising to hundreds on occasions, seemed to confirm the success of the mission.

By August 1551, however, Nóbrega had reached the conclusion that "[t]hey all wish and desire to be Christians; but it appears hard for them to give up their customs."[18] The conversions had been based on the same fascination with ritual and music that Caminha had witnessed and lacked any intellectual basis, any understanding of the theological doctrine that Catholic devotion entailed. The mythologies and codes of behavior governing every aspect of the Indians' social, economic, sexual, and spiritual life, which had taken thousands of years to evolve and were the source of tribal identity, could not be erased through a brief ceremony. Above all, there was the ancestral attachment to traditional lands, which, besides constituting the basis of their economic livelihood, represented their spiritual home, the site of burial grounds and of myths locating them in the past, present, and future. The Fathers quickly recognized this territorial identity as the major obstacle to evangelization, and the mission *aldeias* were their highly effective way of responding to the problem. Slavery, too, rapidly became an acceptable instrument in the effort to win souls to the kingdom of God.

The practice of removing Indian children from their communities, indoctrinating them, and then returning them to their people to spread the Faith, had had limited success. Villagization represented an alternative method, uprooting entire tribes from their traditional territories, close to their buried kin, and concentrating them within the confines of a purpose-built settlement. There the Indian was subject to a totalitarian regime of twenty-four-hour supervision, a chronometrically governed routine intended to leave no room for tribal culture. As well as being permanently exposed to Catholic doctrine and the interrogation of the catechism, this meant the suppression of indigenous rites celebrating birth, puberty, marriage, and death; of the making and drinking of *cauim*, the ceremonial spirit brewed from manioc; of the spiritual role of the *pagé*, or shaman; and of the ritual of human sacrifice. The missions imposed upon the Indians a Western social structure based on the nuclear family and allotted individual dwellings accordingly. This destroyed the complex clan systems of parentage, marriage, and collective identity by which the Indians had lived, putting an end to the fellowship of the communal longhouses and to the easygoing tribal attitude to sexual partnerships. From a seminomadic, hunter-gatherer existence in which tribes roamed over hundreds of miles in their search for game and moved their villages every few years or even months in accordance with slash-and-burn horticultural methods, the Indians had to accept the narrow boundaries of the *aldeia*, the stifling discipline of routine daily plantation labor, and an accumulative economy that was totally alien to their tradition of subsistence.

The mission *aldeias* had one further devastating consequence for the Indians that the Jesuits had not anticipated: their exposure to disease. Gathered together in large numbers in close contact with the colonial population, the Indians were decimated by the common Eurasian and African viruses and bacterial infections to which they had no natural immunity: syphilis, influenza, whooping cough, measles, and smallpox swept across the Atlantic coast during the 1550s and 1560s and repeatedly thereafter and even struck tribes in the interior, killing thousands. Eight thousand died in Rio de Janeiro alone in 1556.[19] The Fathers' response was to care for the sick and dead as best they could, to explain the epidemics as Divine punishment for the Indians' heretical sinfulness, and to replenish the missions again with new reductions from the interior.

Meanwhile, the task of conversion faced a different challenge posed by the linguistic barrier, as Caminha's letter had anticipated, and the Jesuits responded to this, too, with their characteristic intellectual keenness. As well as becoming proficient in the many indigenous languages they encountered and producing aids to learning, such as Anchieta's *Arte de gramática da lingoa mais usada na costa do Brasil* (Art of Grammar of the Language Most Used on the Coast of Brazil), they introduced a kind of lingua franca, the so-called *língua geral,* based on a synthesis of the most common tribal dialects of the Tupi-Guarani group. Still known in Amazonia well into the twentieth century as Nheengatu, its function during the colonial period was to enhance the Jesuits' control over the cultural and geographical diversity of tribal groups, attenuating their sense of linguistic individuality and independence. By retaining an indigenous language as the medium for communication, rather than Portuguese, they also initially limited the degree of access that white settlers might gain to the Indians, although the *língua geral* steadily became spoken across most of the colonial population until the eighteenth century.

This linguistic question contributed to the dual stereotype that was now emerging in the Portuguese perception of the Indian and to its refinement along pseudoethnic lines. As the Tupi-speaking tribes of the coast became annihilated or incorporated into the missions, the image of intractability passed to the Tapuia, or Jê-speaking, groups such as the Aimoré, who had been driven inland by the pre-Conquest migrations of the Tupi. Their distinctive physical appearance—tall, pale, long-haired—their predominantly nomadic culture, and their uncompromising military ruthlessness swiftly became synonymous with a reputation as savagely cannibalistic barbarians. But perhaps of equal importance in the Tapuia resistance to incorporation into colonial society was the fact that their languages were quite unfamiliar and impenetrable to the Jesuits and made the setting up of missions an impossible task.[20]

There is a strong similarity between the dualistic categorization of Tapuias and Tupis and the ethnic stereotyping of Caribs and Arawaks in Spanish America following Columbus's voyage through the Caribbean. For Peter Hulme, the obvious continuities between the classical Mediterranean paradigm and the post-Conquest dualism of fierce cannibal and noble savage, along with the evidence that "anthropophagy" was already operating as the "other" of the still developing concept of "Europe" as early as the thirteenth century, make it tempting to see the colonial discourse on cannibalism as developing in its own separate space hardly affected by actual contact or interchange with the indigenous cultures themselves.[21] Like the reputation of violently man-eating nomadic barbarism attributed to one-half of the native Caribbean population and welded to it linguistically via the transition Carib-Cannibal, the emergence of the category Tapuia in Portuguese America clearly corresponded less to reliable ethnographic observation than to the ideological and political needs of the colonial Europeans, particularly the Jesuits, in their subjugation and administration of the indigenous communities. William Arens has argued that the vast anecdotal folklore of reported acts of cannibalism worldwide springs in the main from a tiny number of apocryphal or at the most, unverifiable accounts, endlessly retold and recycled,[22] such as Hans Staden's seminal "firsthand" testimony of a Tupinambá human sacrifice in 1552, which he was fortunate enough to survive.[23] Arens's claims have been roundly refuted from a number of quarters as the unsubstantiated work of a revisionist whose keenness to deny cultural anthropophagy "under cover of idealism and intellectual high-mindedness, actually leads back to the misrepresentation of the Other."[24]

Nevertheless, while the more recent ethnographic and historical research has reclaimed and reevaluated the significance of cannibalistic practices as an actually existing phenomenon, this does not invalidate the central question posed by Arens: "The significant question is not why people eat human flesh, but why one group invariably assumes that others do,"[25] just as the term "barbarian" or its equivalent in every language has served to define the boundaries of one's own civilization in relation to an external Other to whom this and other such taboo practices may be imputed. Indeed, as Stephen Greenblatt points out, the discourse of cannibalism had even begun to inform the interdenominational rivalry that beset the evangelical mission in the early colonial period; the Catholic Eucharist, in which transubstantiation is interpreted literally rather than metaphorically and in which the bread host and altar wine consumed by the faithful constitute the actual flesh and blood of Christ, was denounced by the French Protestant missionary Jean de Léry as a cannibalistic act.[26] The French philosopher Montaigne, in his famous essay of 1579 "About the Cannibals," compared the anthropophagous rituals ascribed to the Tupinambá Indians favorably to the "cannibalistic" violence and oppression inflicted upon the poor of contemporary French society at the hands of their wealthy compatriots (driving them, on occasions, to eat each other's flesh) or, worse still, in the name of religion at the hands of the Inquisition.[27]

Against this background, and given the crucial role of the evangelical mission in Brazil for the Counter-Reformation project of the Catholic Church, it is not surprising that the Jesuits should have redoubled their efforts to place the practice of cannibalism outside the moral framework of the Christian European world and to identify it exclusively with resistance to the just cause of evangelization. As early as January 1550, less than a year after his arrival in the colony, Nóbrega was contemplating the use of coercion as an instrument in bringing the Indians into the ecumenical fold: "and perhaps they will be converted by fear more quickly than they will do through love, they are so corrupted in their customs and so far from the truth."[28] By 1557, following the death and reported cannibalization of Bishop Sardinha at the hands of the Caeté, force and confinement were judged to be the only sure means of subjecting the Indians to both civil and ecclesiastical control, to "keep them in justice and truth among them as vassals of the King, and subject to the Church."[29] The Natural Law that they had once apparently obeyed instinctively now needed to be imposed upon them: "First the heathen must be subjected and made to live as creatures that are rational, making them keep the natural law."[30] Nóbrega's voice of experience now recommended the slaving expeditions he had previously denounced, as the solution to the joint problems of labor and evangelization that the colony faced. Nowhere is there a more unequivocal example of the identity of economic and ecclesiastical interests, the equation of the Indians' spiritual well-being with the prosperity of the Crown: "and they would have spiritual life, knowing their creator and in subjection to Your Highness, and they will all live better and in plenty and Your Highness would have abundant incomes in these lands."[31]

Nóbrega's pragmatism, the ease with which the Indians' autonomous interests were subordinated to the practical concerns of the evangelical mission and the colonial demand for labor, is all the more striking in the light of the momentous theological and philosophical debate that was taking place during the same years in the Spanish-speaking world. Bartolomé de las Casas's rehabilitation of the moral status of the Indians of Spanish America, his defense of peaceful methods of evangelization, and his denunciation of the *encomienda* system were, if limited in their immediate practical consequences, nevertheless an important advance and an influential precedent for future discussions of tribal Amerindians.[32] For the proponents of just war and natural slavery, such as Vitoria and Sepúlveda, the obstacle that prevented the Indians from taking the crucial step toward the Christian *oikumene* was their "barbaric" condition. The practices of sodomy, bestiality, and cannibalism attributed to the Indians constituted a violation of the natural order and demonstrated their inability to distinguish between the rigid categories that divide up the world; like their failure to develop a literature, this evidence of irrationality barred them from the community of men and confined them to the status of barbarians.

Bartolomé de Las Casas's *Apologetica historia* represented a radical departure from this view, in the first place because it revised the concept of barbarism, discriminating between four categories that had previously been lumped together: the barbarism of the non-Christian; the relative barbarism that was the quality of "foreignness" displayed by an individual in being unable to understand the language of another society; the barbarism of the individual who has lost moral control over himself or herself (a designation that Las Casas found particularly appropriate to the conduct of many Spaniards in the New World); and the absolute barbarism of the true natural slave, the *barbaria simpliciter*, who is unable to interpret the laws of natural justice or to understand the language of his own society.

Las Casas considered only the first two of these categories to be applicable to the American Indian; thus, the Indian's was a relative barbarism, separating him or her from the rest of humanity only by degree and not in essence. In support of this, much of his *Apologetica historia* was devoted to a description of the non-Christian cultural achievements of the New World that were usually ignored by the Aristotelians and to explaining how Amerindian culture differed from European norms, something Pagden considers to be the "first piece of comparative ethnology."[33] A more extensive and influential contribution to this relativistic view of indigenous culture was the sixteenth-century missionary José de Acosta's *Historia natural y moral de las Indias* (Natural and Moral History of the Indies). Defending the value of empirical knowledge, Acosta wrote from his experience of direct, personal contact with indigenous societies; his account of Indian mores conveys a great sense of novelty, an awareness of the unique nature of Amerindian culture and the need to understand it on its own terms, using new language.

Thus, the critical step forward that paved the way for the modern discipline of ethnology was the European's recognition of other cultures as having a validity and existence in their own right, and not simply as perverted or barbarized forms of European, Christian civilization. Remarkably, however, there is virtually no reference to the debate in the Brazilian context until the nineteenth century, when the historian Varnhagen clashed with liberal Indianists over the question of government indigenist policy; moreover, even at this stage Sepúlveda's Aristotelian views on Just War and Natural Slavery received more attention than those of Las Casas. Meanwhile, in order to grasp the terms and logic of the argument as the Jesuits saw it in sixteenth-century Brazil, we must turn to Nóbrega's *Diálogo sobre a conversão do gentio* (Dialogue on the Conversion of the Heathen) (1556-57).

The structure of the dialogue, a classical genre revived during the Renaissance, allowed Nóbrega to confront the missionaries' initial optimism with the evidence of their experience through the mouths of two "ordinary" spokesmen, the friars Matos Nogueira and Gonçalo Álvares. For Nogueira, who apologizes for talking like a blacksmith, the Indians were akin to "cold iron," ready to enter the furnace and be molded to the required shape and purpose, an obvious variation on the image of the tabula rasa. But for Álvares, their very lack of religious sense, far from offering a blank slate, actually presented an obstacle to conversion; the concept of worship, which he defines religiously and politically, was a necessary prerequisite for the assimilation of Catholic doctrine: "If they had a king, they could be converted, or if they worshipped something; but, since they do not know what it is to believe or worship, they cannot understand the sermon of the Gospel, for it is based on making one believe in and worship a single God, and serve him alone; and since these heathen do not worship anything, or believe in anything, everything you say to them will come to naught."[34]

Ministering to the Indians was therefore comparable to casting pearls before swine; indeed, the categories of bestiality and humanity are discussed at some length, for the Indians' right to be considered "próximos," neighbors, and therefore to be admitted into the ecumenical community depended on them. Nogueira takes a different approach to the problem, suggesting that the difference between the Christian and the Indian is not qualitative but quantitative. After the Fall, Adam descended to the status of an animal, with the result that "all of us, both Portuguese and Castilians, Tamoios and Aimorés, became similar to beasts because of our corrupt nature, and in this we are all the same" (p. 63). If, as Álvares protests, the Indians appear so much more bestial than ourselves, it is because civilization has enabled some peoples to transcend their primitive origins, leaving others behind: "That the Romans and other heathen have more politics than the latter did not arise from the fact that they have a better understanding but from their having a better upbringing and being raised more politically" (p. 65). Nevertheless, in spite of their general lack of "culture," a legacy inherited from Noah's cursed son Ham, the Indians are to be credited with some of the signs of civilization: "In the matters that occupy them and in which they deal, they have as fine subtleties, and as fine inventions, and as discreet words as anyone" (ibid.). Nogueira insists that the Indians possess the faculties that constitute the soul: understanding, memory, and will.

Meanwhile, if, relative to the European, the Indian is ignorant, this is an advantage, since it is not intellect (*rezão demonstrativa*) that is required for him to be persuaded of the elements of the Catholic doctrine, but faith (*rezão humana*): "It is easier to convert an ignorant man than one who is cunning and arrogant" (p. 66). In other words, by virtue of their limited mentality, the Indians possessed a correspondingly restricted capacity for corruption and a greater potential for salvation. By illustration, Nogueira remarks that, in comparison with Roman customs and morality, indigenous culture was much less highly developed and sophisticated. As a result, whereas the Indian sinned in only two or three of the Commandments, the Romans had transgressed them all. Álvares can oppose to this philosophical view of tribal morality and amenity to conversion only his practical experience, the experience of working with people who would be baptized in one instant and revert to their primitive "vices" the next. Although it ends on a positive note, recalling the successes of the Mission, the *Dialogue* does not resolve the argument; it simply points up the gulf between the Jesuits' initial expectations of the Indian and their subsequent experience of frustration in the face of a culture whose strength and internal cohesion they did not anticipate or understand.

The *Dialogue on the Conversion of the Heathen* was performed in Brazil on at least three occasions between 1573 and 1584,[35] but its fine points of theology can have meant little or nothing to the more popular and indigenous audiences for whom Anchieta's *autos*, or one-act plays, were intended. Theological debate had now given way to a functional, propagandist literature committed to the immediate and practical task of conversion. For the first time the Indian was given a voice, albeit a highly caricatured one, as a protagonist in the political and ideological drama of Conquest, possessed of the capacity of free will and repentance. Drawing on the late medieval, satirical tradition of Iberian theater, typified by the Portuguese playwright Gil Vicente, Anchieta's tribal characters display a degree of wit and imagination that is a far cry from the mute, infantile ingenuousness of Vaz de Caminha's birdlike innocents. The Edenic Indian of half a century before has eaten from the Tree of Knowledge, losing his mythical moral stature while gaining in human depth and reality.

This development in colonial perceptions of the Indian reflects the social proximity of missionary and Indian in the microcosmic society of the *aldeia*, another expression of which was the execution of the play itself, as performance. Twenty-five dramas were staged between 1557 and 1598 in the halls of the Jesuit colleges, in public squares, and in the *aldeias* with their natural forest backdrop, usually on the occasion of ecclesiastical visits or sacred festivals.[36] Not only were the majority of the audiences of tribal origin, but Indians also enacted the roles written for them by Anchieta. Many of the autos are bi- or trilingual (the case of the present text), juxtaposing Spanish or Portuguese with Tupi-Guarani and sometimes Latin. As well as distinguishing in this way between the dramatic functions of different sections of the plays, this made them more accessible to their primary target, the Indian.

First performed on 10 August 1583 on the Morro de São Lourenço, Niterói, across the bay from the newly founded colony of Rio de Janeiro, *Na Festa de São Lourenço* (On the Feast of Saint Lawrence) was one of Anchieta's most successful dramas and it provided the basic framework for at least three other texts, the *Auto de São Lourenço, Na Festa do Natal,* and the *Auto da Vila de Vitória* or *São Maurício*.[37] Although didactic in aim, it appealed less to the head than to the heart, to the Indians' own religious sensibility, and to their memory of recent military-political events. Indeed, the drama actually sought to alter that memory as part of the process of cultural indoctrination. Its central religious topic, the martyrdom of the patron saint of the settlement at the hands of the Romans, is linked to a moment from the more immediate history of the colony: the war against the Tamoios. An implicit analogy is thus drawn between the early struggles of the Church against its persecutors and the efforts of the Jesuits to bring Christianity to Brazil in the teeth of indigenous hostility and godlessness.

Anchieta appealed both to his audience's sense of humor and to its fear of the supernatural, presenting a simultaneous caricature of the Indian and Roman persecutors of the Church. By turns arrogant and cowardly, they are punished for their tyrannical defiance of Divine authority with the same torture that was inflicted upon the Christian martyrs. However, Anchieta draws an important distinction between the Roman pagans and the modern Indian heathen: whereas the former were historically and morally beyond redemption, the Indians, even those mortal enemies of the Portuguese-Tupinikin alliance, still retained the possibility of repentance. The play's extremely simple structure hinges on this notion of repentance, as the offending Indians are convinced to abandon their scheme of corruption and to serve the Christian martyrs as executioners.

After an initial song commemorating the saint's martyrdom, three devils enter, the "king" Guaixará and his servants Aimbirê and Saravaia. These names were not chosen at random, for it was the Tamoio chief Guaixará of Cabo Frio who, in July 1556, assembled 180 war canoes for a battle against the Portuguese; chief Aimbirê, whose daughter was married to a Frenchman, was seized by the Portuguese during a truce and escaped in his shackles; he went to Iperoig during Nóbrega and Anchieta's visit there and had to be restrained from killing the Jesuits[38]; Saravaia, meanwhile, is thought to have been a spy working for the French.[39] From the very beginning, then, Satan's aides in the archetypal battle between Good and Evil are identified as some of the chief enemies of the joint secular-missionary project to bring about the social and economic integration of the indigenous population.

The chiefs' role in that struggle takes the form of an attempt to repossess the hearts and minds of the Indians who have accepted the regime of the mission *aldeia* and to promote the traditional culture of war making, polygamy, magic, dance, cannibalism, and drunkenness that represented the antithesis of Catholic morality:

My system is pleasing.
I will not have it constrained,
or abolished.
I intend
to stir up all the villages.

It is a fine thing to drink *cauim* until you are sick.
That is most estimable,
that is commendable,
that is admirable!

Here the drunkard chiefs
are held in high regard.
He who drinks until the *cauim* runs out
is brave
and eager to do battle.

It is fine to dance,
to adorn yourself, to paint yourself red,
to cover your body with feathers, to paint your legs,
to turn yourself black, to smoke,
to work cures. . .

Running rampage, killing,
eating one another, capturing *tapuias*,
taking concubines, being dishonest,

a spy, an adulterer
—I will not have the heathen give up these things.

That is why
I live with the Indians,
tricking them into believing in me.
In vain do the so-called "fathers"
come, now, to drive me away,
preaching the law of God.[40]

Ironically, though, in Anchieta's drama, the renegade chiefs are permitted a last opportunity to exercise the illicit practice of cannibalism in the service of their arch-enemies, the martyred patron saints of the colony. In the first of a series of invented links between the Roman persecution of the early Church and the Indians' resistance to the evangelical mission in Brazil, Guaixará recalls that he was responsible for the deaths of Saint Lawrence and his brother-in-arms, Sebastian, the patron saint of Rio de Janeiro. Confronted by the spirit of Saint Lawrence, Guaixará is accused of usurping the only legitimate claim to command the Indians' loyalty, that of their Creator:

—Who, some day,
gave over the Indians to you,
for your property?
It was God himself.
in his holiness,
who shaped their body and soul. (p. 699)

Saravaia's comic attempts at bribery are futile, as the saints lose their patience and imprison the Indian devils. The guardian angel of the *aldeia* then addresses the audience, explaining his mission to protect the village and reciting the history of the Tamoios war and the military and spiritual victory of the two martyrs:

Forever, in truth, they will love
your souls, taking pity on them,
giving them eternal succor,
perfecting them, sanctifying them,
rooting out their old habits.

They will bind the devils,
when the latter wanted you for their prey.
They will not allow them to touch you.
Loving your souls greatly,
they will gather you to them as their family.

Avoid,
from this day onwards, being evil,
so as to extinguish your old habits
—drinking, noisome adultery,

lying, fighting,
wounding each other, warring. (pp. 714-15)

A brief song celebrates the descent of the devils into Hell, and in the third act they are enlisted into the service of the saints for the punishment of their pagan predecessors, the Roman emperors. Thus, the cannibalistic violence and drinking bouts that had previously expressed their heresy and hostility to the missions are now given a legitimate object, as the entire community is invited to collectively devour the historic enemies of the Christian Church:

Whom shall we eat?
—Those who were the enemies of Saint Lawrence.
—Those loathsome chiefs?
Today, herewith, I shall change my name.
Many will be my adopted names!

Excellent! their entrails
will be my share.
—I shall gnaw their hearts.
—Those who remained in our houses shall eat too.
We shall invite them all.

Tataurana,
bring your club!
Urubu, Jaguaraçu,
bring your mace!
Caborê, hurry along
and eat your enemies!

—Here is my stout club.
I shall eat his arms,
Jaguaruçu his neck,
Urubu his skull,
Caborê his legs.

—Here I am,
I'll take his entrails and lungs
to my old mother-in-law.
The cooking-pot has arrived,
they shall cook before me. (pp. 720-21)

Thus, whatever the reliability of reports of tribal cannibalism in sixteenth-century Brazil, its existence was firmly established in the Jesuit literary and historiographical discourse from the last quarter of the century onward. Indeed, although rather more dramatically sensational, Anchieta's representation of the practice bears strong similarities to that provided by his fellow Jesuit Fernão Cardim in his *Do princípio e origem dos Índios do Brasil e de seus costumes, adoração e cerimônias* (About the Beginning and Origin of the Indians of Brazil and their Customs, Worship and Ceremonies), which was completed in 1584, within a year of the auto *On the Feast of Saint Lawrence*:

and then [the victim] is handed over to the butcher or slaughterer, who makes a hole beneath his stomach, in his fashion, into which the children first put their hands and pull out his entrails, until the butcher makes a cut wherever he decides, and what is left in his hand is each person's share, and the rest is divided among the community, except some of the important parts which out of great honor, are given to the most honored guests, and are taken away by them well roasted, so that they will not turn bad, and later in their lands they celebrate over them and drink to them again.[41]

Anchieta's curious ambivalence on this matter—cannibalism is both a defining mark of indigenous barbarism, hostility, and resistance to the evangelical cause yet is also enlisted as a weapon in the world-historic battle of the Church against its enemies—is surely a revealing comment on its enduring symbolic power within the colonial imagination. Like the spectacle of shameless Indian nakedness, its subversive potential could perhaps be better controlled through literary or dramatic representation, provided this was ultimately safely contained within a moral and theological framework as defined by the Church and its historical mission. Against the broader backdrop of a precolonial history dating back to the very origins of Christianity and embracing struggles with other pagan peoples, the Jesuits' encounter with the Amerindian, which had momentarily seemed to herald the dawn of a new paradisiacal kingdom on earth, lost something of its utopian aura, becoming relativized as one more instrumental step in the Church's project of global expansion.

EMANCIPATION, THE EXPULSION OF THE JESUITS, AND THE INDIANIST EPIC

Nevertheless, that initial encounter, as reported in Pero Vaz de Caminha's *Letter*, supplied the Jesuits with the conceptual framework they needed to legitimate the process of cultural and political domination that they sought to complete over the next 200 years. The Indian's consciousness constituted a void, which the Church must struggle to possess and fill, denying it any space for the articulation of an alternative historical memory and silencing those voices that dared to assert the continuity of tribal identity and its resistance to the violent pressures of assimilation.

The second half of the eighteenth century, however, saw the appearance of three epic poems that demonstrate how, far from reaching its successful conclusion, the legitimacy and effectiveness of that struggle were now matters of dispute and were being challenged by new, secular models of negotiation between colonial society and state. In one case, in particular, the Indian is seen to acquire the stature and dignity of a morally constituted political subject, capable of voicing independent, legitimate interests whose claims with respect to the colonial state are not easily resolved. When he speaks, it is not yet with his own words, but in the language of Enlightenment liberalism and rationalism, for whose political and economic projects he is both the model and the sacrificial victim.

These works—*O Uraguay* (1768), *Caramuru* (1781), and *A Muhraida* (1785)—register to varying degrees a crucial ideological ambivalence as regards the relative claims of the Church, the State, and the indigenous population. On one hand, they suggest a growing interest in, not to say sympathy for, the Indians, their culture, and their, by turns, tragic and formative role in the history of the colony. This has encouraged the view that these epics amounted to a minor Indianist movement, anticipating in embryonic, cryptonationalist form the Romantic movement of the next century, following Independence. However, this must be set against the fact that all three authors seem to defend the legitimacy of the imperial regime and the subordination of the Indian communities to it. In Basílio da Gama's *O Uraguay*, in particular, there is an unresolved tension between this formal defense of the repression inflicted by the colonial armies on the rebellious Guarani missions of Sete Povos and the Indian cause itself, as expressed so eloquently by the chiefs Cacambo and Cepé in the libertarian language of the eighteenth-century Enlightenment.

This political-ideological conflict between a loyalty to the imperial monarchy and the dissident ideas of the Enlightenment has been characterized by Carlos Guilherme Mota as peculiar to a dislocated layer of Brazilian intellectuals, the *letrados*, who were becoming increasingly dissatisfied with the regime at a time of growing economic and administrative crisis. Born mainly in the urban centers of Minas Gerais, whose mining boom was by the 1770s entering a period of "decadence," these *letrados* were typically educated in Europe, bringing them into contact with the political and philosophical writings of the French and American revolutionaries of the time. If they thus found themselves temporarily isolated from the colonial world, they tended also, as an exotic, "foreign" minority, to be relegated to the margins of the cultural community in Portugal. At one remove from the rising mood of resentment and agitation in Minas, which was eventually articulated in the form of several abortive republican conspiracies, they could not wholly identify with those popular demands that called for local democracy and autonomy and the abolition of slavery. But as cultural "outsiders" at the metropolitan court, they could be pushed toward what Mota has described as "intermediate forms of thinking," which, while not exactly revolutionary, corresponded to a colonial version of enlightened reformism, both "colonizing" and "critical of colonization."[42] One expression they took was to argue for a renegotiation of the imperial regime in which the status of the Brazilian colony would be elevated to one of equal partnership with Portugal. According to Mota's analysis, these intermediate forms of thinking were symptomatic of the profound crisis that the colonial project was undergoing at that moment, a crisis also manifested in the state's revision of its indigenist policy and its implications for the Jesuits. In order to understand the significance of this moment of ideological and political crisis, then, we need to trace the history of the Jesuit missions from the late sixteenth century to their demise in the mid-1700s.

As settlement and exploration pushed westward, inland into the basins of the rivers Plate and Amazon, the pressure on both the mission villages and on the free Indian populations began to intensify. The colonists of São Paulo were poorer than their counterparts farther up the coast, due to their isolation and the relative weakness of sugar production in the area. The *paulistas*, predominantly descended from the family of the patriarch João Ramalho, depended instead for their prestige and wealth on the trade in Indian slaves. Slaving expeditions soon became organized affairs, led by tough *mamelucos*, the offspring of Portuguese colonists and female Indian slaves, and were known as *bandeiras*. *Bandeiras* of as many as 3,000 men, a large proportion of them Indians, set out each year from 1600 onward, at first against the Carijó Guarani Indians of the region but increasingly in attacks on the Spanish Jesuit missions of the Guairá, situated along the tributaries of the river Paraná. Thousands of Indians were taken captive and forced to march the long route to São Paulo, where they were sold to settlers. The Jesuits were obliged to arm their parishioners illegally and to flee southward, setting up new missions on the river Uruguay and in the region occupied by the modern states of Rio Grande do Sul and Mato Grosso do Sul. Whereas many such missions eventually fell to the *bandeiras*, the Paraguayan missions, including Sete Povos, were extraordinarily successful in resisting these attacks and survived as prosperous and stable communities until the Pombaline legislation of the 1750s.[43]

In the Amazon, meanwhile, which was settled rather later, the Jesuits enjoyed more widespread security and wealth, particularly under the administration of Antônio Vieira. The 1686 Regulations of Missions in the State of Maranhão and Grão-Pará effected a compromise between the interests of the missionaries and those of the colonists. The Indians were divided into three groups: those responsible for supplying the agricultural needs of the *aldeias*, those used by the Jesuits to bring down further "reductions" of Indians from the interior, and a third group available for two-month periods to the government and individual settlers. Later amendments increased the accessibility of the indigenous labor pool to the colonists, but the Jesuits remained firmly in control and were able illegally to divert large numbers of Indians into the mission system, ignoring the prohibition on their use on the tobacco plantations and sugar *engenhos*.[44]

This situation changed dramatically following the signing of the Boundary Treaty in Madrid in 1750 by the Spanish and Portuguese governments. As well as resolving some anomalies concerning the respective possessions of the two powers in the New World, the treaty was, in effect, a ratification of the immense territorial gains achieved by the *bandeiras* along the western frontier, which represented a twofold increase on the area defined by the 1494 Line of Tordesillas. The regime was now faced with the challenge of effectively occupying these acquisitions through settlement and productive exploitation at a time when the colony's mining economy was entering into decline, and the commercial axis of European colonialism had shifted decisively to the northwestern powers and their Caribbean colonies. The response of the imperial regime to this challenge in the north of the country was to launch the first truly modern development project for Amazonia, a precursor of so many other geopolitical strategies carried out on the initiative of the State in the twentieth century.[45] Thus, the marquis of Pombal, the so-called Enlightened Despot who ruled the Portuguese Empire from 1755, set in motion what can be described as the first protocapitalist agricultural scheme for the region, financed by the Greater Pará and Maranhão Company, administered by state directorates and based on a wage labor reserve.

The constitution of this new pool of wage labor was one of the most important and momentous steps in the history of official indigenist policy, for it effectively meant the proletarianization of the great tribal communities of the region, the Indian peoples. This process could be brought to its successful conclusion, however, only by overcoming a formidable obstacle, the power of the Church, in particular, the Society of Jesus, which had for the last two centuries controlled access to indigenous labor via the mission villages, many of which were lucrative farming enterprises in their own right. The great reforms introduced in the sphere of indigenist legislation in the 1750s are therefore inseparable from those decrees that dissolved the Jesuit missions and abolished their role as mediators between Indian and white society. The Jesuits were stripped of their spiritual powers in the colony, the first stage in their eventual expulsion from Portugal and its dominions in 1759. Simultaneously, two edicts, the so-called Laws of Liberty, "freed" the Indians from the slavery legislation of the 1680s and from the regime of the Jesuit missions, whose administration was passed into the hands of lay "directors." Although heavily couched in the language of Enlightenment liberalism, the text of the laws makes transparent the economic aims that lay behind the "emancipation" of the Indians, the promotion of interracial marriage, and the elimination of racial prejudice:

Charter of 4 April 1755. —His Royal Highness, in consideration of the great desirability of populating his American dominions, and of the great degree to which intercourse with the Indians by means of marriage could contribute towards that end, is pleased to announce:

That his subjects in the kingdom and in America, who marry Indian women, should not therefore suffer any dishonor, but should rather become worthy of his royal consideration.

That in those lands where they settle, they should given preference for those positions and occupations that they know to be appropriate to their individual standing.

That their offspring and descendants should be fit and able for any employment, honor or rank, without the need for any special exemption arising from these alliances, those contracted before this law enjoying the same benefit . . .

That it should be strictly forbidden to give the name of caboucolos, or any other similar name, that might be considered insulting, to those subjects married to Indian women, or their descendants; the penalty for those infringing this law, following complaint from the injured party, shall be banishment from the district within a month, without appeal or exception, until His Highness shall order otherwise.[46]

The repeal of the existing slavery legislation, which occupied the second charter of 6 June 1755, was justified by the low numbers of Indians encouraged to settle in the white community as a result of the living conditions of those already there, "to the detriment of the salvation of their souls, and grave harm to the state and to the local inhabitants, who were quite without labor to help them cultivate their lands" (p. 224).

The directorate system was thus an attempt to draw the Indians into the economy as free and willing wage laborers, half of them to supply government needs and the new *aldeia* plantations, the other half to be employed by individual settlers. The failure of the policy and its consequences are discussed briefly in the next chapter, but suffice it to say that conditions were far from liberal: wages were absurdly unrealistic and varied according to levels of production, workers had to endure a ten and a half-hour day beginning at five in the morning, and the result was high rates of death and desertion. The aim to encourage an arable economy had only limited success, and the predominant activity continued to be gathering or extraction of forest products. Much of the labor force was diverted by the government for pioneering and frontier expeditions and for the construction of frontier fortresses to guard against encroachment by the Spanish.[47]

Meanwhile, the political changes resulting from the Treaty of Madrid were not implemented altogether smoothly or without opposition. Such was the case of Sete Povos (Seven Settlements), the Spanish Jesuit missions on the river Uruguay that now found themselves on Portuguese territory and under orders to move across the border. The exact nature of life in the Paraguayan missions has yet to be satisfactorily defined, but the loyalty of the Indians and their determined resistance to the expulsion even after the Jesuits had bowed to the orders of their superiors lend considerable credence to the suggestion that this was a unique social experiment. The totalitarian regime of the mission system found here its most successful example, a prosperous, independent, and self-sufficient state founded on the egalitarian, but highly disciplined, organization of an exceptionally sedentary people, the Tape Guarani. Nevertheless, contemporary and subsequent accounts of Sete Povos justified the offensive against the rebel "republic" by denouncing the wealth amassed by the Jesuits at the expense of their "slaves," whom they kept in the darkest ignorance, inciting them against secular society:

In the hinterland of the aforementioned rivers Uraguai and Paraguai was found established a powerful Republic, which along the banks and territories of those two rivers alone had founded no less than thirty-one large settlements, inhabited by almost one hundred thousand Souls; and as rich and opulent in fruits and fortune for the so-called Fathers, as they were poor and miserable for the unfortunate Indians whom they confined within them like Slaves.[48]

The Indians' obedience was allegedly so blind that they accepted the lashings administered by the Fathers, and then "rising to their feet they go and make their thanks to them, and kiss their hand. . . . These poorest of families live in the strictest obedience, in greater slavery than the blacks who belong to the men of Minas."[49] Whatever the exact nature of the regime, its historical importance lay in the radical challenge that it posed to the political control of metropolitan Portugal, in the person of Pombal, over the colony. The missions represented an obstacle not just to the Portuguese/Spanish boundary changes and economic development of the region but also to the integrity of the Portuguese Empire.

It was thus that, in spite of the Indians' repeated requests that they should be allowed to remain in Sete Povos, joint Spanish and Portuguese forces were sent to implement the results of the Treaty of Madrid. The first campaign of 1754 ended in a compromise that soon proved unacceptable to the European governments. So, in 1756, the allied armies proceeded to carry out a massacre of 1,400 Indians at the Battle of Caibaté. When the soldiers finally entered the deserted missions, it was alleged that great treasures and wealth were discovered, confirming the anti-Jesuit propaganda that claimed the rebellion had been incited by the Fathers in order to defend their illegitimate, tyrannical empire over the Indians.[50]

It is perhaps not surprising, therefore, that before even acquiring the status of a nationalist symbol, the Indian should have emerged within the literary imagination as a focal point of this struggle for the implantation of an Enlightenment, neocolonialist, and capitalist project in Brazil, at the very center of the dispute between the ecclesiastical and secular powers for territorial, economic, and ideological dominance. It cannot be accidental that the resurgence, in late eighteenth-century Brazil, of the epic, celebrating the heroic, founding achievements of a collective national history, should have coincided with the last cycle of colonial development in Brazil, the final effort to reintegrate the disparate ethnic and social elements of the colony under the economic project of the Portuguese imperial state. The historic struggle between Church and State, which in Europe helped established the conditions for the victory of modern capitalism, found a momentary expression in Brazil in the enlightened state's abolition of the Jesuits' feudal monopoly of Indian labor. All three of the Indianist epics are concerned in their different ways with this moment of crisis, with the viability of, on one hand, feudal, ecclesiastical, and religious, and, on the other, liberal, secular, and rationalist mediations between the Indian and the colonial state and with the possibilities for an integration of Indian and State that might be compatible with the economic and political aspirations of the empire.

Thus in Basílio da Gama's *O Uraguay* the Indian appears as the innocent personification of natural law, tragically manipulated by the obscurantism of the "false" Jesuit Fathers and brought to annihilation in the name of a misguided rebellion against the legitimate authority of the Iberian crowns and their implementation of the new Border Treaty. As we shall see, there is a strong case for suggesting that, at least in part, the poem served its author's need to publicly disassociate himself from the Jesuits in the aftermath of their expulsion from the empire.

Conversely, Santa Rita Durão's *Caramuru* fiercely defends the missionary role of the Church in the history of the empire, and its formative contribution to the construction of a stable colonial society. Durão's semimythical pioneering hero, Diogo Álvares Caramuru, is credited with a messianic status amongst the Indians, and, through a fictional device, he is able to subject all the colony's tribal communities to imperial rule. Not only that, he and his indigenous bride, Paraguaçu, are partners in the first *mestiço* marriage to be celebrated in Portuguese writing as the basis for an imperial foundation myth.

The third epic in this group, virtually unknown since its first and only publication in 1819, stands apart from the others in the narrow historical and geographical parameters of its subject matter and the correspondingly acute insight it offers into the reality of contemporary indigenist policy and its application at a local level. Written in 1785 by Henrique João Wilkens, a soldier stationed in the Upper Amazon, *A Muhraida* is a celebration of the "pacification" and settlement of the Mura people in the previous year following a history of bitter conflict with the local white population. As the poem's subtitles—"The Triumph of Faith" or "The Conversion and Reconciliation of the Heathen Mura"—suggest, the work's underlying dynamic arises out of a tension between the "enlightened" developmentalist policy of the lay directorates and the evangelical project of the missions in the management of Indian affairs. While, on one hand, the drama of the Mura conversion is recounted as the result of a divine miracle, the success of their pacification and settlement is simultaneously held up as a tribute to Pombal's emancipation legislation and the lay mission system, precisely at a time when many local administrators and Brazilian-born settlers were advocating a return to militaristic policies of extermination.

THE BATTLE FOR EMANCIPATION ON THE URUGUAY

The year 1755 saw the convergence of three events of such significance for political and cultural perceptions of the Indian as to suggest that this was truly a historical watershed, a crucial moment of opportunity, when the crisis of the imperial order opened up challenging and contradictory options: to realize and confront the full horror of the crimes committed against the Indian in the name of "just war"; even to imagine a new society cleansed of those and other such crimes by a revolution seeking to re-create that harmonious and free association of individuals glimpsed in the "natural" communities of the Indians themselves; or to intensify the process of subjugation, exploitation, and dispossession in order to guarantee the expansion and integration of markets, nation-states, and empires.

As Pombal issued the first set of Emancipation Laws, the allied Spanish and Portuguese forces were preparing their "final solution" for the Guarani missions of Sete Povos. In the same year, 1755, the philosopher Jean-Jacques Rousseau published his *Discourse on the Origin and Foundations of Inequality amongst Men*, whose vision of Natural Man living in self-sufficient freedom and harmony with his world provided one of the most powerful utopian images for the bourgeois revolutions of France and North America.[51] Based on Rousseau's readings of colonial descriptions of Amerindian society, these ideas found their way past the censors in Brazil, where they were taken up by the intellectual community known as the Minas School. Antônio Pereira de Souza Caldas's "Ode ao homem selvagem" (Ode to Savage Man), for instance, was directly inspired by Rousseau's *Discourse*:

Ó Razão, onde habitas? . . . na morada
Do crime furiosa,
Polida, mas cruel, paramentada
Com as roupas do Vício; ou na ditosa
Cabana virtuosa
Do selvagem grosseiro? . . . Dize . . . aonde?
Eu te chamo, ó filósofo! responde.[52]

(Oh Reason, where is your dwelling-place? . . . in the frenzied house/ of crime,/ Refined, but cruel, bedecked/ In the clothes of Vice; or in the blessed/ Virtuous hut/ of the uncouth savage? . . . Tell me . . . where?/ I call you, oh philosopher! answer.)

Another key text of the Enlightenment, Voltaire's *Candide,* may well have offered additional food for thought to the Minas School and, in particular, the author of *O Uraguay,* Basílio da Gama, as far as the relationship between Civilization, Nature, and Reason was concerned. Although there is no verifiable evidence that Da Gama was familiar with *Candide,* he is highly likely to have been, since the book was an instant best-seller following its simultaneous publication in five European capitals in 1759, precisely the year in which he was obliged to leave Brazil following the expulsion of the Jesuits. Furthermore, there is a striking textual link with *O Uraguay,* which would appear to be more than coincidental. Da Gama's Indian protagonist Cacambo, the innocently loyal, but betrayed, defender of the Jesuit missions of Sete Povos, shares his name with Candide's manservant, that "very fine fellow" who is described as "a quarter Spanish, the son of a half-breed in the Tucuman."[53] Indeed, before entering the service of Candide, Voltaire's Cacambo was a servant at a Jesuit college in the Paraguayan missions, and his ingenuous enthusiasm for the Fathers' system of government leads him to persuade Candide to go and fight for them, not against them, as he had intended:

It's a wonderful way of governing they have. Their kingdom is already more than three hundred leagues wide, and it's been divided into thirty provinces. Los Padres own everything in it, and the people nothing—a masterpiece of reason and justice. If you ask me, nothing could be more divine than los Padres making war on the Kings of Spain and Portugal over here and being confessors to the very same Kings back in Europe, or than killing Spaniards here and speeding them on their way to heaven back in Madrid. It appeals to me, that does.[54]

After discovering the brother of his beloved Cunégonde, the baron of Thunder-ten-tronckh, in the guise of a Jesuit colonel and priest and killing him, Candide is then saved from the cannibal Lobeiros by the resourceful and "reasonable" Cacambo, who convinces them that he and his master are, in fact, enemies and murderers of the Jesuits. Concluding that "this half of the world is no better than the other," the two travelers pursue their journey from falsity to reality via Eldorado, the authentic Garden of Eden whose ancient spokesman tells them how its inhabitants have hitherto escaped the colonial destruction suffered by their predecessors the Incas at the hands of the Spanish.

As we shall see, Da Gama's *O Uraguay* certainly shares Voltaire's anticleri-calism but also, more interestingly, something of his ambivalence as regards the paradisiacal, natural goodness of primitive man and the idealism of Rousseau's Noble Savage. Other Brazilian contemporaries drew more clearly radical politi-cal conclusions from the rationalist confrontation between the civilized and natural worlds. Tomás Antônio Gonzaga's *Cartas Chilenas* (Chilean Letters), an uncompromising satire on life under the corrupt and tyrannical administration of the Portuguese, includes what may be the first Brazilian expression of identi-fication with the colony's oppressed indigenous peoples in opposition to the imperial regime:

> Talvez, prezado amigo, que nós, hoje,
> sintamos os castigos dos insultos
> que nossos pais fizeram; estes campos
> estão cobertos de insepultos ossos
> de inumeráveis homens que mataram.
> Aqui os europeus se divertiam
> em andarem à caça dos gentios
> como à caça das feras, pelos matos.
> Havia tal que dava, aos seus cachorros,
> por diário sustento, humana carne,
> querendo desculpar tão grave culpa
> com dizer que os gentios, bem que tinham
> a nossa semelhança, enquanto aos corpos,
> não eram como nós, enquanto às almas.
> Que muito, pois, que Deus levante o braço
> e puna os descendentes de uns tiranos
> que, sem razão alguma e por capricho,
> espalharam na terra tanto sangue![55]

(Perhaps, dear friend, we are feeling/ today, the punishment for the outrages/ com-mitted by our fathers; these fields/ are covered with the unburied bones/ of countless men they killed./ Here the Europeans amused themselves/ by hunting down the hea-then/ as they would hunt down wild animals in the forests./ There was a certain man who gave to his dogs,/ for their daily sustenance, human flesh,/ seeking to excuse such a grave sin/ by saying that the heathen, although/ they resembled us in their bodies,/ were not like us in the matter of their souls./ Well may God, then, raise his arm/ and punish the descendants of those tyrants/ who, for no reason and on a whim,/ scattered so much blood over this earth!)

The emergent liberal and anticolonial consciousness registered by these texts found a certain, limited resonance among the small "middling" layer of traders, farmers, clergy, military, and free coloreds and blacks, who increasingly saw their interests best served by some kind of regional autonomy and a free labor economy based on small agricultural units.[56] Precisely because of this very lo-calized sense of "pátria" and its isolation from the much larger slave population, the movement was incapable of mobilizing any wider popular base for a nation-wide independence struggle. Nevertheless, the several abortive conspiracies that were organized during these years—the Inconfidência Mineira (1788-89), the

Conjuração of Rio de Janeiro (1794), and the Tailors' Conspiracy of Bahia (1798)—were taken seriously by the Portuguese authorities. Five of the leading conspirators of the Inconfidência were deported to Africa, while a sixth, known as Tiradentes, was hanged, and others implicated in the plot, including members of the Minas School, were jailed.

Born in Minas Gerais in 1741, the author of *O Uraguay*, José Basílio da Gama, spent no more than his childhood and adolescence there. After being sent to Rio de Janeiro to study with the Jesuits, he was forced to leave for Europe when, in 1759, the order was expelled from Brazil, and there he remained for the rest of his life. His formal links with the Minas School are therefore extremely tenuous. However, besides the epic for which he is best known, another text suggests that he did share Gonzaga's sense of solidarity with the Amerindian struggle against the European colonial powers. His "Sonnet to Tupac Amaru" is a homage to the *mestizo* descendant of Inca emperors who, in 1781, rallied thousands of Indians to the siege of Cuzco and decreed the liberation of the slaves and the abolition of taxes, before being captured, tortured, and executed by the Spanish authorities:

Dos curvos arcos, açoitando os ares,
Voa a seta veloz do Índio adusto;
O horror, a confusão, o espanto, o susto
Passam da terra, e vão gelar os mares.

Ferindo a vista os trêmulos cocares
Animoso esquadrão de Chefe Augusto
Rompe as cadeias do Espanhol injusto
E torna a vindicar os pátrios lares.

Inca valente, generoso Indiano!
Ao Real sangue, que te alenta as veias
Une a memória do paterno dano.

Honra as cinzas de dor, e injúrias cheias,
Qu'inda fumando a morte, o roubo, o engano,
Clamam vingança as tépidas areias.[57]

(Lashing the air, the ardent Indian's swift arrow is launched from the curved bows;/ Horror, confusion, alarm, fright/ Depart the land and freeze the oceans over.// As their quivering plumes strike one's gaze/ The majestic chief's courageous troops/ Break the unjust Spaniard's chains/ And avenge once more the homes of their countrymen.// Brave Inca, generous Indian!/ The royal blood that fuels your veins/ Is mixed with the memory of the wrongs done to your fathers.// Honor the ashes filled with grief and insults/ For, as the smoke of death, pillage, deceit, still rises,/ The tepid sands cry out for revenge.)

O Uraguay was published in 1769, almost exactly midway between the massacre of the Guarani Indians at the Battle of Caibaté and Tupac Amaru's insurrection in what is now Peru. The immediate circumstances of the poem's composition suggest that Da Gama's need to disassociate himself from the Jesuits, rather than his sympathy for the Indian cause, prompted him to embark on the

project. During a visit to Portugal he was arrested and condemned to be deported to Angola, under suspicion of remaining secretly loyal to the Society of
Jesus. Only after pleading his innocence and writing an "Epithalamium" for the
wedding of Pombal's daughter, was he spared. *O Uraguay* was composed in the
same year and was personally dedicated to Pombal, who enjoyed Da Gama's
enduring loyalty even after his own political downfall. Vania Pinheiro Chaves
situates the text squarely within that considerable body of writing, which, between 1750 and 1773, attacked the Society of Jesus not only from the perspective of Portugal's immediate economic and political interests but also in the
context of the broader international campaign against the order.[58]

The poem certainly seems to enthusiastically embrace the official anti-Jesuit
interpretation of the Sete Povos rebellion. Indeed, such was its impact that a
defender of the Society, Lourenço Kaulen, saw fit to produce in 1786 a 301-
page "Apologetic Reply," republished in 1907 as a "Refutation of the Calumnies
against the Jesuits Contained in the Poem 'Uruguay' by José Basílio da
Gama."[59] Interestingly, however, as Antonio Candido has pointed out,[60] those
passages of the poem most directly concerned with the Jesuits are also the least
successfully executed. Another critic has suggested that the various illogicalities
and factual contradictions in the work can be explained only by accepting that
the propagandistic thrust of the poem was grafted onto it at a late stage in its
composition.[61] Indeed, the painstaking attention devoted in Ivan Teixeira's recent edition of *O Uraguay* and in the accompanying essays to detailing the correspondences between Da Gama's text and the politics of the anti-Jesuit campaign and the Treaty of Madrid tends to overshadow the dramatic and ideological tensions within the text, which strain against its outwardly polemical or
propagandist tone.

Those tensions have more to do with a confrontation between the military-
political implications of the conflict itself, which had taken place when the
author was fifteen years old, the emancipatory rhetoric of Pombal's new indigenist legislation, and the philosophical and artistic currents that Da Gama encountered in Europe, in particular those of the Enlightenment and the Arcadian
movement, which had by then spread from Italy to Portugal. Certainly, the disruption of an American Arcadia, a harmonious, idyllic world, by the violence
and material ambition of modern European civilization, is a central theme of the
work. Ivan Teixeira considers *O Uraguay* not only as a sophisticated and un-
dogmatic intervention in the great debates of its time, from an Enlightenment
perspective, but also as a metonymical synthesis of Brazil's historical formation.[62] The poem opens with a portrayal of the ravages of a colonial war that
seems to anticipate the closing image of the "Sonnet to Tupac Amaru":

> Fumam ainda nas desertas praias
> Lagos de sangue tépidos, e impuros,
> Em que ondeiam cadáveres despidos,
> Pasto de corvos. Dura inda nos vales
> O rouco som da irada artilharia.[63]

(On the deserted shores smoke still rises/ From the lakes of tepid, polluted blood/ In which float naked corpses,/For crows to feed upon. In the valleys the raucous sound/ Of the raging artillery can still be heard.)

The best-known lines of the poem, from the second canto (heard in paraphrased form in Roland Joffe's 1986 screen version of the episode, *The Mission*), are the most unequivocal statement of regret for the trauma of Conquest, the momentous violation of natural barriers by the European:

Gentes de Europa, nunca vos trouxera
O mar, e o vento a nós. Ah! não debalde
Estendeu entre nós a natureza
Todo esse plano espaço imenso de águas. (II, 171-74)

(Peoples of Europe, if only the sea and wind/ Had never brought you to us. Oh! it was not for nothing/ That nature spread between us/ All this huge flat expanse of water.)

Against this background, the Indian characters, although not yet permitted to occupy the center of the stage, display a real human substance, and their arguments, an ingenuous, but natural, legitimacy, beside which the words of the Portuguese commander Gomes Freire de Andrade have the hollow ring of expediency. The more conciliatory of the two tribal envoys, Cacambo, expresses doubts about the political wisdom of exchanging Sete Povos for the Colônia do Sacramento, a hard-won and valuable Portuguese possession. Besides this, he questions the government's economic reasoning, since the agricultural prosperity of the region will inevitably depend on the availability of indigenous labor; at the same time, Da Gama has him unwittingly denounce the Jesuits' tyrannical exploitation of their wards in violation of the supreme authority of the imperial government:

As campinas, que vês, e a nossa terra,
Sem o nosso suor, e os nossos braços,
De que serve ao teu rei? Aqui não temos
Nem altas minas, nem caudalosos
Rios de areias de ouro. Essa riqueza
Que cobre os templos dos benditos Padres,
Fruto da sua indústria, e do comércio
Da folha, e peles, é riqueza sua.
Com o arbítrio dos corpos, e das almas
O Céu lha deu em sorte. A nós somente
Nos toca arar, e cultivar a terra,
Sem outra paga mais que o repartido
Por mãos escassas mísero sustento.
Pobres choupanas, e algodões tecidos,
E o arco, e as setas, e as vistosas penas
São as nossas fantásticas riquezas.
Muito suor, e pouco, ou nenhum fasto. . . .
Vê que o nome dos reis não nos assusta.
O teu está mui longe; e nós os Índios
Não temos outro Rei mais do que os Padres. (II, 86-110)

(These prairies you can see and our lands,/ Without our sweat and toil,/ What use are they to your King? Here we have/ No deep mines, or torrential/ Rivers with sands of gold. This wealth,/ Which bedecks the temples of the blessed Fathers,/ The fruit of their industry, and of the trade/ In the tobacco leaf, and skins, is their wealth./ Heaven, exercising its will over bodies and souls,/ Has given it to them as their lot. Ours is merely/ To plow and till the land,/ With no other reward than the wretched sustenance/ Shared out by meager hands./ Poor hovels, and woven cottons,/ And the bow, and arrows, and the splendid feathers/ Are our marvelous riches./ Much sweat, and little or no fortune./ (. . .)/ See how the name of Kings does not frighten us./ Yours is far, far away; and we Indians/ Have no other King than the Fathers.)

Cepé, on the other hand, appeals directly to the natural justice of age-old land rights, which gives his rebellion the legitimacy of a patriotic defense of the fatherland:

> e todos sabem
> Que estas terras, que pisas, o Céu livres
> Deu aos nossos Avós; nós também livres
> As recebemos dos antepassados.
> Livres as hão de herdar os nossos filhos.
> Desconhecemos, detestamos jugo,
> Que não seja o do Céu, por mão dos Padres.
> As frechas partirão nossas contendas
> Dentro de pouco tempo; e o vosso Mundo,
> Se nele um resto houver de humanidade,
> Julgará entre nós; se defendemos
> Tu a injustiça, e nós o Deus, e a Pátria. (II, 177-88)

(and everyone knows/ That these lands, where you are treading, Heaven gave/ Freely to our forefathers; we too received them freely from our ancestors./ Our sons must inherit them free./ We do not recognize, we abhor any yoke/ But that of Heaven, through the hands of the Fathers./ Before long the arrows will rend/ This feud of ours asunder; and your World,/ If there is a scrap of humanity left in it,/ Will judge between us; whether we defend/ —You, injustice, and we, God, and the Fatherland.)

In opposition to these arguments, the rationale of Gomes Freire de Andrade's discourse becomes fully comprehensible only in the light of Pombal's "emancipation" legislation of 1755, for Andrade's manipulation of the concepts of liberty and slavery exactly corresponds to that of the Laws of Liberty and seems intended to preempt Cepé's impassioned, reiterated appeal to an absolute freedom. For the Portuguese commander, liberty has very specific cultural and political conditions attached to it. To begin with, there can be no genuine freedom in the seemingly structureless society of the Indians, with its nomadic, subsistence economy and its permanent state of intertribal warfare, in other words, in the absence of those institutions, such as the market and the state, that characterize modern bourgeois society:

> Fez-vos livres o Céu; mas se o ser livres
> Era viver errantes, e dispersos,
> Sem companheiros, sem amigos, sempre

Com as armas na mão em dura guerra,
Ter por justiça a força, e pelos bosques
Viver do acaso, eu julgo que inda fora
Melhor a escravidão, que a liberdade. (II, 119-25)

(Heaven made you free; but if being free/ Meant a life wandering scattered,/ Without the company of fellows or friends, always/ With your weapons in your hands, hard at war,/ Having force as your justice, and living/ haphazardly, I believe that slavery/ Would be better than freedom.)

The mission regime has imposed upon the Indians an illegitimate servitude, usurping the "natural" authority of the Portuguese Crown, which, being natural, a "public" cause as opposed to the "private" interests of the Indians, must therefore represent a higher form of freedom:

Mas nem a escravidão, nem a miséria
Quer o benigno Rei que o fruto seja
Da sua proteção. Esse absoluto
Império ilimitado, que exercitam
Em vós os Padres, como vós, vassalos,
É império tirânico, que usurpam.
Nem são Senhores, nem vós sois Escravos.
O Rei é vosso Pai: quer-vos felices.
Sois livres, como eu sou; e sereis livres,
Não sendo aqui, em outra qualquer parte.
Mas deveis entregar-nos estas terras.
Ao bem público cede o bem privado.
O sossego de Europa o pede.
Assim o manda o Rei. Vós sois rebeldes,
Se não obedeceis; mas os rebeldes,
Eu sei que não sois vós, são os bons Padres,
Que vos dizem a todos, que sois livres,
E se servem de vós, como de escravos. (II, 126-43)

(But the kindly King wishes that neither/ Slavery, nor misery should be the fruit/ Of his protection. That absolute/ Unbounded empire, that the Fathers/ Exercise over you, with you as their vassals,/ Is a tyrannical empire, that they are usurping./ They are not Lords, neither are you Slaves./ The King is your Father: he desires your happiness./ You are free, as I am; and you shall be free,/ Not here, but elsewhere./ But you must give up these lands to us./ The private good yields to the public good./ The peace of Europe demands it./ Those are the King's orders. You are rebels,/ If you do not obey; but the rebels,/ I know are not yourselves, they are the good Fathers,/ Who tell you all you are free,/ And use you as they would slaves.)

The language of paternalism, with its play on the Jesuit padres' false claims to fatherhood, is central to legitimating this "liberation" of the Indians and their incorporation into the "free" economy and society of the Portuguese Empire. (Indeed, the principle of state tutelage has remained a key feature of official indigenist policy in Brazil; until the 1988 Constitution, the Indians were defined as "relatively incapable" before the law, sharing the same status as minors and the mentally deficient.) Earlier in the same canto the General bestows upon his "children" the magnanimity of a strict, but merciful, parent:

Torna-lhe o General: Tentem-se os meios
De brandura e de amor; se isto não basta,
Farei a meu pesar o último esforço.
Mandou, dizendo assim, que os Índios todos,
Que tinha prisioneiros no seu campo,
Fossem vestidos das formosas cores,
Que a inculta gente simples tanto adora.
Abraçou-os a todos, como filhos,
E deu a todos liberdade. (II, 26-34)

(The General replies to him: Let us first attempt the measures/ Of kindliness and love; if this does not suffice,/ I shall regretfully carry the struggle through to its end./ With these words he ordered that all the Indians/ Who were held captive in his camp/ Be dressed in the beautiful colors/ That these simple, uncouth folk so adore./ He embraced them all, as if they were his children,/ And gave them all their freedom.)

The closing scene of the poem, when "correct" political relations between the two peoples have been restored, resembles a family portrait, the patriarch at its center with his children gathered around him, seeking his protection. However, before that reconciliation can take place, the rebels must be punished, their disobedience checked with a severity that more than matches Andrade's reply to the defiant Cacambo:

Dentro de pouco tempo um meu aceno
Vai cobrir este monte, e essas campinas
De semivivos palpitantes corpos
De míseros mortais, que inda não sabem
Por que causa o seu sangue vai agora
Lavar a terra, e recolher-se em lagos. (II, 159-64)

(In a short while I shall give the sign/ And this hillside and those prairies will be covered with the half-dead, quivering bodies/ Of miserable mortals, who still do not know/ For what cause their blood is now about/To bathe the earth and gather in pools.)

It is very much in spite of this uncompromising political argument that Da Gama allows his Indian protagonists to achieve an epic stature far surpassing their role as the passive, childlike victims of manipulation we have already seen. More than in the scenes of explicit military heroism that complete canto II, this epic stature is suggested through a secondary, inner narrative that is otherwise superfluous to the historical events of the poem. Cacambo's mission to set fire to the enemy camp, his separation from his lover Lindóia, and his death at the hands of the corrupt Jesuits are all separated from the real, external referent by a new narrative perspective and a special poetic space that is exclusive to the Indian. Antonio Candido has analyzed in detail the cinematic-like sequence in canto IV, which transports the reader across a natural landscape from the Portuguese camp to the mission *aldeia*.[64] A similar technique is used at the beginning of canto III to bridge, yet also emphasize at a mythical level, the physical and cultural distance between Portuguese and Indian. In this respect, the conspicuous paucity of ethnographic detail in *O Uraguay*, by contrast to, say, *Caramuru*, is significant, for those few details that Da Gama does include function precisely to underline the harmony between the Indians and their land, a harmony that excludes the European.

One such instance is his account of the tribal practice of stubble-burning, in order to encourage the top growth of vegetation. For the author, this exemplifies the civilization of the Indian, the principle by which "Art amends Nature." But it also demonstrates the latter's tactical strength, for by abandoning the practice for the duration of the war, the Indians are able to deny their opponents the pasture needed by the horses of their mounted regiments. This alliance between man and Earth, personifying the hostility of the continent towards the imperial invader, produces scenes remarkably similar to those described by Euclides da Cunha at the turn of the twentieth century in his account of the Canudos rebellion,[65] another conflict between the state and "primitive rebels":

Mas agora sabendo por espias
As nossas marchas, conservavam sempre
Secas as torradíssimas campinas,
Nem consentiam, por fazer-nos guerra,
Que a chama benfeitora, e a cinza fria
Fertilizasse o árido terreno.
O cavalo até li forte, e brioso,
E costumado a não ter mais sustento,
Naqueles climas, do que a verde relva
Da mimosa campina, desfalece.
Nem mais, se o seu Senhor o afaga, encurva
Os pés, e cava o chão co'as as mãos, e o vale
Rinchando atroa, e açouta o ar co'as clinas. (III, 30-41)

(But now, knowing through spies/ Which paths our marches took, they kept/ The parched plains dry;/ Nor did they allow, in their war with us, the beneficial flame and cold ash/ To fertilize the arid terrain./ The horse that hitherto was strong, high-spirited,/ And used to no other food,/ In those climes, than the green grass/ Of the lovely prairie, collapses./ No longer, if its Master strokes it, does it bend/ Its legs, and paw the ground with its hooves, and whinny/ Thunderously through the valley, and thrash the air with its mane.)

Similarly, in the second and third cantos the landscape appears actively to participate in the Indians' resistance to the Portuguese. During Cacambo's mission to set the enemy camp alight, the river collaborates by calming its current as the Indian dives into its waters. For the first time the colonial power is viewed from within the tribal universe as an outsider, alien to a people and landscape living in harmonious self-sufficiency.

We now enter another world "on the other bank," in which Cacambo undergoes all the stages of a kind of epic quest in miniature. It begins with the vision or dream of Cepé, who exhorts Cacambo to avenge his death, echoing, as one critic has noted,[66] the appearance of Hector to Aeneas. The vision endows Cacambo with the characteristic isolation of the tragic hero and the transcendent power of his epic, patriotic mission. The epic mood is reinforced by references to Ulysses and the destruction of Troy and, again, by the hero's semi-magical powers over his environment, as he conjures up the animate forces of the fire from two dry sticks. If the tragic hero at the top of the wheel of fortune must eventually fall, his mythical status is nevertheless preserved intact, for it is only after completing this mission that Cacambo returns to meet his betrayal at the hand of his false protector Padre Balda.

The climax of this inner mythical narrative that Da Gama constructs for the Indian is the death of Lindóia after her forced separation from Cacambo. It is the episode that most appealed to the Romantic Indianists, for reasons that are not merely confined to its pathos. On one hand, it allows Da Gama to convey the disruption of the Arcadian, tribal world at an individual level, in terms of the frustrated sexual relationship between the two Indians. On the other hand, Lindóia's intact virginity (she takes her own life rather than yield to Balda's protegé Baldetta) means that the integrity of her special poetic space also remains inviolate. After her vision of the future downfall of the corrupt Jesuit empire, she withdraws into the flower-strewn grotto prepared for her by the old sorceress Tanajura. There, she is discovered by her brother, wrapped in the coils of a snake; after hesitating an ominous three times, he lets loose an arrow, and the animal writhes grotesquely in its own blood and venom, apparently signifying Lindóia's salvation. However, the poison is already working in her veins, allowing her the far preferable death, the *liebestod*, that will reunite her with Cacambo. Denied a proper burial, like her lover, she is left "exposed to the wild beasts and famished birds," reaffirming her integration into the natural order. At the same time she symbolizes, if at a tragically passive level, the vulnerable innocence of her people and their heroic but ultimately hopeless resistance and so becomes the first in a long tradition of Romantic Indianist heroines.

O Uraguay is therefore the first imaginative work in Brazil's literary tradition to dramatize the contradictions inherent in the liberal, progressive idea of indigenous emancipation or integration. In reality, one form of tutelage, that of the Jesuits, was being exchanged for another, the incorporation of the Indian into the political and economic structures of the imperial state. There was no alternative to that project but extermination; just as hundreds of thousands had lost their lives over the previous two centuries in the Christian cause of spiritual salvation, thousands more were now dying at the hands of a new generation of "enlightened" liberators.

CARAMURU, THE COLONIAL MESSIAH, AND THE FIRST *MESTIÇO* MARRIAGE

It is hardly surprising that there should have been some attempt to defend the Church's contribution to the colonial enterprise against the Enlightenment project of a secularized imperial state, as advocated in Da Gama's poem. Santa Rita Durão's *Caramuru* was published in 1781, just twelve years after *O Uraguay*, yet it appears virtually unaffected by those philosophical developments that were increasingly sympathetic to the Indians' cause and that were even drawing revolutionary utopian conclusions from the radical alternative that their culture posed to contemporary European civilization. Most critics have remarked on the artistic limitations of Durão's poem, in particular, its tedious, stylistic conservatism. Less attention has been paid to the vehemently Catholic perspective of the work, which makes it closer in spirit to Anchieta's didactic dramas of two centuries previously.

There are numerous accounts in early colonial chronicles, historical texts, and works of fiction of the story of Diogo Álvares Caramuru, the shipwrecked Portuguese sailor whose life was spared by the tribal inhabitants of the northeastern coast and who married into the family of a local chief.[67] The legend offered fertile sources for a foundation myth celebrating the historical origins of the colonial ruling class of Bahia. Indeed, in the late seventeenth century the satirical poet Gregório de Matos had lampooned the aristocratic, "nativist" pretensions of the local elite in a mock homage "To the Caramurus of Bahia." But it is the Franciscan theologian Durão's peculiarly distorted interpretation of the legend, with its largely fabricated depiction of the hero's missionary role in the nascent colony, that has survived as the received version of the story.

Santa Rita Durão's biography suggests that he was moved to compose his epic by a powerful sense of personal and ideological remorse. After becoming a respected doctor of philosophy and theology in Portugal, ambition led him to enter into a friendship with Dom João Cosme, the bishop of Leiria, whose influence he hoped would benefit his career. To this end he wrote a *Pastoral*, the most violent invective yet against the Jesuits, which was published in his patron's name. However, the bishop repaid Durão's services by taking the entire credit for the piece and disowned his protegé. Durão spent many years traveling throughout Europe recovering from the injury of this ingratitude, pursued by a gnawing sense of guilt that led him to seek an audience with the Pope and to publish a *Retraction* of his earlier libel.[68]

The poem *Caramuru* may be seen as a further attempt to expiate this guilt; in this way it is possible to explain Santa Rita Durão's portrayal of Diogo Álvares as a forerunner of the Jesuit missionaries, with its inflated impression of his religious influence among the Indians. Durão constructs an entire messianic mythology around the arrival of Diogo, combining existing legends with some of his own invention. For instance, one episode tells how Santo Áureo (the Golden Saint) was miraculously transported to a distant, unknown land to bring the Word of God to a dying man, Guaçu. The man had already dreamed of this visit and of the "Venerable, bearded white man"[69] who would fulfill his faith in the ultimate salvation of mankind: "But I never doubted that someone would appear,/ To redeem us from all this misery" (I, 49). On his death the old man is placed on the island to point the way to the "country of the rich metal"—the references to Brazil are obvious, and there is a clear invitation to identify the Golden Saint and Diogo Álvares, whose coming has also been anticipated in the Indian collective unconscious. Durão suggests this by staging a theological debate between Diogo Álvares and the chief of the Tupinambá Indians, Gupeva.

Gupeva expounds a series of theological concepts—the Devil, Hell, Sin, an omnipotent God of truth — which bear no relation to the many accounts of tribal culture previous to its exposure to Catholicism.[70] These beliefs were, according to Gupeva, transmitted down the generations in an unrecognizable form, their true meaning obscured, forgotten, or deliberately suppressed in cases where they conflicted with sinful indigenous customs:

> Outra lei depois desta é fama antiga,
> Que observada já foi das nossas gentes;
> Mas ignoramos hoje a que ela obriga,
> Porque os nossos maiores, pouco crentes,
> Achando-a de seus vicios inimiga,
> Recusaram guardá-la, mal contentes. (III, 80)

(Besides this there is another law of old repute,/ Which was once observed by our peoples;/ But today we are ignorant of its obligations,/ Because our elders, unbelieving,/ Finding it hostile to their vices,/ And displeased, refused to keep it.)

Diogo's arrival has been further prefigured in the legend of Sumé, an itinerant miracle-maker and agent of civilization and probably a fusion of indigenous messianic figures and the Christian evangelist, Saint Thomas (São Tomé)[71]:

> Mas da memória o tempo não acaba,
> Que pregara Sumé, santo emboaba.
> Homem foi de semblante reverendo,
> Branco de cor, como tu, barbado,
> Que desde donde o Sol nos vem nascendo,
> De um filho de Tupá vinha mandado. (III, 80-81)

(But time has not wiped out the memory/ Of Sumé, the holy stranger's preachings.// He was a man of venerable mien,/ White, like you, and bearded,/ Who came from where the Sun is born,/ Sent by a son of Tupá.)

More than all the poem's many other distortions of Indian culture, however, this last idea, "son of Tupá," stands at the center of Durão's messianic interpretation of the Caramuru myth and brings all the previous elements together. If any single image is responsible for the survival of the myth right up to the present, then it is the hero's firing of the musket, which saves him from execution and establishes the origins of his prestige within the tribe. Indeed, among the many, varied explanations for Caramuru's adopted indigenous name, the one that has enjoyed most credibility relates to this prodigious demonstration of European technology and power.[72] The Jesuit chronicler Simão de Vasconcellos, for instance, told the story in the following words:

the man of fire (so he was called) who inflicted injury from afar, and killed, such that those who saw in him the fury of a Volcano swooned, and fled into the forests, giving proof of the valor and superhuman skill (in the opinion of these people) of Diogo Álvares, . . . and here they gave him the name, calling him the great Caramuru.[73]

Although in fact an indigenous term for the moray eel, referring to Diogo's initial emergence from the sea after his shipwreck, this explanation of "man of fire" has remained most popular, suggesting a cultural, as well as military, conquest of the Indian. A brand of fireworks in Brazil still uses the name, and contemporary children's literature perpetuates the image of Diogo firing his musket while the Indians look on in amazement or flee in terror.

Durão's account of the event enhances its epic significance to the full. In most other versions Diogo cooperates with the Tupinambá tribespeople in recovering objects from the wreck, at the same time managing to conceal a musket, powder, and shot, with which he impresses the Indians by killing a bird. Durão, however, is unable to let Diogo humiliate himself by collaborating in his imprisonment. In the poem Diogo has kept, along with the other weapons, a suit of armor that he has somehow hidden in a cave. Durão is thus able to make the hero's subjugation of his captors a more calculated triumph; he first appears in his armor when Gupeva's tribe is being attacked by Sergipe, "the valiant prince," and convinces the Indians that he is the evil spirit Anhangá, transforming the Indians' understandable surprise into quivering, subhuman terror. Then comes Diogo's lesson of technology and European weaponry, the source of his mythical, semidivine status:

> Estando a turba longe de cuidá-lo,
> Fica o bárbaro ao golpe estremecido,
> E cai por terra, no tremendo abalo
> Da chama, do fracasso e do estampido;
> Qual do hórrido trovão com raio e estalo
> Alguem junto a quem cai, fica aturdido,
> Tal Gupeva ficou, crendo formada
> No arcabuz do Diogo uma trovoada.
> Toda em terra prostrada, exclama e grita
> A turba rude, em mísero desmaio,
> E faz horror, que estúpida repita
> —Tupá Caramuru!—temendo um raio.
> Pretendem ter por Deus, quando o permita
> O que estão vendo em pavoroso ensaio,
> Entre horríveis trovões do márcio jogo,
> Vomitar chamas e abrasar com fogo. (II, 44-45)

(Against the mob's furthest expectations,/ the barbarian trembles at the shot,/ And falls to the ground, in the tremendous commotion of flame, and crashing explosion;/ Just as one beside someone who falls at the terrible thunderbolt with lightning and thunderclap, is stunned,/ So was Gupeva, believing a roll of thunder to have sprung from Diogo's harquebus./ Prostrate on the ground, the uncouth mob/ Shouts and exclaims, in a wretched swoon,/ And is awestruck, stupidly repeating/ —Tupá Caramuru!—fearing a lightning bolt./ If he will allow it, they will claim as their God/ This thing that before them in such a frightful trial,/ With terrible thunderclaps from the game of war,/ Is spewing out flames and consuming all in fire.)

Right from the opening stanza of the poem, Caramuru is identified as the "Filho do Trovão" (Son of Thunder), a highly loaded adaptation of the erroneous ety-

mology "man of fire," which was already common currency. Durão was exploiting one of the most widely propagated fallacies concerning the tribal cosmology, namely, that Tupã, "source or mother of thunder," was a supreme
creator god in the tradition of European religions. This was the term commonly
used by the Jesuit missionaries to translate the notion of an omnipotent Christian
God into terms comprehensible to the Indians. Thus, as the Son of Thunder, the
Son of God, Diogo is elevated to the status of a Christ-figure, the archetypal
Messiah of the colonizers' Christian culture. As an American Christ, Diogo has
arrived to reveal the true nature of Indian religion that, as we saw earlier, had
supposedly long since been concealed from the Indians themselves. Following
this line of reasoning, indigenous culture contained within it a latent, disguised
form of Catholicism, whose denial and suppression by the Indians through their
primitive practices constituted an unforgivable blasphemy. One such practice,
which Durão focuses on with a fervor worthy of Anchieta, is cannibalism; indeed, Durão reiterates the Jesuit's comparison between tribal barbarism and the
pagan heresies of the ancient Romans and Greeks:

> Correm, depois de crê-lo, ao pasto horrendo;
> E, retalhando o corpo em mil pedaços,
> Vai cada um, famélico, trazendo,
> Qual um pé, qual a mão, qual outro os braços;
> Outros na crua carne iam comendo,
> Tanto na infame gula eram devassos.
> Tais há que as assam nos ardentes fossos;
> Alguns torrando estão na chama os ossos.
>
> Que horror da humanidade ver tragada
> Da própria espécie a carne já corrupta!
> Quanto não deve a Europa abençoada
> À Fé do Redentor, que humilde escuta?
> Não era aquela infâmia praticada
> Só dessa gente miseranda e bruta:
> Roma e Cartago o sabe no noturno,
> Horrível sacrifício de Saturno. (I, 17-18)

(Discovering this, they run to the awful feast,/ And, dividing the body into a thousand
pieces,/ Each one takes his share, one a foot, another a hand, another the arms;/ Others set to eating the raw flesh,/ So debauched were they in their vile greed./ Some are
cooking their share in burning pits,/ While others roast the bones in the flames.// How
awful to see the corrupted flesh of humanity/ Swallowed by its own kind!/ What does
blessed Europe not owe/ To the Faith of the Redeemer, listening in humility?/ That
infamy was not practiced only by this vile, brute people: Rome and Carthage knew it,
too,/ In the horrible, nocturnal sacrifice of Saturn.)

However, the state of primitive ignorance is unacceptable to Diogo as a justification for this bestial behavior:

> Tornai a culpa a vós; e a vós somente
> (o Heroe responde assim). Se com estudo
> Procurais sobre a Terra o bem presente,

Porque não procurais o Author de tudo?
Para o mais tendes lume, instincto, e mente;
Somente contra Deos buscais o escudo
Em a vossa ignorancia a brutal culpa!
Essa ignorancia he crime, e não desculpa. (III, 10)

(Blame yourselves; and yourselves alone/ (replies the Hero). If by study/ You seek good on Earth, here and now,/ Why do you not seek the Inventor of everything?/ You have light, instinct and intelligence for everything else;/ Only from God do you seek to shield/ Your brutish guilt behind your ignorance!/ That ignorance is a crime, and not an excuse.)

The option of salvation is available, though, and it is offered through the archetypal colonial marriage between Indian and white, which follows the European's military conquest of the territory. Whereas the earlier accounts suggest that Diogo fought with the local Tupinambá against a neighboring Tapuia tribe, Durão augments the scale of the war to an implausible degree. The enemy aggressor, Sergipe, is joined by an impossible alliance of tribes that include the Potiguar from the northeast and the Carijó from the southernmost region of Rio Grande do Sul. By bringing together tribes separated by thousands of miles and representing the entire indigenous population of Brazil, Durão transforms Diogo's local triumph into a global, military conquest of the country.

Diogo's political conquest was achieved, in reality, like that of João Ramalho in São Paulo, by taking full advantage of the Indians' polygamous marriage system and establishing a large patriarchal family. The different accounts of the legend have tended progressively to attenuate the element of polygamy and to offer Paraguaçu (a name probably invented by the Jesuit chronicler Simão de Vasconcellos) as a single representative figure, an ideal symbol of the Indian convert and of the embodiment of the Catholic ethic in the *mestiço* colonial family. Moreover, all the versions of the myth except Durão's attribute the role of evangelization exclusively to Paraguaçu; her vision of the Virgin leads to the discovery of a box containing an image, to which the couple raises a chapel and abbey. In Durão's epic, meanwhile, she has a more secondary, passive function; after Diogo has helped Gupeva defeat the national alliance of tribes, he is offered the daughters of the subjugated chiefs; as one editor of the poem explains, "The Indian chiefs offer their daughters to Diogo Álvares, to honor him with their kinship. The Portuguese accepts the kinship, but not the maidens, out of chaste fidelity to Paraguaçu."[74] This sanitized depiction of the European colonizer's sexual conduct stands in sharp contrast to the instinctive sensuality and even bestiality of the Indian characters. For instance, one of the enemy chiefs, Jararaca (the name of a poisonous snake), plans to abduct Paraguaçu, having seen her asleep in the forest; his brute sensibility is awed by the girl's divine beauty. Even the affable Gupeva is rejected by Paraguaçu, for "Barbarous peoples know nothing of love,/ Nor does the amorous flame burn in their brutish breast" (I, 80).

The most important representative of this notion of an illicit, bestial sexuality is the character Moema, whose tragic exclusion from the central marriage of the Caramuru myth was to appeal to the Romantics more than any other element of

the story. This purely fictional incident developed out of Diogo's departure for
Europe on a passing French ship. In several of the early accounts, his favorite
Indian wife swims out to join him, but from Vasconcellos onward, this idea of
loyal pursuit is transferred to the other wives or "concubines." The notion of the
Indian's self-sacrifice and dedication to her white master is therefore transformed into jealousy, abandonment, and despair. Diogo takes his preferred partner with him, while of the rest, at least one drowns in the attempt to follow, a
picture of desperate sexual rivalry and loyalty that corresponds to Diogo's
global military control over the territory's tribes. His ability to reject all but the
most socially prestigious—the "princess"—enhances his power over the Indians.

But the elements of jealousy, abandonment, and despair imply something
rather different in Durão's version of the story, for he is the first to inscribe a
racial significance onto the death of the drowned girl, whom he names Moema.
According to Gregório's *Contribuição indígena ao Brasil*, "Moema" (also the
name of a town in northern Minas Gerais) is derived from the common Tupi
transitive prefix *mo*, "to make," combined with the particle *ema*, "empty," to
produce the sense of "drive out" or "pour out."[75] The twin notions of rejection
and emotional collapse associated with the character might arguably be supported by the name's etymology, then, although the additional "translation"
cited by Gregório—"extenuada," "frail or languishing, one exhausted by weariness"—is clearly colored by Durão's characterization of Moema in *Caramuru*.
Certainly, Durão was single-handedly responsible for the invention of the tragically abandoned, jealous, and vengeful *índia* whom the nineteenth-century Romantic Indianists would identify with the name Moema on so many occasions.

Let us compare her with Durão's description of her rival Paraguaçu:

> Paraguaçu gentil (tal nome teve),
> Bem diversa de gente tão nojosa,
> De cor tão alva como a branca neve,
> E donde não é neve, era de rosa. (II, 78)

> (Noble Paraguaçu (such was her name),/ Quite different from such repugnant people,/
> Her color as white as the driven snow,/ And where she is not snow-white, she is rose-
> pink.)

Durão goes to great pains to emphasize the physical and moral distance separating Paraguaçu from the other Indians and her consequent proximity to Diogo.
She is described as "Certa dama gentil brasiliana" (One noble Brazilian lady)
and as a "donzela" (maiden) rather than "índia" or "heathen." She displays the
erotic sensibility of a *civilizada*, and her knowledge of Portuguese, conveniently
learned from a captive of the tribe, gives her a special intimacy of communication with Diogo. Antonio Candido rightly sees this ethnic transformation as part
of an ideal cultural union between Europe and America, in which the Portuguese
Diogo praises the marvels of Brazil, adopting a tribal name and certain of the
less controversial aspects of indigenous culture, while the Indian Paraguaçu
speaks for European civilization.[76]

Moreover, the author's reluctance to confront the sexual reality of miscegenation, which is central to the story of Caramuru, brings him to a denial of Paraguaçu's dark Indian blood and to describe what is effectively the marriage of white to white. Meanwhile, he projects the dangerous, dark sexuality of the Indian woman onto the fictitious figure of Moema, who clings hopelessly to the hull of the ship, suggesting a symbolic image of phallic impalement and sexual frustration. Durão does not deny the seductiveness of the forbidden Indian woman for the European male; indeed, he indicates in the poem that Diogo was not immune to the attractive Moema, who complains that he did acknowledge her sexuality in some casual, noncommittal way, ultimately to reject her:

Bem puderas, cruel, ter sido esquivo,
Quando eu a fé rendia ao teu engano; . . .

Porém, deixando o coração cativo,
Com fazer-te a meus rogos sempre humano,
Fugiste-me, traidor, e desta sorte
Paga meu fino amor tão crua morte? (VI, 39)

(Cruel man, you could easily have been aloof,/ When I returned your deceit with loyalty;/ (. . .)/ But, keeping my heart captive,/ Remaining always human to my entreaties,/ You fled from me, traitor, and in this way/ Is my keen love repaid with such pitiless death?)

Moema's death symbolizes for Durão the moral obstacle to any publicly sanctioned sexual union between the white man and Indian woman. Only through a process of racial expurgation, such as that seen in the figure of Paraguaçu, and culminating in her conversion to Christianity, can the marriage take place. The Indian's sexual identity, suppressed in Paraguaçu, is given full expression in the figure of Moema, who bitterly voices her resentment against Paraguaçu:

Por serva, por escrava, te seguira,
Se não temera de chamar senhora
A vil Paraguaçu, que, sem que o creia,
Sobre ser-me inferior, é nescia e feia. (VI, 40)

(I would follow you as a servant, as a slave,/ If I did not fear to call Paraguaçu/ My mistress, she who, though she does not believe it,/ Besides being inferior to me, is foolish and ugly.)

While, on one hand, celebrating a "chaste" colonial marriage, sanctified by the evangelical role assigned to Diogo Álvares and his convert wife, *Caramuru* therefore also brought into being a new tradition—that of the Indian as a tragic victim of social and racial exclusion. For all that Diogo takes on an indigenous name and establishes his political and social authority within the Indian world, he remains, in Durão's account at least, culturally unaltered by the experience. Ironically, it is the angry, defiant Moema, Paraguaçu's alter ego, who survives into the Romantic tradition as an obstinate reminder of the failure to integrate the colonial empire through military and religious conquest.

MIRACLE ON THE UPPER AMAZON: *A MUHRAIDA* AND THE PACIFICATION OF THE MURA

Ever since 1826, when the French intellectual Ferdinand Denis first drew the attention of the new generation of Brazilian writers to *O Uraguay* and *Caramuru*, critics and literary historians have acknowledged the historical role of these two poems in suggesting themes for a nationalist literature and its most characteristic expression, Romantic Indianism. *O Uraguay* went through five new editions between 1811 and 1855, with the 1845 edition organized by the historian Varnhagen also including the text of *Caramuru*. In addition, the latter was republished separately on the instigation of the French journalist Monglave and, as we shall see, was the subject of numerous retellings in prose and verse and on the stage. Durão's fictional character Moema was depicted on canvas by the Romantic artist Victor Meirelles de Lima, and she appears along with other nineteenth-century Indianist heroines, such as Coema, Iguassú, and Iracema, in the sonnet "Lindoya," which the novelist Machado de Assis wrote in 1895 to commemorate the centenary of Da Gama's death.

In 1819, just seven years before Denis made his recommendations to the young artists of the newly independent Brazil, there appeared the first printed edition of an Amazonian "heroic poem," *A Muhraida*, or *The Conversion and Reconciliation of the Heathen Mura*, written in 1785 on the Upper River Negro by a soldier, Henrique João Wilkens. Yet despite the declared Indianist purport of the poem and its concern with recent events comparable to those depicted in *O Uraguay*, there is not a single mention of *A Muhraida* in the critical writings or fiction of those involved in the Indianist movement. Indeed, only since Mário Ypiranga Monteiro's article of 1966 has the existence of the poem begun to be widely divulged and been subject to critical attention.[77]

Among the possible reasons for this disparity in the subsequent fortunes of these works, the first that must be discounted is the antiprovincial prejudice of the literary establishment in the capital, with its eyes on Europe rather than the far north of Brazil. For like *Caramuru* and *O Uraguay*, *A Muhraida* was published by the Royal Press in Lisbon, receiving the additional patronage of the bishop of Eucarpia, "Provisor of the Archbishopric of Évora and member of His Majesty's Counsel."[78] Neither can the issue of artistic quality convincingly be invoked in order to explain its disappearance from literary view; although not a masterpiece, by comparison with *Caramuru*, *A Muhraida* is certainly brief, to the point, and readable.

The origins of the poem's failure to be assimilated into the Romantic Indianist heritage must be sought elsewhere, in the nature of its relationship to the historical events and circumstances that produced it. What most strikingly sets *A Muhraida* apart from the other two epics is that the erotic dimension is completely lacking from Wilkens's text; this alone might suffice to explain its lack of appeal to the Romantics, if one remembers that it is Paraguaçu, Moema, Cacambo, and Lindóia, the Indian protagonists of the amorous episodes from *Caramuru* and *O Uraguay*, who survive into the Romantic tradition, rather than the military or political events in which they are involved.

But the absence of a romantic theme, indeed, of any named, individualized Indian character in *A Muhraida*, is indicative of a more general and fundamental feature of the poem's treatment of its subject: its exclusive concern with a narrowly local and historical context and the immediate political and economic forces at work in it. For all their differences, *O Uraguay* and *Caramuru* enjoyed a similar prestige among the nineteenth-century Romantics as protonationalist Indianist works precisely because their erotic episodes succeeded in adding a mythical dimension to the historical material with which they were concerned, suggesting how local events in colonial history might stand symbolically for much broader narratives of political conflict and state-formation. *A Muhraida* never transcends the context of its own historical narrative and offers instead a correspondingly sharper insight into contemporary attitudes to official indigenist policy and into the reality of its application at a local level.

On one hand, the poem pays homage to João Pereira Caldas, the governor of Pará and an important participant in the execution of the 1750 Boundary Treaty for the Amazon region. Another figure celebrated in the poem is Mathias Fernandes, the director of the Indian mission where the Mura were settled. The example of this mission and the conversion of the Mura as portrayed in the poem are a tribute to the alleged success of Pombal's "emancipation" legislation of 1755, passing administration of Indian affairs into lay hands and "integrating" the indigenous population into the dominant society and economy.

At the same time, the poem is ingenuously frank in acknowledging the other side of the reformist coin of Pombal's Laws of Liberty, the commercial, developmentalist motives of colonization and agricultural exploitation. This undisguised concern with the economic forces underlying the official public rhetoric of emancipation and conversion, no doubt a result of the author's close personal involvement in the events concerned, gives the poem a quality of historical immediacy setting it apart from the other two works with their mythical, epic scale.

Little is known of the life of Henrique João Wilkens, the author of *A Muhraida*, and the details cited by his first critic, Mário Ypiranga,[79] are all taken from Inocêncio Francisco da Silva's *Dicionário Bibliográfico Português*, of 1858-1923. His surname suggests he may have been of English or possibly German birth or descent, but his known biography begins only with his appointment as "squadron corporal of the Imperial militia" in Barcelos, on the river Negro, where he took part in a failed expedition against rebel Indians in the region. He was favored with rapid promotion, being able to offer his skills as an engineer and later as an apprentice to the astronomer Inácio Samartoni, and was awarded the honor of Knight of the Order of Christ. By 1787 we know that he was military commander of the barracks at Ega, since letters addressed to and from him appear among the military correspondence reporting the reduction of the Mura,[80] indicating that he had firsthand knowledge of the events recounted in the poem.

The Mura, or Murá, the name given by neighboring tribes to the Indians who call themselves Buhuraen, are first recorded as inhabiting the right bank of the river Madeira in 1714. They were noted for their hostility toward the Jesuit mission of Abacaxis, founded above the mouth of the Jamary in about 1723 and later transferred downstream. Having been the victims of an act of betrayal by a Portuguese trader who kidnapped and sold some of their number as slaves, they became the scourge of the region for most of the century, resorting to guerrilla-style ambush tactics after an expedition led by João de Souza inflicted great losses on them. By the 1770s they were expanding into the territory north of the Solimões and to the lower Purus, areas that were being increasingly emptied of their indigenous populations as a result of military attacks and the work of the missions.

In 1784, when Brazilian-born colonists were demanding their extermination as the only alternative to the complete collapse of colonial power in the Amazon, and punitive expeditions remained ineffective, the Mura suddenly and unexpectedly made peace with the whites. Five of them entered the village of Santo Antônio de Maripi, on the lower Japurá River, to be followed by other pacific appearances in Tefe, Alvarães, and Borba, where numbers grew within three years to over 1,000. By the end of 1786, when Wilkens had completed his poem, the whole tribe had been settled in permanent villages and continued on peaceful terms with the white community into the nineteenth century, until deep social and racial antagonisms led to their participation in the Cabanagem rebellion.

It seems likely that this decision to abandon their resistance to the military and cultural pressures of colonial society was a result of progressive debilitation through epidemics, increasing contact with non-Indians, and the relentless wars waged on them by the Mundurucú, who were advancing westward from the Madeira.[81] However, in the words of the legendary *sertanista* and ethnologist Curt Nimuendajú, "It is characteristic of the situation of the civilizados that popular belief attributed this event, not to the military expeditions but rather to the impassioned prayers of the bishop Dom Fr. Caetano Brandão."[82] This religious explanation constitutes the miraculous conversion of the poem, "The Triumph of Faith" of the subtitle. As the dedicatee of the poem, Wilkens's superior, João Pereira Caldas, figures in the poem as one of the agents of the divine miracle. The dedication (dated 1789) appeals to Pereira Caldas's memory of the events as incontrovertible evidence of the poem's authenticity, "a circumstance worthy of consideration for whom, like Your Excellency, was not a mere spectator, but after God, was the primary mover and Agent of the opportune means that achieved this outcome that was so beneficial to the service of God and the Sovereign" (p. 85).[83]

The reference to God and the Sovereign in one breath here is the first example of a characteristic duality in the poem's justification of events, the will of Providence and political and economic considerations repeatedly reinforcing each other. In fact, Pereira Caldas's recommendation of a military, rather than conciliatory, policy in dealing with tribes such as the Timbira encouraged the influential traveler and writer Alexandre Rodrigues Ferreira in his skepticism regarding the practical viability of the Pombaline legislation. Experience of the Muras' stubborn resistance and the obstacle this posed to the realization of the agricultural projects proposed for the region "proved" the impracticality of the Laws of Emancipation.[84] Furthermore, in a letter written during the events depicted in the poem, Pereira Caldas expressed some reservations concerning the wisdom of "pacifying" the Mura, when this might leave their enemy, the Mundurucú, in undisputed mastery over the region; the prospect of gaining an ally and reducing the numbers of the enemy, rather than a pious dedication to God's mission of evangelization, prompted him to press ahead with this policy:

I too already knew of the carnage that the other heathen, the Mundurucú, had inflicted on the same Mura; and it would be a bad thing if, after the latter were reduced, the former should infiltrate this river and settle on the Guatazes, so that this waterway, having rid itself of one group, should remain forever infested by another; however there will be fewer of the enemy to fight, and the above-mentioned Mura will be of great help and advantage to us when it comes to their punishment.[85]

As the correspondence edited by Coutinho indicates, the process of "descimento" and peaceful reconciliation was by no means the instantaneous and unreserved success depicted in the poem.

Yet, despite the violent inconsistency, to a modern reader, between the military leaders' preferred faith in a policy of extermination, the pragmatic, tactical criteria for their acceptance of the Mura peace initiative, and the poem's glorification of the divine miracle of conversion, it would be mistaken to view the latter as a hypocritical cloak for the former and wrong to interpret the fiction as a mere falsification, as the elaboration of an official history. For while, as we shall see, justice is certainly not done to the extent of the wrongs suffered by the Mura at the hands of the colonial power, it is also true to say that the poem reflects a coherent code of moral and political reasoning in which economic or military considerations are quite compatible with religious sincerity. After all the evidence cited earlier for Pereira Caldas's pragmatism and even his support for the policy of extermination, another letter, also written in the midst of the events, conveys a readiness to believe in the Mura offer of peace as the work of God:

all of which leaves me content and very pleased; because although we must of course not give entire credence to the promises of those barbarians, and although we must proceed with prudence and caution for the moment with them and some of their intended deceptions; neither must we doubt the infinite mercy of God, that he might permit the completion of such a work of his glory and compassion, as to free these miserable peoples from such a cruel scourge.

On those terms, then, if they return, you should continue, Sir, to offer them the same shelter and all the proper conduct that you can command of them, setting out before them the principal happiness that they will obtain by coming into the community of the church and submitting to the vassalage of our lady Queen, who protects and orders that the Indians be treated with the greatest humanity, even pardoning their insults and crimes.[86]

The documented correspondence confirms, then, the complementary and not contradictory relation between religious compassion and political-economic expediency that characterizes *A Muhraida*. But the preceding extract also raises another possibility, another way of looking at the apparent contradictions within the poem and within the policies of its protagonists that has nothing to do with matters of religion, for the two paragraphs cited reveal to the full the contrast between, on one hand, a position of hostility and distrust, Pereira Caldas's suspicions about "the promises of those barbarians," and, on the other, an attitude of benevolent paternalism, the monarch's order that the Indians should be treated with humanity and tolerance.

This discrepancy is indicative of a crisis in the direction of indigenist policy in the Amazon, an uncertainty over which path to pursue. The skeptical conclusions of Rodrigues Ferreira's *Viagem Filosófica* were reached following the author's travels of 1783-92, over thirty years after the promulgation of the Laws of Emancipation. The effects of these laws, successful or otherwise, should therefore have manifested themselves by this time; in fact, if Rodrigues Ferreira is to be taken as a reliable indicator of the contemporary mood of indigenist opinion, their failure appears conclusive. For Carlos Moreira, Rodrigues Ferreira's attitude is representative of the period between the fall of Pombal and the end of the eighteenth century, when the Portuguese king, Dom João VI, began to institute a number of decrees (Cartas Régias) authorizing "just wars" of extermination against tribes considered "incapable of civilization."[87] At a time when the prevailing mood was for a return to methods of violence and enslavement in dealing with the Indians, the "voluntary reduction in peace and friendship of the fierce nation of the heathen Mura" must have been a source of some embarrassment to the proponents of the new policy. This sense of political embarrassment as well as the compatibility of religious and economic interests for those involved go some way toward explaining the curious combination in the poem of vengeful outrage against the Mura, the hope that they could be "tamed" to enjoy the material, political and spiritual benefits of civilized society, and pious wonder and gratitude before the spectacle of their conversion and baptism.

The synopsis that precedes the text of the poem itself brings these three attitudes together in its summary of the plot. It begins: "The wild, indomitable and formidable Heathen Mura have always been deadly for those navigating the River Madeira" (p. 87) and goes on to describe their intractability, their hostility to other tribes, their reign of terror in which all members of the white community, men, women and children, could be killed without distinction. Set against this reputation is God's instrument in the "reconciliation, conversion and settlement" of the Mura, "a rustic, common man, named Mathias Fernandes," the director of the Imaripi Indian mission, who already enjoyed the confidence of the tribe. Fernandes persuades them to visit the other white settlements and missions downriver, where they are warmly welcomed and showered with gifts, on the recommendation of LieutenantColonel João Baptista Mardel. Mardel is rewarded with "the particular pleasure and spiritual consolation of seeing that, on 9 June of the present Year of 1785, the above-mentioned Mura Chiefs, . . . freely, spontaneously and of their own volition, without any prior persuasion, though not without a special touch from the hand of the Omnipotent judge of human hearts, offered twenty innocent young Mura, children of the same, requesting the Holy baptism, which with inexplicable jubilation, and not without tears of emotion, was granted them and carried out" (p. 91). Following this spectacle of voluntary baptism, at which Mardel acts as godfather, the purpose and value of the new mission villages, established in response to the miracle, are assessed on all their spiritual, political, and economic merits:

the greater honor and glory of GOD; the exaltation and propagation of the Holy Roman Catholic Faith; the conversion of an immense multitude of Heathen; the salvation of their souls, the exceedingly beneficial development of the population of the State of Pará, and the Dominions of Her Faithful Majesty, our August Sovereign; the tranquillity and hope of her fortunate Subjects in the commerce and navigation of this vast continent and its great Rivers and lands, full of precious and interesting goods, useful to the commerce and opulence of the State, that the terror of the cruelties and ferocity of these Heathen had rendered useless or extremely difficult. (pp. 91-92)

In contrast to this promise of peace and prosperity, canto I of the poem itself opens with a description of the state of affairs that prevailed before the relationship between the white community and the Mura was resolved. It is a fascinating inversion of the oppressive view of colonial society that became current from the nineteenth century onward, for here the Indian is not an enslaved victim of the colonist but instead, paradoxically, the prisoner of his own freedom from religious, economic and political law. Like the Tupinambá of Durão's *Caramuru*, he is "the miserable mortal, who, adrift in the bondage of guilt and ignorance," stands in need of God's illumination and guidance. The forest does not represent the world of natural, divine law but a denial of it, by which the Indians, "Abusing the very freedom which that Omnipotent Being granted them," enjoy effortlessly the natural resources surrounding them, while the poor, devout colonist must risk freedom and life in order to win them for himself. In this condemnation of the Indians' illicit freedom there is more than a hint of a rationalization of the envy and resentment felt by European colonists in a region of such natural abundance and economic potential, especially when they saw its indigenous inhabitants satisfying only their immediate needs and obstructing a more lucrative exploitation of its resources. The language of Christian morality by which the poem judges the Mura thus acquires an economic value, as the term "ambition," unknown to the Indian, becomes invested with the capitalist ethos of enterprise.

Having established the political and economic grounds for the repression of the Indians, the poem then provides copious moral evidence to support that repression, in the form of detailed accounts of the atrocities committed against their enemies. Living in the "dense darkness of Heathenism," they hunt their human victims with poisoned arrows, "repugnant to reason and humanity," killing whites and other Indians alike in order to consume their flesh. Devoid of compassion and mercy, the Mura warrior resembles a bird of prey:

Não mitiga o cruel, o feroz peito,
A tenra idade do mimoso infante,
Nem a piedade move, nem respecto
Do decrepito Velho, o incessante

Rogo, e clamor, só fica satisfeito,
Vendo o cadaver frio. (p. 103)

(His cruel, savage breast is not assuaged/ By the darling infant's tender age,/ Nor do pity or respect for the decrepit/ Old man move him, the ceaseless/ Entreaties and out-cry, he is only satisfied/ When he sees the cold corpse.)

In view of this formidable moral and political barrier to integration or even peaceful relations between the two communities, only a miracle, as Wilkens observes, can now explain the actual outcome. Despite the heroic efforts of Jesuits, Carmelites, and Mercenarians to "reduce" the tribe "[w]ith gifts, promises and endearments . . . nothing could appease their indomitable savagery; nothing could prevent their barbarous cruelty." The immediate literary device employed to explain the pacification of the Mura and their sudden deference to the political and economic order that they have combated for so long is a deus ex machina: the visitation of an angel to a Mura warrior in the form of a relative believed drowned. In this situation of apparent hopelessness, God sends his ambassador in human form, who succeeds in convincing the Mura warrior of the existence of his Creator.

However, as much as the angel's words of mystical faith, it is the example of an existing mission *aldeia*, the *tapuia* settlement of S. Antônio de Imaripi, that persuades the Mura to gather the rest of his tribe into the ecumenical and political fold of white society. The *aldeia*'s director, Mathias Fernandes, has protected the *tapuias* from attacks by hostile Mura and has been entrusted by God with bringing the new converts under the paternal wing of João Baptista Mardel, Comissário at Ega. The most substantial argument, the "irresistible force of Truth" that finally prompts the warrior to call his tribespeople to task, is the promise of prosperity:

Tereis nos Povos vossos numerozos
Abundantes colheitas sazonadas.
Vereis nos Portos vossos ventajosos
Comercios florecer, e procuradas
Serão as Armas vossas. Poderozas
Enfim sereis, amadas, invejadas
Serão vossas venturas, finalmente,
Podeis felices ser eternamente. (p. 123)

(You shall have in your many Villages/ Abundant ripened harvests./ You will see profitable commerce/ Flourish in your Ports, and your Arms/ Will be in great demand. In short/ You will be powerful, beloved,/ Your fortunes envied and, finally,/ You can be content forever.)

This, indeed, was the prospect that theoretically lay at the heart of the emancipation legislation: to abandon a subsistence economy for a capitalist one based on wage labor and trade.

However, before the young warrior finally sways the will of his people, the voice of experience and skepticism is heard from an old man who reminds them of the conflicts of the past, the whites' betrayal of offers of friendship and aid.

He is the jealous guardian of the principle of liberty, a principle that, following the arguments of the first canto, has taken on a negative connotation of "lawlessness." This objection, the unreliability of Portuguese promises of peace, is a straw target, raised simply in order to preempt any criticisms of the current indigenist policy. A note refers to the period before Pombal's Laws of Liberty, when colonists could buy Indian slaves in "just war" to provide them with food and labor; the new legislation has abolished such slavery, which continues only through individual violations of the law—abuses of the Indian population can therefore no longer be imputed to government policy and must be dismissed as exceptional aberrations. The point is raised again in canto IV, as the Muras inundate the *tapuia* settlements and are reunited with relatives in a tumultuous welcome and exchange of gifts, healing all the wounds of former conflicts. As he preaches the message of conversion, Mathias is described as a new Moses leading the Mura from the bondage of the devil, as the Israelites were led out of Egypt; and when they arrive at Ega, Mardel greets them as the Prodigal Son returned.

Another biblical metaphor confirms the simultaneously religious and economic success of the "reconciliation" of the Mura: the parable of the sowing and harvesting of the seeds of faith. Within the one image is compressed an entire complex of terms and ideas expressing both the material and political nature of this new "alliance" with the white community and its God:

Plantada pela Mão do Omnipotente,
Na semente da Fé, da Graça o fructo,
Dispõem que da Colheita a innocente
Primicia se lhe offreça, que o producto
Antecipado seja, e permanente
Padrão, do seu Dominio absoluto,
De altos designios Seus, e de alliança
Dispozição, motivo de Esperança. (p. 155)

(Planted by the Hand of the Omnipotent one,/ In the seed of Faith, the fruit of Grace,/ They arrange that the innocent/ First fruits of the Harvest should be offered to Him, that the produce/ Should be hastened, and stand as the permanent/ Model for his absolute Dominion,/ Of His lofty designs, and of the willingness/ For alliance, the motive for Hope.)

The "miracle" of the Muras' unsolicited pacification thus appeared to vindicate the policy of integration, just as figures such as the Governor Pereira Caldas and Rodrigues Ferreira were expressing skepticism about the emancipation reforms and were advocating a return to military coercion. But even the sanction of divine intervention could not ultimately save the experiment of the lay mission system. Within fifteen years many of Brazil's tribal peoples were once again the object of genocidally repressive campaigns, while others were displaying the wretched symptoms of three centuries of colonial rule. It remained to be seen whether an independent Brazil would break with that history and offer them a new kind of relationship founded on the democratic principles of free association and equality that had been defended in the French and American

Revolutions and from which Latin America's nationalist regimes derived their own legitimacy.

NOTES

1. See Roberto Gambini, *O Espelho Índio: os jesuítas e a destruição da alma indígena* (São Paulo: Espaço e Tempo, 1988), for a fuller account of Jesuit-Indian relations.

2. For a summary of the debate concerning Cabral's discovery of Brazil, see Samuel Eliot Morison, *The European Discovery of America: The Southern Voyages 1492-1616* (New York: Oxford University Press, 1974), pp. 210-35.

3. These are thoroughly examined in Sérgio Buarque de Holanda's *Visão do Paraíso: os motivos edênicos no descobrimento e colonização do Brasil* (São Paulo: Companhia Editora Nacional, 1969).

4. George Boas, "The Noble Savage" and "Earthly Paradises," *Essays on Primitivism and Related Ideas in the Middle Ages* (Baltimore: Johns Hopkins University Press, 1948), pp. 139-40, 161.

5. Holanda, *Visão do Paraíso*, p. 157.

6. D. Martín Fernandez Navarrete, *Colección de los viajes y Descobrimientos que hicieron por Mar los Españoles*, 5 vols. (Madrid, 1825-37), quoted in Holanda, *Visão do Paraíso*, p. 14.

7. Serafim Soares Leite, "O tratado do Paraíso na América e o ufanismo brasileiro," *Novas Páginas de História do Brasil* (Lisbon: Civilização Brasileira, 1963), pp. 379-82.

8. See Afonso Arinos de Melo Franco, *O Índio Brasileiro e a revolução francesa: as origens brasileiras da teoria da bondade natural* (Rio de Janeiro: José Olympio, 1976), for a thorough account of this philosophical tradition.

9. Stephen J. Greenblatt, *Marvelous Possessions: The Wonder of the New World* (Oxford: Clarendon Press, 1991), p. 14.

10. Holanda, *Visão do Paraíso*, pp. 1-11.

11. Probably ancestors of today's Pataxó, who still face violence and starvation in their efforts to recover traditional lands to the north, in the state of Bahia; see *Survival International News*, nos. 2 (1983) and 10 (1985), and *Information Pack* BRZ/5/March 1983.

12. Translated from Pero Vaz de Caminha, *A Carta de Pero Vaz de Caminha* (Rio de Janeiro: Livros de Portugal, n.d.), p. 202. Page numbers hereafter refer to this edition.

13. John Berger, *Ways of Seeing* (London: BBC/Penguin, 1972), p. 54.

14. Ibid., p. 55.

15. For a more thorough examination of the Caramuru myth and its evolution, see David Treece, "Caramuru the Myth: Conquest and Conciliation," *Ibero-Amerikanisches Archiv* 10, no. 2 (1984), pp. 139-73.

16. For the following synthesis of early colonial history, the chief source is John Hemming, *Red Gold: The Conquest of the Brazilian Indians* (London: Macmillan, 1978), pp. 10-12, 34-38, 79-114, 120-37; see also C. R. Boxer, *Race Relations in the Portuguese Colonial Empire 1415-1825*, vol. 3, *Brazil and the Maranhão* (Oxford: Oxford University Press, 1963); Alexandre Marchant, *Do escambo à escravidão: as relações econômicas de portugueses e índios na colonização do Brasil 1500-1580* (São Paulo: Companhia Editora Nacional, 1943).

17. P. Manuel da Nóbrega, *Cartas do Brasil e mais escritos* (Coimbra: Acta Universitatis Conimbrigensis, 1955), pp. 21, 51, 54, 65.

18. Ibid., p. 86.

19. Hemming, *Red Gold*, p. 140.

20. Ibid., p. 95.

21. Peter Hulme, "Caribs and Arawaks," *Colonial Encounters: Europe and the Native Caribbean, 1492-1797* (London and New York: Methuen, 1986), pp. 45-87.

22. W. Arens, *The Man-Eating Myth: Anthropology and Anthropophagy* (New York: Oxford University Press, 1979), p. 39.

23. Hemming, *Red Gold*, pp. 30-31.

24. Frank Lestringant, *Cannibals: The Discovery and Representation of the Cannibal from Columbus to Jules Verne* (Cambridge: Polity Press, 1997), p. 7, and notes 15-20, p. 191. See also Francis Barber and Peter Hulme (eds.), *Cannibalism and the Colonial World* (Cambridge: Cambridge University Press, 1998).

25. Arens, *The Man-Eating Myth*, p. 39.

26. Greenblatt, *Marvelous Possessions*, pp. 15, 136.

27. Montaigne, "Des Cannibales," *Oeuvres Complètes*, vol. 2 (Paris: Conard, 1924), pp. 233-66.

28. Nóbrega, 6 January 1550, *Cartas do Brasil*, p. 70.

29. Nóbrega, August 1557, *Cartas do Brasil*, p. 256.

30. Nóbrega, May 1558, *Cartas do Brasil*, p. 278.

31. Ibid., p. 280.

32. Lewis Hanke, *Aristotle and the American Indians: A Study in Race Prejudice in the Modern World* (Ontario: Hollis and Carter, 1959).

33. Anthony Pagden, *The Fall of Natural Man: The American Indian and the Origins of Comparative Ethnology* (Cambridge: Cambridge University Press, 1982).

34. P. Manuel da Nóbrega, *Diálogo sobre a conversão do gentio* (Lisbon: União Gráfica, 1954), p. 53.

35. Lothar Hessel and Georges Raeders, *O Teatro Jesuítico no Brasil* (Porto Alegre: Ed. da Universidade do Rio Grande do Sul, 1972), p. 19; the authors' sympathies with Anchieta's aims should be borne in mind when consulting this text. See also Leodegário A. de Azevedo Filho, *Anchieta, a Idade Média e o Barroco* (Rio de Janeiro: Gernasa, 1966); Oscar Fernández, "José de Anchieta and Early Theatre Activity in Brazil," *Luso-Brazilian Review* 15, no. 1 (Summer 1978), pp. 26-43; Richard A. Preto-Rodas, "Anchieta and Vieira: Drama as Sermon, Sermon as Drama," *Luso-Brazilian Review* 7, no. 2 (December 1970), pp. 96-103.

36. Hessel and Raeders, *O Teatro Jesuítico no Brasil*, pp. 19, 95.

37. Ibid., p. 95.

38. Hemming, *Red Gold*, pp. 130, 134.

39. José de Anchieta, *Poesias* (São Paulo: Museu Paulista, Boletim IV, Documentação Lingüística, 4, Ano 4-6, 1954), p. 695, note 229.

40. Ibid., pp. 685-86; quotations are given only in English translation, since the Portuguese edition is already translated from the Tupi-Guarani of the original text.

41. Fernão Cardim, *Tratados da Terra e Gente do Brasil* (São Paulo: Companhia Editora Nacional, 1939), p. 167-68.

42. Carlos Guilherme Mota, *Ideia de Revolução no Brasil (1789-1801): estudo das formas de pensamento* (São Paulo: Cortez, 1989), pp. 75-77.

43. Hemming, *Red Gold*, Chapters 12, 13.

44. Colin M. MacLachlan, "The Indian Labor Structure in the Portuguese Amazon, 1700-1800," in Dauril Alden (ed.), *Colonial Roots of Modern Brazil* (Berkeley, Los Angeles, and London: University of California Press, 1973), pp. 201-7.

45. Susanna Hecht and Alexander Cockburn, *The Fate of the Forest: Developers, Destroyers and Defenders of the Amazon* (London: Penguin, 1990), Chapters 4-6.

46. In João Francisco Lisboa, *Crônica do Brasil Colonial (Apontamentos para a História do Maranhão)* (Petrópolis: Vozes, 1976), pp. 223-24.

47. MacLachlan, "The Indian Labor Structure in the Portuguese Amazon," pp. 209-22.

48. Sebastião José de Carvalho e Mello (Marquês de Pombal), *Relação Abbreviada da República, que os Religiosos Jesuitas das Provincias de Portugal, e Hespanha, estabeleceram nos Dominios Ultramarinos das duas Monarchias . . .* , in *Recueil de pièces* (Paris: n.p., 1758), p. 6.

49. Ibid., p. 23.

50. Clovis Lugon, *A República "Comunista" Cristã dos Guaranis 1610-1768* (Rio de Janeiro: Paz e Terra, 1977), Chapter 17, pp. 283-305; Hemming, *Red Gold*, pp. 462-74; Capitão Jacinto Rodrigues da Cunha, "Diário da expedição de Gomes Freire de Andrada às Missões do Uruguay," *Revista do Instituto Histórico e Geográfico Brasileiro* 3d series, 16, no. 10 (1853), pp. 137-321. For a detailed account of the historical and ideological framework for da Gama's text, see Ivan Teixeira, "História e ideologia em *O Uraguay*," in José Basílio da Gama, *Obras poéticas de Basílio da Gama* (São Paulo: EDUSP, 1996), pp. 45-98.

51. Franco, *O Índio Brasileiro e a revolução francesa*, pp. 174-210.

52. Antônio Pereira de Souza Caldas, *Poesias Sacras e Profanas*, 2 vols. (Paris: P. N. Rougeron, 1821), vol. 2, p. 129.

53. Voltaire, *Candide and Other Stories* (Oxford: Oxford University Press, 1990), p. 34.

54. Ibid., pp. 34-35.

55. Tomás Antônio Gonzaga, *Obras Completas* (Rio de Janeiro: Instituto Nacional do Livro, 1957), p. 291.

56. Mota, *Ideia de Revolução no Brasil*, p. 84.

57. Gama, *Obras poéticas de Basílio da Gama*, p. 362.

58. Vania Pinheiro Chaves, "A glorificação do Tratado de Madrid, forma original da brasilidade de *O Uraguay*," in Gama, *Obras Poéticas de Basílio da Gama*, pp. 452-55. See also Antonio Candido, "A dois séculos d'*O Uraguai*," *Vários Escritos* (São Paulo: Duas Cidades, 1970), p. 168.

59. See Ivan Teixeira, "Epopéia e modernidade em Basílio da Gama," in Gama, *Obras Poéticas de Basílio da Gama*, pp. 23-25.

60. Candido, "A dois séculos d'*O Uraguai*," p. 175.

61. Waltensir Dutra, "O Arcadismo na Poesia Lírica, Épica e Satírica," in Afrânio Coutinho (ed.), *A Literatura no Brasil*, 5 vols. (Rio de Janeiro: Sul Americana, 1968), vol. 1, p. 344.

62. Teixeira, "Epopéia e modernidade," pp. 20, 52-54.

63. Gama, *Obras poéticas de Basílio da Gama*, p. 197. Subsequent references to textual quotations give the canto and line numbers.

64. Candido, "A dois séculos d'*O Uraguai*," pp. 179-81.

65. Euclides da Cunha, *Rebellion in the Backlands (Os Sertões)* (London: Picador, 1995), pp. 282, 287-88.

66. Mário Camarinha da Silva, editor's note, no. 52, in Basílio da Gama, *O Uraguai* (Rio de Janeiro: Agir, 1964), p. 58.

67. For a more detailed account of the Caramuru myth and Durão's poem, see Treece, "Caramuru the Myth."

68. Arthur Viegas, *O Poeta Santa Rita Durão: revelações históricas da sua vida e do seu século* (Brussels: L'editions d'Art Gaudio, 1914).

69. José de Santa Rita Durão, *Caramurú, poema epico do descubrimento da Bahia* (Lisbon: Na Regia Officina Typografica, 1781), vol. 1, 48. References hereafter give

canto and stanza numbers from this edition. See also Hernâni Cidade (ed.), *Caramuru: poema épico do descobrimento da Bahia* (Rio de Janeiro: Agir, 1961).

70. See, for example, Jean de Léry, *Histoire d'un voyage fait en la terre du Brésil, autrement dit Amérique* (Lausanne: Bibliotèque Romande, 1972).

71. Luís da Câmara Cascudo, *Dicionário do Folclore Brasileiro* (Rio de Janeiro: Edições de Ouro, 1972), p. 836.

72. Treece, "Caramuru the myth," p. 160.

73. Simão de Vasconcellos, *Chronica da Companhia de Jesu do Estado do Brasil* (Officina de Henrique Valente de Oliveira Impressor del Rey N.S., 1663), p. 38.

74. Cidade, *Caramuru*, p. 84.

75. Irmão José Gregório, *Contribuição indígena ao Brasil*, 3 vols. (Belo Horizonte: União Brasileira de Educação e Ensino, 1980), vol. 3, p. 944.

76. Antonio Candido, "Estrutura literária e função histórica," *Literatura e sociedade* (São Paulo: Companhia Editora Nacional, 1967), p. 181.

77. Mário Ypiranga Monteiro, "A Muhraida," *Jornal de Letras* no. 193/194 (May 1966). See the facsimile edition of the manuscript and first printed edition, with accompanying studies, in *Anais da Biblioteca Nacional*, vol. 109 (1989) (Rio de Janeiro: A Biblioteca, 1993).

78. Henrique João Wilkens, *A Muhraida, Senhor ou A conversão, e reconciliação do Gentio Muhra* (ed. P. Cypriano Pereira Alho) (Lisbon: Na Imprensa Regia, 1819).

79. Mário Ypiranga Monteiro, *Fases da literatura amazonense*, vol. 1 (Manaus: Imprensa Oficial, 1977), pp. 142-44.

80. Antonio Carlos da Fonseca Coutinho, "Noticias da voluntaria reducção de paz e amizade da feroz nação do gentio Mura nos annos de 1784, 1785 e 1786, do Furriel Commandante do destacamento do lugar de Santo Antonio do Maripi, no Rio Jupurá," *Revista do Instituto Histórico e Geográfico Brasileiro* 36, first part (1873), pp. 33-92.

81. Julian H. Steward, *Handbook of South American Indians* (Washington, D.C.: U.S. Government Printing Office, 1948), vol. 3, pp. 255-62. See also John Hemming, *Amazon Frontier: The Defeat of the Brazilian Indians* (London: Macmillan, 1987), pp. 19-22; David Sweet, "Native Resistance in 18th-Century Amazonia: The 'Abominable Muras' in War and Peace," *Radical History Review* 53 (1992).

82. Curt Nimuendajú, "As Tribus do Alto Madeira," *Jornal de la Société des Américanistes de Paris*, no. 17 (1925), p. 140.

83. Henrique João Wilkens, *Muhraida ou O Triumfo da Fé, Na bem fundada Esperança da enteira Converção, e reconciliação da grande, e feróz Nação do Gentio Muhúra, Poema Heroico* . . . (Manuscript, 1785); the manuscript is in the Archive of the Torre do Tombo, Lisbon, a Xerox copy having been kindly made available to me by Carlos Moreira. Page numbers refer to the facsimile edition in the *Anais da Biblioteca Nacional*, vol. 109 (1989) (Rio de Janeiro: A Biblioteca, 1993).

84. Alexandre Rodrigues Ferreira, *Viagem filosófica pelas capitanias do Grão Pará, Rio Negro, Mato Grosso e Cuiabá* (Rio de Janeiro: Conselho Federal de Cultura, Departamento da Imprensa Nacional, 1974), Introduction, pp. 9-17.

85. Coutinho, "Noticias da voluntaria reducção," pp. 378-79.

86. Ibid., pp. 329-30.

87. Ferreira, *Viagem filosófica*, p. 14.

2

Exiles of Empire: The Tragedy of Colonialism and the Romantic Indianist Utopia

EXTERMINATION OR INTEGRATION? INDEPENDENCE, CIVIL CONFLICT, AND INDIAN POLICY AFTER POMBAL

By the end of the eighteenth century, Da Gama's and Wilkens's notion of a kind of colonial "social contract," emancipating the Indians from Jesuit rule and from the stateless condition of nature and subjecting them to the economic and political obligations of a secular state, had collapsed. In the Amazonian province of Pará, for instance, the "liberation" of the indigenous communities from the mission regime exposed them to an inexorable process of disintegration and marginalization. Ill prepared to compete socially or economically with the rest of the regional population, these communities became transformed into a dispersed, propertyless mass alienated both from the intact, isolated tribal groups of the interior and from the rural white population. These detribalized Indians, known as *tapuios*, formed a great reserve labor force in Amazonia that was to constitute a potential source of revolt following independence and as such played an important part in the Cabanagem, one of the provincial uprisings that shook Brazil during the 1830s and early 1840s.[1]

The patent social and psychological effects of this process of detribalization were recorded in 1823 by the ethnographers Spix and von Martius, two of the many Europeans who visited Brazil by taking advantage of the newly liberalized customs controls following independence in 1822:

The characteristic feature of the race, sly and taciturn imbecility, which is conveyed above all by the American Indians' morose gaze and bashful behavior, is even more accentuated on first approaching them. . . . The manner in which they are treated by many of today's plantation-owners also contributes to this moral and physical decadence. Neither the national features, nor the physical mutilations (tattoos), nor the habits and customs of these poor survivors of the original native peoples reveal to which tribe they once belonged.[2]

Another traveler who witnessed and documented the condition of the *tapuio* was the French literary scholar Ferdinand Denis, who was to play such a vital role in the development of Brazil's nationalist literature and of the Indianist movement itself. In his geographical surveys of the country, Denis laid considerable emphasis on that sociological distinction between the intact tribal communities of the interior and the *caboclo* or *tapuio* product of contact with non-Indian society. Similarly, the central theme of his fiction and of his immediate followers was a nostalgic mourning of the dispersal and exile of the conquered indigenous races of Brazil and their subsequent degeneration. By contrast, though, the first generation of Brazilian Indianists relied predominantly on sixteenth- and seventeenth-century accounts of indigenous culture and history for their depiction of the tragic outcome of colonial oppression. The contemporary, ongoing social reality of detribalization was not explicitly addressed in Brazil until late in the century, in the fiction of Bernardo Guimarães, for example.

This apparent blindness to the more immediate predicament of the indigenous population should not be taken at face value. It was no mere Romantic escapism, no simple preference for the idealized, Rousseauian image of Natural Man living in a mythical golden age. These early Indianists were doubtless familiar with the documentary and fictional writings of their mentor, Denis, and many must have seen firsthand the evidence of tribal disintegration on their own soil. Indeed, as we shall see, one of their central concerns was to articulate a sense of fellow-feeling between the "exiles" of the Indian world, past and present, and the disfranchised, discriminated, and excluded sectors of contemporary Brazilian society. The problem was that, like the nationalist argument, the postindependence debate on official Indian policy did not have room for ambiguous social categories such as the *tapuio*, nor could it address the possible claims and interests of such groups independently of the Imperial state. For the intellectuals who took part in that debate, many of them prominent literary figures, there were only two alternatives, extermination or integration, the first represented by the oppressive colonial policy of Portugal, from which Brazil was now supposedly liberated as an independent nation-state; while the second reflected the conciliatory ideology of national and social unity that would come to dominate the Second Reign. Between those alternatives there could exist no gray area questioning the value of assimilation into white society from the viewpoint of the Indian's own cultural integrity and identity or denouncing the exploitative nature of the Imperial economy for its more marginalized elements.

This postindependence debate about indigenist policy, which appears remarkably isolated from similar discussions elsewhere in the continent, followed a renewed program of extermination from the end of the eighteenth century. Dom João VI's Royal Charter of 1798 was the first of a series of edicts that abolished the Pombaline legislation of 1755 and ordered military campaigns or "just wars" against particular groups of Indians considered "incapable of civilization": the various tribes inhabiting the provinces of Bahia and São Paulo; the Botocudos of Minas Gerais, who were decimated by eighteen years of wars, and the Timbira of Maranhão, who were the object of particularly vicious methods of extermination, such as the deliberate introduction of disease, in a campaign that lasted from 1798 to 1831. The pioneering expeditions of the seventeenth century, the *bandeiras*, were revived especially for the purpose, and Indian prisoners were given to the captors as slaves for a period of fifteen years, which in most cases meant life.[3]

One of the most serious objections to this policy of extermination was raised soon after independence, early in the reign of Pedro I (1822-31), by the statesman and Enlightenment intellectual José Bonifácio de Andrada e Silva. Having led the delegation that, in January 1822, had persuaded Pedro to assume the government of São Paulo in defiance of the Lisbon parliament, José Bonifácio was appointed Minister of the Empire and Foreign Affairs within a few days of independence being declared and subsequently became known as the "Patriarch of Independence." In July 1823 he resigned from his ministerial post after a series of palace intrigues set him at odds with the Emperor, and, taking up his deputy's seat in the Constituent Assembly, he presented two parliamentary bills for debate.

The first of these, his "Notes for the Civilization of the Savage Indians of Brazil," recommended radical reforms to the existing indigenist policy with a view to the effective integration of the tribal population into the economic and social structures of the newly independent nation. The document is one of the first explicit attempts to link the Indian question to that of the generally oppressive colonial policies suffered under Portuguese rule, including black slavery. Indeed, José Bonifácio's "Proposal to the Constituent Assembly on Slavery," submitted in the same year, foresaw a direct sequential connection between the two reforms: the "general civilization of Brazil's Indians," he argued, would in due course render the slavery of the Africans redundant. As such it marked the first statement in the Indianist movement's ongoing reflection on the possible correspondences between the indigenous and black slave condition and their respective relationships to state and society. Given that this linkage is found in the work of José Bonifácio's most prominent successors, such as Gonçalves Dias, Joaquim Manuel de Macedo, and José de Alencar, one might go so far as to suggest that this, the slavery "problem," actually constitutes a hidden agenda of nineteenth-century Indianism. Certainly, for the first phase of the movement, national independence, the universality of liberal values, and the critique of colonial history could not help but lead, implicitly or explicitly, to a simultaneous defense of the indigenous cause and of the abolitionist cause. The analogies are evident in José Bonifácio's congressional bill; he estimated that 2 million Indians had died at the hands of the colonial regime since conquest, while Pombal's emancipation laws had brought no positive improvement to those who had survived:

According to our laws the Indians should enjoy the privileges of the European race; but this benefit has been illusory, for the poverty in which they find themselves, their ignorance due to lack of education or stimulation, and the continual harassment they face from the whites, make them abject and contemptible like the blacks.[4]

He blamed the white colonist for

the continual, deep-rooted fear in which their former captivity has put them; the contempt with which we generally treat them, the constant theft of their best lands, the labor to which we subject them, paying them little or no wages, not feeding them properly, cheating them in the sale and purchase contracts that we agree with them, and taking them away for years and years from their families and farms in order to work for the State and for private individuals; and finally implanting in them all of our vices, and sicknesses, without conveying to them our virtues and talents.[5]

José Bonifácio's reform proposed, instead, a new program of villagization employing peaceful, rather than coercive, methods of contact and integration, placing emphasis on moral and technical education and, most interestingly, the encouragement of intermarriage between Indians, whites, and mulattos. These proposals were reiterated in a number of the shorter texts written during his period of exile in Europe between 1824 and 1831, in which the possibility of phasing out African slavery is once again envisaged, and there is the glimpse of a fully *mestiço* society. In "The Indians Are Very Imaginative," for instance, he wrote:

The Indians must be progressively mixed with the whites by means of marriages and residence.

As soon as the use of the plow and English cultivation are introduced, there will not be a need for so many slaves using hoes and axes—or for cattle, and artificial and natural pasture for the latter. To expect the Indians to work with the hoe, and to expect them to be the same as the whites, when only the blacks work with it, is to expect the impossible—let us begin by making the Portuguese accustomed to the rural labors of their own farmsteads, with rewards and instruction; then the Indians will imitate them, and the blacks from Africa will not be necessary—the races will blend with each other and be improved.[6]

Independently of José Bonifácio's political proposals, the status of the country's non-European peoples was already being explicitly linked to that of the emergent nation, as some of the press debate surrounding the independence question makes clear. The urgent concern to rehabilitate the Indian, along with the African, in the reconstruction of Brazil's self-image as a distinctly autonomous culture and society was precipitated by antinationalist statements of the kind printed in the *Investigador* in June 1818, which had spoken of "hordes of little blacks," "a land of monkeys, blacks and snakes," and had asked: "[W]ill it not be eminently impolitic to go and bury such glory and patriotism [of the Portuguese] in the forests and wildernesses of Brazil among Indians and Blacks?"[7]

In response to this provocation, there followed a fascinating exchange of open, but semianonymous, correspondence in the same publication, some of it attributed to the future liberal statesman, Evaristo da Veiga. The arguments put forward in defense of the country's ethnic and cultural self-image were identical to the basic guiding principles of the Romantic Indianist writing that was to appear from the 1830s onward, to begin with, the rehabilitation of the "primitive" races within a liberal, fraternal concept of common nationhood:

because I consider it the common Fatherland of men, and the latter all brothers; and that they are neither made greater nor diminished by having been born in Asia, Europe, Africa or America; they are all men; they all have a same origin; they are all prone as men can be to good and evil; and only education, example, temperaments, and free Will, which was granted to them by the SUPREME AUTHOR of Nature, makes them diverge in their feelings and customs.[8]

Second, was the appeal to the notion of a heroic, aristocratic Indian ancestry linking the modern Brazilian to legendary colonial figures such as Antônio Felipe Camarão, who, in alliance with the Portuguese, expelled the Dutch from the northeast in the seventeenth century:

do you not see that when you denigrate the Indians, you denigrate with them the whole of Brazil and the majority of its inhabitants, (and here it pains me to say) who either by alliance or by descendance have something in common with those Indians? With whom did the first Portuguese who came to Brazil contract their alliances which multiplied the human race? Was it not perchance with the very affectionate and solicitous Indian women? It certainly was, and from them are descended very honorable and noble families, who do not therefore cease to be as honorable, noble and Illustrious as those who are descended from the Romans, the Goths, and also from the Moors and Jews may be, who by my frail powers of reckoning are no less people than all the others I have mentioned.[9]

Third, was the notion of the indigenous world and, by extension, of Brazil as a whole, as a utopian terrestrial paradise of freedom and abundance:

Because the customs of their ancestors still prevail in them; and moreover because the natural and spontaneous fertility of this most bounteous Brazil provides them, in exchange for very little toil, with all that their natural and very moderate needs demand for the maintenance of their vigorous health, long lives and beloved, precious Freedoms, whilst our capricious inventions and extolled sciences weaken and consume us.[10]

Finally, there was the liberals' faith in the process of social, economic, and cultural integration of the Indian as a necessary step in the independent nation's progress toward peace and prosperity:

they [the Indian converts] lend us their services when we require them for the navigation of the central Rivers; in which they are outstanding, and for other occupations within their capacity, and this they do very faithfully and with good will, provided that they are given plentiful sustenance and are treated with kindness and sincerity; they provide us with certain kinds of trade, and we always find them willing, whether to conquer the Savage Indians, or to resist their hostilities.

The Indians are no less skilled in the Letters, Arts and Crafts; of this we have abundant experience, and when it becomes more difficult for the Brazilian Population to sustain each individual the Indians will be seen to take their places in Society like the other individuals who constitute it today.[11]

In the same spirit and echoing José Bonifácio's advocacy of Indian integration and his criticism of previous mission systems, which had rendered the Indians "useless to the State," in 1824 José Arouche de Toledo Rendon published his "Memorandum on the Indian Villages of the Province of São Paulo." For Rendon, one of the means of consolidating the nation's independence must be the incorporation of the indigenous population into the mainstream of society:

We are living in the fortunate age of no longer being colonists: Brazil is a constitutional Empire: the most vigorous offspring of the House of Braganza is its First Emperor. It is a question of increasing the forces of this giant by increasing its population: among the various means of achieving this both useful and necessary end there will always be a place for the civilization and conversion of the Indians, who live in wandering hordes in the huge forests of the Brazilian land.[12]

With this aim in mind Rendon recommended four key principles as the basis for a new indigenist policy: an end to military repression; the provision of aid and humane treatment; the settlement of Indians near white communities to encourage them to adopt white methods of farming; and most importantly, the splitting up of families, separating children from their parents for the purposes of "education," the eradication of tribal culture, and the instillation of sedentary habits of work.

However, the integrationist proposals of José Bonifácio and Toledo Rendon were rejected by the conservative assembly of the First Reign, as was Bonifácio's bill for the abolition of black slavery. They had to wait until the Regency, eight years later, when the 1798 Royal Charters were revoked by a Liberal government, and the Indian acquired the status of orphan, subject to a range of new administrative laws designed to open up the interior to more intensive agricultural activity.

The artist Jean Baptiste Debret reproduced the text of one of the new decrees in his celebrated *Voyage pittoresque et historique au Brésil*, which recorded the author's impressions of the country and its people between 1816 and 1831. Debret was a member of the French Artistic Mission that had been invited to Brazil by Dom João VI for the purpose of setting up a native Academy of Fine Arts. A number of Botocudo Indians, almost certainly captured during the "just wars," were brought to Rio de Janeiro to be drawn by him, and the book contains illustrations depicting "índios civilizados," who, he notes, were indispensable intermediaries on his visits to the interior. It is an indication of the extent of detribalization since the Pombaline legislation that Debret refers to the variety of military, civil, and menial domestic positions now occupied by *tapuios* and *caboclos*, from the soldiers employed in the repression of slave revolts in Bahia and in the capture of uncontacted Indians in Curitiba, to the laundrywomen serving the wealthy families of Rio.[13] For Debret, the liberal legislation of 1831 frankly sought to reconcile the economic needs of a young, independent nation with the principles of individual freedom, private property, and enterprise:

the analysis of the physical and moral qualities of the savage Indians must of course be followed by the fully deserved praise for the fraternal philanthropy of the Brazilian legislators who, barely invested with the power to regenerate the prosperity of their motherland, have hastened to abolish the slavery of the Indian prisoners of war and, furthermore, to guarantee their right to ownership of the lands chosen by them to exercise their industry, a judicious means of making them understand the advantages of civilization and accelerating the progress that is so necessary to the Brazilian territory.[14]

However, it was nearly two decades before these integrationist aspirations were to find any effective political expression at a broadly national level. For the next eighteen years, the country was rocked by a series of violent regional revolts and insurrections, at least one of them with important racial implications, which seemed to many to herald the collapse of the unwieldy ethnic, social, and political contradiction that was the Brazilian nation-state. Already in 1824, just two years after independence, the regime had found itself confronted by the Confederation of the Equator, a bid by several northern provinces for autonomy, and by 1828 it had lost the territory that was to become the independent state of Uruguay. Pedro I's forced abdication in 1831 was the culmination of a liberal upsurge that sought to compensate for the Empire's social conservatism by achieving real changes in the political sphere, that is, popular sovereignty via a single governing chamber, and the equation of the nation with the regional "pátrias," or provinces. In the absence of social reforms such as the abolition of slavery, such demands expressed the need to give legitimate substance to the country's nominal independence from Portugal by at least breaking with the centralized structures of the colonial administration. As one representative asked in the Chamber of Deputies in 1831: "How is the new regime to march forward with the same springs as the old regime? How is the national government, newly created and organized, to move onwards whilst keeping all the elements of the old government throughout the country? If this happens there will be upheavals in the provinces, as have already begun."[15]

Indeed, events were already providing their own answer to the congressman's question, as the reforms failed to materialize, and the traditional landed oligarchies of Portuguese descent retained their hold on the archaic colonial power structure that guaranteed their privileged position. In response, a succession of rebellions, riots, political assassinations, and civil wars extended over eighteen years across the entire country. The first wave, lasting until the middle of the decade, expressed the unrest of the urban population in the main capitals and saw the mobilization of the troops or the "povo," or both: six rebellions in Rio de Janeiro (1831-32); the Setembrizada in Recife (1831), the Abrilada in Pernambuco (April 1832); the Pinto Madeira of Ceará (1831-32); the Cabanada in Pernambuco and Alagoas (1832-35); revolts in Pará (April-June 1832); a military uprising in Bahia (October 1832); the attempted assassination of Evaristo da Veiga (November 1832); the federalist revolts in Bahia (February 1832 and April 1833); the military revolt in Ouro Preto (March 1833); street fighting in Pará (April 1833); the killings of Portuguese "mata-bicudos" in Mato Grosso (May and September 1834); the Carneirada in Recife (1834-35), and the *malé* slave revolt in Salvador da Bahia (1835).

The second cycle of unrest, lasting until 1848, reflected the decentralization of power that had come about with the Additional Act of 1834, shifting the focus to the interior and to its social actors: the smallholders, peasants, Indians, and slaves and even some wealthy traders. It included the Cabanagem in Pará (1835-40), with 30,000-40,000 casualties; 5,000 killed out of the 11,000 involved in the Balaiada in Maranhão (1838-41); the 3,000 imprisoned and 1,200 killed in the Sabinada in Bahia (1837-38); the Farrapos war involving 20,000 in Rio Grande do Sul (1835-45); the Bem-te-vi revolt in Piauí (February 1840); the Liberal revolutions of 1842 in Minas Gerais, Rio de Janeiro, and São Paulo; the bloody struggle between "lisos" and "cabeludos" in Alagoas; the Rio Formoso rebellion in Pernambuco (1847); the anti-Portuguese riots in Recife and Rio de Janeiro (1848); and the killings before and during the Praeira Rebellion in Pernambuco (1848-49). As José Murilo de Carvalho puts it, this second wave of struggle, especially, "stirred the deeper layers of the social fabric of the country and uncovered much more serious dangers both for public order and for the country's very survival."[16]

The character of the first twenty years of Romantic Indianist writing, from 1835 onward, is unmistakably shaped by this mood of conflict, instability, and federal disintegration. One incident in particular, the Cabanagem, is of special interest because it involved Indian participation and even provided the material for an Indianist novel. For Carlos Moreira, the racial and social implications of the Cabanagem gave it a revolutionary character that set it apart from the other movements of the period. Military officers and regional politicians themselves perceived the revolt as a conspiracy of the local colored population to do away with the white landowners and traders of the region, whom they identified as their oppressors. The first "exceptional" measures taken in response to the sporadic rebellions that occurred in 1834 were punitive expeditions composed of regular troops, or "patriotas," against the *quilombos*, runaway slave hideouts, and against Indian and *tapuio* settlements. Such raids often served in addition to clear areas for agricultural use, to settle old scores, and to recruit many of the tribes of the upper Amazon into forced labor. However, in the words of the military commander Soares D'Andréa, such repressive measures were the only means of preserving the integrity of Empire from the threats to its ideological and political hegemony, such as military insubordination, disrespect for the Catholic religion, and press libel:

To tell you, Gentlemen, that these have been the causes of the terrible misfortunes experienced by this Province, that these have been the causes of the ills experienced by the Province of Rio Grande de São Pedro do Sul, and that are threatening that of Bahia: that these are furthermore the causes that threaten the existence of the Empire of Brazil, is to tell you quite clearly that you must direct everything that is at your disposal towards the destruction of the germ of so many ills, decreeing measures that are diametrically opposed to them. I shall not now give a detailed exposition of the horrors invented in this fearful revolution in which barbarism has seemed to wish to devour existing civilization at a single stroke.[17]

As we shall see, this apocalyptic association of revolutionary forces with the anarchic barbarism of primitive hordes is one of the chief motors in the work of that most characteristic of the poets of the first Indianist phase, Gonçalves Dias. It also helped to redefine the central stereotype of the movement identified in the previous chapter, contrasting the faceless, intractable savage, on the one hand, and, on the other, the Romantic Indian hero, the loyal friend and servant of the white community.

Among the consequences of the repression of the Cabanagem, which included the destruction of agricultural areas, widespread malnutrition, disease, and depopulation, was a series of official controls over freedom of movement and labor, which served only to reinforce the racial divisions that had been central to the revolt in the first place. Marechal Soares D'Andréa, the officer responsible for implementing the repression, issued a series of "Instructions for the Organization of Workers' Corps" and "General Instructions for the Military Commanders of the Province of Pará." These gave military commanders the responsibility of compiling a register of all households under their jurisdiction, defining the activity of each member, obliging families to hire out their *agregados*, or retainers, to work in some "kind of useful living," and arresting any strangers or "vagrants," generally identified as "homens de cor" (coloreds). Several of the traditional militia corps were abolished, and recruitment for the army was now drawn from respectable white families, barring Indians, *tapuios*, or *mestiços* from any military career as such. Instead, the latter were weeded out, together with those not considered to be engaged in any useful employment, and were conscripted into labor corps under the command of military officers.[18]

THE RISE OF A ROMANTIC INDIANIST MOVEMENT IN BRAZIL

This systematic policy of racial discrimination contrasted starkly with the status that the Indian and African had acquired, as we have seen, within the nationalist debate on the eve of independence in 1821. Among those who contributed to this reappraisal of the indigenous presence within in the society and culture of the Empire was José Bonifácio, who attempted to reform the state's policy toward the Indian communities immediately following independence. Implicated in a restoration conspiracy during the Regency, he was exiled to Europe and there wrote and published a number of poems under the pseudonym of Américo Elísio. Among these was "A Criação" (The Creation), which again revived the myth of the American Terrestrial Paradise, but with an important new development. The initial Fall from grace, which the Edenic Brazil was usually deemed to have escaped, now signified more than simply the universal loss of innocence, for the poem actually depicted a second Fall, the destruction of that American Paradise by the agents of Conquest. In this vision, the monster was no longer the tribal savage of the medieval imagination but the barbarous European who had butchered countless Indians in his lust for gold and whom José Bonifácio described as God's final and most regrettable creation:

Lá de Haiti nas praias assustadas
De ver cavados lenhos, que orgulhosos
Cerram em largo bojo espanto e morte,
Desembarcaram ousados homens-monstros;

E após o estandarte correm, voam,
Que fanatismo, que cobiça alçaram
Imbeles povos, índios inocentes!
Do armado espanhol provam as iras.
Que Deus fizera um mundo, crêem os tigres,
Para ser presa sua. Em toda parte
Americano sangue, inda fumando,
A terra ensopa, e amolenta as patas
Dos soberbos ginetes andaluzes.[19]

(There on the beaches of Haiti, alarmed/ by the sight of hollowed-out barks, that proudly/ Hold in their broad bellies terror and death,/ Insolent monster-men went ashore;/ And rushed, flying, after the banner,/ What fanaticism, what greed/ Did these unwarlike peoples, innocent Indians provoke!/ They taste the wrath of the armed Spaniard./ These tigers believe that God had made a world/ To be their prey. Everywhere/ American blood, still steaming,/ Soaks the earth, and softens the hooves of the proud Andalusian riders.)

But of all the precedents and influences that helped to crystallize a self-conscious Indianist movement, the most important were indisputably the writings and personal intervention of Ferdinand Denis.[20] Born in Paris in 1798, Denis spent three years visiting the towns and interior of Brazil between 1816 and 1819, having interrupted a voyage to India. The parallel between the Europeans' first encounter with the landscape and native people of the colony and this modern "rediscovery" of the New World was not lost on him, for in the opening pages of *Le Brésil . . .*, one of several works that resulted from this visit, he drew his readers' attention to the momentous novelty of that event, inviting them to experience it again as if for the first time: "Let us now do as the old voyagers did, let us witness their encounter with the Indians: there seems to have been in that first act of possession something characteristic, that has escaped all the history books, and that takes as its source the intimate spirit of two nations finding themselves in each other's presence for the first time."[21] Earlier, in his *Scènes de la nature sous les tropiques, et de leur influence sur la poésie* (1824), he had invited French writers to make use of this sense of exotic rediscovery for the purpose of revitalizing the colors and images of their literature. Two years later, in the *Résumée de l'histoire littéraire du Brésil* (1826), he addressed himself to the young artistic elite of Brazil, with the proposal of a new literature that would be consonant with the political independence that the nation had since won. This radical proposal envisaged a new set of literary values, popular, primitive, and medieval, to be found in the figure of the Indian, who was located in a nostalgically remote, pre-Columbian world of innocence:

Our era of mysterious, poetic fables will be the centuries inhabited by those peoples whom we have annihilated, who astonish us by their courage, and who have perhaps reinvigorated the nations who have left the old world: the memory of their savage grandeur will fill one's soul with pride, their religious beliefs will bring the deserts to life; their poetic chants, preserved among some nations, will adorn the forests. The marvelous, which is so necessary to poetry, will be found in the ancient customs of these peoples, and in the incomprehensible force of a nature continually varying its phenomena.

. . . Their struggles, their sacrifices, our conquests, all this offers brilliant tableaux. On the arrival of the Europeans, they believe, in their simplicity, that they are entrusting themselves to gods; but when they realize that they must fight with human beings, they die and are not vanquished.[22]

Ferdinand Denis was not the only European to contribute to the development of new cultural traditions and institutions in Brazil on the basis of indigenous history and society. Following the exile of the Portuguese court in Rio de Janeiro in 1808 and the opening up of the economy to trade and investment, invitations went out to artists, geographers, and scientists to explore and evaluate the material and cultural resources of the country. This was to result, later in the century, in the invaluable travel accounts of Saint-Hilaire, John Mawe, and Spix and von Martius and in the studies of tribal groups made by von den Steinen, Prince Adalbert of Prussia and Koch-Grünberg, which contributed to the birth of ethnography as a serious discipline. It also led to the founding of an Artistic Mission in 1816, at the instigation of the Brazilian foreign minister and the Portuguese ambassador in France. Led by its secretary of fine arts, Lebreton, the academy included architects, writers, sculptors, some of whose names were to remain associated with the Brazilian literary scene for years to come, such as Debret and Auguste Taunay.

Among those keen to introduce Portuguese and Brazilian literature to a European audience and to confirm their place within the Western tradition was Eugène de Monglave, a French liberal journalist. His project to have thirty representative works in Portuguese translated into French, although never completed, was nevertheless responsible for the republication of Durão's *Caramuru* and therefore, indirectly, for its exposure to a new readership in Brazil. Another traveler to Brazil, Daniel Gavet, spent seven years there and in Uruguay, learning the local languages and translating several works from Spanish and Portuguese. Encouraged by Denis's suggestions and by his Indianist short story "Les Maxakalis," he published a reinterpretation of the Caramuru legend, *Jakaré-Ouassou, ou les Tupinambás, Chronique Brésilienne* (1830), in collaboration with Philippe Boucher.[23]

The importance of Gavet and Boucher's *Jakaré-Ouassou* for the history of Brazilian Indianism was that it shifted the central elements of the Caramuru myth, Diogo's cultural "conquest" of the Indians, and his marriage to Paraguaçu into a historical background. In their place is a tragic web of relationships involving Indians and whites, including the now central character of Moema and the oppressive paternal figure of the despotic Portuguese governor. It is a formula that was adopted more than once during the course of the Indianist movement, for which Durão's straightforwardly celebratory foundation myth no longer represented an acceptable view of colonial history. In addition, it established the dominant mood of the first Indianist phase, in which the contemplation of Natural Man and all that he represents increasingly becomes a tragic, nostalgic regret for something that has irrevocably passed away. An epilogue narrates the mournful exile of the remnants of the tribe and bemoans the powerlessness of one good priest against the destruction wrought by Conquest: "'If only all the Portuguese had been like you . . . !!' . . . There was something awful about these confessions of grief made by the savage to the civilized man: it was like a curse uttered from the depths of the wilderness against the old world and its executioners."[24]

Such a perspective was vitally necessary to the mythological underpinning of the liberal ideology that informed this period. On one hand, to acknowledge the survival of a viable, intact tribal society into the present would have militated against the liberal indigenist policy of integration, which proposed the assimilation of the Indians into Brazilian society as the only alternative to their definitive annihilation.

On the other hand, such an admission would also have undermined the mythical status of the Indianist utopia itself, as formulated in Rousseau's *Discourse on the Origin of Inequality*, for Rousseau had stated emphatically in his Preface to the *Discourse* that the "state of nature" he was seeking to reconstruct from the perspective of modern civilized Europe did not constitute an actual or historical reality. Rather, it represented an ideal, hypothetical condition, "a state that no longer exists, that has perhaps never existed at all, and that will probably never exist."[25] Rousseau's account of the shift from "l'état naturel" to "l'état social" was therefore not a historical or anthropological narrative but an abstract, philosophical representation of man's alienation from his natural self. Thus, when he cited specific cases of contemporary tribal culture, such as that of the Venezuelan Caribs, it was not as an example of that abstract ideal but of an intermediate state, a golden age, between the purely instinctive "self-interest" of Natural Man and the rationally cultivated "self-love" of Civil Man:

this period of expansion of the human faculties, keeping a just mean between the indolence of the primitive state and the petulant activity of our *amour-propre*, must have been the happiest and most stable of epochs. The more we reflect on it, the more we shall find that this state was the least subject to revolutions, and altogether the very best man could experience. . . . The example of savages, most of whom have been found in this state, seems to prove that men were meant to remain in it, that it is the real youth of the world, and that all subsequent advances have been apparently not so many steps towards the perfection of the individual, but in reality towards the decrepitude of the species.[26]

The heightened sensibility attributed to even the most "primitive" of human beings allowed him to liberate himself from the immediate dependence on fear for his self-preservation, "and it is particularly in his consciousness of this liberty that the spirituality of his soul is displayed."[27] The Indian enjoyed an ideal condition of physical and spiritual tranquillity, freed from the lower animals' instinctive fears and impulses and from that other kind of anxiety, the unnaturally heightened desires and ambitions of Civil Man. In this way, the Indian's social and political freedom, more than once already posited as a utopian model by European philosophers, now gained a further dimension. It was the supreme liberty of Natural Man in contact with the world through his senses, learning the full extent of his needs and fulfilling them by actions that were sufficient to preserve the tranquillity of his spirit and the harmony of his world.

This utopian vision corresponds closely to the character of the Romantic Indianist writing of the first phase as exemplified by the work of its most significant representative, Gonçalves Dias. The poetry of Gonçalves Dias evoked a special world that, for all its wars, indeed, because of them and their ritual, had remained in perfect harmony with itself until the arrival of the European. Underlying that harmony was a delicate equilibrium, the fulcral, world-historic moment of transition, as it were, in Rousseau's narrative, between the natural and the civil states, balancing the absolute autonomy of the lone human individual, "wandering up and down the forests, without industry, without speech, and without home, an equal stranger to war and to all ties, neither standing in need of his fellow-creatures nor having any desire to hurt them,"[28] and the shared social identity of the tribe, where the solitude of the orphaned marginal can at last find a home. Both dimensions of this liberal equation are found in the Indianist imaginary of Gonçalves Dias—in the defiant chants of individual warrior braves, for whom life is an endless struggle of self-affirmation, and in the dramatic narrative of exclusion and reincorporation into the tribal body-politic, as symbolized by the cannibalist ritual in "I-Juca Pirama." For Gonçalves Dias as for Rousseau, only by carefully nurturing that equilibrium could Indian society sustain the ideal of a harmonious world safe from the specter of revolution and upheaval.

By the late 1830s the cumulative effect of the developments just described had begun to crystallize in the form of a self-conscious artistic and intellectual movement. The Indian had been used as a symbol of the American colony in paintings and illustrations even during the reign of João VI, and after independence the indigenous Brazilian began to appear in statues, on the façades of official buildings, and decorating the walls of aristocratic mansions. As Lilia Moritz Schwarcz observes in her study of Pedro II and the Second Reign, Indianism now entered the political iconography of the Empire, too, becoming incorporated into official ceremonies as part of the representation of Imperial power.[29] In the imaginary of the visual arts later in the century, tragic Indian figures such as Durão's Moema and Gonçalves Dias's Marabá became the subject for paintings by Victor Meirelles de Lima and Rodolfo Amoedo, respectively.

The prestige of indigenous ancestry, even if adoptive rather than real, provoked a minor craze among the Imperial elite. Patriots renounced their Portuguese names in favor of indigenous ones, such as Canguçu, Baitinga, Muriti, Jurema, Araripe, or, in the case of the viscount of Jequitinhonha, Francisco Jê Acaiaba Montezuma. Even Pedro I, as grand-master of the Freemasons, adopted an Indian name, albeit one derived from the more sophisticated civilizations of Spanish America—Guatimozim.[30] Political parties and their publications also sought to affirm their nationalist credentials in the same way; after independence the newspaper supporting José Bonifácio was called *O Tamoio*, the adherents to the restoration cause were called *caramurus*, and the moderate division of the Liberal Party after 1842 was known as the *ximangos*.

Indigenous languages and their influence upon the Portuguese spoken in Brazil became a serious object of interest; indeed, as a result of Pedro II's proposals for the study and teaching of Indian languages, Tupi might also have become available as a university discipline, had it not been for the fall of the Empire. As we see in the next chapter, the arguments in favor of renaming towns and villages with Indian substitutes or of using the Tupi-Guarani language at official state functions were clearly sufficiently pervasive for them to merit public denunciation by skeptics such as the historian João Francisco Lisboa. Legend has it that Pedro II was proficient enough in his command of the Tupi and Guarani languages to have made use of them in Brazil's dealings with Paraguay in the 1860s and to have conversed with a Paraguayan prisoner of war, although such stories came under question at the end of Empire.[31]

We should not underestimate the seriousness of Pedro's commitment to the Indianist movement or the importance of his role in giving it the practical, financial sponsorship and personal encouragement that he did, as well as the Empire's official seal of approval. Such a commitment and the institutional proximity between the movement and the Imperial regime confirm that this was no mere literary fad but a central element in the Empire's project of state- and nation-building. The main forum within which this relationship between Indianism and Empire was articulated, through the patronage of Pedro II, was the Brazilian Historical and Geographical Institute.

Founded in 1838, with the thirteen-year-old Pedro already its official "protector," the Institute was modeled on the French Institut Historique, itself established in 1834 by a group of intellectuals, two of whom— Monglave and Debret—were influential visitors to Brazil, as we have seen. As early as 1839 Pedro made space available in the Imperial Palace for the Institute's meetings and began to frequent its activities regularly following his majority in 1840, as well as financing many of its activities. The group of artists, writers, and historians who met at the Institute from this time constituted the core of the Imperial intelligentsia and its official literary movement, Romanticism. It included the most prominent names in Indianist writing and indigenist debate before Alencar: Gonçalves de Magalhães, Joaquim Norberto de Sousa Silva, Joaquim Manuel de Macedo, Gonçalves Dias, and Francisco Adolfo de Varnhagen.

These were the years in which Indianism was consolidated as a substantive literary movement, a "tradition" of writing consisting of a body of quite ambitious and complex works, as opposed to the rather sporadic, minor efforts that had been ventured in the 1830s. The middle of the decade saw two new editions of Basílio da Gama's *O Uraguay*, the first in 1844 as the inaugural work in the "Biblioteca Brasílica" of the *Minerva Brasiliense* journal, the second as Varnhagen's academic edition, copublished in 1845 with Santa Rita Durão's *Caramuru* under the general title *Épicos Brasileiros*.[32] That these two works were now perceived as the foundational texts of the movement is clear from the number of new texts (especially dramas) that, as we see later, recycled the cast of Indian characters invented by Da Gama and Durão, in particular their romantic heroines Lindóia, Paraguaçu, and Moema. By the end of the decade most of the Indianist poetry of Gonçalves Dias had been published, and there were serious experiments with more extended forms, such as Teixeira e Sousa's verse narrative *Os Três Dias de um Noivado* (The Three Days of a Marriage, 1844) and Martins Pena's drama *Itaminda ou o Guerreiro de Tupã* (Itaminda or the Warrior of Tupã), published in 1846.

From the early 1850s, when Pedro was presiding personally at most of its sessions, the Historical and Geographical Institute and its members became, as Lilia Moritz Schwarcz argues, not only an important center of research but also the essential link between the country's intellectual life and the political sphere of state officialdom, a kind of "think tank" with a central role in constructing national unification at the cultural level.[33] However, this official endorsement and sponsorship of the Indianist movement through the Institute did not guarantee that the relationship between individual writers and their Imperial patron was always a comfortable one or that the movement uniformly reflected a consensual view of the official self-image of Empire. We shall see how, as well as depicting a devastatingly critical vision of Empire through the Indianist prism, Gonçalves Dias wrestled bitterly with the question of his personal dependence on the Emperor's largesse for the publication of his work. Pedro may have financed Carlos Gomes's operatic adaptation of Alencar's novel *O Guarani*, but there was no lack of friction on both literary and political matters between the Emperor and Alencar himself, not least over his public attack on one of Pedro's pet projects, Gonçalves de Magalhães's epic *A Confederação dos Tamoios*.

Much of the output of the Historical and Geographical Institute was published in its own journal, whose first editions reflect the growing and varied scientific and scholarly interest in indigenist matters: reproductions from manuscripts of a "Treasure Discovered on the Upper River Amazon" and a "Notice regarding the Tupinambá Indians," a "History of the Horsemen Indians or Guaycurú Nation," Sousa Caldas's "Ode to Savage Man," and an essay by Januário da Cunha Barbosa entitled "Whether the Introduction of African Slaves into Brazil Hinders the Civilization of Our Indians, Exempting Them from Work That Has All Been Entrusted to Black Slaves." But there were other academic vehicles, too, for the movement's literary, political, historical, and ethnographic output, such as the multidisciplinary journals *Niterói, Minerva Brasiliense*, and *Guanabara*, which was founded in 1849 by Porto Alegre, Gonçalves Dias, and Joaquim Manuel de Macedo and became the arena of a crucial debate on indigenist policy.

Meanwhile, another, perhaps more reliable indicator of the broader penetration of the movement among Brazil's educated elite was the popularity of Indianist themes as a subject for drama. Indianist plays and musical works occupied the stage on numerous occasions. As early as 1846, Martins Pena, who was largely responsible for establishing a national theatrical tradition in Brazil using local themes, produced *Itaminda ou o Guerreiro de Tupã*. But it was in the 1850s that Indianist drama really flourished: Joaquim Norberto de Sousa Silva provided the Indianist libretto for Domingos José Ferreira's *Colombo* (1854), while the opera *Volta de Columella* (1857), staged in the theaters of São Januário and São Pedro, was the first to be performed by Indian actors.[34] These trends were encouraged by the organization of a competition under the auspices of the Brazilian Dramatic Conservatory. Among the submissions were three works based on traditional Indianist themes: *Lindoya*, "a lyrical tragedy in four acts," by Ferreira França, *Moema e Paraguaçu*, by Francisco Bonifácio de Abreu (1859), and another version of the Moema episode; in addition there exists an undated "Historical Drama in Four Acts, Caramuru" by Eduardo Carijé Baraúna.[35] The most popular Indianist drama was Joaquim Manuel de Macedo's *Cobé* (1854), which, after its first performance in 1859, enjoyed a period of particular success during the 1860s and is included in Sábato Magaldi's *Panorama do Teatro Brasileiro* under the heading "Drama to the Public Taste."[36] Carlos Gomes's famous opera *Il Guarani*, based on Alencar's novel, was first performed at La Scala, Milan, in 1870 and elsewhere in Europe thereafter. By then, however, Indianism had moved on to quite different concerns from those expressed in the first texts published over thirty years before.

COMPATRIOTS AND COMRADES-IN-ARMS

The earliest extant texts of the Indianist movement, by the poet Ladislau dos Santos Titara, offer clear evidence of the relationship between the atmosphere of political conflict, the struggle for nationalist self-assertion, and the combative mood of Indianist writing, which is characteristic of the first phase. Born in 1801 in Capuame, in the province of Bahia, the son of a lawyer, Titara began training in his father's profession, but his studies were interrupted by the independence movement. He took part on the nationalist side and, following the example of many of his compatriots at this time, changed his name from the original Ladislau do Espírito Santo Mello, so as to disown his Portuguese ancestry. According to Sacramento Blake,[37] he was both a prominent military officer and a writer of some standing; he gained several honors, including the Order of the Rose, was a member of the Historical and Geographical Institute, and produced a number of works on military law. As a poet he was very prolific, publishing eight volumes between 1827 and 1852,[38] and was a pupil of the Indianist playwright Ferreira França.

The "Metamorphose Original—Moema, e Camorogí" (first published with *Paraguassú* in 1835) marks the beginning of that strand of Indianism that sought to foster a sense of national identity through the fusion of landscape and myth. The poem concerns two Indians, Moema and Camorogí, who are united by "The God of marriage" on the banks of the river Pitanga in Bahia. The link between myth and geography is reinforced by the choice of name, for Camuruji was a town in the municipality of Taperoá, also in Bahia. In addition, a number of indigenous terms designating animals and plants peculiar to the Brazilian landscape, for example, *jacarandá*, *potumujus*, *oyticica*, are included to reflect linguistically this sense of a distinctive American identity. The familiar name of Moema, meanwhile, now removed from the original tragic context of Durão's *Caramuru*, had acquired its own tradition of sentimental associations.

The poem purports to explain the origin of the *dorminhoco*, the bird of indolence: Moema wakes at dawn and urges her new husband to join her in exploring their idyllic home together. He, disturbed from his sleep, becomes enraged and almost kills Moema, who calls for protection from the spirit of the forest and is transformed into a bird. Camorogí returns home downcast, led on by the singing voice of his wife; the god Tupá takes pity on him and transforms him, too, into a bird, the voiceless Dorminhoco:

> E só, se incauta mosca vai pousar-lhe
> No cabis-baixo bico, mal disperto,
> Come-a, coxila, e languido redorme.[39]

(And alone, if an unwary fly settles/ On his downcast beak, half awake,/ He eats it, yawns, and lazily falls asleep again.)

As well as contributing in this way to establishing a national folkloric tradition, the poem offers a mythical explanation for the disappearance of the Indian; rather than suffering a drawn-out process of extermination and marginalization, the Indian is placed in a prehistoric world, a poetic space that preserves the indigenous ideal intact.

Titara's epic poem *Paraguassú* is quite different, for it demonstrates for the first time the overtly political function of Indianist writing in its initial phase, supplying the independence cause with an ideological and historical legitimacy. Here Titara reinterprets the foundation myth of Durão's *Caramuru* so as to highlight the role of the Indian heroine as the precursor of the nineteenth-century independence forces. During much of the poem, the name Paraguassú has a token significance, recalling both the legendary mother of the Colony and the particular geographical context from which she derives her name: the river Paraguaçu, which flows into the Bahia de Todos os Santos, for the text concerns that part of the independence campaign in which the poet himself participated in his native province. Actually written in 1831 and therefore before most of the provincial revolts of the Regency, which might have put the story in a different light, the poem is dedicated to the viscount of Pirajá, who led the campaign in its early stages. It is preceded, and each canto followed, by extensive lists of credits to all the officers involved in the campaign.

The first canto sees the viscount besieging the town from which he gained his title; meanwhile, as Portuguese aid is being sent from Lisbon, the future emperor, Pedro I, is visited in a dream with the advice that he must support the *baianos* with forces from the capital. The "Spirit of Brazil" who appears to him carrying a bow and defending the principles of "Liberty, Courage, Unity and Glory," is unmistakably a tribal warrior, with long black hair, and a feather headdress, while "do hombro espaçoso/ Pende envolto o carcaz em lindas pelles/ De bi-color Panthéra" (from his expansive shoulders/ Hangs the carcass of a piebald Panther/ Wrapped in lovely skins).[40]

As the cantos progress through battle after battle toward the final triumph of the independence struggle, the myth of indigenous ancestry and the common cause of Brazilian and Indian is brought into play. Tribal names are invoked frequently, sometimes referring to white nationalist forces, the "Novos Tupinambás," for example, and sometimes to the regiments of conscripted Indians who also took part in the campaign. As a result, Brazilian and Indian soldiers fighting under the same banner become indistinguishable, and their cause and the fatherland they are defending become identical. The officer Carvalhal is thus able to encourage his men with the example of a tradition of tribal bravery and self-sacrifice that is at once their own: "Que o morrer pela Patria he vida honrosa,/ Muito ha, Tupiniquins, que sabeis bravos" (You have long since known, Tupiniquin braves,/ That to die for one's Fatherland is an honorable life).[41] In canto IV, the commander Pirajá appeals to unrecruited local tribes, again uniting both Indian and Brazilian interests against a common colonial enemy:

> Os contrarios não são outros d'aquelles,
> Em quem vexame, opprobrio, e iniquas mortes
> Punistes mais, que bravos, tendo à frente
> Heroína, cujo Neto ser me ufana:
> Contra Toimocês vís, Tupá socorre.[42]

> (Our adversaries are none other than those/ Whose outrage, infamy and iniquitous killings/ You braves have punished, having at your head/ The Heroine, whose grandson I am proud to be:/ The God Tupá comes to our aid against the vile Toimocês.)

Here Pirajá offers his own ancestral credentials in support of his argument, claiming descent from Paraguaçu, the Indian mother of the founding family of Bahia, the Caramurus.

Meanwhile, Diogo Álvares, the white, Portuguese hero of the colonial legend, is not even mentioned by name but appears briefly in an explanatory note as the husband of Paraguaçu and the captive of the despotic governor of Bahia, Pereira Coutinho. As in other nineteenth-century accounts of the legend, the female Indian protagonist assumes the heroic role, defending the first capital of Brazil against the colonial tyrant:

> she had her fellow countrymen gathered together, and at the head of them, the Tamoyos and other tribes, whom she had summoned from the Recôncavo, she besieged the City and after bloody battles and strong resistance from Coutinho, who lost in them a son, they forced him into flight together with his men, who sheltering on board the ships, escaped to Ilhéus, leaving Bahia rid of those torturers.

Titara's *Paraguassú* thus laid one of the cornerstones of the Romantic Indianist discourse of the first phase: the mythology of a heroic indigenous ancestry and of a shared tradition of anticolonial military resistance, through which the Brazilian national and the Indian could be identified as partners in a natural alliance. The symbolic usefulness of this mythology to the invention of a nationalist tradition is all the more striking when one remembers that, by comparison with the violence of the national liberation struggles elsewhere in the Americas, Brazil could hardly be described as fighting an independence war as such.

However, it was not this but another poem from the 1830s that came to be recognized as the seminal text of the movement and was even described by the important late nineteenth-century literary historian Sílvio Romero as the first authentic example of "poesia americana" in Brazil.[43] Rodrigues Silva's obituary "Nênia" (lament or dirge) was written in 1837 to commemorate the death of

Francisco Bernardino Ribeiro, a prestigious poet and lecturer at São Paulo's law faculty. First published in the literary, scientific, and political journal *Minerva Brasiliense*, it was subsequently reproduced in various nineteenth-century anthologies and cited in contemporary debates on the development of the Indianist aesthetic.

Rodrigues Silva's innovation lay in his personification of Niterói, his own birthplace and that of Bernardino Ribeiro, as a bereaved Indian mother. The name already held considerable symbolic, nationalist significance as the original indigenous settlement facing modern Rio de Janeiro across the Bay of Guanabara and had been adopted in the year preceding Rodrigues Silva's "Nênia" as the title of the first journal of Brazilian Romanticism. Although its etymological origin is debatable, most commentators agree in translating it as "sheltered, hidden or safe water or bay,"[44] referring to the Bay of Guanabara; indeed, Santa Rita Durão confirms that interpretation when, in canto VIII of *Caramuru*, he writes: "Nhigheteroi se chama a vasta enseada,/ Que estreita boca, como vasta barra encerra" (Nhigheteroi is the name of the immense bay/ That a narrow mouth encloses, like a vast bar). According to Lilia Moritz Schwarcz, the name was found in the sixteenth-century travel narrative of the French missionary André Thevet, where it was seen to have suggested that association between indigenous culture and the American continent that lay at the heart of the Romantics' nativist nationalism.[45] Similarly, in Rodrigues Silva's poem Ribeiro, one of the most eminent representatives of the postindependence cultural establishment, is embraced and mourned by the indigenous maternal symbol of the national capital as the son and heir of an uninterrupted native identity:

> Sem dó, nem compaixão roubou-me a morte
> Do meu cocar a penna mais mimosa,
> A joia peregrina de meu cinto,
> O lirio mais formoso das campinas,
> O lume de meus olhos!—Oh! meu filho,
> Inda canta a araponga, e o rio volve
> Na ruiva areia a lobrega corrente;
> Inda retouca a laranjeira a coma
> Verde-negra de flôres alvejantes,
> E tu já não existes!!—Sol brilhante,
> Numen de meus pais, que he do meu filho?
> Ó Tupá, ó Tupá, que mal te hei feito?[46]

(Without pity or compassion, death has robbed me/ Of the loveliest plume in my headdress,/ The matchless jewel of my girdle,/ The most beautiful lily of the fields,/ The light of my eyes! —Oh! my son,/ The *araponga* still sings, and the river stirs/ Its murky current across the ruddy sands;/ The dark-green mane of the orange-tree is still crowned with gleaming white flowers,/ And you are no more!!—Blazing sun,/ Spirit of my fathers, what is become of my son?/ Oh Tupá, oh Tupá, what wrong have I done you?)

In the last stanza the reiterated appeal to an incomprehensible, wrathful god is interrupted by the chorus of nature's sounds, waves upon the shore, wind in the forests, and the echoes across valleys and mountains. The Brazilian landscape, its mythical indigenous inhabitants, and the modern representative of the national culture are thus identified in a single image of maternal loss.

DRAMAS OF RACIAL EXCLUSION, REVENGE, AND EXILE: MARTINS PENA, TEIXEIRA E SOUSA, AND GONÇALVES DIAS

No sooner had the viability of the Indianist theme as an expression of nationalist sentiment been established, than a new generation of writers began to explore its more complex possibilities, including its potential for commenting, if obliquely, on the internal contradictions within the new, independent Empire. However, after Rodrigues Silva's "Nênia" it was not until the middle of the next decade that a substantial body of work, in verse and for the stage, began to emerge with a clear set of shared preoccupations. One might speculate as to whether the seven years' silence in Indianist writing until the appearance of Teixeira e Sousa's *Os Três Dias de um Noivado* (The Three Days of a Marriage) in 1844 was a direct consequence of the civil unrest that, as we have seen, had by this time spread across the provinces of the north, northeast, southeast, and south of the country. Certainly, the new cycle of Indianist writing closely coincided with the formation of that core group of writers and artists within the newly founded Historical and Geographical Institute and the beginning of its efforts self-consciously to build a national intellectual and cultural tradition for the country. What is at least certain is that the broadly pessimistic and critical thematic focus of the mid- to late 1840s *was* informed by the atmosphere of ethnic, social, and political conflict and violence that extended until nearly the end of the decade. Whereas the first Indianist writers could celebrate the notion of uninterrupted indigenous identity through the myths of a shared Indian ancestry and an anticolonial military alliance, the new writing was marked by a sense of rupture; the legacy of colonialism was one of irreparable social disruption, the disintegration and dispersal of whole peoples.

This shift in perspective is clearly illustrated by the changing function of the deity Tupã, to whom the maternal indigenous figure of Niterói appeals, in Rodrigues Silva's "Nênia," as she seeks an explanation for the loss of her native son. By the time we come to Martins Pena's stage play *Itaminda ou o Guerreiro de Tupã* (Itaminda or the Warrior of Tupã, 1846), Tupã has taken on an Old Testament or classical role as the wrathful, merciless god of the Tupinambá tribe, presiding over a tragic drama of betrayal, revenge, and exile that now speaks of the colonial experience in its entirety. As we shall see, these became central themes of the Indianist movement during this phase, explored first in Teixeira e Sousa's verse narrative *The Three Days of a Marriage* and then fully developed in the poetry of Gonçalves Dias, culminating in his apocalyptic interpretation of Brazil's colonial history.

The setting for Martins Pena's *Itaminda . . .* is the very outset of Conquest, as an alliance of Tupinambá and Tamoio tribes faces the recently arrived vanguard of Portuguese colonialism in mid-sixteenth-century Bahia. The prospects for a unified campaign of resistance are threatened, however, since the Tupinambá chief Itaminda has fallen in love with Beatriz, the captive daughter of the colonial governor, raising not only the possibility that he might be tempted to betray his people but also locking him into conflict with a rival warrior, Tibira, who has his own designs on the young Portuguese woman. The web of relationships is further complicated by the addition of two female characters derived, in part, from the eighteenth-century epics of Santa Rita Durão and Basílio da Gama. Itaminda's sister is Lindóia (recalling the virginal tragic heroine from *O Uraguay*), who, despite the governor's execution of her mother, has been persuaded by Itaminda to befriend and protect Beatriz. Moema, meanwhile, draws even more explicitly on the vengeful character of her predecessor in Durão's *Caramuru*, for as Itaminda's abandoned lover and the mother of his son, she is intent on avenging her betrayal and soon sets about plotting to poison Beatriz.

These destructive forces begin to converge by act 2, when Itaminda returns from the middle of the military campaign to find that Lindóia has foiled Moema's murder attempt but that Beatriz has meanwhile been abducted by his rival Tibira. Hearing his leaderless warriors utter the chant of defeat, now exposed as a traitor to his people, disowned by his father, and having lost Beatriz to Tibira, he declares himself an outcast ("I have no tribe, I have no father, I have no friends!"[47]) dedicated only to self-destructive, personal revenge. His fellow tribesmen take up the theme collectively, as they prepare Beatriz's captive lover, the Portuguese soldier Dom Duarte, for the ritual of cannibalism in exchange for the wrongs they have suffered: "Foreigner, Tupã gave us this land, and your people wish to steal it from us. In it rest the bones of our forefathers, and the feet of your warriors profane the bones of our forefathers. War for war, torment for torment! You shall die and your body will be served at our banquet. May all your people end thus!"[48]

Itaminda now perversely turns his thirst for revenge on his own tribespeople, leading a party of Portuguese soldiers back to the Tupinambá camp in order to free Dom Duarte. He has become the personification of willful betrayal, unbridled vengeance, and self-destruction: "Exterminate them, exterminate them! How soft to my ears is that terrible echo of death! Oh, vengeance is such sweet pleasure! Sitting alone in the smoking ruins of this village, I shall intone the chant of vengeance and my voice will resound fatefully in the silence of the forests!"[49] Now stricken with guilt and grief, as his father dies in his arms, cursing him, Itaminda's final intended act of betrayal and revenge is a further reversal, to turn once more against the Portuguese and lead his warriors in a last, hopeless battle. He has again been imprisoned by the Portuguese, but calling on the Anhangá, the terrible spirit of evil, he cruelly tricks Moema into freeing him with false protests of remorse and renewed promises of loyalty to her and their son. Defeating Tibira in a hand-to-hand combat on a mountain-top, he emerges fatally wounded from a raging torrent, only to find that Moema, betrayed for a second time, has now locked Beatriz and Lindóia in a hut and set it alight. He is too weak to save them, and they are rescued instead by Dom Duarte, as Itaminda collapses, dying, at the feet of Beatriz. Moema, her revenge only half satisfied, is left to shake her arms threateningly at the heavens and at Tupã.

In Martins Pena's drama, then, the colonial encounter, in both its military and sexual forms, is depicted as setting in motion a relentless cycle of internal conflict, betrayal, and destructive revenge, hardly the model for a celebratory Indianist mythology of preindependence history as a formative process, laying the imaginary foundations for a secure sense of nationhood rooted in a continuity with the past and with the Indians' cultural legacy. In fact, until the mid-1850s, Indianism was dominated by this tragic ethos; moreover, its two leading proponents during these years—the celebrated Indianist poet Gonçalves Dias and his lesser known contemporary Teixeira e Sousa—went even further in questioning the foundational assumptions that underpinned the official promotion of Indianism as part of the project of state-building and national unification. As a dissident, if minor, tendency within Brazil's Romantic movement, their work, within the limited political space available to them, made use of the Indianist scenario to draw implicit, but disturbing, comparisons between the forms of oppression suffered by Brazil's subject races under colonial rule and the continuing denial of social and political freedoms to the majority following independence. The existence of slavery, a stifling culture of patronage, and political disfranchisement for the overwhelming mass of Brazilians suggested that the ongoing nationalist celebration of the Empire's emancipation from the metropolitan yoke served to mask the unbroken bonds of class and ethnic domination that still tied the country to its colonial past. Not only that, but for Gonçalves Dias at least, the failure of the Empire to break with its colonial legacy also posed a dangerous threat to the very fabric and survival of the independent nation, which was felt to be hovering on the verge of collapse.

Unlike the most eminent apologists of the Imperial status quo, such as Gonçalves de Magalhães, Porto Alegre, or Alencar, these writers did not enjoy the advantages of financial security, ancestral respectability, or prestigious political, diplomatic, or military careers. Rather, there are good reasons to suppose that an acute sense of their disadvantaged racial and social origins provided them with the critical distance that explains their pessimistic vision of life under Empire. As such, they were well placed to relate their own experience to that of the wider layer of free colored and white Brazilians who existed outside the structures of the dominant axis of the economy—slavery—and who by the same token found themselves relegated to a situation of redundancy, disfranchisement, and social invisibility. As Maria Sylvia de Carvalho Franco puts it in her study of freemen in the slaveholding order,

Thus, in a society where there is a concentration of the means of production, where there is a slow but progressive growth of markets, there is formed in parallel a body of free and expropriated men who have not known the rigors of forced labor and who have not become proletarianized. Rather, it was a "rabble" that was formed, that grew and drifted across four centuries: men who were strictly speaking dispensable, disconnected from the processes that were essential to society. Mercantile agriculture based on slavery simultaneously opened up a space for their existence and left them without any raison d'être.[50]

Indeed, for Richard Graham, one of the functions of the Imperial system of patronage was precisely to exert some kind of control over such a dislocated population with a potential will of its own:

[V]irtually every institution served to stress the social hierarchy, insisting that for every individual there was a very particular place, even if the most important distinction lay between the propertied and the poor. Measures of social control were all the more necessary because of obstacles to its imposition in Brazil, particularly the geographical mobility of the landless free.[51]

As we shall see, the work of Teixeira e Sousa and Gonçalves Dias is, in large part, driven by their awareness of this ambiguity and tension in the relationship between the "landless free" and Imperial society, caught as they were between the powerlessness of their social marginalization and the dependency of patronage. "Favor was our quasi-universal social mediation,"[52] writes Roberto Schwarz in his pioneering study "Misplaced Ideas . . . ," which reevaluates the importance of relations between masters and free dependents for an understanding of nineteenth-century Brazilian literature. While Schwarz's focus is primarily prose fiction and the work of Machado de Assis in particular, we can now see how the novelistic exploration of the theme of patronage was actually prefigured rather earlier, in the verse writing of the Indianists Teixeira e Sousa and Gonçalves Dias.

Antônio Gonçalves Teixeira e Sousa was the eldest of five children, born to a Portuguese trader and his black mistress in Santa Helena, Cabo Frio, in 1812. The independence crisis led his father into heavy debt, and Antônio, who was already studying Latin, was obliged to become apprenticed as a carpenter. While still a young man he suffered the deaths of his entire family and in 1840 moved permanently to Rio de Janeiro, where he had completed his apprenticeship. [53] There he met and began a lifelong friendship with the future publisher Francisco de Paula Brito (1809-61), also a mulatto from a modest family of artisans. The association with Paula Brito requires some comment, since it confirms the evidence of Teixeira e Sousa's *The Three Days of a Marriage* and of the poetry of Gonçalves Dias that points to the existence of a distinctive mulatto and *mestiço* consciousness within the Brazilian intellectual community.

Jean-Michel Massa describes Paula Brito as a self-made man; certainly, it was due to his idealism, generosity, and willingness to take risks in the face of considerable financial difficulties that many young writers were encouraged and their first works made available to the public.[54] More specifically, he gave Teixeira e Sousa the moral support and stimulus that were denied to him elsewhere in the artistic establishment on account of his social origins.[55] As a source of continuity and personal encouragement, Paula Brito probably offered the solidarity needed by mulatto writers who, like himself, found the material obstacles to self-improvement multiplied by virtue of their race. Indeed, another mulatto, Machado de Assis, was also employed by Paula Brito during the early years of his career, before he began publishing his first volumes of poetry and novels. The poems of Machado's *Americanas*, a late contribution to Brazilian Indianism, belong to the third phase of the movement and are considered later;

but their concern with the problem of social marginalization suggests a significant point of continuity with Teixeira e Sousa's bitterly pessimistic brand of Indianism.

Having helped Paula Brito open a printer's and stationer's shop, Teixeira e Sousa began to earn a meager living writing dramas, novels, and poetry: the *Cantos lyricos* and *The Three Days of a Marriage* (1844). In 1847 he published the novel *As Tardes de um pintor ou As intrigas de um jesuíta* (The Evenings of a Painter or The Intrigues of a Jesuit), which, though not strictly an Indianist work, holds some interest due to its historical setting: Gomes Freire de Andrada's campaign of 1754-56 against the Guarani Missions in Uruguay, the subject of Basílio da Gama's Indianist epic. The novel's central narrative strand concerns the scandalous love affair of a Jesuit priest, and much of the historical detail focuses on the power of the missionaries, their enormous landed properties, theocratic tyranny, and military and sexual exploitation of the Indians. Training them to fight against other tribes, they "turned to their advantage the natural proclivities of the Indians, both of one sex and the other."[56]

Teixeira e Sousa also specified a precise historical location for his more successful Indianist poem, *The Three Days of a Marriage*. The date of 1715 is given, indicating a period of well-established colonization, long after the initial confrontation between white and Indian. The geographical context is also precisely defined, for this longish narrative poem opens with a description of the tropical landscape of the coast at Cabo Frio, the poet's home region. According to Joaquim Norberto de Souza Silva,[57] Teixeira e Sousa often walked in the Narandyba forest depicted in the poem, was familiar with the chapel of the Virgin of Saquarema that appears in it, knew the cliffs and cave off Itaúna with their strange wailing sound that was the inspiration for one of the poem's key episodes, and would have heard there the traditional tale of Corimbaba and Miry'ba, which forms the basis of the plot. Whatever the accuracy of these details, the explicit location of the action in the poet's native region confirms the tendency for the Indianist writers of this period to express their *nativismo* in terms of an identification with local landscapes as much as with the independent nation as a whole.

As far as the social condition of its characters is concerned, though, the poem marks a departure from the first Indianist texts, for the protagonists are a converted, "civilizado" Guarani and a *mestiça* woman. *The Three Days of a Marriage* deals, then, not with the first, archetypal colonial clash of the races in the golden age of unadulterated tribal culture but with its social and cultural aftermath. The marriage is a childless, futureless one, interrupted after three days by the tragic weight of history, racial conflict, and alienation. As such it allows Teixeira e Sousa to make some of the most acerbic denunciations of social and racial marginalization under Empire that are to be found in the literature of the period.

The young couple, Corimbaba and Miry'ba, return newly married to the idyllic setting of a village in Cabo Frio and enjoy the traditional tribal celebrations. However, the success of the marriage is marred by Miry'ba's memory of the occasion that brought them together, her mother's death, and by her increasing sense of exile and isolation from the community. At this time Corimbaba witnesses a curious incident in which a boy, in trying to save a small dove from the clutches of a falcon and then from a snake, kills both snake and dove. This is interpreted as an ill omen by the Indian Coapara, and, sure enough, the boy is later killed by a falling tree as it is struck by lightning.

On the day following their wedding night, Corimbaba contradicts his wife's wishes and accompanies his friends on a hunting expedition, during which he becomes separated from the others and drifts far around the coast in his canoe. Inland he comes across an ancient hermit, who tells him of his disillusionment with humanity and advises Corimbaba to visit the magical "cave of mysteries." There, an oracle unravels the mysterious symbolism of the earlier incident involving the boy and the dove; it is a parable of jealousy and hasty conclusions that anticipates the tragic outcome of the story, for, waiting in despair for the return of her husband, Miry'ba has fainted in the arms of a stranger who knocks at the door; it is her Portuguese father, who, believed dead, has been searching for her since he was shipwrecked. However, when Corimbaba returns to the house and sees his wife in the arms of another man, he hastily jumps to conclusions and stabs Miry'ba, who has time only to reveal the truth before she dies, quickly followed by the suicide of Corimbaba.

The bare bones of the plot, then, appear to tell the story of a marriage destroyed by mistrust and jealousy, confirming the old man's pessimistic view of the human condition and conforming to the fatal forces of the oracle's premonition. But the characters' social origins and experiences constitute a more oppressive background that hangs over the marriage and invests the tragedy with disturbing racial implications.

In the first place there is Corimbaba, reputedly descended from invincible chiefs of the Guarani nation but whose conversion to Christianity has brought about a transformation such that "quem o tractara/ O crêra cidadão da antiga Europa" (whoever had dealings with him/ Would believe him to be a citizen of the old Europe).[58] The narrator comments that this transformation is to be responsible, in part, for the tragedy to follow: "Mais feliz fôra,/ Si tranquilo vivendo em seu deserto,/ Em menos aprendesse" (Happier would he have been,/ If, living peacefully in his wilderness,/ He had had less learning) (canto I, xlvii). It is clear that the harmony of their world, which should have been confirmed by the couple's marriage, has long since been undermined.

As he tries to dispel Miry'ba's feelings of alienation and foreignness among the strangers of her new home, Corimbaba recounts the historical facts of colonial greed, violence, and exploitation that must unite all those who, with indigenous blood in their veins, have been its victims. This is the first of a series of remarkably frank indictments of the historical treatment of the nonwhite races in Brazil, which gives the lie to the dominant Indianist rhetoric of a united, integrated nation of Indians, whites, and *caboclos*:

Somos uma nação . . . antes reliquias
De uma grande nação! . . . Dispersos restos,
Escapados às ondas tormentosas

Dos mares da cubiça! A nossa raça,
Só porque habitára um paiz rico . . .
Nefando crime aos olhos da politica
Lá das terras dos brancos, (assim chamam
Seu saber a respeito aos outros povos)
Ou ante os vãos pretextos religiosos,
Perseguida, assolada a ferro, e fogo
Foi quase exterminada! Longo tempo
Proscriptas estas raças descorreram
Pelos vastos sertões! as que escaparam
Ao ferro d'ambição, apavorados
Emigraram p'ra sempre, e se esconderam
Lá pelas virgens matas do Amazonas! (canto III, xxiv)

(We are a nation . . . rather relics/ Of a great nation! . . . Scattered remnants,/ Who have escaped the stormy waves/ On the seas of greed! Our race,/ Merely because it inhabited a rich country. . ./ A heinous crime in the eyes of politics/ Over in the white man's lands, (so they refer in their way to other peoples)/ Or in the face of vain religious pretexts,/ Persecuted, ravaged by sword and fire,/ Was almost exterminated! Long/ Banished these races roamed/ The vast wildernesses! those who escaped/ The steel of ambition,/ Emigrated in terror forever, and hid/ In the virgin forests of the Amazon!)

But Teixeira e Sousa does not stop at this denunciation of Conquest; in the first of several passages that resonate with echoes of contemporary, Imperial Brazil, he has the old hermit of the forest speak of the colonial legacy of racism in an ambiguous past tense:

Não vi mais que a injustiça em toda parte!
A cor do homem, accidente mero,
(Fallo pois dos cabouclos destas terras)
Foi à perseguição pretexto infame!
Teve-se em menor conta os seus serviços,
E olhou-se com desprezo os seus talentos,
Seus feitos, seu valor, suas virtudes!
E a baça cor da pelle era barreira
Aos empregos, e premios merecidos! (canto IV, liv)

(I have seen nothing but injustice everywhere!/ A man's color, a mere accident,/ (For I am speaking of the *caboclos* of these lands)/ Has been the foul pretext for persecution!/ Their services have been held in lower esteem,/ And their talents, their deeds, their courage,/ Their virtues have been looked upon with contempt!/ And the dull color of their skin was a barrier/ To the occupations and rewards they deserved!)

Only the most willfully narrow reading of this passage could ignore its historical ambiguity, its thinly veiled allusion to the continuing discrimination suffered by the free, nonwhite population of nineteenth-century Brazil, made more pointed by the author's, surely ironic, disclaimer in parentheses. Admittedly, the liberal revision of colonial history following independence might justify a more one-dimensional interpretation. But to this must be added the autobiographical weight of Teixeira e Sousa's origins and experiences as a mulatto, which must undeniably have made him acutely aware of the disadvantages of being poor and colored in a society where power depended on the ownership of land and slaves and the exercise of patronage.

Moreover, even more striking parallels between the lives of the author and his central character, Miry'ba, make this analysis particularly compelling. Both Miry'ba and Teixeira e Sousa were of mixed race, both were orphaned, the poem being dedicated to the author's parents (Teixeira e Sousa also lost his four brothers and sisters), and both were separated from their family home, obliged to live in an unfamiliar environment in poverty, dependent on the favor of others. For the first time in Brazilian writing we are confronted with the tragic predicament of the *mestiça*, who inhabits a stateless limbo between two communities, races, and classes, condemned to a future of exile and dependency:

> Irei, sem vós, vagar na terra estranha
> (Continúa outra vez) sem esperanças!
> Hei de comer o pão da caridade,
> Molhado pelo pranto da miséria!
> Ao passar pela estrada os caminhantes
> Me dirão—alli vae uma estrangeira,
> Vagabunda entre nós: seus paes nasceram
> Aonde ninguem sabe; e nem cuidaram
> Em lhe deixar sustento; —e desta sorte
> Todos me julgarão filha lançada,
> Alta noute, nas portas dos visinhos!
> Ah! que eu serei olhada com desprezo,
> Obrigada a pedir, ou condemnada
> A servir, como escrava, e assim a vida
> Me será mais penosa do que a morte! (canto II, lxxvi)

> (Without you, I shall wander in an alien land/ (She continues once more) without hope!/ I shall eat the bread of charity,/ Moistened with the tears of misery!/ As they pass along the road the wayfarers/ Will tell me—there goes a foreigner,/ A vagabond among us: her parents were born/ Noone knows where; and they did not even care/ To leave her any sustenance; —and so/ Everyone will regard me as a daughter cast out,/ In the middle of the night, on the neighbors' doorstep!/ Oh! I shall be looked upon with contempt,/ Obliged to beg, or condemned/ To serve as a slave, and thus my life/ Will be more grievous to me than death!)

Miry'ba's lament on her orphanhood and her song of exile, whose intensity and emphasis are otherwise difficult to account for, thus acquire a secondary significance, speaking both for the author and for a whole, marginalized sector of Brazilian society under Empire:

> Por graça em mesa alhéa
> Feliz quem não comeu;
> Feliz quem não bebeu
> Nas festas dos estranhos! (canto III, xii)

> (Happy the one who has not eaten/ At another's table, out of favor;/ Happy the one who has not drunk/ At the feasts of strangers!)

Teixeira e Sousa's tragic *mestiça* heroine obviously invites comparison with the rather more familiar, nearly homonymous protagonist of a shorter poem, "Marabá," by his contemporary Antônio Gonçalves Dias. Gonçalves Dias's Marabá is, like Miry'ba, so named because of her mixed-race parentage, which, as in Teixeira e Sousa's poem, is the source of her estrangement from the community of the tribe. Gonçalves Dias explained in a note that the episode was suggested to him by a passage in the Jesuit historian Vasconcelos's colonial *Chronicle of the Society of Jesus*: "A certain old woman had buried alive a child, the son of her daughter-in-law, on the same spot where she had given birth to him, because he was a child they call *marabá*, which means of mixed race (an abominable thing among these people)."[59] What gives this account of sexual rejection its special significance is that, as in *The Three Days of a Marriage*, Marabá's isolation is due to her white, rather than her indigenous, parentage. Gonçalves Dias therefore inverts the racist tradition of tragic, dark-skinned heroines, such as Durão's Moema, who are the victims of their forbidden, exotic sexual appeal. Marabá's beauty is ironically that of the classic European Virgin, pale and blue-eyed:

> Meus olhos são garços, são cor das safiras,
> Têm luz das estrelas, têm meigo brilhar;
> Imitam as nuvens de um céu anilado,
> As cores imitam das vagas do mar! . . .
> É alvo meu rosto da alvura dos lírios,
> Da cor das areias batidas do mar;
> As aves mais brancas, as conchas mais puras
> Não têm mais alvura, não têm mais brilhar.

(My eyes are turquoise, they are the color of sapphires,/ They have the light of the stars, they have a tender gleam;/ They mimic the clouds of an indigo sky,/ They mimic the colors of the ocean's waves! . . ./ My face is pale white, as pale as the lilies,/ The color of the sands pounded by the sea;/ The whitest birds, the purest shells/ Are not whiter, do not have a brighter gleam.)

Although steeped in the natural imagery of the tribal environment, it is precisely that European model of beauty that is spurned by the Indian warriors:

> Se algum dos guerreiros não foge a meus passos:
> —"Teus olhos são garços,"
> Responde anojado, "mas és Marabá:
> "Quero antes uns olhos bem pretos, luzentes,
>   "Uns olhos fulgentes,
> "Bem pretos, retintos, não cor d'anajá!". . .
> Se ainda me escuta meus agros delírios:
>   —"És alva de lírios,"
> Sorrindo responde, "mas és Marabá:
> "Quero antes um rosto de jambo corado,

"Um rosto crestado
"Do sol do deserto, não flor de cajá."

(If one of the warriors does not flee from my steps/ —"Your eyes are turquoise,"/ He replies with displeasure, "but you are Marabá:/ I would rather have bright black eyes,/ Shining eyes,/ Black eyes, jet-black, not the color of the anajá palm!". . ./ If he still listens to my bitter ravings/ —"You are pale as the lilies,"/ Smiling he replies, "but you are Marabá:/ I would rather have a face the color of the red jambo fruit,/ A face tanned/ By the desert sun, not the yellow of the mombin flower.")

The Marabá may seductively protest her attractions, but her words of amorous affection will remain unspoken and the symbol of her virginity, the *arasóia* "feather girdle," will remain forever intact. The virginal beauty of the European feminine stereotype is thus symbolic, in this tribal context, not of virtuous chastity but of sexual frustration and social exclusion.

As we shall see, these were familiar experiences to Gonçalves Dias himself, and by inverting the gender of the protagonist, earlier readings of "Marabá" have linked it to the event that may also have inspired "Tu não queres ligar-te commigo" (You Will Not Have Me for Your Partner)—the rejection of a marriage proposal to his friend's cousin, Ana Amélia, on the grounds of social or even racial prejudice. Biographical readings of this kind are speculative, of course. The figure of the social outcast appears in a number of Gonçalves Dias's non-Indianist poems, too, such as "O Assassino" (The Murderer), "O Baile" (The Dance), and "Agar no Deserto" (Agar in the Desert), and it should not be forgotten that exile and the solitude of the human individual are stock Romantic themes. While we should guard against narrowly reductionist biographical intepretations of the work, there is, nevertheless, a strong argument for viewing the treatment of these themes in the Indianist writing of Gonçalves Dias as fully comprehensible only in the light of the specific character of nineteenth-century Brazilian society as he perceived it. Both his personal and professional life, his nonfictional writings and his Indianist poetry together bear witness, as did the experience of other mixed-race, lower-middle-class intellectuals of his generation, to a powerful sense of social alienation, an acute consciousness of racial and economic disadvantage, and a bitter disgust with the oppressive conditions upon which the prosperity of the Empire was based.

However, although, like Teixeira e Sousa, he represents a rather atypical, dissident tendency within the predominantly conservative framework of the movement, Gonçalves Dias never went so far as to question the basic integrationist assumptions of Indianist thinking. His work and career demonstrate the same accommodation of radical liberal principles to the interests of a centralized, oligarchic, and slave-owning state that characterizes the movement as a whole. What makes the Indianism of Gonçalves Dias so interesting is that this ideological compromise exists in a state of tension that gives his work an intensity not to be found elsewhere in those of his generation.

It is perhaps here that an explanation must be sought for the unprecedented contemporary success of Gonçalves Dias's poetry among the educated elite of Brazilian society, a success, incidentally, that contrasts with the relative obscurity of Teixeira e Sousa during his lifetime, despite his outstanding talent.[60] Gonçalves Dias touched a vital nerve in the consciousness of a new, fragile, and unstable grouping within Imperial society. Echoing Otávio Tarquínio de Sousa, Raymundo Faoro notes that the radical wing of the Liberal Party, the *exaltados*, "originated from that part of the population that was as yet socially undefined, without a stable position." As regent, Feijó was governing an illusory social base, supported by a "middling class" that had no structural function within Brazil's master-slave, plantation economy and therefore no coherent social identity.[61] As the voice of that contradictory, compromised generation, Gonçalves Dias wrote some of the most passionate indictments of black slavery and of the genocide of the Indian and linked to these a bitter denunciation of social marginalization under Empire. But not once did he challenge the integrationist, nationalist mythology upon which the continuity of the Imperial status quo depended. Indeed, his fears of federal disintegration and social anarchy were fully consonant with the prevailing political rhetoric of the Second Reign.

In any case, the Indianist poetry of Gonçalves Dias certainly struck a chord in the Brazilian and even European imagination. Until the publication of the "Poesias Americanas," the number of texts devoted to Indianism was small and of very limited public success; it was Gonçalves Dias who, in terms of sheer commercial volume, "popularized" the movement within the restricted readership of the nineteenth century. After the initial success of the *Primeiros Cantos* in 1847, he was offered Crown sponsorship for the publication of the *Segundos Cantos*. With the appearance of a complete edition of the *Cantos* in Leipzig in 1857, articles and translations into German were produced, and by the end of the decade the entire first editions of the *Primeiros*, *Segundos*, and *Últimos Cantos* were sold out. Two thousand copies of the first Leipzig edition were sold in Brazil, with customs duties being officially waived for their entry into the country, and after two years the edition was almost sold out in Europe, too. The demand for copies led to commercial wrangles between the publishing houses of Brockhaus and Garnier over the third edition and to the unauthorized introduction of some copies into Brazil. The poet was celebrated in France, Spain, Germany, and England and was compared favorably with Zorilla, Victor Hugo, and Longfellow.

Antônio Gonçalves Dias was born on 10 August 1823 in political and social circumstances that must have given him an acute awareness of the important issues of his time. He was illegitimate and of mixed blood and was born while his parents were fleeing the xenophobic political reprisals that followed the declaration of independence in the northern province of Maranhão. His father, João Manuel, was a small shopkeeper from the backward region of Trás-os-Montes in Portugal, and his mother, Vicência Mendes Ferreira, was probably a *cafusa*, a *mestiça* of Indian and African parentage. During the two years that João Manuel spent in exile in Portugal, the child lived alone with his mother on a small farm at Boa Vista, not far from Caxias. The poet's early childhood, then, was spent in the midst of the rural Brazilian landscape, surrounded by black slaves from the cotton plantations and by the detribalized Indians who came to trade in the towns and villages.[62]

After returning to Brazil in 1825, Antônio's father abandoned Vicência, moved back to Caxias, and married Adelaide Ramos de Almeida. Although he left little written mention of his natural mother, we do know that Antônio retained a deep affection and regard for her throughout his adult life, visiting her whenever he was in Maranhão and supporting her financially. By contrast, he found little love in the new environment of his stepmother's home and was forbidden as a child from seeing Vicência. His father had taught him to read and write, and, having impressed his schoolteacher, it was decided that he should go to study at the University of Coimbra in Portugal. Dona Adelaide reluctantly paid for his education, but only after some concerned local civic dignitaries had offered to put up the money. Antônio left for Portugal in 1838, aged fifteen.

However, only through the hospitality and generosity of a group of *maranhense* friends in Coimbra, including his lifelong confidant Alexandre Teófilo de Carvalho Leal, was he able to continue his education, for Dona Adelaide was one of those conservative *cabanos* who suffered financial losses as a result of the liberal Balaiada revolt in 1839. Now cut off from his source of support in Brazil, he entered the university in 1840 to study French, English, and German. There he became exposed to the influence of the major figures of contemporary Portuguese and French literature, such as Herculano, Castilho, Garrett, Hugo, Lamartine, and Chateaubriand, and contributed to the *Crónica Literária*, directed by the medievalist Serpa Pimentel. He had also begun to write his own poetry by this time and composed the two dramas, *Patkul* and *Beatriz Cenci*. Although he obtained a degree in law and was optimistic of a career in the profession, a family incident prevented him from proceeding to take his doctorate, and he returned penniless to Brazil in 1845.

After a brief reunion with his mother, which necessitated a journey by canoe up the river Itapicuru, he moved to Caxias and there experienced the first of many moods of alienation and exile, the sense of being "a foreigner in his own land." He also felt the humiliation of economic dependence, which a strong sense of pride repeatedly resisted but which absolute necessity forced him to accept. He became an active member of the group of *cabanos* surrounding the newspaper *O Brado de Caxias* and was gaining a name for himself as a poet, but his personal life was far from happy, and in 1846 he moved to São Luis and the more convivial family atmosphere of the home of his student friend Teófilo. The latter arranged a legal post for him in Rio, and there Gonçalves Dias entered a period of greater optimism. He had the *Primeiros Cantos* published in 1847 and was able to use the libraries for his historical researches; he planned a Brazilian epic and a history of the Jesuits in Brazil and wrote the play *Leonor de Mendonça* and the medievalist poems of *Sextilhas de Frei Antão*.

Despite this flurry of activity, for some while Gonçalves Dias had no regular source of income until two other friends, Serra and Alves Branco, obtained for him the post of "secretary and assistant professor of Latin" in the newly created Lycée at Niterói. After the publication of the *Segundos Cantos* in 1848 he was completely occupied with journalistic activities: while working as correspondent for the *Jornal do Comércio* for proceedings in the Senate, he reported on the debates in the Lower Chamber for the *Correio Mercantil*. He wrote literary criticism for the *Correio da Tarde* under the pseudonym of Optimus Criticus and published regular columns of social comment and short works for the theater. For his reporting of the parliamentary debates he was appointed as a teacher of Latin and history at the Imperial College Dom Pedro II, and after the publication of the visionary *Meditation* on the Emperor's birthday he was made a Knight of the Order of the Rose. Meanwhile he was working on the literary review *Guanabara* with Joaquim Manuel de Macedo and Porto Alegre and had become a member of the Historical and Geographical Institute.

At the first session of the latter its president, Pedro II, assigned research projects to its most prominent members, the subject selected for Gonçalves Dias being a comparative study of the tribal peoples of the Pacific Islands and Brazil. This allowed the poet to pursue his own research interests in greater depth and bore fruit in the form of *Brasil e Oceânia*, which he read to the members of the Institute during sessions extending over almost a year. Lúcia Miguel Pereira describes it enthusiastically as "the first work of Brazilian ethnography"[63]; certainly, as Fritz Ackermann has shown, much of the detailed ethnographic material contained in it also found its way into the Indianist poetry.[64]

During his preparation of the *Últimos Cantos*, published in 1851, Gonçalves Dias abandoned his political reporting and was subsequently appointed by the government to survey the state of public education in the north of the country and to collect various historical documents from the region. About this time he made a proposal of marriage to Ana Amélia, a cousin of his friend Teófilo. This met with refusal, a snub that, for him and his biographers, was attributable, in part, to the family's racial prejudices. He then embarked on a series of unsatisfactory sexual encounters that punctuated the rest of his life, adding syphilis to an increasing list of ailments. The search for sexual fulfillment and for the social intimacy of the family life that he had never enjoyed still remained unresolved when he did eventually marry.

From this point on, Gonçalves Dias devoted his mind, above all, to history and ethnography. As secretary of foreign affairs he received a dispensation to visit Europe with his wife, and there their only child, Bibi, died at the age of two. The poet was celebrated and welcomed by literary circles in Portugal, and he spent a good deal of time with Ferdinand Denis in Paris, where he reported on the International Exhibition. In 1856 he was appointed to lead the Ethnography Section of the disastrous Scientific Exploration Committee that was sent to evaluate the scientific and cultural resources of northern Brazil. In 1861 he resigned from the post and traveled to Maranhão, where he visited family and friends and nearly stood as a Conservative candidate for parliament, withdrawing only at the last minute. He continued his work for the committee in isolation from his colleagues, at the same time investigating the state of education in the Solimões, Negro, and Madeira regions of Amazonas Province. These travels were much more satisfactory and, enduring quite elemental conditions at times, Gonçalves Dias visited the deep interior, reaching Venezuela and Peru, and brought back a valuable collection of tribal artifacts.

By now, the several editions of his lyric poetry had sold well, and he had made an important contribution to Brazilian ethnography with *Brasil e Oceânia* and his *Dictionary of the Tupi Language*. Despite these achievements, though, he suffered from an increasing sense of demoralization and depression; the four published cantos of the epic *Os Timbiras* had not been well received, and the *History of the Jesuits* remained unfinished. In 1863, having completed his last tour of Europe, he embarked as the only passenger on a ship bound for Brazil, suffering from a chronic inflammation of the liver and a lung disorder as well as his many other complaints. The ship foundered off the Brazilian coast near Guimarães and was abandoned by its crew; it is not known for certain whether Gonçalves Dias was still alive when the ship went down, taking the poet and the manuscripts of two of his major works, the *History of the Jesuits* and *Os Timbiras*, with it.

CONQUEST, APOCALYPSE, AND THE SLEEPING GIANT OF HISTORY

If the career of Gonçalves Dias leaves a single outstanding impression, it is the ambiguity of his relationship to the political and cultural establishment and particularly to the Emperor himself, Pedro II. His student friends at Coimbra had all been liberals, and the prose writings such as the *Meditação* (Meditation) are unequivocally the work of an abolitionist. Yet he twice flirted with active Conservative politics and succeeded in finding a secure, if not spectacular, niche within the nepotistic career structure of the Second Reign. For someone like Gonçalves Dias, who had experienced a degree of poverty and economic dependence on friends, the issue of patronage was a very sensitive one. When under pressure to accept Crown sponsorship for the publication of the *Segundos Cantos* in return for dedicating the book to the Emperor, he protested vehemently against this assault on his artistic independence:

So I refused; I hadn't accepted the money, and I wouldn't accept it on such a condition; I held fast, and said loud and clear that they could all go to hell—Serra, Alves Branco, the Emperor, the Princesses and the three hundred *milréis*. What have I got to do with them, what have they done for me, what relationship is there between me and them, that I should dedicate my work, my year-long studies to them?

. . . Besides I'm not a courtier and I don't wish to be; I especially don't want to appear something that I'm not to those scoundrels . . . you have to have some courage, when one of these people has just been applauded, to confront with certainty, in the opinion of the common people—the epithet of flatterer or toady! It's something I could never do, even if I had all the will in the world: I can't, I don't know.[65]

Nevertheless, although he refused to grant the dedication and received his membership of the Order of the Rose with indifference, even annoyance, he did accept the money, and the Emperor's name appeared at the head of several other texts, such as "Entusiasmo Ardente" and the four published cantos of *The Timbiras*.[66] The poet's comments on this episode and the atmosphere at Court echo other contemporary descriptions of the day-to-day reality of clientelism under Empire, which "cast it explicitly in terms of bowing and scraping before the Emperor in order to gain the coveted power to appoint."[67] They are an expressive example of the "anxiety" that Richard Graham identifies as the characteristic emotional response to the patron-client relationship and its arbitrary distribution of "favor," leaving the individual's sense of self-esteem and social place hanging in the balance.

Gonçalves Dias's ambivalence toward the Imperial establishment that sponsored his artistic career also extended to his more overtly political statements during the same period. It might be expected that his experience as a parliamentary correspondent would have produced some coherent perspective on the recent political development of his country. But, as Manuel Bandeira has noted, all that emerges is a vaguely resentful monarchism and a general cynicism with regard to politicians and to the political process as a whole: "[P]olitics, as he saw it practiced in Brazil, did not attract him. He believed in the need for monarchical government, he liked the Emperor and recognized in him 'qualities of a literate king,' but for him 'in Brazil, anywhere, whatever the political color, politics is nothing more than individualism, it's never anything but that!'"[68] The other dimension of this cynicism was his irrational, apocalyptic interpretation of Brazilian history, which, as we shall see, informs so much of the Indianist poetry itself.

It is, then, once again a demonstration of the contradictory nature of this generation of the intellectual community, as well as of the Indianist movement itself, that an essentially loyal, if reluctant, apologist for the Imperial regime, one of the beneficiaries of its paternalistic career structure, should have written in prose and verse one of the most searing indictments of Brazil's treatment of its nonwhite races. The most obvious and fundamental change that nineteenth-century Indianism brought to literary perceptions of the country's tribal population was its massive revision of colonial history. For the writers of the eighteenth century and before, such as Durão and even Basílio da Gama, the slavery, military repression, and cultural disruption of Conquest (rarely represented as such) were vindicated by the success of the economic schemes for which they were the preparation, whether the Jesuit mission system or Pombal's project of Amazonian occupation and development.

By contrast, for a Romantic Indianist such as Gonçalves Dias, Conquest constituted a historical disaster of cataclysmic proportions, a shameful episode in the country's development, with incalculable social and psychological consequences for its victims and grave moral implications for the legitimacy of the modern, Imperial order of things.

The poet's own interest in colonial history dated back to his student days and his readings of the texts of the chroniclers and travel writers. A few years later, about the time of the publication of the *Primeiros Cantos*, he began to gather material for a projected series of historical novels about his native province, including various documents concerning a "decree on the freedom of the Indians," probably the 1831 anti-extermination legislation or perhaps Pombal's Laws of Liberty. His most sustained and ambitious historical project, however, which he began about the same time, was the *History of the Jesuits*, his intended entry for a competition organized by the Historical and Geographical Institute. Ten years later, when in Europe, he was still gathering material for the work.

Although, unfortunately, nothing of the manuscript survived apart from some proposed plans submitted to the Institute, remarks elsewhere confirm that he saw the role of the Jesuits in the administration of the Indian populations as fundamental to the understanding of the nation's social and cultural history.

Of the extant historical texts, his "Reflections on the Historical Annals of Maranhão by Bernardo Pereira de Berredo" was the most contentious and polemical, as it was an uncompromising denunciation of what amounted to a genocidal process, for which responsibility was largely attributed to the Society of Jesus. First published in 1849 in the journal *Guanabara*, it provoked a minor controversy, leading to an exchange of views between the poet and a number of interested historians. These included a fellow *maranhense*, João Francisco Lisboa, a vigorous critic of what he saw as the Indianist mania, "this false backwoods patriotism" promoted by Pedro II through the Historical and Geographical Institute and by Gonçalves Dias in his poetry and whose extravagances, in his capacity as a historian of the rationalist European tradition, he could not tolerate.[69]

However, Lisboa revised his dismissive attitude to Gonçalves Dias's defense of the Indian a few years later, when confronted with the reactionary views of Francisco Adolfo de Varnhagen. As a result of this new debate on indigenist policy, examined in the next chapter, Lisboa remained convinced of the essential barbarism of the Indians but acknowledged that Gonçalves Dias had performed a valuable service in raising the issue of tribal rights. As we shall see, it led him to a new judgment, "in which condemnation of the invaders is inevitable,"[70] and to the conclusion that the basic interests of the Indians could and should be reconciled with the economic needs of the nation as a whole.

Meanwhile, it is worth quoting at length from Gonçalves Dias's "Reflections . . ." in order to reveal just how profound the poet's understanding was, not only of the sheer extent of the crimes committed but also of the consequent problem of social marginalization suffered by the mission Indians:

Unconcern for the morrow, resignation and heroism, that is the Indian.

All this is Indian, all this is ours; and all this is as though lost for many years to come.

Yes, the slavery of the Indians was a great mistake, and their destruction was and will be a great calamity. It was right that someone should reveal to us the full extent to which that mistake was unjust and monstrous, the extent of those calamities in the past, and their likely extent in the future: that is history.

All [the Indians] were defeated, routed and enslaved: when they [the Portuguese] could not do so by force of arms they would send them a priest from the Company [of Jesus] with a crucifix and words of peace, who would bring them bowed and captive to languish and die on our plantations . . .

The greed of wanting to be able to expand the Company, the greed of setting foot in America as they had already done in India, the greed of infiltrating the nascent population with the milk of their doctrine, the greed in short of conquering a world . . .

Thus we cannot consider the Indian in the state of conversion as anything but a being in transition . . . in this state the Indian was neither savage nor civilized, neither heathen nor catholic; but, shifting instantaneously, without preparation, from one state to another, he had become equally incapable of either—of living in the towns with the men we call civilized or of living in the jungles among those we called barbarians.[71]

However, after these perceptive observations, Gonçalves Dias's analytical historical method seems to give way to an apocalyptic fatalism; the genocide of the Indians is at first ironically explained as the inevitable sacrifice necessitated by the evolution of the Brazilian nation, before being attributed despairingly to the wrath of a vengeful God:

> With the last stage of the total extinction of the American race in Brazil appointed in the book of eternity, the Jesuits were the precious instrument of Providence in order that over the corpses of that race, decimated by hunger and by drudgery, broken down by physical and moral suffering, another, younger, stronger, finer race should rise up . . .
> . . . —we shall have twice the justification for arguing that they [the Jesuits] were, not the weapon of the Portuguese to put an end to the American customs, for they were already finished long ago; but God's instrument to extinguish that race which was perhaps thwarting His lofty plans.[72]

An important distinction needs to be made, though, between Gonçalves Dias's appeal to a divine explanation for Conquest and that of Indianists such as Santa Rita Durão or Gonçalves de Magalhães. Whereas the latter subordinated everything to the glory of the divine plan and therefore justified all the atrocities committed in its name, for Gonçalves Dias the destructive hand of providence remained incomprehensibly ruthless, and he did not allow it to compromise his sense of moral outrage: "But because he had discovered in this 'the hand of Providence,' he could not therefore 'worship the scourge that it sends us, nor the tool that it uses.'"[73] The roots of this irrational, apocalyptic vision of history are to be found in his experience and perception of contemporary political events. The Indianist poetry is, on a second and perhaps more disturbing level, an expression of this view of the historical process, a process that is not progressive but repetitive, cataclysmic, and destructive.

I argue that the connection between Conquest and Empire, although rarely made explicitly in the poetry, is nonetheless a real and powerful motor behind the tragic intensity of the Indianism of Gonçalves Dias. There is one text, however, in which that historical connection is laid bare, in which the barbarously oppressive conditions suffered by the majority of Brazilians, past and present, are condemned uncompromisingly: that text is the *Meditation*. Although finished in May 1846, the *Meditation* did not appear in the review *Guanabara* until 1849, and the poet's advice to his friend Alexandre Teófilo on editing the second chapter indicates an awareness of the bold, controversial nature of the views expressed in it: "Cut out ruthlessly—whatever you consider wrong—or dangerous to print."[74]

The work is an apocalyptic vision of Brazil's political and social system, whose economic and racial groups are arranged in concentric circles, the white ruling elite at the center and the colored, subject classes radiating from it. The register throughout is that of an Old Testament narrative, recounting the rise and eventual destruction of a kind of American Babylon. The narrator, a representative of the Imperial regime, is first shown the spectacle of mass black slavery, upon which the prosperity of the country's white ruling class is based:

E os homens de côr preta teem as mãos presas em longas correntes de ferro, cujos anneis vão de uns a outros—eternos como a maldição que passa de pais a filhos! . . .

Mas grande parte de sua população é escrava—mas a sua riqueza consiste nos escravos—mas o sorriso—o deleite do seu commerciante—do seu agricola—e o alimento de todos os seus habitantes é comprado à custa do sangue do escravo! . . .

E nos labios do estrangeiro, que aporta ao Brasil, desponta um sorriso ironico e despeitoso—e elle diz comsigo, que a terra—da escravidão—não póde durar muito.[75]

(And the hands of the black men are held fast by long iron chains, whose rings pass from one to the next—on and on forever like the curse that passes down from father to son! . . . / But much of its population is slaves—but its wealth consists of slaves—but its smile—the delight of its businessman—of its farmer—and the nourishment of all its inhabitants is bought at the expense of the blood of the slave! . . . // And on the lips of the foreigner who arrives in Brazil there appears an ironic, contemptuous smile—and he says to himself, that the land—of slavery—cannot last long.)

He is then confronted by an old man, the witness to the nation's history, to whom he promises a future of progress, achieved through the patriotism of the country's citizens, in which the institutional problems of its early Independence will have been ironed out. The old man replies by comparing the freedom of the land's indigenous peoples before Conquest to the subsequent tyranny of the white man:

Ouvia-se de instante a instante o som profundo, cavernoso e agonisante de uma raça que desapparecia de sobre a face da terra.

E era horrível e pavoroso esse bradar do desespero como seria o de milhões de indivíduos que ao mesmo tempo se afundassem no oceano.

E cadaveres infindos, expostos à inclemência do tempo e à profanação dos homens, serviam de pasto aos animaes immundos.[76]

(From one moment to the next could be heard the deep, cavernous and agonizing sound of a race that was disappearing from the face of the earth.// And that cry of despair was terrible and awful, like that of millions of individuals swallowed up all at once by the ocean.// And countless corpses, exposed to the harshness of the weather and the desecration of men, served as food for the vile animals.)

But the most interesting passage of the work concerns the surviving "free" Indian and colored populations and their discussion of the future facing them. These two ethnically and historically distinct social groups are, nevertheless, united by a common condition of marginalization. Rendered economically redundant by the exclusive labor structure of master and slave and therefore alienated from the machinery of power, they occupy a dispossessed limbo of "idleness," vulnerable to the manipulation of warring political forces:

E os homens de raça indigena e os de côr mestiça—disseram em voz alta:—"E nós que faremos?"

"Qual será o nosso logar entre os homens que são senhores, e os homens que são escravos?

"Não queremos quinhoar o pão do escravo, e não nos podemos sentar à meza dos ricos e dos poderosos.

"E no entanto este sólo abençoado produz fructos saborosos em todos os quadros do anno—suas florestas abundam de caça—e os seus rios são piscosos.

"Os brancos governam—os negros servem—bem é que nós sejamos livres.

"Vivamos pois na indolência e na ociosidade, pois que não necessitamos trabalhar para viver.

"Separemo'-nos, que é força separarmo'-nos, lembremo'-nos porém que somos todos irmãos, e que a nossa causa é a mesma.

"E seremos felizes, porque os individuos carecerão do nosso braço para a sua vingança, e os homens politicos para as suas revoluções.

"Deixar-nos-hão no ocio, porque precisarão de nós—e porque a nossa ociosidade lhes será necessaria.

"E nós seremos felizes."[77]

(And the men of Indian blood and those of mixed race—said aloud:—"And what shall we do?"/ "What will be our place among the men who are masters, and the men who are slaves?/ We do not wish to share the bread of the slave, and we cannot sit at the table of the rich and powerful./ And yet this blessed soil produces delicious fruits in all the seasons of the year—its forests abound with game—and its rivers are teeming./ The whites govern—the blacks serve—it is right that we should be free./ Let us live then in indolence and idleness, for we do not need to work to live./ Let us be separate, for we must be separate, but let us remember that we are all brothers, and that our cause is the same./ And we shall be happy, because individuals will need our hands for their revenge, and the politicians will need us for their revolutions./ They will leave us in idleness, because they will need us—and because our idleness will be necessary to them. And we shall be happy.")

If one reads the poet's notion of contented idleness metaphorically rather than literally, then this vision of the marginalized "tribes" of landless freemen bears a close resemblance to an identifiable sector of nineteenth-century Brazilian society, the poor and alienated *tapuios*, *mestiços*, and whites who, as we saw, rose up in the many provincial revolts that shook Brazil during the Regency period. Like Teixeira e Sousa's orphaned *mestiça* Miry'ba, Gonçalves Dias's Indian and mixed-race exiles have much in common, too, with that very numerous caste of free dependents, or *agregados*, who for want of other income might be attached to the family or estate of a landowner and who in return for the right to raise subsistence crops on some outlying patch of land were required to pay him military or political allegiance. Richard Graham cites the following observation of the phenomenon given by an engineer, João da Rocha Fragoso, during the latter years of the Empire:

[O]ne notes a great number of people who settle there with the permission of the landowner or planter and who are called *agregados*. These *agregados*, far outnumbering the slaves, are poor citizens. . . . By their dependence on the owners these *agregados* constitute an enslaved class, which, although not subject to any tribute in money or labor, . . . are so, nevertheless, by the electoral tax [i.e., their vote], that they pay at the right moment at the ballot box, or else risk eviction.[78]

An even broader reading of the same extract from the *Meditation* might also plausibly embrace that other group out of which Gonçalves Dias himself emerged and whose marginalization was experienced at a different level: the landless class of white and mulatto artisans, traders, and civil servants who, in the industrial countries of Europe, constituted an emergent petty bourgeoisie but who remained an impotent and marginal force within the archaic slavocratic regime of Imperial Brazil. This layer of society spawned the liberal movement for reform, which, although effectively silenced with the majority of Pedro II, had allied itself with the country's urban and rural poor in a potentially revolutionary wave of unrest. Significantly, in Gonçalves Dias's apocalyptic vision that revolutionary potential is not repressed and contained, as was historically the case, but erupts into the final cataclysm, as the city is set alight, and blood flows like wine at a banquet.

These twin elements of his perception of colonial and Imperial society, the oppression and marginalization produced by Conquest and slavery, and the monster of radicalism and revolution, are the two contradictory forces that give the Indianism of Gonçalves Dias its characteristic drama and intensity. The same language of cataclysm and revolution occurs briefly in his nonpolemical, scientific study *Brasil e Oceânia*. This was the comparative study of Pacific and Brazilian tribal peoples commissioned by Pedro II and written between 1852 and 1854. Here Gonçalves Dias takes a more measured look at the history and culture of the Indians and makes his contribution to the debate on indigenist policy.

The great upheaval experienced by the Tupi races before Conquest was the mass migration to the Atlantic coast, which came to be explained in tribal mythology as the result of some natural catastrophe: "Their traditions speak of a great cataclysm, after which they must have settled in these parts. Perhaps they used this figurative language to express a great revolution or emigration as the Mexicans use the same figure of speech to refer to an invasion of barbarian peoples."[79] In at least one text from the "Poesias Americanas," as I shall demonstrate, Gonçalves Dias makes use of this mythological tribal perception of historical events to convey the psychological trauma of Conquest for the Indian.

Another general feature of the poetry that has parallels in *Brasil e Oceânia* and reflects the author's ideological outlook is the fragmentation of tribal society. Addressing the question of whether the Indians were enjoying a period of cultural ascendancy or undergoing a decline, Gonçalves Dias notes that intertribal conflict was an important source of weakness in the struggle against the European invader: "Those primitive elements that held them together as a society were gradually disintegrating: they were beginning to break up, and the tribes were becoming mutually hostile families."[80] In the poetry a significant distinction is made between the normal ritual warfare of tribal culture, with its accepted cycle of reprisal and revenge, and the divisive, internecine conflicts fomented by the Portuguese in order to weaken their enemy. It perhaps comes as no surprise to discover that Gonçalves Dias's fear of social and political disintegration, such as he portrays it in the Indianist poetry, leads him to advocate the same liberal, integrationist policy toward the Indians that was to characterize the "conciliatory" Second Reign:

I should like this to be considered not as the eulogy of a race, which rather deserves our commiseration than praise; but as a cry, however weak, in favor of the conversion of the Indians. At a time when there is so much concern with foreign colonization, whose usefulness and advantages I am far from questioning, it would be a good thing if we were to return to our forests for a while, and consider whether there is any antipathy between philanthropy and the love of the nation's prosperity, or whether there is anything repellent to the notion that conversion and colonization should advance under the same impulse.[81]

There are few poems among the Indianist writing of Gonçalves Dias in which the great historical burden of slavery and oppression, described so thoroughly in his prose works, is not present in some form or other. On some occasions it provides the text with its central scenario, while on others it stands as a tragically ironic background, an imminent fate of which the reader, but not the Indian protagonist, is aware. "O Canto do Piaga" (The Shaman's Chant) contains something of both methods; here the *piaga*, "shaman," reveals to his tribe his nocturnal vision of the evil spirit Anhangá and the latter's warning of an approaching "phantom" from across the sea. The key to the poem's effectiveness lies in its dramatic structure, which is based on a progressive shift in the narrative perspective. In part 1 the shaman himself describes the prodigious apparition of Anhangá and then the physiological sensations of fear he inspires:

> Abro os olhos, inquieto, medroso,
> Manitôs! que prodígios que vi!
> Arde o pau de resina fumosa,
> Não fui eu, não fui eu, que o acendi! . . .
>
> O meu sangue gelou-se nas veias,
> Todo inteiro—ossos, carnes—tremi,
> Frio horror me coou pelos membros,
> Frio vento no rosto senti.[82]

(Anxious, fearful, I open my eyes,/ Manes, what wonders I saw!/ The smoking, resinous branch is in flames,/ It was not I, it was not I, who set it alight! . . . // My blood froze in my veins,/ From head to foot—flesh and bones, I shook,/ An icy terror ran through my limbs,/ I felt a chill wind on my face.)

The meter of the poem, based on Gonçalves Dias's preferred rhythmic unit, the anapaest, contributes to the sense of drama; in the first section it suggests the urgency of the shaman's appeal to his tribe. In part 2 the same rhythm reinforces the accusatory tone of the Anhangá, whose voice takes over the narrative, reprimanding the shaman for failing to understand the signs of the impending disaster. In the following section it imitates the tread of an inexorably advancing doom, as the monstrous apparition emerges on the horizon, and its shape and form gradually become distinguishable. Here, in an unprecedented imaginative leap, Gonçalves Dias constructs an image of the arrival of Conquest as if perceived by the Indians, in terms of the visual resources available to them in their immediate environment. The ship's masts are therefore depicted as the trees of the forest, its rigging as a dense web of tropical creepers, its hold the belly of the monster itself, and its sails a host of white wings. As well as conveying an impression of the tribal psychology, the poem thus sustains in a dramatic form the historical irony of the situation, in which the full significance of the monster's arrival, the devastating tragedy of Conquest, remains hidden from the Indian until it is too late.

Thus, the final section is divided exactly in two by the question: "Não sabeis o que o monstro procura?/ Não sabeis a que vem, o que quer?" (Do you not know what the monster is seeking?/ Do you not know why it is coming, what it wants?). But only with the beginning of a new stanza is its true intent revealed: "Vem matar vossos bravos guerreiros,/ Vem roubar-vos a filha, a mulher!" (It is coming to kill your warrior braves,/ It is coming to steal your daughters, your wives!), in other words, to defile tribal culture, to enslave the Indians in their thousands, and to drive the rest into exile. By now we have forgotten that this is still the shaman repeating the words of the Anhangá; they now have the effect of an anonymous prophecy that derives not from dreams and omens but from the inevitability of history.

The trauma of Conquest is suggested more directly in "Deprecação" (Prayer), which takes the form of a prayer addressed to the "god" Tupá in the wake of an Indian massacre and the dispersal of the tribe into the interior. It is our first example of the poet's apocalyptic interpretation of Conquest, by which he appears to share the Indians' shock and incomprehension, their disbelief at seeing their world and the power of their cosmology so easily shattered. If, as Diogo Álvares Caramuru proved, men can also wield the lightning bolt, then even the gods may be overthrown. In spite of the depth of his historical knowledge—overwhelmed by it, perhaps—Gonçalves Dias turns, like his Indians, to providence for an answer:

> Anhangá impiedoso nos trouxe de longe
> Os homens que o raio manejam cruentos,
> Que vivem sem pátria, que vagam sem tino
> Trás do ouro correndo, voraces, sedentos.
> E a terra em que pisam, e os campos e os rios
> Que assaltam, são nossos; tu és nosso Deus:
> Por que lhes concedes tao alta pujança,
> Se os raios de morte, que vibram, são teus?

> (Merciless Anhangá brought to us from afar/ The bloody men who wield the lightning bolt,/ Who live without a fatherland, who wander aimlessly/ Greedily, thirstily in pursuit of gold./ And the land on which they tread, and the fields and rivers/ Which they ravage, are ours; you are our God:/ Why do you grant them such lofty might,/ If the lightning bolts of death, that they hurl forth, are yours?)

The material devastation of Conquest is expressed in the simple language of loss and emptiness; the shores that were once peopled with brave warriors and their canoes now bear nothing but the ebb and flow of the tide. Even the ritual removal of the dead warriors' remains to their place of exile has become a difficult task, so few are the survivors.

If the tight construction of these short poems allows Gonçalves Dias to convey the dramatic immediacy of the emotional and psychological trauma of Conquest, the longer, freer verse forms provide space for depicting the actual processes by which thousands of Indians were killed or enslaved. In the poem "Tabira (poesia americana)," from the *Segundos Cantos*, the role of the Portuguese in the manipulation of intertribal conflict is made explicit. Tabira is the legendary chief of the Tobajaras who, after converting to Christianity, has negotiated an alliance with the Portuguese or *caraíbas*. Stanzas 4 and 5 of the poem denounce the betrayal with which the Tobajaras' loyalty was rewarded, the slavery into which they were unwittingly led:

> Hão de os teus, miserandos escravos,
> Tais triunfos um dia chorar!
> Caraíbas tais feitos aplaudem,
> Mas sorrindo vos forjam cadeias,
> E pesadas algemas, e peias,
> Que traidores vos hão-de lançar!

(Your people, miserable slaves,/ Will one day mourn such victories!/ The caraíbas applaud such deeds,/ But amid smiles they forge chains for you,/ And heavy manacles, and shackles,/ Which they will treacherously cast upon you!)

The alliance, symbolized by Tabira's renunciation of his tribal beliefs, draws the Tobajaras into a fatal conflict with their Potiguar neighbors. Although defeated, the Potiguar have at least escaped the fate of those Tobajara warriors who survived only to be enslaved and to recount the downfall of their people:

> Insepultos na terra inclemente
> Muitos dormem; mas há quem lh'inveja
> Essa morte do bravo em peleja,
> Quem a vida do escravo maldiz!

(Many sleep unburied/ On the hostile soil; but there are some who envy them/ That death of the brave in battle,/ Who curse the life of the slave!)

Perhaps the most unusual and interesting of the texts that deal with Conquest is "O Canto do Índio" (The Indian's Chant), from the *Primeiros Cantos*. My inclusion of the poem under this heading may be surprising, for it is normally, when examined at all, taken at face value: as the love song of an Indian for the white woman he discovers bathing naked in the forest. Lúcia Miguel Pereira encourages this interpretation when she notes that it was written during the poet's canoe journey up the river Itapicuru to his mother's home in 1845, and she speculates that it may have been inspired by an analogous incident along the way.[83] However, besides the historically implausible nature of the encounter (European women rarely being found among the early colonizers' ranks), the poem's overtly religious imagery and its structure support a more disturbing analysis, one that reflects Gonçalves Dias's understanding of the central role of the Jesuit missionary and the catechesis in the process of tribal subjection and integration.

The poem shifts between two metrical forms, corresponding to the two levels of discourse at which the text functions and that culminate together in the Indian's promise to abandon his freedom and culture for the woman as she appears in her complete, seductive nakedness. A series of quartets of *redondilha maior* (the most popular form in the Portuguese lyric tradition) conveys the emotional and psychological impact of the vision, gradually revealing her beauty as she emerges from the water. Alternating with this are stanzas of decasyllabic lines that describe the sacrifices he is prepared to make in exchange for the right to contemplate her; these, too, form a progression, from his acceptance of physical pain, even death, for a glimpse of her, to the renunciation of his tribal liberty and sovereignty in order that she should become his queen and govern his people. The combination of stunningly sensual imagery, psychological insight, the interplay between sexual attraction and self-abnegation, and the historical irony that holds these elements together make this poem one of Gonçalves Dias's finest achievements.

The opening stanzas delicately invoke a natural scenario at sunset with its characteristic sounds and birdsongs, suggesting the richly sensuous life of the forest. Out of this setting appears the sparkling vision of the bather, which at first can elicit no more than the astonished exclamation: "Eu a vi, que se banhava" (I saw her bathing), and images of limpid springs and stars. Over the course of the following quartets of *redondilhas* her hair and neck are revealed, then her smiling face and lips uttering incomprehensible words. Finally, she rises naked from the water, presenting an irresistible sight to the Indian:

> Bem como gotas de orvalho
> Nas folhas de flor mimosa,
> Do seu corpo a onda em fios
> Se deslizava amorosa.

(Just like dew drops/ On the leaves of a lovely flower,/ The ripples trickled/ Lovingly from her body.)

Meanwhile, the impassioned appeals that accompany the apparition—"Ó Virgem, Virgem dos Cristãos formosa" (Oh Virgin, beautiful Virgin of the Christians)—suggest that the Indian's seduction is working at more than simply an erotic level. The language of his "Chant" draws on a biblical and specifically Iberian tradition (with which the medievalist poet Gonçalves Dias would have been intimately familiar), in which religious and sexual adoration are expressed in identical terms, blurring the distinction between the two. The Old Testament "Song of Songs," for instance, or the medieval Cantigas de Santa Maria of Alfonso X, in which the Virgin Mary assumes the same role as that of the aristocratic Lady, interceding with God on behalf of her devotee just as the mistress pleads for her knight. Through its religious vocabulary and use of capitals, the poem plays on this ambiguity so as to expose the insidious power that Christianity exercised over the Indians who were exposed to the influence of the Jesuits. The white Virgin's erotic allure resembles the fascinating aesthetic attraction of the Catholic ritual, which, as we saw in Chapter 1, helped to draw many Indians into the repressive regime of the missions.

As well as conveying this sense of awestruck fascination, the poem also suggests how the Christian discourse of self-sacrifice came to legitimate the sacrifice of the Indians' lands, liberty, and cultural identity to the Portuguese project of colonization. Speaking the language of martyrdom—"Calcara agros espinhos" (I would tread on harsh thorns)—the Indian protests to the Virgin that, in return for her love, he would endure pain and ignominious death at the hands of his enemies, that he would abandon his people's cult of war:

> Sem que dos meus irmãos ouvisse o canto,
> Sem que o som do Boré que incita à guerra
> Me infiltrasse o valor que m'hás roubado.

> (Without hearing the chant of my brothers,/ Not letting the Boré's call to war/ Invade the courage that you have stolen from me.)

and, finally, that he would renounce his freedom and his hatred of the Portuguese and exchange his warrior's club for the iron manacles of a slave:

> Vencer por teu amor meu ódio antigo,
> Trocar a maça do poder por ferros
> E ser, por te gozar, escravo dêles.

> (Overcome my ancient hatred for your love,/ Exchange the club of power for shackles/ And be their slave, in order to have you as my own.)

The irony that renders the beauty of the seduction so insidious and the Indian's innocent faith so tragic is the depressing historical fact that he and his people did undergo all those trials and humiliations, that the Jesuit mission of evangelization was the principal tool, apart from sheer force, in clearing thousands of acres of tribal lands of their inhabitants and in supplying the colony's demand for mass slave labor. In this poem Gonçalves Dias shows us the psychological and social forces of that process at work and their dependence on the Indian's trust and ignorance of the real motives behind the white priest's promises of salvation. Enchanted by the Virgin's incomprehensible words, he allows them, literally, to "captivate his life, his will and his strength" and so unwittingly surrenders himself to his betrayers:

> Outra vez—dentre os seus lábios
>   Uma voz se desprendia;
> Terna voz, cheia de encantos,
>   Que eu entender não podia.
> Que importa? Esse falar deixou-me n'alma
> Sentir d'amores tão sereno e fundo,
> Que a vida me prendeu, vontade e força.

(Again—from her lips/ There issued a voice;/ A tender voice, full of charms,/ That I could not understand./ What does it matter? Those words left in my soul/ Such a serene, profound feeling of love,/ That they have captivated my life, my will and strength.)

This drama of the Indian warrior's voluntary enslavement to the feminized colonizer will return more than once in the literature of the Indianist movement, as we see in the next chapter. As retold by Macedo and Alencar, however, it undergoes a vital alteration, as the critical irony at the heart of Gonçalves Dias's vision of the colonizing process is replaced by a celebratory account of indigenous self-sacrifice in the interest of the survival and well-being of the colonial state.

Thus far, the connection between the colonial exploitation of the Indian and the contemporary oppression of the nonwhite population under Empire has remained confined to the prose texts. In the preceding poems, Gonçalves Dias invites his readers to share his outrage at the atrocities committed on Brazilian soil before his nation's independence, but he does not oblige them to confront the ethical contradictions of their own society, founded as it was on a new cycle of inhumanity and tyranny.

The four extant cantos of the epic *Os Timbiras*, which were published late in the poet's career, in 1857, are another matter altogether, for, in addition to the now familiar historical pattern of Conquest and enslavement, the poem includes a lengthy denunciation of the legacy of annihilation and slavery bequeathed to the modern, "progressive" era of the nineteenth century. Furthermore, the poet's particular choice of subject matter, a war between the Timbiras and Gamelas, suggests that he wished to remind his readers that the nightmare of Conquest, the white man's persecution of the Indians and seizure of their lands, did not end in 1600 or even in 1755 but had continued on into their own century.

It is perhaps for these reasons that, as Gonçalves Dias discovered to his irritation, Pedro II kept his copy of the poem for some time in a drawer without apparently having read it.[84] The Emperor may, of course, have judged that the text, incomplete as it was, did not deserve the attention and recognition he had awarded to his other works. He had, after all, granted Gonçalves Dias membership of the Order of the Rose for his *Meditation*, which was far more openly critical of Empire. On the other hand, the poor reception given to the poem may simply reflect Pedro's lack of artistic judgment. Only the previous year, 1856, he had sat through an entire reading of the ten long and tedious cantos of Gonçalves de Magalhães's *A Confederação dos Tamoios* and was now defending it in public. More significantly, this was no longer 1847, when Gonçalves Dias had originally written the text of his epic poem, when the liberal abolitionist language of the *Meditation* was still acceptable, and when the regime could consider banning the traffic in slaves from Africa; this was 1857, times had changed, Paraná's conservative government of "conciliation" had just ended, and a new generation of Indianist writing had arrived on the scene to endorse, not criticize, the Imperial order.

By contrast, *Os Timbiras* belongs unequivocally to the first phase of the movement. In the third canto of the poem, Gonçalves Dias takes an unprecedented approach in his denunciation of Conquest, stepping outside the dramatic context of the story itself in order to assume a direct, personal voice of condemnation. The reader is reminded that the tribes of Itajuba are now fossils beneath the earth's crust, concluding just one chapter in a history of extermination and exploitation that continues into the present age:

> —Chame-lhe progresso
> Quem do extermínio secular se ufana;
> Eu modesto cantor do povo extinto
> Chorarei nos vastíssimos sepulcros,
> Que vão do mar ao Andes, e do Prata
> Ao largo e doce mar das Amazonas.
> Ali me sentarei meditabundo
> Em sítio, onde não oiçam meus ouvidos
> Os sons freqüentes d'europeus machados
> Por mãos de escravos Afros manejados:
> Nem veja as matas arrasar, e os troncos,
> Donde chorando a preciosa goma,
> Resina virtuosa e grato incenso
> A nossa incúria grande eterno assolam.

(He who glories in the centuries old extermination/ May call it progress;/ I the modest bard of a deceased people/ Shall weep over the great vast tombs,/ That reach from the sea to the Andes, and from the Plate/ To the broad, freshwater ocean of the Amazon./ There I shall sit in contemplation/ In a place, where my ears will not hear/ The ongoing noise of European axes/ Wielded by the hands of African slaves:/ Nor shall I see them lay waste to the forests, and tear down the trunks,/ That weep the precious gum,/ The virtuous resin and welcome incense/ That we left neglected for eternity.)

Two factors converge here to suggest that Gonçalves Dias may have had in mind the new waves of deforestation in his native province and the threat they posed to the region's Indian communities and its untapped resources of native latex. *Os Timbiras* was written just five years after the discovery of the vulcanization process, which accelerated the emergence of this new commodity onto the international market, culminating in the first rubber boom at the end of the century:

The full economic and demographic impact of the rubber trade would only be felt with the onset of the Amazon's "golden years"—roughly 1880 to 1910—but as early as the mid-nineteenth century, rubber exports were having a highly visible impact on Pará's "vital statistics." The provincial population nearly doubled between 1850 and 1872, and the city of Belém grew at an average rate of 3.65 percent per year in the same time span. Provincial income, derived from export taxes, increased by over 100 percent between 1852 and 1865; and by the latter year, rubber already constituted two-thirds of the value of Pará's exports.[85]

In order that such an expansion could take place and the new population be securely settled without interference from the tribal groups whose lands were being expropriated, large numbers of Indians were exterminated. While in Pará the main areas of rubber production, besides the islands district near the mouth of the Amazon, were located upstream along the rivers Xingu and Tapajós, frther north war was declared against the Waimiri and Atroari tribes, and hundreds of Indians were massacred by the armed expeditions sent from Manaus by the provincial government.[86] Gonçalves Dias himself saw the effect of this military and economic onslaught on the tribal people of the region when he visited the Rio Negro in 1861 and observed the atrocious living and working conditions endured by the Indians:

Can you believe that an Indian on the Upper Rio Negro, rowing like a Christian in a Moorish galley, works five days to earn a yard of American cloth? And that those five days may give him work for a further ten or fifteen, as is the case, without him receiving a wage, nor a canoe for the return journey, nor even flour to feed him, as is also the case?[87]

We can only speculate, although with a good degree of certainty, as to whether Gonçalves Dias had these developments in mind when he wrote the last passage quoted from *Os Timbiras*. His prose works indicate, though, that he was only too aware of the policy of "just war" waged against a number of tribes during the reigns of João VI and Pedro I. One of the chief areas of repression was Maranhão, the poet's home province, which he frequently visited and which provides the setting for *Os Timbiras*. Moreover, the Timbiras were one of the tribes that suffered most from these campaigns, along with a subgroup, the Gamelas or Canelas:

In Maranhão the violence against the Indians was no less. Since production there was of cotton and rice, cultivation was not advancing because the whole of the right bank of the river Itapicuru was "infested with Gamela and Timbira heathen, who occupy the richest lands of that continent as far as the river Tocantins, plaguing those farmers day by day, and causing them considerable damage, sometimes with raids, killing the slaves and whites they encounter, and sometimes burning the plantations and granaries." "This hindrance suffered by agriculture is crying out for measures," wrote Manuel Antônio Xavier in 1822, referring to the armed forces that waged war on the heathen adjacent to the plantations, "the governors and generals of the Province having aided these expeditions with troops of the foot regiment."[88]

It can hardly be coincidental that Gonçalves Dias chose as the subject of his Indianist epic the disintegration and extermination of the two tribes of his native region, which, just twenty-five years before, had been the target of a ruthless, official campaign of military repression and were now being exposed to new forms of economic conquest. On the contrary, his point was that the official and unofficial atrocities committed against the Indian by white society were not a thing of the past, not simply the mark of an oppressive Portuguese colonialism that independence had abolished but that the resumption of such policies after

1822 was evidence that Empire signified continuity rather than a break with the colonial regime.

Like Teixeira e Sousa before him, Gonçalves Dias drew much broader and more disturbing conclusions from this interpretation of Indian policy before and after independence. The following extract, clearly modeled on Cacambo's speech from Basílio da Gama's *O Uraguay* ("Peoples of Europe, if only the sea and wind/ Had never brought you to us"), challenges the emancipatory rhetoric of independence that Indianist writing in the previous decade had echoed:

> América infeliz, já tão ditosa
> Antes que o mar e os ventos não trouxessem
> A nós o ferro e os cascavéis da Europa?!
> Velho tutor e ávaro cubiçou-te,
> Desvalida pupila, a herança pingue
> Cedeste, fraca; e entrelaçaste os anos
> Da mocidade em flor—às cãs e à vida
> Do velho, que já pende e já declina
> Do leito conjugal imerecido
> À campa, onde talvez cuida encontrar-te!

> (Unfortunate America, once so happy/ if only the sea and winds had not brought/ To us the shackles and rattlesnakes of Europe?!/ The greedy old guardian lusted after you,/ Weak and helpless ward, you gave up/ Your rich inheritance; and entwined the years/ of your blooming youth—with the white hair and life/ Of the old man, who wanes and droops now/ From the undeserved marriage bed/ Towards the tomb, where he perhaps still believes he will find you!)

The first three lines express, like Cacambo's lament, regret that Conquest ever took place, the shackles and rattlesnakes evoking as much the slavery and economic poison of the nineteenth century as that of the sixteenth. The grotesque sexual imagery that follows points, however, to something else: a perverse, incestuous relationship between the colony and its former ruler that promises not the birth of new, prosperous generations of free Brazilians but a sterile afterlife in which the potential wealth of the young nation is sacrificed in order to sustain the needs of a declining European power. As Portugal, Brazil's aged guardian, lusts after his nubile ward and her rich inheritance (the *Dicionário Novo Aurélio* gives for *pingue* "fertile, fecund; productive, profitable, lucrative"), she is forced to spend the first years of her economic womanhood in the marriage bed with an old man who has one foot in the grave. Despite her maturity and fertility, Brazil remains in the clutches of her European power who, far from giving her freedom, has exchanged his overt paternalism for a perverted form of wedlock, symbolized by the continuing dynastic link with the Portuguese Crown through Pedro I.

Once again, however, the poet responds to this vision of renewed social and economic oppression with an irrational, apocalyptic despair, surrendering to the inevitability of some form of divine retribution or cosmic punishment for the accumulated wrongs of humankind:

Aos crimes das nações Deus não perdoa;
Do pai aos filhos e do filho aos netos,
Porque um deles de todo apague a culpa,
Virá correndo a maldição—contínua,
Como fuzis de uma cadeia eterna.
Virão nas nossas festas mais solenes
Miríades de sombras miserandas,
Escarnecendo, secar o nosso orgulho
De nação; mas nação que tem por base
Os frios ossos da nação senhora,
E por cimento a cinza profanada
Dos mortos, amassada aos pés de escravos.
Não me deslumbra a luz da velha Europa;
Há de apagar-se mas que a inunde agora:
E nós! . . . sugamos leite mau na infância,
Foi corrompido o ar que respiramos,
Havemos de acabar talvez primeiro.

(God does not forgive the crimes of nations;/ From the father to his sons and from the son to the grandsons,/ So that one of them may wholly erase the guilt,/ The curse will pass swiftly on—continuous,/ Like the links in an eternal chain./ Myriads of wretched shades/ Will appear at our most solemn feasts,/ To mock, and wither our nation's pride;/ But a nation whose foundation/ Is the chill bones of the mistress nation,/ And whose cement is the defiled ashes/ of the dead, bound to the feet of slaves./ The light of old Europe does not dazzle me;/ It will be snuffed out but for now let it flood forth:/ And we!. . . we suckled evil milk in our infancy,/ The air we breathed was polluted,/ We shall perhaps be finished first.)

This recourse to the idea of nemesis expresses, on one hand, the poet's sense of incomprehension and outrage at the sheer extent of the horrors unleashed by Conquest. But it is also rooted in Gonçalves Dias's perception of the violent political upheavals of his own time. A comparison between the Indianist poetry and those texts that depict the provincial conflicts of the Regency reveals the same apocalyptic language, the same nightmarish vision of futile destruction. History, like the eternal round of ritual war and reprisal in the Indian world, is not progressive but cyclical; both processes are afflicted by inexplicable cataclysms that appear, in their horror and chaos, to be the retribution of a wrathful God.

This specter of chaos rears its head most dramatically, perhaps, in "A Desordem de Caxias" (The Disorder of Caxias), which depicts the Balaiada, the revolt that shook the poet's native province of Maranhão between 1838 and 1841. Gonçalves Dias is unable to analyze this upheaval in terms of a struggle between classes or between conflicting political projects, such as absolutism, liberalism, republicanism, or federalism. Instead, he sees only material collapse, human carnage and distress, a nightmare in which the perpetrators of violence cannot be distinguished from its victims. The forces being unleashed are compared to the elemental clashes of nature that are impersonal, uncontrollable, and inexplicable:

Como, quando o vulcão prepara a lava
Nas entranhas da terra, e à noite lança,
Pela sangrenta rábida cratera,
Mais viva chama em turbilhão de fumo; . . .
Assim tão bem, quando abafadas rosnam
Sanhas do povo, antes que em fúrias rompam,
Propaga-se confuso borborinho,
Cresce a agitação naquele e neste,
E um quê de febre lhes transtorna o siso.

(Just as when the volcano prepares its lava/ In the bowels of the earth, and at night
spews forth,/ From the glowing, bloody crater,/ The vivid flame in a swirl of smoke,
. . ./ So too, when the stifled fury of the people/ Growls, before it breaks out into
rage,/ A confused murmuring spreads,/ The tumult grows in this man and the next,/
And a kind of fever deranges their minds.)

"Curse you!," the poet utters at the rebels, for abandoning God, worshiping the
"cult" of politics, and sacrificing human blood "on the altar of cannibalism."
This and other familiar references to "miserable, unburied warriors" give added
weight to a comparative reading of the overtly "political" poetry and the Indianist texts as reflecting a common, apocalyptical vision of history. But with a
difference: until Conquest, when the Portuguese exploited the Indians' cultural
propensity to war beyond its "natural," controlled limits, conflict in the tribal
world was for Gonçalves Dias ritualistic and self-sustaining, a perpetual cycle of
victory and defeat within which Indian society continued to flourish.

It is in the light of these preoccupations, then, that one should read the Indianist poems, with their depiction of intertribal warfare and Conquest. The conflicts that divide the Tobajaras and Potiguaras in "Tabira" or the Timbiras and
the Gamelas in the epic *Os Timbiras* leave them vulnerable to their cataclysmic
destruction as nations at the hands of an alien power, the Portuguese. But if, as
in the case cited before, Gonçalves Dias was sometimes able to apply a coherent
political analysis to the crisis he feared was imminent, there is also a stronger,
more irrational dimension to his pessimism that we have seen reflected equally
clearly in his Indianist writing: the expectation of divine retribution for an accumulation of crimes committed throughout the nation's history. Political unrest
and unresolved social injustices, such as slavery and the oppression of the Indian, were to explode in some cathartic convulsion. An essential ambiguity underlies this expectation of nemesis, though, for the anticipation of a supernatural
punishment beyond the control of man is inseparable from the poet's barely articulated fears of revolutionary social upheaval. As in the extract already cited
from the *Meditation*, there is merely the vague, prophetic sense of an impending
crisis as the nation moves closer and closer to the limits of moral and political
collapse. Similarly, in 1861 Gonçalves Dias warned: "Brazil seems to be to be
nearing a crisis, very soon, and I can see no remedy for it."[89]

The most explicit formulation of this vision of nemesis and apocalypse is to
be found in "O Gigante de pedra" (The Giant of Stone), which situates the
events of the colonial and Imperial eras within a much broader, cosmic history.
Narrated in a timeless present tense, Brazil's geological, ethnic, and political

evolution is witnessed by the indifferent eye of the Sleeping Giant, not as a teleological, organic sequence of events but as an eternally repeated cycle of growth and destruction, rather like that described in the poem "História":

Triste lição de experiência deixam
Os evos no passar e os mesmos atos
Renovados sem fim por muitos povos,
Sob nomes diversos se encadeiam.

(A sad lesson of experience is left/ By the ages as they pass and the same acts/ Endlessly repeated by many peoples,/ Are linked together under different names.)

One section of "The Giant of Stone" recounts the successive phasees of the Indians' history, the emergence of internal disunity, internecine conflict, and their eventual downfall at the hands of the Portuguese. But within the endless, futile cycle of life witnessed by the Giant, this is a brief, insignificant moment quickly overtaken by other conflicts and upheavals:

Com soberba indiferença
Sente extinta a antiga crença
Dos Tamoios, dos Pajés;
Nem vê que duras desgraças,
Que lutas de novas raças
Se lhe atropelam aos pés!

(With supreme indifference/ He knows the ancient beliefs/ Of the Tamoios, of the Shamans, have been extinguished;/ And does not see that grim misfortunes,/ That the struggles of new races/ Are hard upon their heels!)

The quotation from Victor Hugo's "Le Géant" that prefaces the poem ("Ó guerriers! ne laissez pas ma dépouille au corbeau;/ Ensevelissez-moi parmi des monts sublimes,/ Afin que l'étranger cherche, en voyant leurs cimes,/ Quelle montagne est mon tombeau!") encourages an interpretation of the Brazilian Giant as the nation's dormant martial spirit that must some day awaken and reclaim its glory. Certainly, against the formless, meaningless background of history that he has witnessed, the Giant, as the personification of the Brazilian land, offers the only focus of stability and continuity. Like the image of the Sugar Loaf mountain embracing the Southern Cross, the Giant symbolizes that identity of beliefs—nationhood and religion—that must survive and transcend the disruptive conflicts of the country's history.

But Gonçalves Dias's description of the Giant, together with the warning that ends the poem, suggests that he anticipates more than a simple revival of this spirit of nationalism as the key to Brazil's salvation. Despite the apparent immutability of the Giant in his dumb indifference, there are threatening indications that his sleep is tense and restless: "With his arms crossed nervously at his chest/ . . . He was surely keeping watch deep in furious thought." The same primeval cataclysm that first petrified him into his granite silence may at any moment be repeated, only this time to unleash long-repressed forces of revenge:

Em duro granito repousa o gigante,
Que os raios sòmente poderam fundir. . .
De lavas ardentes seus membros fundidos
Avultam imensos: só Deus pode
Rebelde lançá-lo dos montes erguidos,
Curvados ao peso, que sobre lhe 'stá.

(In hard granite rests the giant,/ Whom the lightning alone could melt. . . / Cast in burning lava his limbs/ Loom immense: only God can/ Cast him rebellious down from the mountains that were raised up,/ Bent under the weight, that bears down upon him.)

There will come a moment in the arrogance and pride of human history when the unity of "faith and fatherland" is abandoned for chaos and doubt, when even the most basic assumptions will fall apart, and more powerful forces will take their revenge:

Porém se algum dia fortuna inconstante
Poder-nos a crença e a pátria acabar,
Arroja-te às ondas, ó duro gigante,
Inunda estes montes, desloca este mar!

(But if one day capricious fortune/ Should destroy our faith and fatherland,/ Hurl yourself into the waves, oh unyielding giant,/ Flood these mountains, cast aside this sea!)

The myth of nemesis is therefore a fusion of the two contradictory, but related, responses of Gonçalves Dias to the historical iniquity of Conquest and the contemporary injustices of Empire. They are essentially two sides of the same coin: on one hand, an outraged appeal for some kind of apocalyptic judgment and punishment of those crimes, for a natural or supernatural stroke of atonement and catharsis; and, on the other hand, his fears of the form that that retribution might take in reality, that is, radical sociopolitical upheaval, even revolution, and the disintegration of the nation-state.

But this was only one dimension of the Indianist poetry and thinking of Gonçalves Dias. For alongside that vision of apocalyptic disintegration was its radical utopian antithesis, the longing to recuperate the absent or lost harmony of the tribal universe and to imagine an ideal, integrated society in which the exiled or marginalized individual might rediscover a place within the community.

THE RETURN OF THE EXILE AND THE UTOPIA OF INTEGRATION

During an expedition to Amazonia, Gonçalves Dias wrote to his friend Antônio Henriques Leal of the refuge and consolation that this world offered to one whose faith in human society and nationhood had been destroyed by the events of his time:

You who, like me and so many others, perhaps without reason, are saddened or angered by the way our affairs are going, perhaps because the sun no longer shines so brightly in the firmament of your imagination, —you who, in a fit of depression, have come to hate the land whose sons you are and to lose your faith in the men whose brothers you are, — come and spend a quarter of an hour here on a quiet moonlit night . . . and you will find yourself changed, and, as in the happy times of your youth, still capable of lush illusions, unbounded confidence, a robust faith in events, in men, in the future, and, if just for a few moments you are capable of feeling, you will feel proud to call yourself "Brazilian" too.[90]

This sense of a spiritual affinity with the universe of the Indian dated back to the poet's earliest Indianist writings. In "Visões.1—O Índio" (Visions.1—The Indian), written in Portugal in 1844 but excluded from the first published volumes of poetry, Gonçalves Dias depicted an archetypal dialogue between the poet, "The Bard," and "The Indian," the son of the last Tupi chief. The problem of the artificiality of such a meeting is not avoided; rather, the poet draws attention to the role of the fictional imagination in making it possible—"E noutro quadro da minha alma os olhos/ Mais distinta visão me figuraram" (And in another scene in my soul my eyes/ Pictured a much different vision)—for only there, in the imaginary space of the poem, can he confront his nation's guilty conscience with the figure of its victim and at the same time rediscover the humanity he finds lacking in his own society. The dialogue goes right to the heart of the central ideological contradiction that, as I have argued, characterizes Romantic Indianism: the notion of a socially and racially integrated nation rooted in the shared anticolonial identity of Brazilian and Indian, yet founded simultaneously on the genocide, slavery, and marginalization of its nonwhite population. The Indian of the poem registers the terrible irony that his jailer and executioner should be the one to speak the language of reconciliation:

(O Cantor)	Não somos nós irmãos—a tua pátria
	Não é a pátria minha? Ali marcada
	Não tinhas outra vida—outro futuro?
(O Índio)	És dos grandes também—tu que assim falas.
	Desses que aos índios têm no rol de escravos?
	Irônico sorrindo me inquiria.

((The Bard) Are we not brothers—is your fatherland/ Not mine? Did you not have/ Another life reserved for you—another future?// (The Indian) You too are one of the great ones—you who speak thus./ One of those for whom the Indians number among their slaves?/ He inquired of me, smiling ironically.)

However, he recognizes in the poet someone different, a kindred spirit whose flights of imagination seek the same liberty that the Indian finds in his forest and whose vision allows him to face the truth of Conquest with honesty and sincerity. It is in recognition of this special relationship that the Indian invites the poet to sit with him and hear the history of his people, the apocalyptic omens of destruction, the anger of their gods, and their defeat, slavery, and exile. Ultimately, though, in spite of the poet's privileged insight, there can be no reconciliation between the two societies; the myth of a common nationhood remains a myth, for the white man and the Indian inhabit two irrevocably separated worlds:

> Adeus, Cantor—adeus! que a minha pátria
> Não é a tua, não—mas este vasto
> Frondoso praino—estes vestidos serros,
> E o imenso azul dos céus.

> (Farewell, Bard—farewell! for my fatherland/ Is not yours, no—but this vast/ Verdant plain—these hills bedecked in foliage,/ And the immense blue of the heavens.)

The remaining Indianist poems examined here can be understood as an extension of this dialogue, in which the poet attempts a kind of imaginative communion with the spiritual and cultural self-sufficiency of tribal society and at the same time dramatizes the struggle of the exile and marginal to find a place within it. Central to his effort to convey this sense of an organic, integrated world is a key stylistic technique, exemplified by texts such as "Canto do Guerreiro" (The Warrior's Chant): the rejection of traditional Iberian meters (i.e., those based on syllable counting) in favor of meters based on rhythmic units, in particular, the anapaest (a practice also found in other Indianist writers outside Brazil, such as the North American Longfellow). For Manuel Bandeira, this choice serves to reinforce certain sentiments associated with the tribal character, "wherever there are bellicose movements or sentiments of pride, indignation or revolt."[91] But more than that, this rhythmic emphasis is allied to an overall simplicity of form through which Gonçalves Dias achieves a ritualistic, musical effect. Taking the form of pseudofolk poetry and tribal songs or chants commemorating aspects of tribal life and tradition, these poems represent the utterances of men and, occasionally, women, attempting to fix their existence within the shifting natural cycles of life and death. Structures tend to be limited to repeated, interchangeable stanzas free from narrative development and capable of standing alone as independent, self-contained units.

"The Warrior's Chant" also illustrates the other key element in this depiction of an organic tribal identity—the military ethos:

> Valente na guerra
> Quem há, como eu sou?
> Quem vibra o tacape
> Com mais valentia?
> Quem golpes daria
> Fatais, como eu dou?
> —Guerreiros, ouvi-me;
> —Quem há, como eu sou?

> (Courageous in war/ Who can compare to me?/ Who wields his club/ With greater courage?/ Who could deal such lethal/ Blows, as I do?/ —Warriors, hear me;/ —Who can compare to me?)

Indeed, with a few conspicuous exceptions, the Indianist poetry is dominated by this ethos, its figures celebrating, preparing for, fighting, and recounting perpetual wars. The critical consensus has seen this concern with military values as a simple variation on the medievalist or chivalresque Romanticism to which Gonçalves Dias was introduced during his student days in Coimbra. For instance, in reference to "I-Juca Pirama," José Guilherme Merquior suggests, "The existence of the forest people is presented in a heroic tone, as if our Indians had emerged from the romances of chivalry."[92] Antonio Candido goes further:

It should be noted that the Indianism of Gonçalves Dias is a relative of the medievalism of Coimbra, which he practiced in loco and which must have influenced his aim to apply to his country the same criterion of lyrical and heroic exploration of the past. *As Sextilhas de Frei Antão*, "O Soldado Espanhol," "O Trovador (medievalist poems) could be considered symmetrical pairs with *Os Timbiras*, "I-Juca Pirama," and the "Canção do Guerreiro" [*sic*], through the reduction of the Indians to the model of the chivalresque genre.[93]

It is certainly true that the Indianist and medievalist movements are analogous in their attempt to locate ideal values in a past, mythical age. But such a reductionist account of the poetry of Gonçalves Dias ignores both the specific historical and moral perspective that underlies his vision of tribal society and the peculiar character of the military ethos as it is depicted in the poetry. Taking up Antonio Candido's example of the *Sextilhas de Frei Antão* (Sextets of Friar Antão), it needs to be said that the martial spirit is here underpinned by a cultural and political project—the Christian reconquest—that has no direct parallel in Gonçalves Dias's Indianist poetry. While, as we have seen, the colonial Conquest of Brazil was denounced as a criminal, apocalyptic act to which the church was a guilty accomplice, the medieval wars are unequivocally portrayed as a legitimate religious struggle against the Islamic infidel, who is depicted in frankly racist terms:

São homens de fero aspeito,
Homens de má condição,
Que vivem na lei nojenta
Do seu nojento alcorão. ("Loa da Princesa Santa")

(They are men of savage appearance,/ Men of evil condition,/ Who live under the loathsome law/ Of their loathsome Koran.)

The intertribal wars of the Indianist poetry, meanwhile, are not fought for the possession of land or wealth or in defense of a religion, but for the affirmation of personal and collective identity, the identity of the warrior and the tribe. As such, they function as ritual, as symbolic, if brutal, conflicts between moral equals. Courage is the right of the defeated as well as of the victorious; the enemy exists not as an evil to be eliminated or subjugated but as a challenge and test of the rival's military prowess.

In addition, the tribal culture depicted in the Indianist writing of Gonçalves Dias is a typically masculine environment, from which the psychology and drama of sexual relationships are generally excluded. Significantly, the few instances of female Indians in the poetry record experiences of sexual failure, frustration, or alienation. The protagonist of "Leito de folhas verdes" (Bed of Green Leaves) can be seen precisely as the victim of an exclusively masculine, militarist culture in which heterosexual love does not figure very highly; she waits in vain for her lover, who, we may speculate, prefers the company of his fellow warriors or the excitement of the hunt to the intimacy of a sexual encounter. But whereas in "Marabá," as we have seen, the woman's rejection has historical and racial origins, here her abandonment and frustration are linked to the natural order of the forest and its temporal cycles of growth and reproduction.

The poem does not explain the lover's absence; rather, it records the passing of a moment of potential sexual fulfillment that remains unrealized in the indifferent, random environment of nature. In the central metaphor of the poem, the Indian girl appears as a virgin flower of the forest that time has left unfertilized in the few hours granted to it before it must fade. One of Gonçalves Dias's most finely structured and executed pieces, the text expresses the sentiment of frustration and disappointment indirectly, through the subtle, but meaningful, passage of time. It opens with the breeze of dusk and the aromas of the forest, evoking a sensual atmosphere of expectancy as the girl prepares her bed of leaves and flowers. The third stanza suggests an image of sexual ripeness, the flowers opening their petals and releasing aphrodisiac perfumes in a delicately veiled gesture of erotic invitation:

> Do tamarindo a flor abriu-se, há pouco,
> Já solta o bogari mais doce aroma!
> Como prece de amor, como estas preces,
> No silêncio da noite o bosque exala.

(The tamarind flower has not long opened,/ The bogari now lets forth the sweetest scent!/ Like a prayer of love, like these prayers,/ The grove breathes in the silence of the night.)

Exactly midway through the poem, the fifth stanza brings this metaphor of potent, fecund expectancy to its crucial point of tension, as the girl prepares for the unique, unrepeatable moment of self-realization:

> A flor que desabrocha ao romper d'alva
> Um só giro do sol, não mais, vegeta:
> Eu sou aquela flor que espero ainda
> Doce raio do sol que me dê vida.

(The flower that unfolds at the break of dawn/ Blooms for just one turn of the sun, no more:/ I am that flower still awaiting/ A sweet ray of sun to give me life.)

But in the very interval as she is speaking, declaring her virginity and loyalty ("My eyes have never looked upon another's eyes"), the moment has passed unaltered, night has turned to day, and the flower now "lies half-open," intact and redundant; the dawn that should have brought her lover to her finds her still alone, still a virgin. Within the contingent world of nature and the masculine, militarist environment of Gonçalves Dias's Indian society, women are thus condemned to a destiny of passivity and abandonment.

Moreover, the arrogance and bravado of the male Indians, their competing claims of superior strength and prowess, have a strong sexual content of their own. One might go so far as to speculate that, in part at least, the poetry represents the sublimation of a sexual impulse that the poet's own unsuccessful marriage and extramarital affairs were unable to satisfy. As we see in Chapter 4, the phallic overtones of "The Warrior's Chant" ("Who wields his club/ With greater courage?/ Who could deal such lethal/ Blows, as I do?") were certainly evident enough to later Indianists such as Bernardo Guimarães, who was moved to write an obscene parody of Gonçalves Dias's poem.

"The Warrior's Chant" exemplifies a further aspect of intertribal warfare as portrayed in the Indianist poetry: its harmonic, organic character. War, the hunt, and even death are integral elements of a self-sufficient way of life; violence, whatever the number of dead, does not have the devastating power of the colonial wars between Indian and white. Instead, it is a ritualistic and natural process, a collision of elemental forces springing out of the forest environment:

> E então se de novo
> Eu toco o Boré;
> Qual fonte que salta
> De rocha empinada,
> Que vai marulhosa,
> Fremente e queixosa,
> Que raiva apagada
> De todo não é,
> Tal eles se escoam
> Aos sons do Boré.

> (And if then I once more/ Sound the horn;/ Like a spring that leaps from a lofty cliff,/ Pouring forth in a tremulous,/ Querulous torrent,/ Whose rage is not quite quenched,/ So do they rush forward/ At the sound of the horn.)

As ritual, tribal war does not disrupt the basic harmony of indigenous society but reinforces it; like the symbolic, token confrontations between birds and animals, it reproduces an ever-changing pattern of victory and defeat while allowing the organism as a whole to survive and flourish. Affirming his respect for this principle in the fourth canto of *Os Timbiras*, the wise stranger who lives among the Gamelas opposes the renewal of war against the Timbiras because it is unnecessary, an unjust defiance of the proven supremacy of the Timbiras. The Gamela chief has been fairly defeated and must allow his rival to savor the victory, for both defeat and victory are necessary to the harmony of their world:

> Se o filho de Jaguar trazer-nos manda
> Do chefe desditoso o frio corpo,
> Aceite-se . . . se não . . . voltemos sempre,
> Ou com ele, ou sem ele, às nossas tabas,
> Às nossas tabas mudas, lacrimosas,

Que hão-de certo enlutar nossos guerreiros,
Quer vencedores voltem, quer vencidos.

(If the son of Jaguar has the cold body/ of the ill-fated chief brought to us,/ Let it be accepted . . . if not . . . let us still return,/ With it, or without it, to our villages,/ To our silent, tearful villages,/ Which will surely deck our warriors in mourning,/ Whether they return victorious, or defeated.)

"Canção do Tamoio" (The Tamoio's Song) explores a further aspect of this organic tribal cosmology, the relationship between life and death. Gonçalves Dias describes the tradition upon which the poem is based in his ethnographic work *Brasil e Oceânia*. The newborn child is given a bow and arrows, and the father sings a "birth song" that prepares the child for the struggle of life, for the need to be strong and confront death:

By a philosophical antithesis, in the colors with which they painted him in the cradle they depicted life and bereavement; and if in the grave they sought to give to the corpse the position that the foetus had in the womb, counterposing the grave to the cradle: so too when focusing on life they pointed towards the end that awaited them, as if the child's babbling cry and the dying man's last sigh formed a single hiatus, and the first "ah!" of existence were the first step towards death.[94]

Life is a dynamic battle whose motivation is not pleasure or the fear of death but the struggle itself; the short lines and familiar rhythm of the Indianist poetry suggest the urgency, intensity, and brevity of the life experience, which demand that it be lived to the full:

Não chores, meu filho;
Não chores, que a vida
É luta renhida:
Viver é lutar.
A vida é combate,
Que os fracos abate,
Que os fortes, os bravos,
Só pode exaltar. . . .
As armas ensaia,
Penetra na vida:
Pesada ou querida,
Viver é lutar.

(Do not weep, my son,/ Do not weep, for life/ Is a hard-fought battle:/ To live is to fight./ Life is a struggle,/ That crushes the weak,/ That can but ennoble/ The strong, the brave. . . ./ Test your weapons,/ Enter into life:/ Whether burdensome or cherished,/ To live is to fight.)

Death is, therefore, not a tragic end but an extension of life that must be faced with vigor and courage. It is described in the natural imagery of biological collapse and decomposition in the forest, such as when a tree is struck down by a lightning bolt and falls back into the cycle of decay and renewal. The death of the Gamela chief in the first canto of *Os Timbiras*, for example, appears as the conclusion of a magnificent, organic clash of natural elements:

> o colosso verga,
> Inclina-se, desaba, cai de chofre,
> E o pó levanta e atroa forte os ecos.
> Assim cai na floresta um tronco anoso,
> E o som da queda se propaga ao longe!

([T]he colossus buckles,/ Bends, topples, falls abruptly,/ And raises the dust and sends echoes thundering powerfully away./ So too an aged trunk falls in the forest,/ And the sound of its falling is heard far and wide!)

The tribal ethos of war thus defines Gonçalves Dias's vision of Indian society as an integrated, organic world whose rituals and life cycles incorporate the individual into a collective and cosmic identity. Conquest, on the other hand, signifies the irremediable disruption of that world, the distortion and manipulation of the ritual culture of war, the rupture of tribal alliances and the wrenching of the individual out of his perfectly integrated society. In exploring this dimension of the impact of Conquest, Gonçalves Dias clearly drew on his own experience as one of a marginalized sector of nineteenth-century Brazilian society, economically dependent on the ruling oligarchies of slave-owning *latifundiários* yet excluded from the political process by a lack of property or capital and denied social acceptance by virtue of their racial and class origins.

That condition of marginalization is revealed most explicitly in "Estâncias" (Stanzas), perhaps the most personal and overtly autobiographical of his reflections on the sense of solidarity and community evoked by tribal culture in a world of utter solitude. Motivated by the death of his daughter, the poem testifies first to the isolation of grief in the midst of an atomized society of lonely individuals, comparable only to the terrible alienation of the Indian following Conquest:

> Ando como ele incessante,
> Forasteiro, vago, errante,
> Sem próprio abrigo, sem lar,
> Sem ter uma voz amiga
> Que em minha aflição me diga
> Dessas palavras que fazem
> A dor no peito abrandar!

(Like him I wander ceaselessly,/ A roving, drifting stranger,/ Without a refuge of my own, without a home,/ Without a friendly voice/ To speak to me in my distress/ Those words that soothe/ The pain in one's breast!)

But the similarity between these two fragmented societies is only partial, for while the Indian has seen families and tribes shattered and scattered across the interior of the country, the inner cohesion and integrality of his people have not been destroyed. Carrying the remains of his dead about with him in his wanderings, the Indian continues to live in constant communion with his tribe:

Por isso onde quer que chega
Da vida n'amplo deserto,
Como que a pátria tem perto,
Nunca dos seus longe está!

(Therefore wherever he goes/ In the vast desert of life,/ In a way his fatherland is close by,/ He is never far from his people!)

By contrast, for the poet the loss of his daughter signifies the irremediable rupture of family bonds; death is definitive, casting the individual into a social void, the empty space that separates him from her place of burial:

Mas qual teu jazigo? e onde
Jazem teus restos mortais?. . .
Esse lugar que te esconde,
Não vi: —não verei jamais.

(But where is your grave? and where/ Do your mortal remains lie?. . . / That place that hides you,/ I have not seen: —I shall never see.)

Gonçalves Dias's most celebrated Indianist text, "I-Juca Pirama," represents the high point of this drama, the disintegration of family and community, the exile of the individual and his search to recover the sense of solidarity and belonging within the integrality of tribal culture. Because it recounts the struggle of a young captive warrior to protect his dying father in the face of his own imminent execution, it is tempting to see in the poem the triumph of a Western morality of filial devotion over the martial tribal culture of courage and resistance. But this is to ignore the dramatic structure of the text in its entirety, for while the bond of paternity is an important theme, it is subordinated to the main climax of the poem, which is the moment of tribal reconciliation and reintegration. The father disowns his son because, ironically, he has tearfully asked that his life be spared in order to care for the old man and has therefore betrayed the highest values of tribal stoicism and courage. Reacting to this rejection and to the accusation of cowardice at the climax of the poem, the warrior gives proof of his bravery and so reaffirms his identity as a worthy Indian captive. Consequently, he is restored to his father's bosom and, more important, is able to resume his role in the symbolic ritual of tribal communion and incorporation—death by cannibalism.

At first sight, this ritual around which the dramatic and emotional movement of the poem revolves appears to remove it from any notion of historical time. After weeping before his captors, the young prisoner demonstrates his true bravery and filial devotion, reconciling himself once again to the community, reconfirming tribal values and leaving Indian society intact. Nevertheless, that reconciliation derives its full force only from the historical context, which, although not usually acknowledged, is clearly established early in the poem. In the first section we read that the prisoner is a stranger, the member of some remote tribe, while in the third section it is indicated more enigmatically that he is bereft of both tribe and family. The mystery is unfolded in the "death chant," in which he is allowed to tell his story:

Vi lutas de bravos,
Vi fortes—escravos!
De estranhos ignavos
Calcados aos pés.

E os campos talados,
E os arcos quebrados,
E os piagas coitados
Já sem maracás;
E os meigos cantores,
Servindo a senhores,
Que vinham traidores,
Com mostras de paz.

Aos golpes do imigo
Meu último amigo,
Sem lar, sem abrigo
Caiu junto a mi!

(I saw the struggles of braves,/ I saw the strong—made slaves!/ Trampled underfoot/ By vile strangers.// And the fields laid waste/ And the bows broken in pieces,/ And the poor shamans/ Without their rattles;/ And the gentle chanters,/ In the service of masters,/ Who came treacherously,/ With signs of peace.// At the enemy's blows/ My last friend,/ Without a home or shelter/ Fell by my side!)

He and his father are the last survivors of a Tupi tribe that has fallen victim to the European invader and his treachery; they have been wandering in exile as if only in order finally to rediscover their lost world in another place, among the Timbira who are holding the warrior prisoner. He is given an opportunity to reaffirm the traditional values of his people within the honorable context of his captivity, through some act of bravery. This he does, giving new life to his old, decrepit father and to the tribe that Conquest appeared to have destroyed:

Era ele, o Tupi; nem fora justo
Que a fama dos Tupis—o nome, a glória,
Aturado labor de tantos anos,
Derradeiro brasão da raça extinta,
De um jacto e por um só se aniquilasse.

(It was he, the Tupi; nor would it have been right/ That the fame of the Tupis—their name and glory,/ The untiring labor of so many years,/ The last emblem of the deceased race,/ Should be extinguished all at once, at a stroke.)

The rhythmic diversity and richness of the poem's individual sections and their dramatic function have been thoroughly analyzed elsewhere,[95] but it should be added that those meters based on the poet's preferred rhythmic unit, the anapaest, appear precisely at the moments of greatest structural and dramatic importance, for example, section IV, the "death chant," section VII, the father's curse on his son, or section II, where the prisoner has been prepared for his execution and sits awaiting his death, urged on by the poem itself to face it honorably:

> Folga morrendo; porque além dos Andes
> > Revive o forte,
> Que soube ufano contrastar os medos
> > Da fria morte.

(Rejoice in your death; for beyond the Andes/ The strong one,/ Who proudly resisted the fear of chill death/ Returns to life.)

The intervening sections are descriptive or narrative passages, linked and swept on by the dramatic and rhythmic force of the ritual; this impulse drives the poem to what seems an inevitable conclusion; the inner momentum and law of the Indian cosmos dictate that the ritual must be fulfilled, and the execution must take place. The old man's respect for this law overrides the imminent loss of his son; noticing, in spite of his blindness, that the warrior's tribal mane of hair is missing, he realizes that his son has been a captive and has therefore, by going free, violated the code of execution. In the belief that he has been released out of generosity, he returns with his son to the Timbira village to request that the sacrifice should go ahead: "Em tudo o rito se cumpra!" (Let the ritual be performed in full!)

But on hearing that his son has betrayed the values of his people by weeping in the face of death, he condemns him to the worst fate possible for one born into the communal world of the tribe—exile. The biblical curse that follows is a terrible invocation of absolute exclusion, the sum of those experiences and fears voiced by Gonçalves Dias throughout his work, and the shattering negation of the social cohesion that he sees as characteristic of the Indian world:

> "Possas tu, isolado na terra,
> Sem arrimo e sem pátria vagando,
> Rejeitado da morte na guerra,
> Rejeitado dos homens na paz,
> Ser das gentes o espectro execrado;
> Não encontres amor nas mulheres,
> Teus amigos, se amigos tiveres,
> Tenham alma inconstante e falaz!"

("May you wander solitary on the earth,/ With nothing, noone to lean on and no fatherland,/ Rejected by death in war,/ Rejected by men in peace,/ The abominated specter of human beings;/ May you find no love in women,/ May your friends, if friends you have,/ Be fickle and deceitful souls!")

The restoration of his son to him, after he proves his bravery by a furious onslaught against the whole tribe, is correspondingly absolute in its force and significance. It is expressed in the language of the Prodigal Son's homecoming:

O guerreiro parou, caiu nos braços
Do velho pai, que o cinge contra o peito,
Com lágrimas de júbilo bradando:
"Este, sim, que é meu filho muito amado!
"E pois que o acho em fim, qual sempre o tive,
"Corram livres as lágrimas que choro,
"Estas lágrimas, sim, que não deshonram."

(The warrior stopped, and fell into the arms/ of his old father, who gathers him to his breast,/ Crying out with tears of rejoicing:/ "This truly is my beloved son!/ And as I find him at last, as he was ever mine,/ Let the tears I weep flow freely,/ Yes, these tears which are no disgrace.")

For the chief of the Timbiras, too, the warrior has been restored to his rightful place as a member of tribal society; having earlier rejected his cowardly flesh as unfit for brave tribesmen to feast upon ("we will not weaken/ The strong with wretched flesh"), he now invites him to prepare for the death that he has earned: "'Basta, guerreiro ilustre! assaz lutaste,/ E para o sacrifício é mister forças'" ("No more, illustrious warrior! you have fought enough,/ And you will need your strength for the sacrifice"). The ritual that is about to be enacted thus confirms the Indian's rediscovery of his tribal identity in both physical and symbolic terms. His gesture of filial devotion does not usurp the dominant militarist culture of his people but momentarily questions it, only to leave it reinforced and enriched. By honoring the ritual and accepting his incorporation into the body of the tribe, he is fulfilling the role laid out for him within the social and cosmic order of the Indian world: I-Juca Pirama—"o que há de ser morto, e que é digno de ser morto" (he who must be killed, and is worthy of being killed).

It was noted before that the force and significance of this drama of tribal reintegration depend on the historical antecedents given at the beginning of the poem: the defeat, dispersal, and virtual annihilation of the Tupi community, whose last exiled survivors are the old man and his son, following Conquest. The mythical isolation of the Timbiras provides an imaginary space in which the bonds of collective tribal identity can be reconstituted. Most remarkable about the poem is its particular interpretation of the practice of cannibalism as a means of enacting and ritualizing this reincorporation of the individual into the tribe. In offering a reading of the practice that comes close to the modern anthropological wisdom on the matter, Gonçalves Dias broke with the entire tradition of Indianist writing in Brazil, which for three centuries had represented and caricatured cannibalism as proof of the Indian's primitive barbarism, as we saw in the last chapter. Indeed, he is unique within nineteenth-century Indianism for this interpretation, and not until the Modernist movement was the ritual significance of cannibalism once again reasserted. Such a radical revision of one of the cornerstones of colonial discourse speaks volumes for this poet's remarkable contribution as one of the most powerful dissident voices within the Romantic Indianist tradition.

142 • *Exiles, Allies, Rebels*

NOTES

1. Carlos de Araújo Moreira Neto, "A Política Indigenista Brasileira Durante o século XIX" (mimeo.), (doctoral thesis, Faculdade de Filosofia, Ciências e Letras de Rio Claro, São Paulo, 1971), p. 5.

2. J. B. von Spix and C.F.P. von Martius, *Viagem pelo Brasil* (trans.) (Rio de Janeiro: Imprensa Nacional, 1938), vol. 1, p. 197.

3. José Oscar Beozzo, *Leis e Regimentos das Missões: política indigenista no Brasil* (São Paulo: Loyola, 1983), pp. 71-74. As Manuela Carneiro da Cunha confirms, the name Botocudo became virtually synonymous with Tapuia or "índio bravo" in nineteenth-century terminology, as opposed to the "índio doméstico ou manso." See Manuela Carneiro da Cunha, "Política indigenista no século XIX," in *História dos Índios do Brasil* (São Paulo: Companhia das Letras/Secretaria Municipal de Cultura/FAPESP, 1992), p. 136.

4. José Bonifácio de Andrada e Silva, *Projetos para o Brasil* (São Paulo: Companhia das Letras, 1998), p. 100. See also Emília Viotti da Costa's biographical portrait of José Bonifácio: "José Bonifácio de Andrada e Silva: A Brazilian Founding Father," *The Brazilian Empire: Myths and Histories* (Chicago and London: University of Chicago Press, 1985), pp. 24-52.

5. Andrada e Silva, *Projetos para o Brasil*, p. 91.

6. Ibid., pp. 142-43.

7. Anon., "Justa Retribuição dada ao compadre de Lisboa em desagravo dos brasileiros offendidos por varias asserções, que escrevo na sua carta em resposta ao compadre de Belem, pelo filho do Compadre de Rio de Janeiro, que offerece, e dedica aos seus patricios" (Rio de Janeiro: na Typographia Regia, 1821), pp. 3-4.

8. Anon., "Carta do Compadre do Rio de S. Francisco do Norte, ao filho do compadre do Rio de Janeiro, na qual se lhe queixa do parallelo, que faz dos indios com os cavallos, de não conceder aos homens pretos maior dignidade, que a de reis do rozario, e de asseverar, que o Brazil ainda agora está engatinhando; E crê provar o contrario de tudo isso, por J.J. do C.M." (Rio de Janeiro: na Impressão Nacional, 1821), pp. 3-4.

9. Anon., "Carta do Compadre do Rio de S. Francisco do Norte," p. 6.

10. Ibid., p. 8.

11. Ibid.

12. José Arouche de Toledo Rendon, "Memoria sobre as aldeias de indios da Provincia de S. Paulo, segundo as observações feitas no anno de 1798—Opinião do auctor sobre a sua civilisação," *Revista do Instituto Histórico e Geográfico Brasileiro*, vol. 4 (1842), p. 295.

13. Jean Baptiste Debret, *Viagem pitoresca e histórica ao Brasil* (trans.), 2 vols. (São Paulo: Círculo do livro, n.d.), vol. 1, pp. 14, 20, 39.

14. Debret, *Viagem pitoresca e histórica*, vol. 1, p. 71.

15. Paulo e Souza, cited in José Honório Rodrigues, *Conciliação e Reforma no Brasil: um desafio histórico-cultural* (Rio de Janeiro: Nova Fronteira, 1982), p. 49.

16. José Murilo de Carvalho, *Teatro de sombras: a política imperial* (São Paulo: Vértice, 1988), p. 14. See also Rodrigues, *Conciliação e reforma no Brasil*, pp. 51-53.

17. Moreira Neto, *A política indigenista brasileira*, pp. 18-19.

18. Ibid., pp. 2-26.

19. José Bonifácio de Andrada e Silva, *Poesias de Américo Elísio, Obras de José Bonifácio de Andrada e Silva*, vol. 1 (Rio de Janeiro: Imprensa Nacional, 1946), pp. 29-30.

20. For a general study, see Paul Hazard, "De l'Ancien au Nouveau Monde: les Origines du Romantisme au Brésil," *Revue de Littérature Comparée* (1972), pp. 111-28.

21. Jean Ferdinand Denis, *Brésil, par M. Ferdinand Denis, L'Univers, ou Histoire et Description de tous les peuples, de leurs religions, moeurs, coutumes etc.* (Paris: Firmin Didot Frères, 1837), pp. 2-3.

22. Jean Ferdinand Denis, *Résumé de l'histoire littéraire du Portugal suivie du Résumé de l'histoire littéraire du Brésil* (Paris: Lecointe et Durey, 1826), p. 529.

23. Antonio Candido, *Formação da literatura brasileira (Momentos decisivos)*, 2 vols. (São Paulo: Martins, 1962), vol. 1, p. 329; see also David Treece, "Caramuru the Myth: Conquest and Conciliation," *Ibero-Amerikanisches Archiv* 10, no. 2 (1984), pp. 145-46.

24. D. Gavet and P. Boucher, *Jakaré-Ouassou, ou les Tupinambás: Chronique Brésilienne* (Paris: Timothée de Hay, 1830), p. 364.

25. Jean-Jacques Rousseau, "A Discourse on the Origin of Inequality," *The Social Contract and Discourses* (London, Melbourne, and Toronto: Dent, 1973), p. 39.

26. Ibid., p. 83.

27. Ibid., p. 54.

28. Ibid., p. 72.

29. Lilia Moritz Schwarcz, *As Barbas do Imperador: D. Pedro II, um monarca nos trópicos* (São Paulo: Companhia das Letras, 1998), p. 142.

30. Nelson Werneck Sodré, *História da literatura brasileira: Seus Fundamentos Econômicos* (Rio de Janeiro: Civilização Brasileira, 1969), pp. 273, 274, 276.

31. Schwarcz, *As Barbas do Imperador*, p. 131 and note 16.

32. Ivan Teixeira, "Bibliografia ilustrada de *O Uraguay*," in José Basílio da Gama, *Obras Poéticas de Basílio da Gama* (São Paulo: EDUSP, 1996), pp. 134-40.

33. Schwarcz, *As Barbas do Imperador*, p. 127.

34. Ferdinand Wolf, *O Brasil literário (história da literatura brasileira)* (trans.) (São Paulo: Companhia Editora Nacional, 1955), p. 341.

35. Augusto de Freitas Lopes Gonçalves, *Dicionário histórico e literário do teatro no Brasil* (Rio de Janeiro: Cátedra, 1979), vol. 3, pp. 90, 201, 229; J. Galante de Sousa, *O Teatro no Brasil*, 2 vols. (Rio de Janeiro: Instituto Nacional do Livro, 1960), vol. 2, p. 244.

36. Sábato Magaldi, *Panorama do Teatro Brasileiro* (São Paulo: Difusão Européia do Livro, 1962); Wolf, *O Brasil literário*, p. 334. See also Tania Rebelo Costa Serra, *Joaquim Manuel de Macedo ou os Dois Macedos: A Luneta Mágica do II Reinado* (Rio de Janeiro: Fundação Biblioteca Nacional/Departamento Nacional do Livro, 1994), p. 493.

37. Augusto Victorio Alves Sacramento Blake, *Diccionario Bibliographico Brazileiro*, 6 vols. (Rio de Janeiro: Imprensa Nacional, 1899), vol. 5, pp. 279-80.

38. Nelson Werneck Sodré, *História da literatura brasileira: Seus Fundamentos Econômicos* (Rio de Janeiro: Civilização Brasileira, 1969), p. 121.

39. Ladislau dos Santos Titara, *Obras Poéticas* (Bahia: Typographia do Diario, 1835), vol. 3, p. 26. See also Antônio Joaquim de Mello's "Os Cahetés" and "Itaé," *Biografias de Alguns Poetas, e homens illustres da Provincia de Pernambuco*, 3 vols. (Recife: Typographia Universal, 1858), vol. 2, pp. 100-103, 218-29.

40. Titara, *Obras Poéticas*, vol. 4, p. 7.

41. Ibid, p. 61.

42. Ibid., pp. 159-60.

43. See Sílvio Romero, *História da Literatura Brasileira*, 5 vols. (Rio de Janeiro: José Olympio, 1943), vol. 1, pp. 75-79; Péricles Eugênio da Silva Ramos, "Uma Nenia formosa," *Estado de S. Paulo, Suplemento Literário* (12 September 1964); and Candido, *Formação da Literatura Brasileira*, vol. 1, pp. 308-313, 331.

44. Irmão José Gregório, *Contribuição Indígena ao Brasil*, 3 vols. (Belo Horizonte: União Brasileira de Educação e Ensino, 1980), vol. 3, pp. 1249-51.

45. Schwarcz, *As Barbas do Imperador*, p. 129.

46. Firmino Rodrigues Silva, "Nenia, ao meu bom amigo O Dr. Francisco Bernardino Ribeiro," *Minerva Brasiliense*, vol. 2, no. 18 (15 July 1844), p. 560.

47. Martins Pena, *Obras*, vol. 2: *Dramas* (Rio de Janeiro: MEC/INL, 1956), p. 215.

48. Ibid., p. 218.

49. Ibid., p. 221.

50. Maria Sylvia de Carvalho Franco, *Homens livres na ordem escravocrata* (São Paulo: Instituto de Estudos Brasileiros, 1969), p. 12.

51. Richard Graham, *Patronage and Politics in Nineteenth-Century Brazil* (Stanford, Calif.: Stanford University Press, 1990), p. 24.

52. Roberto Schwarz, "Misplaced Ideas: Literature and Society in Late-Nineteenth-Century Brazil," *Misplaced Ideas: Essays on Brazilian Culture* (London: Verso, 1992), p. 22.

53. Joaquim Norberto de Souza Silva, "Noticia sobre Antônio Gonçalves Teixeira e Sousa e suas obras," *Revista do Instituto Histórico e Geográfico Brasileiro* 39, 1st part (1876), pp. 197-216.

54. Jean-Michel Massa, *A Juventude de Machado de Assis (1839-1870): ensaio de biografia intelectual* (Rio de Janeiro: Civilização Brasileira, 1971), pp. 82-83. See also Eunice Gondim, *Vida e Obra de Paula Brito* (Rio de Janeiro: Livraria Brasiliana, 1965).

55. Candido, *Formação da Literatura Brasileira*, vol. 2, p. 126.

56. Antônio Gonçalves Teixeira e Sousa, *As Tardes de um Pintor ou As Intrigas de um Jesuita* (Rio de Janeiro: Três, 1973), pp. 175-82.

57. Silva, "Noticia sobre Antônio Gonçalves Teixeira e Sousa e suas obras."

58. Antônio Gonçalves Teixeira e Sousa, *Os Três Dias de um Noivado* (Rio de Janeiro: Typ. Imparcial de Paula Brito, 1844), canto I, stanza xlvii.

59. Antônio Gonçalves Dias, *Poesia completa e prosa escolhida* (Rio de Janeiro: José Aguilar, 1959), p. 679.

60. Candido, *Formação da literatura brasileira*, vol. 2, p. 377.

61. Raymundo Faoro, *Os Donos do Poder: Formação do Patronato Político Brasileiro*, 2 vols. (Porto Alegre: Globo, 1979), vol. 1, p. 317.

62. The chief sources for Gonçalves Dias's biography are Lúcia Miguel-Pereira, *A vida de Gonçalves Dias* (Rio de Janeiro: José Olympio, 1943); Manuel Bandeira, "Gonçalves Dias: esboço biográfico," *Poesia e Prosa*, 2 vols. (Rio de Janeiro: Aguilar, 1958), vol. 2, pp. 617-804, republished in a condensed form in Gonçalves Dias, *Poesia completa e prosa escolhida*; Antônio Henriques Leal, *Gonçalves Dias* (Lisbon: Imprensa Nacional, 1874).

63. Miguel-Pereira, *A vida de Gonçalves Dias*, p. 102.

64. Fritz Ackermann, *A Obra Poética de Antônio Gonçalves Dias* (São Paulo: Conselho Estadual de Cultura, 1964), pp. 92-99.

65. Miguel-Pereira, *A vida de Gonçalves Dias*, pp. 91-92.

66. Ibid., pp. 101 & 205.

67. Graham, *Patronage and Politics*, p. 211.

68. Bandeira, "Gonçalves Dias: esboço biográfico," p. 673.

69. João Francisco Lisboa, *Crônica do Brasil Colonial (Apontamentos para a História do Maranhão)* (Petropolis: Vozes, 1976), p. 159.

70. Ibid., p. 579.

71. Antônio Gonçalves Dias, *Obras Posthumas*, 3 vols. (São Luiz: Typographia de B. de Mattos, 1867/68), vol. 3, pp. 197-224; Miguel-Pereira, *A vida de Gonçalves Dias*, pp. 309-10.

72. Miguel-Pereira, *A vida de Gonçalves Dias*, p. 312.

73. Ibid.

74. Bandeira, in Gonçalves Dias, *Poesia Completa e Prosa*, p. 22.

75. Gonçalves Dias, *Obras Posthumas*, vol. 3, p. 17.

76. Ibid., p. 81.

77. Ibid., pp. 93-94.

78. Graham, *Patronage and Politics*, p. 21.

79. Antônio Gonçalves Dias, *Brazil e Oceania: estudo ethnographico* (Rio de Janeiro: Felix Ferreira, 1879), p. 16.

80. Ibid., p. 255.

81. Ibid., p. 255.

82. Gonçalves Dias, *Poesia completa e prosa escolhida*, p. 106. Unless indicated otherwise, all subsequent citations are from this edition.

83. Miguel-Pereira, *A vida de Gonçalves Dias*, pp. 55-56.

84. Ibid., p. 215.

85. Barbara Weinstein, *The Amazon Rubber Boom: 1850-1920* (Stanford, Calif.: Stanford University Press, 1983), pp. 37-38.

86. "The Final Attack on the Waimiri and Atroari," *Survival International Review* 7, nos. 3-4 (Autumn/Winter 1982), p. 40.

87. Bandeira, "Gonçalves Dias: Esboço biográfico," p. 755.

88. José Honório Rodrigues, *Independência: Revolução e Contra-revolução*, 4 vols. (Rio de Janeiro: Francisco Alves, 1975), vol. 2, p. 109.

89. Miguel-Pereira, *A vida de Gonçalves Dias*, p. 272.

90. Bandeira, "Gonçalves Dias: Esboço biográfico," p. 751.

91. Ibid., p. 788.

92. José Guilherme Merquior, *De Anchieta a Euclides: breve história da literatura brasileira—1* (Rio de Janeiro: José Olympio, 1977), p. 67.

93. Candido, *Formação da literatura brasileira*, vol. 2, pp. 83-84.

94. Gonçalves Dias, *Brasil e Oceania*, p. 193.

95. Bandeira, "A poética de Gonçalves Dias," *Poesia e Prosa*, vol. 2, pp. 788 ff.

3

Slaves and Allies: The Conservative Mythology of Integration

THE POLITICS OF CONCILIATION AND INDIGENIST POLICY IN THE SECOND REIGN

Teixeira e Sousa's *The Three Days of a Marriage* and the poetry of Gonçalves Dias were a far cry from the first Indianists' celebratory nationalism, with its mythology of shared ancestral origins and anticolonial struggle. Testifying instead to a divided, prejudice-ridden society haunted by the exiled "tribes" of landless, powerless freemen, these texts also bore little relation to the kind of Indianism that emerged in the mid-1850s: the conservative Romantic mythology of Indian-white relations based on miscegenation, self-sacrifice, and conciliation.

The radical thematic and ideological shift that occurred at this stage of the Indianist movement marked a new political atmosphere that provided the conditions for the most stable and prosperous years of the Empire. In her study of the historian, novelist, and Indianist playwright Joaquim Manuel de Macedo, Tania Rebelo Costa Serra describes the decade following 1851 (the year in which Gonçalves Dias published his *Últimos Cantos*) as one in which the Brazilian urban middle class reached full maturity, confident in its role alongside the coffee-growing elite in the construction of the "country of the future." If, in the words of historian Capistrano de Abreu, this decade represented the "apogee of Imperial brilliance,"[1] for Serra the cultural and ideological expression of that atmosphere, its bourgeois consciousness, owed a good deal to the ethical model provided by Macedo's writing: "the 'ethos of the bon sauvage,' of the man who is pure and good, of the good Catholic, of disinterested love."[2] In referring to this "ethos of the bon sauvage," Serra does not seem to have Macedo's Indianist drama *Cobé* (1854) specifically in mind, and she does not examine the text in any detail. However, as we shall see later, Cobé's selfless, self-sacrificing Indian corresponds very closely to that ethical model, and as such it paved the way for the more famous indigenous heroes of José de Alencar's novels *O Guarani* (The Guarani Indian, 1857) and *Iracema* (1865).

Alencar took upon himself the task of elaborating, in its most sophisticated and fully developed form to date, a foundational mythology that could "reconcile" the Romantic, liberal values personified by the figure of Natural Man with the interests of the postcolonial Imperial state at this time of optimism and stability. Moreover, in the wake of a reform that had abolished the traffic in slaves from Africa, while still denying the existing slaves their freedom, Alencar's Indianist mythology of voluntary servitude and self-sacrifice offered the middle-class reading public what it needed—an ethical rationalization of the system that was to underpin its well-being for another forty years or so.

That well-being depended, as José Honório Rodrigues has described, on the confidence of the ruling, landowning elite in its hegemony for the foreseeable future, neutralizing the threat posed by the more radical reformist pressures that had emerged during the Regency:

Conciliation and non-conciliation, a bloody and bloodless history alternate in Brazil's historical process, but it was from 1849 onwards that a formula was sought to avoid the liberals, the conservatives' natural allies, participating in the radical *mestiço* currents and threatening, through their more powerful and intelligent collaboration, the economic power of the landowning class; the latter required peace and order to carry out its business.[3]

Thus, by the middle of the century, the violent ideological and civil conflicts that had characterized the first three decades of independence and that informed the Indianist writing of that period were provisionally resolved by a combination of carrot and stick, with the collusion of rival political interests in a kind of pact. On one hand, the early majority of the adolescent Pedro II followed up the military repression of the rebellions unleashed under the Regency by imposing a strict return to centralized rule. At the same time the erstwhile opponents of such measures were co-opted into the new dispensation by the granting of certain significant, but nevertheless only partial, concessions to liberal reformism, bolstered by a systematic policy of compromise between the two parliamentary parties. As José Murilo de Carvalho explains, the political task of the so-called *regresso* or return of the Imperial order

consisted of devolving to the central government the powers it had lost with the decentralizing legislation of the Regency, particularly with the Additional Act of 1834 and with the 1832 Code of Criminal Process. In 1840 the Additional Act was interpreted, in 1841 the Code was reformed. With this, the state assemblies ceased to have jurisdiction over functionaries of the central government; the entire staff of the justice system and the police came under the control of the Minister of Justice; the only elected judge, the justice of the peace, lost a good proportion of his powers to the chiefs and deputy-chiefs of police. The Minister of Justice acquired the power to appoint and dismiss, by direct or indirect means, from the judge of appeal right down to the prison warder. With the majority [of Pedro II] in 1840, the Moderating Power also became fully functional again and the Counsel of State, extinguished by the Additional Act, was re-established.[4]

The liberals who initially revolted against these laws in 1842,

on returning to power in 1844, maintained a purely rhetorical opposition to them, for they had realized their usefulness for the exercise of power. During four years in power they did not alter at all the scheme of the *regresso*. Their return to power had also removed from them the fear of a conservative dictatorship and had revealed the important role of the Crown in avoiding the monopoly of power by factions. The only unconvinced faction was that of the Liberals of Pernambuco which revolted in 1848. Its defeat signified the end of the process of acceptance of parliamentary monarchy by the rural elites. An acceptance that was problematic but provided the system with its basic legitimacy.[5]

Between 1853 and 1857 this politics of consensus was formalized under the "Conciliation" government of the marquis of Paraná. For its advocates, Conciliation signified the renunciation by both Conservative and Liberal Parties of their narrow partisan and personal antagonisms, the abandonment of nonconsultative, coercive methods of government and decision making, and a willingness to consider new ideas, all for the sake of the "national good":

Conciliation was meant to be the "forgetting of all disagreements and grievances," a truce, a neutral politics, devoid of passion, that would reestablish the normality of the constitutional regime through the cooperation of all those who understood that "above the cause of parties was the cause of Brazil."[6]

The policy was defended in the Chamber of Deputies by Nabuco de Araújo, in the press by Sales Torres Homem, and in the army by the duque de Caxias, who had directed the "pacification" of the provincial revolts in the early 1840s, so paving the way for this new era of "peace and cooperation." Figures such as Caxias represented the principle of a moderating influence, taming and subduing the country's revolutionary forces in order to promote a "one Nation" ethos, the notion that "the Brazilian on the opposite side is a Brazilian too, and must not be excluded, but incorporated."[7]

At the other end of the political spectrum, for Nabuco, the objective of a government of conciliation was to harness certain extreme, intolerant elements within the Brazilian establishment, those whose wealth, property, and position gave them a special interest in the institutions of authority. These elements were not to be challenged or provoked but groomed, tempered, and turned to the public good.[8] Even a conservative opponent of conciliation, such as Justiniano José da Rocha, shared this view that some form of compromise between the radical, extreme forces at either end of the political spectrum was indispensable and urgent if revolution were to be avoided. In his 1855 political pamphlet *Ação; Reação; Transação*, he wrote:

If, however, the opportunity is missed; if the years from 1855 to 1856 are as fruitless for the great cause of transaction as were the three years that preceded them; if power so misunderstands its duty to the fatherland that it continues to magnify still further its gains, then . . . Ah! who knows whether the defenders of the national cause, the cause of liberty and order, may not have to go to its defense against the excesses of a new democratic reaction at the extreme limits of social order, may not have to defend it, not against those who wished for the suppression of the senate, the ruin of essential institutions, but against those who assaulted the entire political edifice, and the entire social edifice, against those who want a constituent assembly![9]

The new, official indigenist policy of the Second Reign was a typical expression of this political atmosphere, in which a liberal language of tolerance and pluralism claimed to incorporate and reconcile antagonistic interests, while in reality speaking for the maintenance of a conservative status quo, ensuring that any challenge to the power and authority of the traditional *latifundiários* was postponed indefinitely.

The campaign for a humane Indian policy that had been pursued unsuccessfully during the First Reign by José Bonifácio and Toledo Rendon was resumed after the majority of Pedro II in 1840, with the aim of reinstituting and consolidating the reforms that had been introduced in 1831 during the Regency. Gonçalves Dias was not alone in calling for a decisive repudiation of the colonial policy of extermination and enslavement carried out under João VI and continued under Pedro I and for the implementation of a liberal project of social and economic integration. In 1845 José Joaquim Machado de Oliveira wrote a report for the Historical and Geographical Institute on the mission villages of São Paulo, condemning "the idée fixe of exterminating, butchering and despoiling men and objects." Speaking of that legacy of colonial rule, Machado de Oliveira's report argued the following:

In vain has one sought to legitimate by these results the great offense of Indian slavery: neither those results nor the impotent and indeterminate Portuguese legislation concerning the Indians of Brazil have been able to justify to civilized Europe, in the face of common sense, the barbarism and inhumanity of the Portuguese government, whether in authorizing and tolerating that slavery, or in disregarding the preponderance and energy that ought to have been employed in order that those legislative measures should have in their execution the efficacy attributed to them.[10]

In the same year a new regulation was issued, that officially replaced the repressive indigenist policy of Just War with a more conciliatory program of integration. Manuela Carneiro da Cunha describes this Regulamento das Missões as the only general indigenist document of the Empire: "More an administrative document than a political plan, . . . it prolongs the system of village settlements and understands it explicitly as a transition towards the complete assimilation of the Indians."[11] Certain guarantees were now offered to those Indians who had survived extermination, and administration of the mission villages was handed over to Italian Capuchin friars. Equally, if not more significant, was the 1850 Lei de Terras (Land Law), which effectively consolidated the power of the *latifundiários*, guaranteeing them access to this new pool of labor. Along with smallholders and *sertanejos* (backwoodsmen), the Indians could now be evicted from their traditional lands and moved to areas where they would be more closely subject to economic and social control.

These changes in agrarian legislation had important links with another concession to the pressures for liberal reform. In 1850 the Queiróz Law was passed, banning the traffic in slaves from Africa, and, although the internal slave trade continued alive and well, this advance went some way toward neutralizing abolitionist opinion and toward preserving Brazil's moral image abroad. The new indigenist policy was, in part, a response to the increased demand for labor that occurred in certain areas and was anticipated elsewhere, as a result of the abolition of the African slave traffic. Carlos Moreira describes the relationship between tribal integration and the slave economy during Empire as follows:

The rural status of the Indian, and his acceptance of a labor regime in conditions of servitude preserved without any essential modifications in these areas during the entire course of the century, made him the most fitting solution to the chronic shortage of manpower in those areas. All efforts to integrate the Indian into national society, accompanied by the inevitable speeches and projects regarding the redemption of the forest dweller from his condition of savagery and misery, were integrally subordinated to the objective of his likely use as docile and cheap labour.[12]

Nevertheless, the 1845 Regulamento and the Land Law of 1850 were not welcomed by all; the policy of replacing black with Indian labor was opposed by Senator Vergueiro and other powerful farmers whose capital was invested in slaves or who were committed to colonization projects using European immigrants. One defender of such interests was the historian Francisco Adolfo de Varnhagen; his "Memorial Orgânico" (Organic Petition) launched a polemic whose parallels and connections with the contemporary literary debate concerning the Indianist movement have not previously been recognized, even though, as we shall now see, the participants in both cases were prominent intellectuals and writers, many of them Indianists.

One of the chief vehicles for liberal views on abolition and indigenist policy was the artistic, scientific, and literary review *Guanabara*, edited by Porto Alegre, Gonçalves Dias, and Joaquim Manuel de Macedo during the years 1849-55. Besides these political contributions, *Guanabara* published historical and social commentary, such as Gonçalves Dias's "Reflexões sobre os Anais Históricos do Maranhão" and his *Meditação*, as well as literary material of an Indianist nature—Macedo's drama *Cobé* and a short story, "Aricó e Caocochee ou Uma voz no deserto" (Aricó and Caocochee or A Voice in the Desert), by João Henrique Helliot.

In the light of the journal's predominantly liberal character, it is not difficult to understand the storm caused by Varnhagen's "Organic Petition" when it appeared in *Guanabara* in 1851. Flying in the face of the prevailing thinking, Varnhagen proposed a colonization program for the interior that would give considerable advantages to the European immigrant while excluding both the African and Indian from any participation in its realization or benefits. The Indian was considered a physical obstacle to this development strategy and to the progress of civilization under Empire; a nomadic invader, he had neither a right to possession of the land he occupied nor the moral or intellectual capacity to govern himself. Furthermore, as "a people alien to the social pact," an outlaw and barbarian, the Indian was a legitimate target of the Aristotelian principle of "just conquest," for which purpose the *bandeiras* and the legislation of 1798 might be revived. Quoting Senator Vergueiro, Varnhagen offered a definition of the civil status of the Indian that, although not institutionalized in his own time, closely anticipated the indigenist legislation of the post-1964 military regime:

The Indian race does not have the necessary capacity to rule itself. Either because their nature has less aptitude for civilization, or because they are still far from this, what I observe is that the grandchildren and great-grandchildren of the villagized Indians do not make anything of themselves, they do not progress at all. As a consequence, therefore, of this incapacity or difficulty in reaching civilization, there results the need for tutelage: they cannot govern themselves, they are not equal to this, they cannot be independent, and in their villages that tutelage was to be found in their directors . . .

But, if we consider them to be alien to the social pact, if we regard them as a foreign nation that is troublesome and harmful to us, we have every right to conquer them, and there is no more just right of conquest than that of civilization over barbarism. "A barbaric people that does not recognize the duties of humanity and the laws of war," says the famous American jurist Bello, "must be treated as an enemy of human kind."[13]

One of the first published responses to these statements was the article "Civilização dos Indígenas" (Civilizing the Indians, 1852) by Manuel Antônio de Almeida, whose highly popular novel *Memórias de um Sargento de Milícias* (Memoirs of a Militia Sergeant) began to appear in serialized installments in the *Correio Mercantil* in the same year.[14] Basing his reply on liberal, humanitarian principles and likening Varnhagen to European "barbarians" such as the colonial governor Mem de Sá, "the ravager of the Tamoios," Almeida exposed the concept of tutelage as a new form of slavery and the arguments on Just War as a pretext for a rapacious neocolonialism.[15] Also in 1852 the influential historian, critic, novelist, playwright, and poet Joaquim Norberto de Sousa Silva wrote his "Historical and Documented Memoir on the Indian Villages of the Province of Rio de Janeiro," winning the Imperial Prize with its praise of the *aldeia* mission system and its attack on coercive colonial practices:

One day the times to come will ask America about her original forests, her original inhabitants, and how will she reply?

Here are the earth and sky, as for the rest . . . ask the hunger, the plagues and the slavery brought from Europe by the peoples who came after them to these parts; ask the treefeller's ax and the incendiary torch that have leveled and reduced to ashes the produce of the seeds that the earth carried within its fertile bosom, that germinated to the sound of God's voice, that flourished and thrived through the rolling of centuries and centuries![16]

Fueling the debate, the second volume of *Guanabara* (1854) carried an article by Henrique de Beaurepaire Rohan entitled "Considerações acerca da conquista, catechese e civilisação dos selvagens no Brasil" (Considerations on the Conquest, Conversion and Civilization of the Savages in Brazil). Rohan refuted from firsthand experience Varnhagen's claim that the Indians had nothing to contribute to Imperial society and voiced his aversion to the methods of the Capuchin missionaries, the so-called *barbadinhos*:

[A]nyone, like myself, who has observed them in their savage dwellings, and has had occasion to study their aptitude for industry, their peaceful nature and their natural propensity for social life, will recognize for sure their inestimable importance for the future aggrandizement of Brazil. Meanwhile, our government considers that it is doing much in their favor, when it presents them with a *barbadinho*! For his part, it is the *barbadinho's* understanding that he is thoroughly fulfilling his mission by preaching fasting and chastity to these people! These are facts that would have made me laugh a thousand times, if I had not been overwhelmed by the grievous sense of my country's miseries![17]

Rohan even went so far as to condemn the liberal Regulamento of 1845 as a worthless sham, "more an administrative fiction than a true means of making effective the thinking that dictated it. It is eight years since it was published, without, to this day, it having improved in a single respect the lot of the savages."[18]

The debate was given a fresh impulse when Varnhagen published his highly acclaimed *História Geral do Brasil* (1854), with its Preface "Os Indios perante a Nacionalidade Brasileira" (The Indians in the Face of Brazilian Nationality). Here, accompanying an unashamedly contemptuous account of tribal culture, he presented a baldly anti-Rousseauian view of the Indian: "Unfortunately, the profound study of human barbarism, in all countries, proves that, without the ties of laws and religion, the sad mortal tends so much towards savagery, that he is almost metamorphosed into a wild beast."[19] Conquest, meanwhile, was a just retribution for the Tupi Indians' own expulsion of the previous inhabitants of the Atlantic coast, the Tapuias: "The day of expiation had to come to them in their turn. It was brought by discovery and colonization, carried out by Christian Europe."[20]

Early in his career, paradoxically, Varnhagen had strengthened his nationalist credentials by associating himself with figures such as Ferdinand Denis and the eminent explorers Humboldt, Von Martius, and Prince Maximilian von Neuwied, who had recommended him to the Emperor, Pedro II. On presenting a letter from Von Martius to the Historical and Geographical Institute, he had "taken the opportunity to speak in defense of the civilization of our Indians, who in his opinion were in danger of extinction."[21] As we saw in the previous chapter, in 1845 he also published an academic edition of the eighteenth-century Indianist epics *O Uraguay* and *Caramuru*. For José Honório Rodrigues, Varnhagen, the son of an immigrant German family, was representative of a neocolonialist perspective influenced by the new current of European racist thinking. It was a perspective that could quite happily maintain a view of tribal society as biologically and culturally degenerate, alongside an idealized, folkloric image of the Indian "para inglês ver," for external consumption.[22] Thus, Varnhagen was able to make his own, idiosyncratic contribution to the literary Indianist movement without compromising his reactionary position with regard to state indigenist policy.

By way of illustration, an 1853 anthology of Brazilian poetry included Varnhagen's popularized version of the Caramuru story, which was republished separately for wider consumption in 1859 and 1861 in "Liliput" format, measuring a couple of inches square. In Varnhagen's comic ballad account of the legend, the heroic figure of the mythical founding colonist, Diogo Álvares, is drastically diminished to the stature of a common, feckless sailor who deserts his ship and is forced to shelter behind the formidable authority of his Indian wife, Paraguaçu.[23] This lampoon of the ancestral symbol of pioneering colonialism may well have been linked to a campaign pursued by members of the Historical and Geographical Institute, Varnhagen among them, to denigrate the monarchist Restoration movement associated with the newspaper *Caramuru* and the "Patriarch of Independence," José Bonifácio.[24]

Varnhagen's other Indianist work, *Sumé, Lenda Mytho-Religiosa Americana* (Sumé, American Mytho-Religious Legend, 1855), was a rather more serious attempt to defend his ideas concerning Just War through a reinterpretation of the legend of Sumé, the evangelist saint who attempts in vain to bring the gospel to the Indians. After being received with ridicule and hostility by the lawless, debauched tribes of the Caribbean and Maranhão, Sumé eventually encounters a people, led by the chief Serigy, that seems to respect the God-given principles of legality, authority, and social hierarchy:

And Sumé, seeing that these peoples punished rebellion, judged them to be respectful of the institutions of civil society, and thought that they would listen to him.

For civil society cannot subsist without the idea of punishment.

For the multitudes who hold no fear become unruly and barbarously arrogant.

And sometimes the predominance of honest reason, which is the supreme law, constant, immutable and eternal for men, can only be achieved by means of force . . .

Providence, which subjected animals to man, made men subject to each other, since he created them physically and intellectually unequal.

And this inequality, far from being harmful to mankind, is an indispensable condition for life and the preservation of the social body.

And equality among men, as some would understand it, without mature examination, is a veritable chimera, which you will only find in the silence of the tombs.[25]

However, having been helped to victory by Sumé, Serigy and his tribespeople thanklessly revert to their former ways, leaving the prophet to lament the generations of apocalyptic destruction that must ensue, culminating in their annihilation or assimilation at the hands of a superior race:

Then the people fled like madmen, and the tribes scattered as nomads, and waged war on each other and had no territory for a homeland, and the frontiers of their nations extended no further than the range of their bows and arrows and they exterminated each other or at least were all weakened.

And sitting on a granite rock Sumé mourned the fate of the condemned people, which must perish or melt into another people through the presence of some conqueror stronger in spirit and heart and beloved by the Lord.[26]

This apocalyptic defense of Conquest and Just War, as necessary steps in the working out of God's will for his chosen people, was strongly influenced by the ideas of Joseph de Maistre, who is cited in Varnhagen's introduction to the *História Geral*. One of the most vehemently reactionary opponents of the Enlightenment and of the French Revolution, de Maistre had ridiculed, in his *Study of Sovereignty*, Rousseau's comparison between the "natural" and "social" states of man; no such distinction could be drawn, argued de Maistre, since all of existence was God's creation and therefore natural, while primitive tribal man, in the infancy of his development towards wholeness, could not yet be considered a full and proper expression of this providential Nature. In the *Seventh St. Petersburg Dialogue*, meanwhile, de Maistre glorified the violence of war as a cathartic, self-consuming process of sacrifice fulfilling God's will for the destruction of evil:

Thus is worked out, from maggots up to man, the universal law of the violent destruction of living beings. The whole earth, continually steeped in blood, is nothing but an immense altar on which every living thing must be sacrificed without end, without restraint, without respite until the consummation of the world, the extinction of evil, the death of death.[27]

Between these two positions, that is to say, Varnhagen's advocacy of Just War and extermination for social outlaws and barbarians, and the liberal pro-Indianism of Gonçalves Dias, Almeida, Sousa Silva, and Rohan, there was nonetheless a third option. Interestingly enough, one of the most vigorous responses to Varnhagen's views came from the historian João Francisco Lisboa, himself a critic of the literary Indianist movement. Writing under the pseudonym of Timon, he first advanced an evaluation of tribal culture that seems to differ little from that of Varnhagen:

Timon concludes, in view of so many facts attested to by writers of such number and authority, that our ancient savages were not only an uncouth, ferocious, cruel and bloodthirsty people, but also indolent, inert, profoundly corrupt, given to drunkenness and dissipation, and abandoned in the midst of that coarse barbarity to all the vices and perversions of the most refined Tiberian civilization.[28]

Indeed, Lisboa objected to the Indianists' idealization of tribal culture, their rehabilitation of the Indian as the cornerstone of Brazilian nationality to the detriment of the other elements that had contributed to colonization:

Someone proposes that at official acts and in Parliament only the General or Tupi language should be used; someone else regrets, given our towns and villages are known by Portuguese or saints' names, that they are not henceforward renamed, on the principle of rehabilitation, with Tupinambá terms or words; another declares that these fine, venerable ancestors lived here happily and peacefully until the time of conquest, and that the time has now come to make a grand and solemn reparation for its iniquities. Now, if all this does not constitute a school organized for the complete rehabilitation of the defeated races—the near extinct races, we should say—of ancient savages, it does at least reveal a tendency and formal reaction, as exaggerated as it is indiscreet, against the formerly prevailing ideas.[29]

But if he mocked the Indianists' proposals and their literary expression, as, for example, in the poetry of Gonçalves Dias's *Cantos*, he nevertheless took seriously the poet's denunciation of colonial abuses as a valuable opening for serious discussion of the separate issue of Indian rights:

> But it is time for us to move on to the resolution of other matters. Were the aborigines owners of the lands on which they trod, and did they have an exclusive right to their possession, repelling the European invaders? And was it in reality a misfortune for these regions that in the struggle that was waged victory should be declared by the crossbow and the sword against the arrow and club?[30]

It was time, then, to question Varnhagen's simplistic analysis of the available alternatives—Civilization or Barbarism:

> Could Brazil really not become civilized without the slavery of the Indians, achieved by force and war? Are the gentle, persuasive methods of catechesis really vain and illusory, mere empty-headed fantasy? Or put another way, and generalizing these ideas, are coercion and terror, slavery and war the great and true instruments of civilization and religious propaganda?[31]

Lisboa's solution to the problem, the policy of integration, typified the spirit of ideological and political accommodation that was expressed in the politics of Conciliation and that lay at the heart of the Romantic Indianist movement itself. It hinged on the following quotation from the French historian and political theorist Alexis de Tocqueville, who, in his *Democracy in America*, had discussed the related questions of black slavery and the liberty of the Indian. For Tocqueville and Lisboa, slavery clearly deprived the African of a fundamental human right: the individual's possession of his or her own person. Yet the Indian, despite an appearance of freedom, also remained deprived of the genuine condition of liberty so long as he or she refused to acknowledge the social and economic obligations of law and labor, which are the mark of civilization:

> The Europeans never could modify entirely the character of the Indians; and while they had the power to destroy them, they never had the power to police or subjugate them. The Negro is located at the extreme bounds of slavery, the Indian at the bounds of liberty. And to be sure, slavery produces results in the former that are no more disastrous than those produced by independence in the latter.
> The Negro has lost his very ownership of his person, and could scarcely dispose of his own existence without committing a kind of theft against his master.
> The Indian is master of himself provided he is capable of working. It can be said that he has never known the authority of the family. His will has never bowed to the will of any of his fellow-men; and no one has ever been able to teach him to distinguish reasoned, voluntary obedience from shameful subjugation. He does not even recognize the name of—law—, and in his understanding liberty is an exemption from all social ties. He is happy in this barbarous independence, and would rather perish, than sacrifice the slightest part of it. Civilization will be able to do little or nothing with a man of this temperament.[32]

Lisboa's analysis of the prospects for the civilization of the Indian was rather more optimistic than this. It did depend, though, on Tocqueville's definition of liberty as the social realization of the individual through the exercise of legal responsibilities and through the activity of labor. Integration, as well as ensuring the peaceful coexistence of Indian and colonist to their mutual benefit, would reconcile these liberal principles with the economic aspirations of those wishing to open up the Brazilian interior to more intensive agricultural development:

> Without doubt, however barbarous they were, the Indians had a right to their own preservation, by means of the gifts provided by the land, whether spontaneously or solicited through labor. But that right could be reconciled, and made even fuller, more real and effective, with the simultaneous occupation of the Europeans; for civilization, as well as improving the moral condition of the savages, should at the same time make the pleasures and conveniences of life easier for them. The iniquity, then, consisted, not in the occupation of an empty and uncultivated land, but in the abuse of the oppression and harassment inflicted on the wandering hordes.[33]

There is no better illustration of this policy in action and of how it operated through the kind of political accommodation described earlier by Murilo de Carvalho than the case of the entrepreneur Teófilo Ottoni and the Indians of the Mucuri Valley. Ottoni was secretary of the Republican United Friends' Club, the revolutionary liberal movement centered in Minas Gerais that had been crucial to the abdication of Pedro I. Following the split between the radical "exaltados" or "luzias" and the moderates, a consequence of the frustration of the other constitutional reforms demanded by the party, he attempted to reunite the two wings, leading the campaign for the Additional Act. This was passed in 1834, abolishing the moderating power of the monarchy and the upper house, granting autonomy to the provinces, and creating a federation. After the conservative reaction of 1840 and the emasculation of the act by means of the "law of interpretation," there was a rebellion in Minas, during which Ottoni was arrested. Thereafter,he was known nationally as a prominent *luzia*, returning to parliament in 1845 to take a subdued part in the liberal/monarchist coalition until Paraná's government of Conciliation was installed in the 1850s.

For the next twelve years Ottoni turned to business and to a radical scheme to develop communications links between the Minas interior and the northeastern coast of the province. In 1847 his family textiles firm, Ottoni e Cia., presented to the government its "Conditions for the Incorporation of a Company for Trade and Navigation of the River Mucuri, which will be called the Companhia do Mucuri." The legalization of the company brought with it considerable privileges, tax exemptions, and exclusive rights; for Ottoni's biographer and chief apologist, this program of colonization, navigation, and road building represented an entrepreneurial, capitalist challenge to the conservative interests of the resident landowning oligarchies:

> The Companhia do Mucuri was a retort to the sugar-mill owners. With its vast industrial platform—colonization, navigation, roads—it was certainly the dynamic, democratic economy, free and joyous, in opposition to the stagnant landowning and slaveowning aristocracy.[34]

However, the Mucuri Valley was also the homeland of the Giporoks and other groups of Indians, remnants of the Botocudos, who had been the victim of systematic campaigns of extermination under Dom João VI. Ottoni's first observations of these tribes displayed a degree of humanitarian, albeit highly paternalistic, outrage and compassion that was worthy of the early Indianists such as Gonçalves Dias:

It pains me in my soul to have to express to you, Sirs, my conviction that the poor savages have not found here that disinterested and noble protection that is their right. I was forced to stifle my feelings of hatred, which are excused by the deaths of the Viola family, the only attack committed many years ago by the Indians in this municipality, and which is mitigated by various circumstances, especially by the consideration that the Giporok chief, when he committed that act of violence, was trying to free his children, who were held in slavery. And I cannot but bring to your attention that a vile traffic has been carried out with the children of the savages, as is public knowledge here. I have written to the Magistrate of this district to send forces to the area, not so much to defend the inhabitants, but to protect the poor Indians, who, according to the eloquent expression they themselves use, are as tame as turtles.[35]

Nevertheless, by 1852, when Ottoni announced, "Aqui farei a minha Filadélfia!" (Here I shall build my Philadelphia!) on the site where a town would later be named after him, the project had experienced the first attacks by the Botocudo communities on whose lands it had encroached. These attacks, combined with several severe outbreaks of malaria, led to mass desertions on the part of his workers. Ottoni's response to this crisis demonstrates the remarkable facility with which liberal thinking could draw a qualitative moral distinction between slavery and a comparably exploitative system of wage labor. He converted a number of friendly Indians from the locality and employed them, rather unsuccessfully, on one of his road-building projects. Pragmatism and expediency, as Pinheiro Chagas is lamely forced to admit, could work wonders with unprofitable political principles:

And he who did not want slaves working for the Companhia do Mucuri, finds himself forced by the lack of manpower to engage them, saying melancholically, in his report of 1853: "there is no philosophy to rival experience!"[36]

Ottoni soon found other, more persuasive arguments within his liberal reasoning, though, with which to rationalize this exploitation of indigenous labor. The Companhia do Mucuri now acquired a missionary role of "rehabilitation" through the medium of the work ethic; the Indians' integration into the "free" labor regime of capitalism was to lead to their full self-realization as human beings awakened to the "natural" concepts of individual enterprise and private property:

I am convinced of the advantages of a new plan of conversion, which I strongly wish to see attempted under conscientious leadership. The means of villagizing the Indians used up to now, consists of obliging them to work together, under the administration of directors, who are the true owners of all that the labor of the settled Indians produces.

Since the time of the Jesuits, this method has had as its sole result to keep the Indians peaceful and obedient in the settlement, serving as an instrument for the prosperity and undeserved profits of the catechists, without the intelligence of those catechized progressing in the slightest. I have sought to advance along a different path in the Mucuri. Since family ties are so strong among the Nak-Nanuks, I have attempted, out of that love of family, to make the sense of property blossom amongst them, advising them to establish themselves on the soil, and to cultivate it to their own benefit.[37]

The company's "protection" of the Indians, Ottoni argued, thus guaranteed their basic human rights to liberty, security, property, and freedom from oppression: "Democracy had imbued the Mucuri with its substance. It had ended the exploitation of man by man. It had extinguished the slave traffic. It had brought dignity to the family. It had established the right of the Indian over the land. It had defended his liberty and increased his self-worth as a human being, through free and remunerated work."[38]

Ottoni reported these achievements in his "Notice about the Savages of the Mucuri" of 1858, which had been requested by Joaquim Manuel de Macedo as material for his own "Memoir" to the Brazilian Historical and Geographical Institute. Ottoni invoked as his inspiration the example of the North American occupation of Pennsylvania. Indeed, the legal agreements by which the Nak-Nanuks "freely" surrendered their title over ancient tribal lands to the Companhia do Mucuri closely resemble those that had arbitrarily dispossessed the North American Indians of their territories earlier in the century: "The lands are divided up with a great spirit of justice. Those which, by common agreement, fall to the Indians, have their ownership duly registered, which guarantees them sure rights."[39]

This was the reality that lay behind Ottoni's liberal mission of integration, then: the seizure of Indian lands and the destruction of the collective subsistence economy of tribal culture so as to exploit the Indian within a capitalist framework of wage labor. This reality has enabled a more recent commentator to attack the hypocrisy of Ottoni's arguments, if from a more reactionary position as a nostalgic monarchist. As Leônidas Lorentz states, the liberal Ottoni was a slave owner by his own admission; not only did the company have at its disposal 100 black slaves, but Indian slaves were also numbered among its assets in its report to the shareholders. Teófilo's brother, Augusto Benedito, was "Director of the Indians of the Mucuri and Todos os Santos," with control over a further 100 Indians.[40] As Pinheiro Chagas is forced to confirm, the Indians were effectively abandoned after the collapse of the company. They were not given the lands or tools they had been promised, and they were deprived of their fishing and hunting grounds and were consequently forced to work as virtual slave laborers, while Ottoni and his family enriched themselves as newfound *latifundiários*.[41]

Ottoni's practical experiments with the Nak-Nanuks, like Lisboa's theoretical contribution to the indigenist debate, represented the liberal search for an equilibrium between the two views that had been polarized by Varnhagen's provocative statements: on the one hand, the Rousseauian libertarian ideal (found reflected in the poetry of Gonçalves Dias) of the Indian tribe as a roaming collective of autonomous, self-sufficient individuals exempt from the obligations of a modern state and society; and, on the other hand, Varnhagen's reactionary, inverted reading of that natural state, in terms of the lawless freedom of the Indian as outlaw and barbarian, alien to the social pact and therefore needing to be subjugated to the repressive, but legitimate, rule of civilized government. If, as Tocqueville had put it, the absolute freedom of the Indian was as abominable as the absolute bondage of the slave, then Lisboa's new interpretation of the integrationist model represented the liberal solution to that dilemma, a form of compromise or social contract between the interests of sovereign liberty and the obligations of the civilized state. In its turn, this solution was also an expression of the ideological equation that underpinned the politics of Conciliation at the height of Second Reign: the accommodation of liberal principles to the interests of slave owning and latifundist power. That same accommodation, as we shall now see, lay at the heart of the new narrative of Indian-white relations that emerged within the literary Indianist movement, as it moved into its next phase.

THE IDEAL INDIAN SLAVE

The central fictional offspring of this conservative Indianist mythology of conciliation was a new heroic figure, the Indian who, while jealously defending his right to move freely within the natural environment of the forest, at the same time voluntarily and loyally engaged his special powers in the service of the colonial community and in opposition to those forces threatening its survival from within and without. Alencar's Guarani warrior, Peri, was the ideal, voluntary "slave" who successfully reconciled the liberal principle of individual autonomy, which was so central to the first, radical, postindependence phase of the Indianist movement, with the notion of social responsibility and the obligation to defend the state from revolution.

As we have seen, far from occupying a purely imaginary sphere of literary invention removed from the practical social and political concerns of Imperial life, the Indian "question" had been explicitly linked to the issue of black slavery consistently since independence: in the legislative proposals of José Bonifácio, in the debates about the labor regime of the Imperial economy, in Gonçalves Dias's critique of the social iniquities underlying the prosperity of the Empire, and in João Francisco Lisboa's response to Varnhagen's regressive interpretation of official indigenist policy. Although less overt in its articulation of these parallel concerns, Alencar's writing between 1856 and 1865, in particular the Indianist novels and "abolitionist" plays, offered the most complex artistic representation of the role of the colored non-European, both Indian and African, in the postcolonial Brazilian family. As such, these works should be seen collectively as the mature culmination of the Imperial intelligentsia's efforts to develop an imaginary model of social and political integration for the nation, a mythology of multiracial heroism, self-sacrifice, and reconciliation that could promise the survival of the Empire in essentially unaltered form for the foreseeable future. Alencar was not, however, the first writer to envisage a role for the Indian as a self-sacrificing ally of the postcolonial community; there was a more tragic precedent to Peri's loyal Indian "slave," and that was Joaquim Manuel de Macedo's stage hero, Cobé.

Macedo had achieved literary fame in 1844 with his instantly successful novel *A Moreninha*, which sustained his reputation as Brazil's leading writer of fiction until the appearance of Alencar. Besides his other literary activities as poet, playwright, and critic and his career as a teacher of history in the Colégio Pedro II and for the Emperor's children, he wrote for liberal newspapers and journals such as *A Nação* and *Guanabara* and represented the party in the provincial and federal congresses during much of the Second Reign. Yet, as José Honório Rodrigues argues, like many others of his generation, "whether as a journalist, or as a congressman, Macedo is formally a liberal, but a conservative in substance."[42] His was an extremely conservative liberalism, a heresy practiced by the liberal majority that defended black slavery, that had distanced itself from the more radical liberalism of 1817, 1824, and 1848-49.

Indeed, Macedo's late abolitionist work, the three propagandistic novellas of *As Vítimas Algozes* (The Victim-Executioners, 1869), demonstrates very clearly that peculiar combination of political reformism and social and economic conservatism that characterized Brazilian liberalism during most of the Empire. Rather than denouncing the inhumanity and cruelty of slavery for its victims, these didactic morality tales served as warnings to the unwary or negligent plantation owner to guard against the "enemy within." While the slaves' treachery, corruption, and bestiality were formally attributed to the institution that has created them, Macedo's caricature of these "victim-executioners" was so unsparing that the liberal notion of their incorporation into a common brotherhood of man or as responsible citizens following emancipation is barely imaginable.[43]

By contrast, in Macedo's Indianist drama *Cobé*, the redemption of the (Indian) slave and the community that has imprisoned him is made possible through a heroic act of self-sacrifice. Cobé's martyrdom could be interpreted simply from the perspective of a postindependence historical revisionism, as just another example of the price paid by Brazil's indigenous forebears for their resistance to Portuguese colonialism. Nevertheless, the language and structure of the play make a strong appeal to a different tradition, one that legitimates the acceptance of pain and sacrifice as the means to salvation. The survival of the ruling, white community, personified by the Portuguese nobleman's daughter Branca, is the priority to which all else must be sacrificed, including the freedom and life of the Indian.

The play is set in the now familiar territory of the early colonial war between the Portuguese and the French-Tamoio alliance. A prisoner of the Portuguese and slave to the household of Dom Rodrigo, the young Indian Cobé is torn between two conflicting sets of loyalties. On one hand, his love for Rodrigo's daughter, Branca, compels him to accept his captivity, but, on the other, his sense of guilt and the bitter reproaches of his mother move him to escape and rejoin his tribespeople. Branca, meanwhile, who loves Estácio, a soldier of lower birth, is oblivious to Cobé's feelings for her; she has resolved to commit suicide since she has been promised by her father to the villain Dom Gil, who is one of the Indians' most hated oppressors.

The play is steeped in the literal and metaphorical language of slavery, which defines each of these relationships set up by the plot. Cobé's mother, Agassamu, curses her son for submitting voluntarily to the slavery that has subjected an entire race under the colonial yoke:

"Escravo! escravo! os olhos tens erguido
Até a filha do senhor que serves;
Ousas amar a filha de um fidalgo,
E a seus pés tua honra sacrificas.
Pois bem; cede aos impulsos desse afeto:
Fica! e consuma a obra da vergonha!
Devorador remorso há de pungir-te;
Em toda parte te acharás com ele,
Como um espectro vingativo e fero.
Bastardo vil da geração dos bravos,
Fica, que os bravos corarão de olhar-te
Vivo, e te negarão morto uma cova!"[44]

(Slave! slave! you have raised your eyes/ To the daughter of the master whom you serve;/ You dare to love the daughter of a nobleman,/ And you sacrifice your honor at her feet./ So be it; yield to the impulses of that affection:/ Remain here! and complete your work of shame!/ Devouring remorse will torment you;/ It will be with you everywhere,/ Like a vengeful, savage specter./ Mean bastard of a generation of braves,/ Remain here, for the braves will blush at seeing you/ Alive, and they will deny you a grave in death!)

Cobé himself realizes, meanwhile, that if his own relationship to Branca is doomed from the outset by the barriers of race and class, his status as her servant will become intolerable upon her marriage to Dom Gil, the archetypal colonial tyrant. Branca innocently describes Cobé's impossible situation when she sings her song of the captive Indian, an adaptation of the medieval Portuguese *cantiga de amor*:

Pobre tamoio cativo
Jovem fidalga adorou,
Sua paixão extremosa
Com façanhas ilustrou.
Era belo, forte e bravo,
Mas era também escravo.
. . .
Pobre tamoio cativo
Que adoras com tal primor,
Está mui alta quem amas,
Lá não chega o teu amor.
Tu és belo, forte e bravo,
Mas ai que és também escravo.
. . .
Pobre tamoio cativo
Foge para a solidão
Se não queres ver o escárnio

Pagar a tua paixão,
Não és nem forte, nem bravo,
Porque sofres ser escravo.[45]

(Poor captive Tamoio/ Adored a young noblewoman,/ He demonstrated with exploits/ His devoted passion./ He was handsome, strong and brave,/ But he was also a slave./ . . ./ Poor captive Tamoio/ You love to such perfection,/ The one you love is high above you,/ Too high for your love to reach./ You are handsome, strong and brave,/ But oh! you are also a slave./. . ./ Poor captive Tamoio/ Flee into solitude/ If you do not wish to see your passion/ Repaid with scorn,/ You are neither strong, nor brave,/ For you allow yourself to be a slave.)

Cobé is thus a "slave" to his love for the white woman, yet ironically is prevented by his servile condition from consummating that love.

Branca, meanwhile, whose name obviously links her symbolically to the cause of the white community, is to become the slave of a colonial tyrant whom she is forced to marry. By contrast, she protests to Dom Gil that her heart is the willing captive of the man she truly loves, Estácio:

"Presa tenho a minh'alma, e até confesso
Que amo, que beijo meus queridos ferros.
Eis o que eu sou . . . eis o que eu sinto e penso.
Senhor Dom Gil, não posso nunca amar-vos;
Em respeito a meu pai seguir-vos hei-de.
Vossa escrava serei, não vossa esposa."[46]

(My soul is captive, and I further confess/ That I love, I kiss my beloved shackles./ This is what I am . . . this is what I feel and think./ Dom Gil my lord, I can never love you;/ out of respect for my father I am bound to follow you./ I shall be your slave, not your wife.)

Later, when Cobé holds in his hands the fatal poison that could deliver her from her torture, she declares, begging on her knees: "És agora o senhor . . . eu sou a escrava" (You are now the master . . . I am the slave).

The act that dissolves all these different bonds of slavery and restores social relations to their "just" state is Cobé's decision to take the poison himself and then kill Dom Gil. In so doing, he avenges his personal honor and the crimes against his people, saves the heiress of the white community from its oppressor, and resolves his own impossible love. This is not a martyrdom imposed on the Indian by an unjust society but a free and rationally meditated decision that he chooses in ultimate deference to the values and legitimacy of the white community. For, just as his love for Branca redeems him from his heathen, savage condition ("When her eyes turn towards me,/ My savage fury disappears"), his self-sacrifice also receives the consecration of white civilization, in the form of the Christian oath by which he swears to save Branca.

The redemptive, taming influence of the white mistress; the remoteness of the mistress from her adoring slave, suggestive of the code of courtly love; the self-sacrifice of the Indian dedicated to her survival; and his implicit conversion to Christianity—these elements are all familiar ingredients in *The Guarani Indian*, which Alencar began writing just two years later. We can speculate as to whether Cobé actually provided the blueprint for Alencar's ideal slave, Peri. What is at least certain is that the play reflects a mythical, ideal conception of social relations and obligations according to which the interests of the indigenous colonial subject might legitimately, even voluntarily be subordinated to the needs of the postcolonial state. By the time we come to *The Guarani Indian*, however, the tensions and distortions arising out of the attempt to square liberal principles of equality and freedom with the reality of Empire have largely disappeared. The contradictions remain, but the tragic intensity of the Indianism of Gonçalves Dias, Teixeira e Sousa, and Macedo has been replaced with a mythology that is self-assured and confident in its ability to resolve the struggle between reformism and conservatism, rebellion and authority, freedom and servility.

REWRITING THE INDIANIST EPIC: ALENCAR'S CONSERVATIVE MYTHOLOGY OF CONCILIATION

In 1856, in the wake of the debate surrounding Varnhagen's "Organic Petition" and as the Indians of Teófilo Ottoni's Mucuri Company were discovering the true meaning of "the dignity of labor," the serialized installments of Brazil's first Indianist novel, José de Alencar's *O Guarani* (The Guarani Indian), began to appear in the *Diário do Rio de Janeiro*. Published in its entirety in 1857, the last year of Paraná's Conciliation government, the novel marked a major watershed in the history of Romantic Indianism for two reasons.

In the first place, *The Guarani Indian* depicted the "marriage" between a Brazilian-born white woman and her former Indian slave as the only means of guaranteeing the survival of a colonial community threatened by internal subversion and by invasion from a hostile, savage tribe. As such, the novel ushered in a radically new mythology of political, social, and racial relations that was, in effect, a vindication of the politics of Conciliation; that is to say, the defense of an exploitative, conflict-ridden state against revolution, by means of a "liberal" accommodation of antagonistic forces and a rhetoric of tolerance, pluralism, and integration.

Second, in order to establish this mythological model for the conservative, Imperial nation-state, Alencar was forced to challenge and break the hegemony of a literary establishment whose reactionary leadership, in the person of Gonçalves de Magalhães, the "father of Brazilian Romanticism," left no doubt that the first Indianist phase had by now been emptied of all its critical and utopian possibilities. In the same year, 1856, Magalhães published his own Indianist epic, *A Confederação dos Tamoios* (The Confederation of the Tamoios), which he had begun nearly twenty years earlier. The Emperor Pedro II financed this first edition as well as two Italian translations, and his patronage extended to sitting through seven hours' live reading of the text, no mean test of his loyalty to his protegé, were this even a modestly stimulating or original work. What is more, the Emperor was among those who publicly defended the poem, under the pseudonym "O Outro Amigo do Poeta" (The Poet's Other Friend), after Alencar launched his devastating critique of it in the pages of the *Diário do Rio de Janeiro*.[47]

Despite his historical role in formally instituting a Romantic school in Brazil, with his "Discourse on the History of Brazilian Literature" (1836), a critical consensus has identified in Magalhães's work a conservative combination of the neo-classical aesthetic traditions that persisted in Brazil well into the nineteenth century and the Christian sentimentalism and nationalism that shaped the ideological character of the First Reign, immediately following independence.[48] *The Confederation of the Tamoios* suggests that, more than this, Magalhães's conservatism remained fundamentally at odds with the liberal pro-Indianism of Romantics such as Gonçalves Dias.

The first generation of Indianists had lamented Conquest and the slavery of the Indians as bequeathing a tragic legacy of oppression and divisiveness that must be confronted by the postcolonial, Imperial order if it, too, were not to be overturned or collapse into chaos. In Magalhães's epic account of the Tamoio war and the founding of Rio de Janeiro, by contrast, the Indians' claims to liberty are subordinated to a triumphant historical project of evangelization and nation-building whose culmination and realization are Empire itself. Thus, the Indians emerge as mythical heroes, not for defending their homeland against the colonial Portuguese invaders but because their deaths were a necessary and glorious sacrifice to the working out of God's plan for the creation of the future capital of the independent Empire. They are represented no longer as comrades-in-arms engaged in a common anticolonial struggle on an equal footing with the forerunners of Brazilian nationalism but as the sacrificial foot soldiers upon whose corpses another civilization was to be founded: "Victory, after all, belongs to civilization and to the future," wrote Magalhães in a note to the poem.[49]

The Tamoios' military defeat is thus turned into a moral triumph, all the more so because, without their heroic but futile defense of their territory, the Portuguese commander Mem de Sá would never have hastened to found the city and prevent the French from establishing themselves there. In the sixth canto, the Indian Jagoanharo is carried high above the colony by Saint Sebastian, its patron saint, in order to glimpse the country's future and to witness the vindication of his people's annihilation:

> Vê dos Tupis as descendentes tribos,
> Um só povo formando, unidas todas,
> Como ali se recordam que pelejam
> Contra os filhos dos seus perseguidores . . .
> E a nova cidade do Janeiro,
> Que em breve tem de ser ali fundada
> Co'a minha proteção . . .
>   . . . cabeça ilustre
> De todo o vasto Império Brasileiro,
> Do qual a Cruz será o alçado emblema
> Da sua liberdade e independência.[50]

(See the tribes descended from the Tupis,/ Forming a single people, all united,/ As they remember then that they are fighting/ Against the sons of their persecutors . . ./

And the new city of Janeiro,/ Which soon must be founded there/ With my protection . . ./. . . the illustrious head/ Of the whole vast Brazilian Empire,/ Of which the Cross will be the raised emblem/ Of its liberty and independence.)

The final act of national emancipation, however, is achieved by the monarchs João VI and Pedro I, who bow to God's plan in recognition that "a single will, and a single sceptre/ Can no longer unite different Nations." Even Pedro I's subsequent abdication, which had actually occurred as a result of liberal protests against his increasingly absolutist, pro-Portuguese rule, is reinterpreted as a further sacrifice, entrusting the nation with the care of his children as he returns to Portugal to guard the throne against the illegitimate claims of his brother Miguel.

Pedro II's interest in defending Magalhães's epic celebration of colonial history, as the necessary preparation for the Imperial regime, is therefore obvious. Nevertheless, the structural balance of the work is ultimately incapable of sustaining that idea of celebration in the face of the overwhelmingly tragic weight of the historical material that it so ponderously conveys. The entire first eight cantos are devoted to the war against the Tamoio-French alliance, while the remaining events—the peace negotiations conducted by the Jesuits Anchieta and Nóbrega and the final Portuguese victory—are compressed somewhat anticlimactically into the last two cantos. A contemporary Portuguese critic of the poem, Alexandre Herculano, understood that if the role of the Indians in this process of nation-building was no more than that of military and political self-sacrifice, there could be no cultural legacy capable of founding an authentic sense of epic national identity worthy of the name:

The conquistadors and races that imposed themselves on the original races by annihilating them might inherit the sum of their few or many material possessions: what they do not inherit from them, and do not appropriate to themselves is the sum of their traditions, their longings, their collective feelings; in short their epic poetry.[51]

This gap between Magalhães's historical perspective and the foundational aims of the text is reflected in his inability to recognize, let alone identify, with the cultural universe whose destruction he defends as the precondition for the birth of the Brazilian nation-state. The tribal landscape, for example, far from symbolizing the utopian terrestrial Eden announced at the beginning of the poem, is instead a hostile domain of uncontrollable elemental forces, not so much an ideal space of freedom as a Gothic "mansion" of fear:

> Desta negra mansão o horror redobra
> O funebre clamor da voz nocturna,
> O echo dos ventos que entre as folhas gemem,
> O echo do rio que o trovão simula,
> E lento se prolonga reboando;
> E o echo inda mais funebre e monotono,
> Como o som do martelo sobre a incude,
> Da imovel araponga, que soluça
> De ancião jequitibá na altiva coma.

Esta é a voz da Natureza em luto,
Voz terrível que os homens apavora,
E a ideia lhes desperta do infinito.[52]

(The funereal clamor of nocturnal voices/ Redoubles the horror of this dark mansion,/ The echo of the winds moaning among the leaves,/ The echo of the river mimicking the thunder,/ And slowly resounding on and on;/ And the even more funereal, monotonous echo,/ Like the sound of the hammer on the anvil,/ Of the motionless *araponga*, sobbing/ In the lofty mane of the age-old Jequitibá tree./ This is the voice of Nature in mourning,/ A terrible voice that strikes terror into men,/ And awakens in them the idea of the infinite.)

Meanwhile, the few evocations of indigenous culture in the poem have a very specific purpose, that of emphasizing not a utopian sense of the alterity of tribal identity but the Tamoios' proximity to white civilization and their consequent amenity to conversion and assimilation into the Catholic empire. The Tamoios' innate cultural affinity for the Catholicism of the colonizers already predisposes them to identify with civilization rather than nature. Those individuals who intransigently reject the offer of civilization, like Aimbire, the supreme representative of liberty and nature, must perish.

This, then, was the glaring ideological contradiction at the heart of Magalhães's Indianist epic: for all its attempt to prefigure the successful independence struggles of the nineteenth century, the depiction of the Tamoios' annihilation at the hands of the colonial power pointed not to a chain of continuity or evolution linking the Indians' history to the civilization of the Imperial nation-state; rather, it exposed an irremediable rupture between the two.

It was precisely this sense of historical and cultural alienation that Alencar, writing under the pseudonym Ig., identified in his critique of *The Confederation of the Tamoios* and that he explicitly sought to overcome in his own literary project. Leaving aside his stylistic objections to the poem, the main thrust of his attack concerned what was essentially Magalhães's antipathy to the people and culture that were his subject. Alencar, by contrast, proposed to immerse himself in the tribal world, to identify not the sources of antagonism between the Indian and white, in particular the colony's genocidal military history, but those elements of the tribal culture and psychology that had been assimilated by Brazilian society and that might therefore foster the process of national conciliation:

If some day I were to be a poet, and I wished to sing of my land and its beauties, if I wished to compose a national poem, I would ask God to make me forget for a moment my ideas as a civilized man.

A child of nature I would wend my way through these age-old forests; I would contemplate God's marvels, I would see the sun rise on its golden sea, the moon glide across the blue of the sky; I would hear the murmuring of the waves and the profound, solemn echoing of the forests.[53]

Afrânio Coutinho summarized the shift in literary perspective that Alencar sought to bring about as follows:

What was new was the integration of the Indian, his incorporation into literature with the cosmogony, the conception of life, the habits, tastes and ideals that are peculiar to him. . . . It does not matter that the poet conveys or transfers to the indigenous ideology something of his own Christian thinking. What matters is that he places himself "inside" the mind of the savage.[54]

It was no longer the achievement of political independence that was at issue, then, but an identification with the cultural universe of the colonial experience as the basis of Brazil's postindependence formation. Miscegenation therefore plays a central role in Alencar's mythology of collaborative Indian-white relations, both at the literal level of interracial fusion and as a metaphor for the dialogue between antagonistic cultures, social classes, and political forces.

Elsewhere Alencar explained how his entire artistic project as a novelist corresponded to this conception of the evolution of Brazilian society as the product of an intercourse between the colonizing and indigenous cultures. Dividing his country's history, and his fiction, into three phases of development—precolonial, colonial, and independent—Alencar defined the second phase as a formative period of miscegenation:

> The second period is historical: it represents the intercourse between the invading people and the American land, which received its culture, and reciprocated in the outpourings of its virgin nature and in the reverberations of a splendid soil.
>
> In the shelter of this teeming creation, temperaments are refined, fantasy takes flight, language is imbued with softer tones, other customs take shape, and a new existence, guided by a different climate, begins to emerge.
>
> It is the slow gestation of the American people, which had to depart from its Portuguese lineage, in order to continue in the new world the glorious traditions of its parent.[55]

Interestingly, although there is no evidence of a direct, explicit connection, Doris Sommer plausibly argues that Alencar was effectively aligning himself with the German naturalist Karl Friedrich Philipp von Martius, whose winning submission to the Historical and Geographical Institute's 1847 essay contest defended much the same view. "How the History of Brazil Should Be Written" pointed to the contribution of Brazil's novel racial mixture to its historical evolution, concluding: "We will never be permitted to doubt that providential will predestined this mixture for Brazil."[56] It should be noted, however, that while Von Martius's triumvirate of races includes the African, the latter is pointedly excluded from Alencar's scheme, which is concerned less with the eugenics of *mestiçagem* than with its broader social, political, and cultural symbolism. In any case, Von Martius was by no means the first to defend the role of miscegenation in Brazil's social and cultural formation; as we saw in the last chapter, as early as the First Reign, José Bonifácio had envisaged a *mestiço* society emerging in the wake of his legislation to abolish slavery and integrate the Indians into the Empire.

There are two dimensions to the process of cultural miscegenation and reconciliation as it appears in Alencar's Indianist fiction. One, examined chiefly in

The Guarani Indian but also reproduced in a series of regionalist novels, is the power struggle between the white patriarch, the representative of the colonial and Imperial ruling class, and a marginal, socially inferior figure, such as the Indian. The extreme forces of authoritarianism and rebellion that these figures embody are eventually reconciled through the intervention of a number of Christian formulas, the myths of sacrifice and salvation, and particularly through the mitigating influence of a female character, the daughter of the patriarch. She, as the motor of sexual contact and standing at the center of the conflict, acquires a psychological maturity and consciousness of her identity as a Brazilian, the symbol of a new generation that has learned to exercise power without stifling the indigenous spirit of freedom and rebellion.

This leads to the other dimension of the process, the sexual union itself, which provides the new, Brazilian generation with a truly *mestiço* identity. Whereas *The Guarani Indian* created the ideal, mythical conditions within which this union could take place, Alencar's later Indianist novel, *Iracema*, followed the narrative of the colonial marriage through to its historical conclusion, exploring, albeit still at a mythical level, the patterns of seduction, sacrifice, betrayal, and guilt that shaped this marriage. Iracema's exiled offspring, drifting afloat on the ocean, symbolizes the *mestiço* identity whose origins the modern Brazilian must confront in order that the colonial burden of guilt might be lifted from the shoulders of the Empire without the latter necessarily being obliged to question its own legitimacy.

Something that has been left unmentioned until now but that is central to the effectiveness and coherence of Alencar's mythology of racial conciliation is the fact that *The Guarani Indian* is the first novel of the Indianist movement. As we have seen, dramas and verse-forms dominated the first twenty years of Indianist writing—short verse-forms, on the whole; the few attempts to use the extended epic genre met with little success and tend to have been overwhelmed by the historical or narrative material that was thrust upon them. For Alencar, by contrast, the novel offered a structural breadth that was able to accommodate both the intricacies and details of narrative plot and the grand scale of his myths of racial and social democracy. Indeed, the Portuguese term *romance* is more suggestive of the mythical potential of the genre than is the English word "novel."

These two innovations, the use of the novel form and the elaboration of nationalist mythologies within that novelistic structure, invite one to seek possible affinities between Alencar and other, non-Brazilian writers from the same literary tradition. Indeed, comparison with a number of authors Alencar is known to have read reveals some important parallels as regards the function of the novel in the construction of a national consciousness. Chateaubriand and Fenimore Cooper might be considered obvious choices for comparative study, given their explicit recourse to the Indianist theme. However, as the following analysis of *The Guarani Indian* and *Iracema* shows, Chateaubriand's preoccupation with the philosophical, Rousseauian implications of the European adventure in the New World has little meaning within Alencar's perspective; here the natural Brazilian landscape is not an exotic objective correlative of human solitude or dissatisfaction but constitutes the fertile locus of a national cultural identity.

Similarly, Cooper's antimiscegenist viewpoint, his horror of any real social approximation between the races other than the isolated fraternal relationship between pioneer and Indian in the forest, is the antithesis of Alencar's ideal of *mestiçagem*.

The work of Victor Hugo offers some more genuine points of affinity, although there is little evidence of any direct influence on Alencar's writing. The connection lies in both authors' interest in myth and in the biblical sources for the mythologies underlying their texts. Pierre Albouy has traced the development of this Romantic interest in the Judeo-Christian mythical tradition back to the seventeenth-century notion that "mythology is nothing but an enormous 'plagiarism' of the Bible." Comparative religious studies in the following century removed Christianity from the center of this relationship and began to recognize parallels between Western mythologies and those of primitive tribal cultures. For instance, Lafitau discovered what he believed were links between the folkloric traditions of North American Indians and the legends contained in the Bible and the works of Homer. A quotation from Hugo's *La Fin de Satan* (1854) illustrates his conviction, following the voyages of his exile, that there is an intimate unity between all religions:

Trimourti! Trinité! Triade! Triple Hécate!
Brahma, c'est Abraham; dans Adonis éclate
Adonai; Jovis jaillit de Jéhovah.

The location of this "christianisme antérieur" in the primeval universe of nature allows us to incorporate Alencar into this tradition: "This identity of religions and mythologies derives, not from a primitive revelation gathered and transmitted by the priests, but from the universality of the only primitive bible: nature."[57] As we shall see, a whole series of Christian formulas, such as salvation, self-sacrifice, and redemption, endow the actions of Alencar's Indian characters with their natural moral legitimacy. In *The Guarani Indian*, Peri instinctively dedicates himself to the salvation of the White Virgin of his dreams, "rising again" from his intended martyrdom at the hands of the Aimoré savages in order to redeem the colonial community and lead its young representative, Ceci, into a new Eden. In *Iracema*, meanwhile, the landscape of Ceará provides the Edenic setting for an adaptation of the Genesis myth. Alencar makes the most of the similarities between indigenous traditions and biblical mythology, such as the twin flood legends of Tamandaré and Noah. His poetic work *Os Filhos de Tupã* (The Sons of Tupã) constructs an entire mythology to explain the genealogy of Brazil's tribal peoples, including elements of the Old Testament narrative of Cain and Abel.

However, it is Balzac and Walter Scott who offer the most illuminating points of comparison with Alencar's vision of his country's political and social formation. The Romantic novels of Scott are known to have formed the staple literary diet of his domestic family life as a young man, while the linguistic difficulties that Balzac's work posed for the student Alencar made his readings of the author very much a labor of love. Josué Montello has observed that Balzac and

Alencar had a similar conception of their role as artists and of the novelistic genre itself in the life of the nation.[58]

In addition, they shared some fundamental ideological convictions, even though these were born out of different historical conditions: the same legitimist faith in constitutional monarchy and the same Catholicism. Moreover, Balzac experienced the same disparity that faced Alencar, between his social and political ideals and the reality of national political life, in his case that of French society after the Restoration, hence, according to Pierre Barberis,[59] his belief in the ideal principle of aristocracy as "the thinking of a society" yet his criticism of the contemporary French aristocracy as "a failed and egotistical class." Preferring to uphold the ideal rather than the reality, Balzac resorted to the same method of historical revisionism, the substitution of myth for actuality, that Alencar was to adopt in *The Guarani Indian*. The brutal repression of the republican conspirators of the *charbonnerie* was thus erased from Balzac's account of the Restoration monarchy:

How could one reconcile the formulation of an ideal of rational monarchy with a reality of monarchism that was utterly remote from it? Quite simply, by straightening out the facts, by idealizing the Restoration, lending it, despite the descriptions made of it, an orientation that would normally annul that appearance.[60]

There are similar ideological parallels between the two writers' interpretation of the relationship between conqueror and conquered, authority and rebel. Like Walter Scott, Balzac attributed the right of social ascendancy not to the recent colonial invader but to the indigenous subject race. Alencar must have been familiar with the struggle between patriotic Saxons and the Norman regime in Scott's *Ivanhoe*. In his own novels, as elsewhere in the Indianist movement, the legitimacy of the Indian's battle against the European colonist is rarely questioned. More significant is the link between the American "savage" and the European peasant, both representing a potential force for rebellion or revolution:

In Balzac, the savage hero, that figure whom one discovers in surprise beyond the spectacular oppositions between liberalism and the Ancien Régime, is in the first place the peasant (first Marche-à-Terre, then Father Fourchon); he is the deserter and the "chauffeur," the semi-bandit (Butifer in *Le Médecin de campagne*, Farrabesche in *Le Curé de village*), the man who refuses conscription.[61]

Now it will be clear from what has been said so far that the categories of European liberalism, "the masses" and "la classe bourgeoise" on which this analysis of Balzac's France depends, cannot be transferred uncritically to the Brazilian Second Reign, with its very specific ideological and class character. Nevertheless, at the general level of struggle between the marginal or rebel and the center of power, the comparison still stands; in the France and Brazil of the Restoration and Regresso, respectively, Balzac and Alencar both defended the "middle" way, the way of constitutional monarchy, the moderating power that existed to negotiate a delicate balance between aristocratic absolutism and revolutionary liberalism.

Moreover, more than one critic has noted the conscious association that Balzac established between the "stark antagonism, the brute ferocity, the endless hostilities" that lie close to the surface of Fenimore Cooper's *Leatherstocking* novels and the atmosphere of struggle in the *Comédie humaine*. For H. Levin, "the poor relation, Lisbeth Fischer, is the Mohican in ambush, the eternal revolutionary,"[62] while the "primitive warfare over possession" that occupies *Les Paysans* is explicitly related to the natural environment of the tribal world, where civilization is seen to break down:

One need not travel to America, remarks the journalist Étienne Blondet, in order to behold Cooper's redskins. "After all, it's an Indian's life surrounded by enemies, and I am defending my scalp," announces Vautrin, when he makes his appearance on the stage. "Paris, you see, is like a forest in the new world, agitated by twenty sorts of savage tribes—Illinois and Hurons living on the products of the different social classes," so he warns Rastignac in *Le père Goriot*. "You are hunting after millions."[63]

Balzac's *Les Chouans* (1827), originally entitled *Le Dernier Chouan* and closely modeled on Fenimore Cooper's *The Last of the Mohicans*, offers further examples of the peasant/Indian analogy and interesting parallels with Alencar's model of indigenous culture and its "medievalist" tradition of loyalty and service. The Breton peasant evinces the same combination of simplicity, ancient superstition, respect for tradition and heroism as are displayed by Alencar's Indians Peri or Poti:

There, feudal customs are still respected. There the ancients find the monuments of the druids still standing, and the spirit of modern civilization is afraid to penetrate through the immense primordial forests. An unbelievable ferocity, a brutal obstinacy, but the faith of the solemn oath, too; the complete absence of our laws, of our mores, of our modes of dress, of our new currencies, of our language, but patriarchal simplicity and heroic virtues, too, concur in making the inhabitants of these fields poorer in intellectual ingenuity than the Mohicans and Redskins of North America, but just as great, just as artful, just as tough as them.[64]

When confronted by the figure of Francine de Verneuil, the primitive simplicity of the *chouan* is expressed in terms identical to Peri's awed worship of Cecília, the white Virgin of his vision:

The *chouan* put his red woolen cap back on his head, remained standing, and scratched his ear in the manner of someone embarrassed, when he saw Francine appear to him as if by magic.
— Sainte Anne d'Auray! he cried.
Suddenly, he dropped his whip, joined his hands together and stood in ecstasy. A faint flush illuminated his coarse countenance, and his eyes gleamed like diamonds lost in the mire.[65]

As in Alencar's novels, female characters such as Francine play a special role as agents of a shift in the balance of power between the peasant rebel and the aristocratic patriarch of the ancien régime, offering the possibility of an alternative, ideal world where such conflicts are held in check:

[I]t is to be noted that they always function as a sign of optimism and openness and that the possibility of a reconciliation between woman and savage hero is always a sign that a chance remains in the world and that one can find in it, if not a future then at least a possible meaning.[66]

In the same way, the Indian Peri and the marginal figures from Alencar's regionalist novels are "tamed" by the mediating influence of the female representative of a new generation, while their essential quality of independence is tolerated and indulged in defense of the regime's survival.

Further similarities with this representation of conciliation, an accommodation of antagonistic political forces through the agency of a moderating power, can be found in the work of Walter Scott. The notion of an unspoken contract or political equilibrium between the center of power and its margins appears in what was probably Scott's most popular novel and one with which Alencar must have been very familiar. Toward the end of *Ivanhoe*, the "King of Outlaws," Robin Hood, who has aided Richard Coeur-de-Lion in the overthrow of his tyrant brother, John, feasts his king in Sherwood Forest. However, noticing that his men are encouraged by the drink and merriment to boast of "their successful infraction of the laws," he thinks it wise to cut short the celebration. In his own words: "And know, moreover, that they who jest with Majesty even in its gayest mood, are but toying with the lion's whelp, which, on slight provocation, uses both fangs and claws."[67] Ivanhoe likewise recognizes the delicate balance of power, the danger of conflict that exists between his defiant outlaws and a jealous guardian of authority. Richard, too, is equally aware of the value of reconciliation and of a government of tolerance and generosity, if the rebellious tendencies of the outlaw are to be curbed:

He once more extended his hand to Robin Hood, assured him of his full pardon and future favor, as well as his firm resolution to restrain the tyrannical exercise of the forest rights and other oppressive laws, by which so many English yeomen were driven into a state of rebellion.[68]

In his classic study of the historical novel, Georg Lukács defines Scott's conception of English history in terms that could equally be applied to Alencar and his vision of Brazil's formative development. For Lukács, the conservative Scott repeatedly fathoms the whole of England's evolution through his fiction in order to find a "middle way" between warring extremes. It is the task of his heroes

to bring the extremes whose struggle fills the novel, whose clash expresses artistically a great crisis in society, into contact with one another. Through the plot, at whose center stands this hero, a neutral ground is sought and found upon which the extreme, opposing social forces can be brought into a human relationship with one another.[69]

In this light Alencar's work can be seen as belonging to a broader nineteenth-century tradition of post-Restoration historical fiction that sought to construct a conservative nationalist model of an "imagined community" (in Benedict Anderson's phrase[70]), safe from conflict and subversion, on the basis of an accommodation or negotiation of power between antagonistic social forces. Such an interpretation of the fiction is supported by the more overtly political views that Alencar expressed during his parliamentary career and as a newspaper columnist. Between 1854 and 1855, the height of the Paraná government, Alencar contributed to the pages of Rio de Janeiro's *Correio Mercantil* with the regular *crônicas*, or columns, entitled "Ao Correr da Pena," which proved very successful until they were considered too controversial and were terminated. Among other comment of a topical and political nature, one can find here his views on the politics of Conciliation.

On one hand, as the following extract from a piece on the birthday of Pedro II illustrates, he considered the official version of Conciliation, as implemented under the Second Reign, to be utterly dependent on the system of royal patronage, the balanced distribution of "graças," or favors, to those "whose services the Imperial munificence has judged fit to remunerate":

this year . . . the favorable circumstances of a current period of calm and serenity have permitted the Imperial munificence at once to pay the nation's debts and assist in the realization of the thinking of union and concord, which is the program of the government of Sr. Dom Pedro II and his most ardent desire as a Brazilian and as the sovereign.

. . . this year tolerance had passed its sponge over all those names of *guabiru* and *praieiro, luzia* and *saquarema, exaltado* and *conservador* [rival political factions], which political hatreds had formerly forced to play the roles of Guelphs and Ghibellines in the bloody struggle between the parties.[71]

As Alencar remarked elsewhere, the guiding principle of this system was that "everything has its price," including justice and the integrity of the country's statesmen. The consequence of such a policy was the replacement of a genuine debate between clearly defined ideological positions by the false, spineless conciliation of idle "chitchat," in which principles disappeared, convictions became blurred, and opinion followed the dictates of expediency and personal ambition. Alencar's critical view of the politics of Conciliation came very close to that of the Conservative statesman Justiniano José da Rocha, for whom the term "transação" (from the title of his 1855 pamphlet *Ação; Reação; Transação*) best expressed the ethos of interparty consensus, whose pre-condition was "the extinction of passions, struggles, the disarming of spirits."[72]

As an alternative to this travesty of the political ideal, on the other hand, Alencar recommended creating a new party of conciliation, to be born out of the "confusion of extreme ideas," but nevertheless committed to a truly dynamic exchange of viewpoints, an authentic dialectic between government and an effective opposition:

Let us rehabilitate this fine idea of the conciliation of spirits, let us avoid it being replaced by a conciliation of individual interests; let all those who wish to join in it be

accepted, but let no one be pleaded with to join; let all minds be called upon to collaborate for the good of the country, but let there be no demand for an immoral compromise
that may not be lasting: let all opinions be respected and let the opposition be entirely
free, for if it is loyal, it will assist the government; if it is licentious, it will discredit itself. (OC, IV, p. 748)

It was not for these opinions, however, that Alencar's column began to be
censored, forcing him to leave the *Correio Mercantil*, but for his attacks on economic speculation and the vice of "lucro," profit. Together with some friends he
attempted an enthusiastic revival of the waning *Diário do Rio de Janeiro* as a
vehicle for his ideas on Conciliation, but with little commercial success. At this
time his father named him in his will, requesting that he continue the family tradition of active, liberal militancy. Alencar seems to have lacked confidence and
faith in that tradition, however, and he failed to win the parliamentary election
for his home province when he stood as a candidate in 1856, the same year in
which he published his criticisms of Magalhães's epic poem and began writing
his own novel, *The Guarani Indian*.

In 1858, after returning from his literary activities to advocacy, he was appointed to a post in one of the new government departments through the influence of Senator Nabuco. Alencar's increasing alienation from his family's political traditions must be seen against the background of widespread shifts in
party allegiance during this period; prominent Conservatives such as Nabuco,
Saraiva, Zacarias, and Paranhos formed a new dissident grouping called the
Liga Progressista. The appointment of a new Conservative administration in
1859 led to Alencar's promotion to a senior post within the Ministry of Justice.
When, after his father's death in the following year, he stood for the second time
as an electoral candidate for his home province of Ceará and won his seat, it was
not as a Liberal but as a Conservative.

In 1865, anxious to return to politics after a long period of illness and the
publication of two further novels, *As Minas de Prata* and *Iracema*, Alencar began to publish the anonymous "Letters from Erasmus," in which he resumed his
discussion of Conciliation, calling for a truly representative electoral system
along the lines of the British parliamentary monarchy. Fundamental to his revised conception of political conciliation was the role of the monarch as a disinterested arbitrator, the voice of the national conscience restraining the excesses of government and opposition:

The Moderating Power is the national ego, the enlightened conscience of the people. Just
as the human creature in the course of its life is reprimanded by an inner sense that
obliges it to reflect upon the morality of the act that it is about to commit; so the nation
receives the same service from the monarch; and very often the anticipated remorse of an
evil passion preempts its consequences, obliging the people to reflect. (OC, IV, p. 1085)

However, as far as the current moderator Pedro II himself was concerned, Alencar's opinion shifted from admiration and faith in his capacity to fulfill this
role—"Monarch, I love and respect you, you are in these calamitous times of
indifference and unbelief an encouragement and faith for the people" (OC, IV,

p. 1050, November 1865)—to an increasingly critical stance, demanding a more responsible exercise of his political duties. Looking back over the history of the Second Reign, he concluded that, during the Conciliation period, Pedro had made insufficient use of his powers to dissolve the lower chamber, while in the earlier and more recent periods of party conflict he had taken too little account of public opinion. This led Alencar to his sustained attacks on what he saw as an absolutist tendency in the current regime, an abuse of "Personal Power," which even prompted him to collaborate temporarily on the newly founded opposition paper, A República. These criticisms of Pedro's political conduct earned Alencar the hostility of the Emperor, who is supposed to have said of him: "He's stubborn, that priest's son," and although his name was the most voted out of a list of three candidates nominated for a vacancy in the Senate in 1869, his appointment was vetoed by the Emperor.[73]

If, for Alencar, the continued stability and prosperity of Empire depended on a political system of tolerant government, effective opposition, and the moderating power of the monarch, its economic base, slavery, was for him equally indispensable. Thus, the novelist, while praising the 1850 Queiróz Law, which abolished the traffic from Africa, nevertheless opposed the Law of the Free Womb of 1871, which was to herald the virtual end of slavery in Brazil. The conditions of slavery could be improved so as to make them "humane," a view he implemented during his period of office as minister of justice, when he ended the practice of open slave auctions at the Valongo market. But as for the institution itself, "precisely because it is an institution condemned by morality, an outdated institution, it cannot be modified: it will become extinct one day, but it cannot be altered."[74] Alencar viewed total and immediate abolition as a prelude to inevitable economic collapse and civil war. Such a step would constitute a dangerous interruption of the natural, but gradual, evolution of Brazilian society toward universal emancipation:

What could be observed was simply the continual, gentle and natural progress of the inner revolution that has long since been under way in Brazil and that is tending towards the achievement of emancipation through the improvement of customs, through the generosity of the Brazilian people, through our civilization that flourishes with an immense vigor.[75]

Alencar's gradualist position on the slavery question can be traced, furthermore, to a pair of plays that he wrote for the stage between 1857 and 1860, precisely during the years immediately following his first successful novel, The Guarani Indian, and before his second Indianist work, Iracema (1865). According to João Roberto Faria, both dramas—O Demônio Familiar (The Family Demon, 1857) and Mãe (Mother, 1860)—were extraordinarily well received and consolidated his reputation as the renovator of a homegrown theatrical tradition, equal to the service he had performed for Brazil's national fiction.[76] Even independently of the argument being made here, for a structural relationship between the Indianist theme and the slavery question, one might expect some broad ideological affinity between these four texts, given that they were produced in fairly close succession during the heyday of the Second Reign. The truth is rather more surprising, however, for when examined together these texts point to a closely analogous set of concerns, central to which is the master-slave relationship and the contribution of the dark-skinned non-European to the well-being of the postcolonial Brazilian family.

Each pair of texts—*The Guarani Indian* and *The Family Demon*, on one hand, and *Iracema* and *Mother*, on the other—mythologizes a nearly identical gendered role for the Indian/African servant of the Creole community. In the case of *The Guarani Indian* and *The Family Demon* it is the male guardian spirit of the nation's household, whose tranquillity and survival hinge on his intervention, whether as the benign Indian protector Peri or the mischievous, manipulative house-slave Pedro, as genie or demon. As we shall see, the "reward" granted to the slave in both cases for his actions is his freedom, but the meaning and effect of this act of emancipation differ according to whether the context is that of the mythical colonial New World or the more contemporary realist setting of the nineteenth-century bourgeois family.

The common pattern shared by *Iracema* and *Mother*, meanwhile, is that of the self-sacrificing, non-European mother (Iracema or Joana), who dies before her mixed-race son can come to know her as such. The *mestiço* or mulatto inheritor of the postcolonial order must thus live out his life as an orphan but as one who, in surviving his mother and remembering her act of sacrifice, both acknowledges the historical guilt of his maternal non-European origins and is simultaneously unburdened of responsibility for them, remaining free to make his own history. But if one accepts the parallelism between these two sets of Indianist novels and dramas of slavery, what conception of the postcolonial social and political order is suggested by the central figures that link them—the ambivalent, but emancipated, guardian spirit of the Brazilian family and the tragically self-sacrificing, non-European mother?

There has been ample disagreement over the years as to whether *The Family Demon* and *Mother* should be interpreted as abolitionist works. Putting considerable store by Alencar's own statements on the matter, João Roberto Faria sympathizes with Brito Broca's verdict that they constitute Realist and Romantic critiques of the "peculiar institution," respectively. Thus the first exposes the pernicious social and moral effects of slavery on its victims (both the "innocent" slave boy himself and his manipulated masters), appealing to the audience's ethical sense; while the second speaks to their hearts, exalting the slave as a virtuous and tragically misused creature who transcends her captive condition by exemplifying the ideal, universal quality of maternal self-sacrifice.[77]

These are plausible readings, if one considers the slave characters as no more than repositories of the given values of mischievousness and maternalism. But they do not adequately explain the outcome that awaits each of the characters, in order that the dramatic structure can be brought to a reassuring close, that is, the liberation of Pedro and the death of Joana. As the contemporary mulatto critic Paula Brito argued, if for an abolitionist the greatest prize that a slave could be granted was his freedom, then how could Pedro's emancipation constitute a punishment for his misguided intrigues, as Eduardo intends that it should?[78] And if the modern young protagonist Jorge can acknowledge the slave woman Joana as his mother without hesitation (so already straining at the bounds of historical plausibility, as Décio de Almeida Prado has pointed out[79]), then why does Alencar insist on her suicide as the "self-sacrifice necessary so that Jorge will not fail to belong to white society"?[80]

Neither of these dramatic denouements can be convincingly translated into a straightforward pro-abolitionist position, that is, the advocacy of immediate universal emancipation, however much the dramas may denounce the social ills engendered by slavery. What they point to, instead, is a much more conservative kind of reformism that, as we have seen defended by Alencar elsewhere, would leave the economic core of the institution—mass plantation slavery—intact for the time being, while mitigating its more distasteful aspects where these were visible to the urban bourgeois population. Thus, the act intended to leave the bourgeois household safe from the maleficent infiltration of the family demon, the dark-skinned "enemy within," is the option of individual manumission for the domestic slave. It is proposed not as the slave's legitimate, overdue right but as a liberally educative, corrective measure designed to transform the irresponsible child into a citizen answerable to the edifying obligations of work and law:

I shall correct him, making of the automaton a man; I shall restore him to society, however I shall expel him from the bosom of my family and close to him forever the door of my home. (*To Pedro*) Here: these are your emancipation papers, they will be your punishment from this day forward, for your failings will fall back exclusively on you yourself; for morality and the law will require of you a severe account of your actions. Free, you will feel the need for honest labor and you will appreciate the noble sentiments that today you fail to comprehend. (OC, IV, pp. 135-36)

Likewise, Joana's suicide, while rehabilitating the moral status of the slave, simultaneously promotes a myth that must have been intensely attractive to a troubled slave-owning elite for whom abolition, although postponed for the moment, could not be put off indefinitely. For Jorge has already emancipated this woman who, unknown to himself, is actually his mother (and who, in any case, he "never considered to be [my] slave"), when she not only insists on maintaining the pretense but also persuades him to remortgage her in order that he can pay off his friends' urgent debts. That is, Joana's entire raison d'être as Jorge's unconfessed mother and protector depends on her position as a domestic slave, a role that she is determined to cling to even in a voluntary capacity: "Massa can't make me . . . I'm not freed! . . . I don't want to be! . . . I don't want to! . . . I'm my master's slave! . . . And he shan't go wanting for anything! . . . Did you ever see such a thing, a woman in the house with nothing to do, not good for anything at all?" (OC, IV, p. 325). When the truth is finally revealed, and his newfound social and racial origins put Jorge's respectability in jeopardy, then Joana's suicide is simply the logical extension of her selfless, slavish dedication to his well-being and the willing effacement of her own image and interests.

Far from implying Alencar's advocacy of some thoroughgoing structural reform, let alone abolition, of Brazil's key socioeconomic institution, then, the central formulas of these two dramas—the taming of the dangerous "enemy within" through the civilizing effects of emancipation and the self-effacement of the voluntary slave and martyred non-European mother—served, on the contrary, to offset the need for universal social reforms by means of individual acts of manumission and self-sacrifice. This was by no means the stuff of artistic fantasy, for it is well known that before and after abolition, many emancipated ex-slaves did, indeed, remain on the plantations as loyal "agregados," or retainers, since this was often their only hope of access to land and protection:

The manumission of slaves . . . encouraged good behavior, for it demonstrated that loyalty and obedience would be rewarded . . . Sometimes owners manumitted a slave on the specific condition of continued faithful service for a fixed number of years or until the death of the master, and the law even provided that manumission could be revoked for such acts of ingratitude as hurling insults at the former master.[81]

What is more, the close correspondences between these dramas and the narratives of *The Guarani Indian* and *Iracema* suggest that Alencar saw in the colonial scenario of the Indianist novel the ideal space, away from the more immediate, contemporary social setting of his plays, in which to articulate on a grand scale this mythology of the colored races' reconciliation and sacrifice to the interests of the postcolonial order.

Once combined with the concept of miscegenation, Alencar's mythology acquired an ideological force that reached far beyond the Indianist movement itself, for this notion of a conciliatory, collaborative relationship between the races, on the basis of a history of intimate social and sexual contact, is the first manifestation of the most influential tradition of thinking about race relations and national identity in Brazil to date: a tradition of *mestiço* nationalism that is best known in its twentieth-century form as elaborated by Gilberto Freyre and associated with the phrase "racial democracy."[82] Essentially, the theory proposes that the character of Brazilian society is such that the progressive integration of racial groups into the national community, as "Brazilians," has been able to transcend the class interests that normally divide a nation and set it into conflict. The unique flexibility of race relations in Brazil exempts them from the kinds of analysis that might be applied to other societies, such as the Marxist concept of class struggle. Thus, for the apologists of the theory, such as João Camillo de Oliveira Torres, even before the advent of the French Revolution, Brazil boasted a classless society: "America was the paradise of the isolated pioneer, of the adventurer. In Brazil all this amounted to a 'racial democracy.'"[83]

In his landmark account of the plantation system of northeastern Brazil, *Casa Grande e Senzala* (The Masters and the Slaves, 1933), Freyre argued that the peculiar sociability of Portuguese and Africans had fostered a domestic and sexual intimacy between the slaves and their owners, that dissolved the otherwise violent antagonisms of race and class in the aftermath of abolition. The "commonsense" evidence of widespread miscegenation "confirmed" this lack of racial prejudice, the large mixed-race population blurring any clear demarcation along the black-white continuum. In his later work *Sobrados e Mucambos* (The

Mansions and the Shanties, 1936), Freyre suggested that this progressive miscegenation of Brazilian society had led to the evolution of "so-called individual
and, at the same time, ethnically and culturally mixed, forms of family, economy
and culture, equal in number from that time, in Brazil, to those patriarchal families of Portuguese origin that day by day were becoming less powerful, and ethnically and culturally less pure."[84] The apparently inflexible social structure
produced by a slave economy had been progressively eroded, subverted even,
by the democratic impulse characteristic of Brazil's history of miscegenation:

> Integration, maturation and disintegration . . . have never been witnessed independ-
> ently of that other process that is equally characteristic of Brazil's formation: the amal-
> gamation of races and cultures, the chief dissolving agent of everything inflexible in the
> limitations imposed by the more or less feudal system of relations between people on
> situations not only of race but of class, groups and individuals. . . .
> Until what was most obstinately aristocratic about the patriarchal organization of the
> family, economy and culture was affected by that which was always contagiously demo-
> cratic or democratizing and even anarchizing, in the amalgamation of races and cul-
> tures.[85]

It is far from coincidental, then, that Freyre should have been one of the most
enthusiastic admirers of Alencar's literary project and of his foundational Indianist mythology. As we shall now see, this mythology of gradual democratiza-
tion or conciliation, mitigating, but never ultimately questioning, the unequal
balance of power between master and slave, patriarch and rebel, colonist and
Indian, landowning elite and liberal opposition, Imperial state and the disfranchised, marginalized majority, was central to both Alencar's political thinking
and the significance of his Indianist novels. Referring to another of his works, he
asked:

> But is the society where the scenes of the novel take place surely not open and demo-
> cratic? Where two poor and unknown young men are invited to dinner, having just got to
> know each other in a quick meeting the same morning? Where the nobility is represented
> by titled persons of low birth, such as a baron who was once a trooper, a count who was
> once a coachman, and a counselor who has a dispatch-house?[86]

SLAVE, REBEL, AND ALLY: *THE GUARANI INDIAN*

The Guarani Indian, published in the last year of the Paraná ministry, may be
described as the classic novel of Conciliation, reproducing on a mythical level
the elements of Alencar's thinking that have previously been outlined: the evolution of a democratic, contractual negotiation of power between the forces of
the state and its subjects; the achievement of this through the cultural agency of
miscegenation and the "political" mediation of a moderating figure, restraining
the absolutist and revolutionary tendencies of those locked in conflict; and,
emerging from this process, the growth of a new national consciousness, a
shared cultural identity.

In fact, so successful was Alencar's first, Indianist version of this model of a conciliatory social contract that he effectively reproduced the same narrative structure in a whole series of regionalist novels representing the same power struggle and its successful resolution. As we shall see in the next chapter, *O Tronco do Ipê*, *Til*, and *O Sertanejo* all depict the crisis of a patriarchal regime ruled by an oppressive rancher or plantation owner (Joaquim Freitas, Luís Galvão, or Capitão-Mor Campelo), the more contemporary equivalent of the nobleman Dom Antônio de Mariz, the colonial patriarch of *The Guarani Indian*. Each of these novels sets the patriarch into conflict with a marginal figure (Mário, Jão Fera, or Arnaldo), distanced from the source of power by his social circumstances, racial origins, or special relationship with the indigenous, natural world and refusing to submit to the arbitrary tyranny of the *senhor*. The conflict is resolved through the mediation of an adolescent female figure, the patriarch's daughter (Alice, Berta, or Dona Flor); while her love for the marginal succeeds in taming his rebellious, destructive instincts, she is also able to temper the excessive authoritarianism of her father, reaching a mature awareness of her own Brazilian identity in the process.

However, of all the different versions of this basic scheme, *The Guarani Indian* was, significantly, the most popular during the author's lifetime and has remained so. As well as Scalvini's Italian libretto for Carlos Gomes's operatic setting, *Il Guarany* (1870), which played at La Scala, Milan, and London's Covent Garden, the novel gave rise to a drama in three acts, *Guarany ou O Amor no deserto* (Guarany or Love in the Wilderness) (1875), and even an illustrated literary journal under the same title. In the present century, too, the text has been adapted for the cinema screen on several occasions.[87]

The plot of the novel concerns the family of the Portuguese *fidalgo*, or nobleman, Dom Antônio de Mariz in its isolated "fortress" somewhere between Rio de Janeiro and São Paulo at the beginning of the seventeenth century and the events that lead to the destruction of all but two of its members. The son and heir, Dom Diogo, is sent away early in the novel and thus survives to reappear in a later work, *As Minas de Prata* (The Silver Mines); the daughter Cecília is saved by a Goitacá Indian, Peri, who adores the white virgin and is dedicated to her protection. The destruction of the patriarchal community on the Paquequer River is brought about by internal and external forces: the undermining of its unity by a mutiny of its resident band of "aventureiros," led by the power-crazy renegade missionary Loredano; and by the attacks of the local Aimoré Indians, sparked by the killing of one of the tribe's women at the hands of Dom Diogo.

Given his close knowledge of the colonial and Imperial texts that were his sources for the plot and judging from his own writing on the subject, it is indisputable that Alencar was well acquainted with the history of slavery, dispossession, and genocide to which soldiers such as Dom Antônio de Mariz, rewarded for his services in the devastating war against the Tamoios, would have contributed.[88] Yet, while the reality of racism and violence is acknowledged in the novel, the text is chiefly concerned with a set of characters and social relationships that are distinguished by their exceptional nature within the colonial context. Dom Antônio is presented as owning no slaves, Indian or African; as a virtuous knight, a man of his word, and not a slaughterer of Indians; as someone who will strip his own son Diogo of his right to defend the family as an honorable knight and expel him from the community for the accidental killing of an Indian woman—an extraordinary condemnation of an event that must have been commonplace:

a knight who kills a weak and harmless creature commits a lowly, unworthy act. . . . for me, when the Indians attack us, they are enemies whom we must fight, when they respect us they are vassals of a land we have conquered; but they are human beings! (OC, II, p. 50)

Alencar does not present this attitude as universal within the society of the novel but as a special, advanced view of the colonial relationship that prepares the *fidalgo*'s daughter for the momentous transformation of the book's climax. Dom Antônio's militaristic stance toward the Indians is a defensive one, the fortification of the "house on the Paquequer" and the maintenance of a band of "adventurers" for the protection of the family. However, Alencar seems unable to disguise the real, historical function of such bands, and Chapter 3 of the novel reveals the name "aventureiro" to be a euphemism for *bandeirante*:

In those times the name "bandeiras" was given to those caravans of adventurers who penetrated the hinterlands of Brazil in search of gold, precious stones and emeralds, or discovering still unknown rivers and lands. (OC, II, p. 33)

The description leaves something to be desired, of course, for as the notes to the text indicate, albeit somewhat cryptically, the principal source of income for the wealthy colonist was the profits from the *bandeiras'* slaving expeditions, their "explorations and forays through the interior." It is even suggested that Dom Antônio participated in such raids, since his "niece" Dona Isabel is rumored to be the "offspring of the old fidalgo's love for an Indian woman he had captured on one of his explorations" (OC, II, p. 32). As if to rectify this stain on his character and restore his special moral status, we read in a narrative "flashback" in the second part that he subsequently saved an Indian woman from the hands of his men and that this woman was the mother of Peri. This is the initial step in the evolution of the mutually contractual relationship between the novel's two archetypal male figures, the white patriarch and the Indian warrior.

That relationship develops against a background of racial prejudice and hostility that is expressed particularly through the character of Dom Antônio's *paulista* wife, Dona Lauriana. Whereas her husband instinctively allies himself with Cecília, she sides with her son, defending his killing of the Indian girl. When Cecília voices her fears for Peri's life, Dona Lauriana remarks: "It would be no great loss," and she campaigns to have him expelled from the household, claiming that he deliberately plotted to terrorize the family with his captive lynx. Her attitude epitomizes the denial of the indigenous contribution to Brazilian nationality and culture against which the novel is working: "this caste of people, who are not even human, can only live properly in the forests" (OC, II, p. 75).

Even Isabel, herself half-Indian, is infected by the prejudice of which she is a victim; she would like to erase the stigma of her indigenous parentage, to remove the barrier that defines her as no more than Cecília's half sister. While Cecília ironically envies her dark skin, she declares: "And I would give my life to have your pale complexion, Cecília" (OC, II, p. 46). This hatred of her racial identity as a *mestiça* is the basis of her aversion to Peri and her attraction to Dom Álvaro; born not of the utopian interracial marriage Alencar envisages at the end of the novel but from an oppressive colonial relationship, the rape of the Indian, Isabel's *mestiça* has no future but that of the tragically marginalized *marabá*:

In Isabel the Indian had made the same impression that was always caused in her by the presence of a man of that color; she had remembered her unfortunate mother, the race from which she originated, and the cause of the contempt with which she was generally treated. (OC, II, p. 101)

Dom Antônio's downfall is not simply an accident of fate, then, but obeys an internal necessity for change. The Aimoré attack on the Paquequer and the killing of the Indian girl that precipitates it are symptoms of the colonial community's inability to adapt to the racial and cultural milieu in which it is embedded. That alienation is to be overcome on a mythical, ideal level by the new, independent generation of Ceci. As the opening description of the landscape surrounding the settlement suggests, Alencar believed that there was another world of social relationships imaginable beyond the rigid, inflexible hierarchy of master and slave. At first the relationship between the two rivers seems to confirm that hierarchical structure of power, in which the Paquequer is lord over the cliffs but is itself subordinate to its "king": "It might be said that, a vassal and tributary of this king of the waters, the little river, arrogantly towering over the cliffs, humbly bows at the feet of its sovereign" (OC, II, p. 27). But Alencar also glimpses an alternative "natural" order farther upstream, where the tributary preserves its independence from the master's tyranny:

It loses then its savage beauty; . . . a submissive slave, it endures its master's whip. It is not there that it should be seen; but three or four leagues above its mouth, . . . still free, like the indomitable child of this country of liberty. (OC, II, p. 27)[89]

Something stands in the way of this utopian ideal of liberty for the archetypal colonial community, however, and that is Dom Antônio's relationship to the metropolitan powers, Spain and Portugal. The novel is set at the beginning of the seventeenth century, when Portugal and, therefore, Brazil were under Spanish rule. In loyalty to his country, Dom Antônio has laid down his arms rather than serve the Spanish and has isolated himself in his "little Portugal" on the Paquequer (echoing Silviano Santiago, Doris Sommer reminds us of the parallels here with João VI's flight from Lisbon in 1807, when the Portuguese court was moved to the safety of Rio de Janeiro in the face of a threatened Napoleonic invasion[90]). As a first-generation colonist, a "foreigner" in an alien land, Dom Antônio is asserting in this way his obstinately Portuguese identity, his attachment to the Old World: "Here I am a Portuguese, . . . In this land that was given me by my King and conquered by my hand, in this free land, you will reign, Portugal, as you will live on in the souls of your children. I swear it!" (OC, II, p. 30). Profoundly embedded in this sense of Portuguese identity is the medieval ethic of chivalry. There are many clear references to the fortress as "a feudal castle in the Middle Ages," Dom Antônio's men as "vassals" protected by the "rico-homem," his "squire" Aires Gomes; his very appearance—"he was immediately recognizable as a fidalgo by the loftiness of his countenance and his knight's costume" (OC, II, p. 46)—and the chivalric code of behavior, which demands that Dom Antônio expel his son and recognize Peri as a "knight" in the guise of an Indian.

These instances have generally been presented as proof for the claim that Alencar's Indianism is simply a Brazilian variant on the current of Romantic medievalism represented, in Europe, by Walter Scott or Alexandre Herculano. However, this is to ignore the ultimately negative, anachronistic nature of this medievalism as it appears in the novel. Aires Gomes, for instance, is Portuguese chivalry at its most comical and anti-Brazilian, totally at odds with the New World and its inhabitants, such as Peri, who ties him to a tree for his troubles: "curse the savagery of such a land! Oh! if only he were amongst the gorse and heaths of his homeland!" (OC, II, p. 120). The spirit of chivalry prevents Dom Antônio from leaving the Paquequer when it is threatened with destruction—he is a part of the old order, and must perish with it:

Such was the sentiment of honor in those old knights, that not for a moment did Dom Antonio admit the idea of escape to save his daughter; if there had been any other means, he would surely have accepted it as a favor from heaven; but that was impossible. (OC, II, p. 252)

Thus, the obsolete nature of Dom Antônio's patriarchal, medievalist values and his continued attachment to Portugal make the destruction of his regime necessary, so that a new generation, that of Cecília, can create a modern, democratically independent Brazilian society.

The novel's narrative structure is therefore of fundamental importance to the understanding of its ideological significance. In the first of the text's four parts appear all the elements of conflict that motivate the rest of the plot: Isabel's despair in the face of her racial identity and her attraction to Álvaro; Dona Lauriana's hatred of Peri and her attempts to have him expelled from the community; Dom Diogo's killing of the Indian woman and the discovery of her body by her tribespeople; and Loredano's conspiracy with the disloyal adventurers Bento Simões and Rui Soeiro.

Despite its appearance of calm and stability, the patriarchal community of the Paquequer contains an inherent quality of precariousness that is symbolized by the location of the fortress, dominating the vicinity but perched on the edge of a precipice. This precipice represents the way toward change, an abyss between two worlds that must be crossed but that carries with it the danger of destruction. The chasm outside Cecília's window is the scene of several such moves toward change: it is there that Loredano drops the bracelet, Álvaro's gift to Cecília, and so attempts to disrupt the conventional love match between the couple; Peri must descend into its depths at risk to his life in order to retrieve the bracelet and restore the well-being of the community; by passing across a flimsy plank over the chasm, Loredano hopes to enter Cecília's room and abduct her, realizing his destructive dream of power. On several occasions Loredano comments on the symbolic meaning of this precarious journey to power, such as when he convinces his accomplices of his irresistible influence over them: "Once you have set a foot over the precipice, my friends, you must walk across, if you are not to tumble down to the bottom. So let us walk" (OC, II, p. 86). The Aimoré Indians eventually invade the house by scaling the cliffs of the "abyss," thus destroying the barrier of apparent security that separated the community from chaos; and lastly, by crossing the bridge formed by a palm tree bent over the precipice, Peri and Ceci escape to their new world, fulfilling the movement toward change that is prefigured so early in the novel.

Another symbol of the momentous transformation depicted by the novel is the cataclysmic potential of the river, one of the natural forces to which human activity is normally oblivious. At the end of the novel these forces assert themselves; in defiance of the order and hierarchy that it seemed to confirm in the opening pages, the river awakens like Gonçalves Dias's Sleeping Giant, to announce the apocalyptic moment of change:

At that moment the river gasped like a giant writhing in convulsions, and flung itself back down on its bed, uttering a deep, cavernous moan . . .

One might say that some enormous monster, such as one of those tremendous boa constrictors that live in the depths of the waters, snapping at the base of a cliff, was spinning its immense tail, squeezing between its thousand coils the forest that stretched along its banks.

Or that the Paraiba, rising like a new Briareos in the midst of the desert, was stretching out its hundred titanic arms, and squeezing to its chest, strangling it in an awful convulsion, all that age-old forest that had been born with the world. (OC, II, p. 272)

The flood is linked explicitly to the biblical myth of Noah, by means of the nearly identical indigenous legend of Tamandaré, which Peri recounts to Ceci in the closing pages. The point here is that the myth does not impose a closed structure on the novel, as Afonso Romano de Sant'Anna suggests,[91] but an open one; God, saddened by the wickedness of man on his Earth, decides to destroy him but allows his favorite, Noah, to survive and "replenish the earth," to begin mankind afresh, like Tamandaré and his "companion." It is this new, ideal society of the future that Peri and Ceci are permitted to create after nature, avenging itself by an act of purification, sweeps away the old, decadent order so as to recover the primeval innocence and harmony of the Terrestrial Paradise.

Let us now examine the process by which this new society, based on a completely different set of relationships to that of the colonial regime, is made possible. The social conventions of the medieval code of chivalry, reflecting the structures of power imposed by colonialism, point in the novel to an expected marriage between Álvaro and Cecília, preserving an all-white, Portuguese-dominated patriarchal order. Isabel looks upon this relationship with resigned hopelessness, seeing herself inevitably excluded, her only future that of solitude and marginalization, or suicide. However, from the outset, Álvaro's own feelings for Cecília are by no means free of ambiguity; his love has neither the sensual passion of Loredano nor the idolatry of Peri but is the conventionalized "afeição" of the chivalresque code of courtly love:

> In Álvaro, a discreet and courteous knight, the sentiment was a noble and pure fondness, full of that gracious timidity that perfumes the first flowers of the heart, and of the chivalresque enthusiasm that lent such poetry to the lovemaking of those times of faith and loyalty. (OC, II, p. 59)

Conventional, restrained, and traditionally unrequited, Álvaro's chivalresque sentiments are inevitably overwhelmed by the much more powerful attraction of Isabel, her "irresistible power of seduction." From the moment when she returns to him the flower intended for Cecília and thereby, in a manner characteristic of the novel, establishes a strand of communication, the image of Isabel begins to replace that of the other woman in his mind:

> [H]is thoughts were quite far away and were flitting about the image of Cecília, next to whom he could see the dark, velvety eyes of Isabel rapt in a melancholic languidness; it was the first time that that dark face and that ardent, voluptuous beauty had mingled in his dreams with the fair angel of his loves. (OC, II, p. 114)

The remainder of the novel traces Álvaro's struggle with his sense of guilt for the betrayal of his duties as a knight, his promise of marriage given to Cecília's father, and the admission of his true feelings for Isabel. This admission, a Romantic rejection of classical conventions and also of the obsolete code of Portuguese chivalry, can come only at the moment of death, when the house is being besieged by the Indians. Until that final *liebestod*, Álvaro cannot compromise his code of honor; like Dom Antônio, he cannot survive the collapse of the old order:

> Then, close to the end, at the edge of the grave, when death had released him from the earth, with a final sigh he could stutter the first word of his love: he could confess to Isabel that he loved her.
> Until then he would fight. (OC, II, p. 205)

Cecília's liberation from the conventional marriage to Álvaro, toward her final union with Peri, follows a similar path, although it is complicated by the structures of power and subjugation that exist between the white mistress and her Indian slave. Her childish dreams are at first filled with myths of chivalry, the fantasy that a gallant knight will come and "fall timid and supplicant at her feet" (OC, II, p. 42). This image is initially strong enough to dispel the melancholy and repulsion aroused by the intrusion of an Indian figure into her dreams. But when her inherited colonial prejudices are overcome, the feeling of revulsion turns to pity:

But the supplicant slave would raise his eyes with such a look of pain, so full of silent prayers and resignation, that she would feel something inexpressible, and would become so, so sad, until she would run away and weep. (OC, II, p. 205)

Throughout most of the novel it is this attitude of pity, determined by Peri's social status as a slave, which characterizes their relationship. However, from the very beginning Cecília's sensibility is instinctively attracted to the Indian's natural world; her clothes and the decoration of her room incorporate the skins and feathers of the forest animals and birds, and she experiences the delight of what she is eventually to recognize as her own, native environment:

Everything held for her an inexpressible magic; the night's teardrops trembling like jewels on the leaves of the palm-trees; the butterfly that with its wings still benumbed would await the sun's heat to be revived; the little widow-bird which, hiding in the foliage, would tell its companion that day was breaking; everything made her utter a cry of surprise and pleasure. (OC, II, p. 67)

Cecília gradually realizes the superficial nature of her love for Álvaro, recognizing that it has been artificially exaggerated by the rivalry of Isabel. When she deliberately encourages the affair between Isabel and Álvaro, first by returning the latter's gifts and then diverting them to Isabel, hers is less an act of self-sacrifice than of self-liberation, in order that she can pursue her more genuine feelings for Peri.

Peri's relationship to Cecília, meanwhile, recalls Gonçalves Dias's "Indian's Chant," with the Indian's religious worship of the white Virgin as a divine source of authority and consolation. In Chapter 2 of the second part the narrator recounts Peri's first encounter with Dom Antônio and Cecília; the relationship begins with two reciprocal acts of salvation, the first of several Christian formulas that are to bring about the ultimate reconciliation of white and Indian. In spite of the state of war between the two races, Dom Antônio has rescued Peri's mother from the adventurers; two days later Peri saves Cecília from a falling boulder—to him, this angelic apparition is the embodiment of the "mistress of the white men," the image of the Virgin Mary that he found in an abandoned church and that later returned to him in a dream:

In the night Peri had a dream; the lady appeared; she was sad and spoke thus:
—Peri, free warrior, you are my slave; you will follow me everywhere, just as the great star accompanies the day.
The moon had returned with its red bow, when we came back from the war: every night Peri saw the lady in her cloud; she did not touch the earth, and Peri could not climb up into the sky . . .
And so Peri was sad.
The lady did not appear again; and Peri always saw the lady in his eyes . . .
His mother came and said:
—Peri, son of Arare, white warrior saved your mother; white virgin too.
Peri took up his weapons and left; he was going to see the white warrior to be a friend; and the daughter of the lady to be a slave.

The sun was reaching the middle of the sky and Peri was also reaching the river; he glimpsed your big house from afar.

The white virgin appeared.

She was the lady whom Peri had seen; she was not sad like the first time; she was happy; she had left the cloud and the stars behind. (OC, II, pp. 98-99)

Incarnation and salvation, two of the central formulas of Christian theology, are thus combined in a mythological explanation for Peri's desertion of his society and culture and his devotional relationship to Cecília, the devotion of the medieval knight to his feudal *senhora*, of the slave to his mistress. The reenactment of these Christian dramatic motifs is the basis for the reconciliation of the two alienated cultures and races, but the burden of sacrifice is shouldered overwhelmingly by the Indian, while its beneficiary is the survival and consolidation of the postcolonial state.

Peri's love for Cecília is therefore totally selfless, "a cult, a kind of fanatical idolatry, into which not a single thought of egotism entered" (OC, II, p. 59). He is the ideal guardian of the patriarchal society of the Paquequer, "a beneficent genie of the forests of Brazil" (OC, II, p. 97); like a guardian angel, he uses semi-magical, supernatural powers to ensure Cecília's well-being and to preserve her, and thus the future of the community, from danger. He protects her from animals and insects, from the arrows of the hostile Aimorés, and from the evil Loredano, even dreaming of a moonbeam to guard over her. His plan to foil the Aimoré attack involves poisoning his own body, so that by consuming his flesh in the ritual of cannibalism, the enemy warriors will also die. Although saved at the last minute from execution, Peri seems bound to die from the effects of the curare, which is already working in his veins. His mysterious journey into the forest, where a communion with nature brings him from a deathlike sleep to a miraculous revival, resembles the biblical Resurrection of Christ, the archetypal savior figure.

His final act of salvation is to carry Cecília away from the scene of destruction before the old colonial community is annihilated in the explosion that Dom Antônio has prepared; even as the floodwaters rise and threaten to engulf her, he tears a tree from its roots with superhuman strength, willing the survival of the land's "chosen people": "Tu viverás!" (You will live on!).

Like Dom Antônio and Cecília, then, Peri has a special, ideal status in relation to the reality of colonial history; he wanders virtually as he pleases in the household on the Paquequer, having abandoned his family and tribe for a life of voluntary servitude. In order to reinforce the special status of his Indian hero, Alencar draws on the stereotype whose tradition, as we have seen, has its roots in the earliest contact between missionaries and Indians—the stereotype of the amenable, civilized Tupi and the intractable, savage Tapuia. His description of the Aimoré Indians, "a people without a fatherland or religion, which fed on human flesh and lived like wild beasts on the ground and in dens and caves" (OC, II, p. 81), is a classic caricature of the faceless, anonymous tribe, the pack of savage beasts devoid of the intelligence that marks out the member of human society:

His ruddy hair fell across his brow and completely obscured the noblest part of the face, created by God as the seat of intelligence and as the throne where the mind must reign over matter.

His rotting lips, drawn back by a contraction of the facial muscles, had lost the gentle, sweet expression that smiles and words impress upon them; they had turned from a man's lips into the mandibles of a wild beast, accustomed to shouting and roaring.

His teeth, as sharp as a jaguar's fangs, no longer had the lustre which nature had given them; both weapons and feeding instruments at once, blood had stained them the yellowish color that the teeth of carnivorous animals have. (OC, II, pp. 208-9)

Peri, meanwhile, is the individual singled out from the collective body of the tribe by his special qualities and therefore ready to be integrated into Alencar's *mestiço* society. He is one of the Goitacá (Waitacá), a tribe that, like the Aimorés, was not, in fact, native to the area that provides the setting for the novel. As Alencar notes, though (OC, II, p. 105), these Indians were famous for their skill as archers and swimmers and for their bravery and mobility in war. The Goitacá chief, Peri, reveals his cultural and moral superiority to the Aimorés in the battle that leads to his deliberate capture. Having proved his physical mastery over them, he surrenders voluntarily yet remains psychologically in absolute control of his situation:

He rose, and with supreme disdain stretched out his fists to the savages who at the old man's order set about tying his arms together: he seemed more like a king giving an order to his vassals, than a captive submitting to his conquerors; such was the arrogance of his demeanor, and the contempt with which he faced the enemy. (OC, II, p. 212)

However, Peri's special qualities of loyalty and self-sacrifice are not sufficient alone to bring about the transformation, the *mestiçagem* of colonial society that is anticipated by the developments so far. In order that his final act of salvation can take place, and a new society can be born, a fundamental change is necessary in the relationship between the Indian, and the *fidalgo* and his daughter, a change in the exercise of authority. From the moment when Peri agrees to remain in Cecília's service, she becomes aware of her power as mistress and heir to her father's absolute rule:

To see that savage soul, as free as the birds gliding in the air, or as the rivers running through the meadows; that strong, vigorous nature that performed wonders of strength and courage; that will as indomitable as the torrent leaping off the mountain-tops; prostrate itself at her feet, submissive, defeated, a slave! (OC, II, pp. 106-7)

But the limitations of Peri's apparent freedom as a voluntary slave in the household are tested and exposed only when there is an open conflict of wills. This occurs at a critical moment in the novel when Dom Antônio and his daughter forbid him to sacrifice his life in the Aimoré camp, a sacrifice that Peri knows is their only hope, forcing him to violate the normally unspoken law of obedience to his colonial masters:

Cecília rose with an instantaneous movement; standing pale, magnificently angry and indignant, the previously gentle, gracious girl had suddenly been transformed into an imperious queen. . . . Throwing back her fair little head over her left shoulder with a vigorous gesture, she stretched out her hand towards Peri:
—I forbid you to leave this house!. . .
Peri took a step towards the door; Dom Antônio stopped him:
—Your mistress, said the knight coldly, has just given you an order; you will carry it out. Do not worry, my child; Peri is my prisoner.
Hearing this word that destroyed all his hopes, that made it impossible for him to save his mistress, the Indian withdrew and took a leap, landing in the middle of the room.
—Peri is free! . . . he cried, in a frenzy; Peri will not obey anyone any more; he will do what his heart commands. (OC, II, pp. 207-8)

Peri's predicament, his rebellion against the authority of the patriarch and their final reconciliation, as Dom Antônio knights the Indian and confides his daughter to his safekeeping, demonstrates the necessarily precarious balance of power that must be nurtured if the community is to survive. On one hand, it must be remembered that Peri never actually challenges the principle of patriarchal authority itself; he seeks only to temper it, to moderate its absolutist excesses and thereby create a space within which his own instinct for autonomy is permitted to function for the benefit of the regime as a whole. It is worth, in this respect, comparing Peri's momentary clash with patriarchal authority and Loredano's more revolutionary attempt to overthrow Dom Antônio's regime. An Italian fisherman's son "of low extraction," Loredano is intent on a fundamental transformation, not just of the exercise of power but of the entire structure of society. He is inflamed

by the moral impossibility that his status created, by the barrier that was raised between him, a poor settler, and the daughter of Dom Antonio de Mariz, a rich nobleman with his manor and coat of arms.
In order to destroy that barrier and level their positions, an extraordinary event would be necessary, a fact that would completely alter the laws of society that in those times were stricter than today; one of those situations was needed in the face of which individuals, whatever their hierarchy, nobles and pariahs, are leveled; and they rise or sink to the condition of mere men. (OC, II, p. 59).

Alencar's demonic characterization of Loredano as the agent of such a revolution allows us to put into perspective his invocation of the principle of liberty in the novel. Rather like Gomes Freire's manipulation of the concept in *O Uraguay*, here liberty has only limited, relative claims that are ultimately subordinate to the survival of the existing state. Peri's willingness to sacrifice a proportion of his freedom actually appears to give the ideal society of the novel a greater "liberal" legitimacy; the Indian symbol of liberty has been freely incorporated into a new, more mature regime.
Loredano, by contrast, in challenging the very sovereignty of Dom Antônio, is questioning and threatening the entire edifice of political hierarchy, whose theological underpinning is divine authority itself. In the first chapter of Part II he is exposed as a former Carmelite priest who abandons his ministry on discov-

ering the existence of an immense store of hidden treasure. His first step in pursuit of this obsession is to betray the trust of a dying man to whom he is giving absolution and to keep the vital map for himself. Repudiating his religion, he becomes the archetypal fallen angel, defying his God:

[S]till shaking and pale with terror, the reprobate raised his arm as if challenging the ire of heaven, and uttered a terrible blasphemy:
—You may kill me; but if you spare my life, I shall become rich and powerful, against the will of the whole world!
There was in these words something of the impotent fury and rage of Satan cast down into the abyss by the Creator's irrevocable sentence. (OC, II, p. 95)

Thus, when he is finally brought to justice and burned at the stake in a crude auto-da-fé, it is as much for his crimes as a heretic as for his attempt to usurp the power of Dom Antônio.

Against Loredano's diabolical revolutionary, then, Peri is the "good rebel," an Indian Robin Hood; as Dom Antônio is forced to recognize, his freedom and identity as a marginal living in the limbo between civilization and nature, society and forest, are vital to his role as guardian of Cecília and of the white community. He knows that in the historical reality of colonial, patriarchal Brazil, the Indian could enter white society only as a slave and by accepting its laws; as such he could not protect Cecília: "If Peri were a Christian, and a man wished to insult you, he could not kill him, because your God commands that one man should not kill another. The savage Peri respects no one; whoever offends his mistress is his enemy, and will die!" (OC, II, p. 163).

Only in the ideal, perfectly integrated, and democratic society glimpsed in the Epilogue of the novel, the new Eden after the flood, can Peri's freedom be reconciled with the survival of an authentically Brazilian society and culture. After the destruction of the fortress on the Paquequer, Cecília wakes to find herself alone in the forest with Peri. A fundamental rupture has taken place between past and present; the loss of her parents and her expulsion from the isolated security of the fortress into the real world of her native land have brought about her maturity from a girl into a woman. It is a maturity that gives her a new view of things, a special communication with nature:

Going back over the past she wondered at her existence, as one's eyes are dazzled by the light after a deep sleep; she did not recognize herself in the image of what she had previously been, in that irresponsible, mischievous little girl.
Her whole life was changed; and misfortune had effected that sudden revolution, and another as yet confused feeling was perhaps about to complete the woman's mysterious transformation.
Everything about her was touched by this change; colors had harmonious shades, the air had intoxicating perfumes, the light had velvet-like tones, that were unfamiliar to her senses. (OC, II, p. 260)

A major element of that rupture with the past is the change in the relationship between mistress and Indian; removed from the physical and social structures of the patriarchal community that have until now alienated Cecília from the forest, the barrier between the two characters is broken down. The relationship can no longer be defined by the hierarchies of class and race, only by their common link to the natural, forest environment that is to be the new Brazil:

> In the midst of civilized men, he was an ignorant Indian, born of a barbarous race, whom civilization repulsed and consigned to captivity. Although to Cecília and Dom Antonio he was a friend, he was only a slave friend.
> Here, however, all distinctions disappeared; the son of the forests, returning to his mother's bosom, regained his liberty; he was the king of the wilderness, the lord of the forests, wielding power through the right of strength and courage. (OC, II, pp. 261-62)

The couple can now exchange roles and cultures: Ceci (her new, "indigenized" name echoing that of her partner) takes the part of the guardian angel as Peri lies exhausted in the canoe: "Sleep, she said, sleep; Ceci is watching over you"; while Peri accepts the Christian faith. Refusing to let him leave her with her relatives in Rio, Ceci enters Peri's world, abandoning her Western clothes for the costume of the Indian and setting adrift the canoe that is their link with white society. Choosing between the white-dominated, colonial order now represented by her disgraced brother Diogo and the liberal, fraternal society of her new "brother," Peri, she recognizes that she belongs, like him, to this world, the Brazil in which they were both born and have grown up: "We shall live together as we did yesterday, as we have today, as we shall tomorrow. Can you imagine? . . . I too am a daughter of this land; I too was raised in the bosom of this nature. I love this beautiful country" (OC, II, p. 270).

In the kiss that ends the novel, the new relationship between Peri and Ceci changes from one of brother and sister, to that of man and woman; from a fraternal love that, therefore, has no future beyond their own lives, to a sexual love capable of "replenishing the earth," as Noah and his family do in the Old Testament myth. Recognizing herself as "a daughter of the forests, a true American" (OC, II, p. 267), Ceci is asserting her nationality as a Brazilian and at the same time is defining that nationality in terms of a new set of "natural" values. Or rather, they are the traditional Christian values of love and self-sacrifice, overlaid with the liberal principles of equality and freedom and renewed by the natural world. In making endless sacrifices, dying and being resurrected, Peri is announcing a new Christianity for Brazil, an Empire of conciliation and democracy in which the sins and conflicts of the colonial past will have been wiped away.

Such a marriage between a white woman and an Indian warrior must have posed a daring challenge to the racist bourgeois mentality of Alencar's readership, for all that Peri's threateningly primitive virility is largely emasculated by his voluntary conversion to Christianity. However, this postdiluvian Paradise Regained was, in any case, no documentary reconstruction of colonial history but a mythical utopian substitute for the social and political emancipation that independence and Empire had failed to deliver to the majority of the country's people. The egalitarian partnership between Peri and Ceci could survive only in the imagined seclusion of the forest, safe from the historical truths of slavery, patronage, and dispossession that awaited them outside in the real world.

ORIGINAL SIN IN THE BRAZILIAN EDEN: THE NEW CONSERVATIVE GOSPEL OF *IRACEMA*

Alencar's fanciful marriage between the Guarani warrior Peri and the heiress to the colonial community, Ceci, had thus established in the Indianist imaginary the dream of reconciliation and regeneration for the Imperial nation-state. Thus far, however, Alencar had projected the drama of miscegenation only into a postdiluvian future still empty of history. His next Indianist novel, *Iracema*, published in 1865, resumed the narrative of interracial marriage, but this time within a more sophisticated pseudohistorical framework derived from an entire complex of biblical myths from the Edenic Fall to the birth of a new redeemer. This was Alencar's second attempt to substitute a mythical narrative of nation-building for the unresolved legacy of structural contradictions inherited by inde-pendence, which were soon to return to the surface of Brazil's political life. In the same year the War of the Triple Alliance against Paraguay launched the Empire into a new phase of upheaval that marked the definitive end of the mythical political consensus fostered by the years of Conciliation.

Alencar was not the only Indianist writer of the postconciliation period to look to a "universal" grand narrative such as provided by the Old and New Testaments, within which the more local history of state-formation might confi-dently be inserted. The poet Fagundes Varela (1841-75), after a stormy, youth-ful career spent moving between the bohemian intellectual circles of São Paulo and his family's estates in the interior of Rio, produced a religious verse epic, *Anchieta ou O Evangelho nas selvas* (Anchieta or The Gospel in the Jungle, 1871). A radical departure from his earlier Byronic writing, *Anchieta. . .* was an expression of faith not only in the possibility of individual salvation but also in the idea of Empire as the realization of the historic goal of redemption prefig-ured in the Jesuits' colonial evangelical project. As such, it may well have been a response to a moment of moral crisis, a search for spiritual regeneration or direction after the years of alcoholism and domestic chaos: "Left to roam the forests, in a poor financial state, it is possible that the bourgeois showed through from time to time in the bohemian, punishing him with the remorse, that was not so much individual as characteristic of his group, for a career without prospects, a drop in living-standards."[92]

In Varela's epic the military-religious crusade against the Tamoio confedera-tion unfolds as its leader, Anchieta, recounts to his indigenous disciples the drama of the Old and New Testaments from the Fall to the Crucifixion. Scrip-ture, dream, and historical events are juxtaposed so as to present the conflict between rival Indians as a reenactment of Cain's bloody crime, the jealous slaughter of God-fearing man by his brother. By the same token, the death of Anchieta recalls Christ's martyrdom, as he dies at the hands of the people he wishes to save. The parallels are completed with the slow death of the Tupinikin girl Naída, a symbol of innocence, as Anchieta brings the Crucifixion story to its climax in the Last Supper and the Gethsemane episode. In effect, the entire Christian mythology of fall, betrayal, sacrifice and redemption has been reproduced in the colonial history of the New World, whose Indians are the latter-day persecutors of Christ, as well as his disciples.

In the epilogue of the final canto, as Anchieta lies dying, he speaks of the "Universal Church" that will be built by God's chosen people on these historical foundations. Before uttering the final words, "Farewell! Our mission is complete!," he reveals that this ecclesiastical empire, the realization of God's kingdom on Earth, is nothing less than the political Empire of the Second Reign with all its institutions:

> Mas, entre o sólio e o povo resplandece
> O sinal da aliança, a nívea pomba,
> Sustendo o verde ramo de oliveira,
> Descansa aos pés do soberano ilustre
> Que há de elevar o templo do futuro,
> Arca sublime das grandezas pátrias,
> E reviver o século de Augusto
> No ciclo de ouro da brasílea história![93] (X, viii)

> (But, between the throne and the people/ Gleams the sign of alliance, the snow-white dove,/ Holding aloft the green olive-branch,/ The noble ark of the fatherland's glories/ Rests at the feet of the illustrious sovereign/ Who will raise up the temple of the future,/ And relive the century of Augustus/ In the golden cycle of Brazil's history!)

Like Gonçalves de Magalhães before him, then, Varela identified Empire with the redemptive, historic triumph of Christian civilization over a sinful colonial order. But it was again left to Alencar to address the nation's subjective legacy of guilt for the Indians' sacrifice to that triumph. Only by assuming and internalizing the contradiction between the European's capacity for violence and betrayal and the Indian's material and cultural sacrifices could the Brazilian conscience be reconciled with itself. The point about such a reconciliation, of course, is that it dispensed with the need for any objective change to the social and political order inherited by independence.

This was achieved in Alencar's novel *Iracema* by reconstructing within the colonial scenario the biblical narrative of fall, betrayal, sacrifice, and the redeemer's birth, all of whose events are completed early in the country's history. With the birth of the archetypal *mestiço* Brazilian, Moacyr, all that remains is for him to grow to maturity, to emerge from his exile between two lands, two peoples; independence signifies not a political or economic rupture with the past but a growth out of it.

The plot is deceptively simple and is based on the events that led to the colonization of Alencar's native province, Ceará, in the northeast of the country. The Potiguar Indians were the largest and most unified of all the coastal tribes, and through their populous villages and relatively advanced farming methods they gained a reputation as a civilized people. They were allied with the French, who were the earliest European presence in the region, against their traditional enemy, the coastal Tobajara of Olinda and their Portuguese allies. However, a truce at the end of the sixteenth century meant that the Potiguar now joined the Portuguese in their campaigns into the interior against other tribes, including another group of Tobajara.

Martim Soares Moreno participated in one such campaign in 1603, taking part in the defeat of thirty villages on the Camocim River, the last to fall being that of Chief Irapuã. Soares Moreno subsequently pushed expansion farther west, with the intention of opening up the territory to European settlement, and to prove that colonization was viable, he took a *mestiço* son born in Ceará back with him to the governor general of Brazil. He personified the policy of alliance and miscegenation, fighting, tattooed and painted, alongside the Indians, and was befriended by both the main tribes. In particular, he gained the loyalty of the Potiguar warrior Poti, or Antônio Filipe Camarão, whose biography Alencar wrote during his youth and who earned the unprecedented esteem of the Portuguese after his services to them in the wars against the Dutch. However, because of the harsh geographical conditions of the region and in spite of the efforts of Jesuits and laymen alike, it was some years before serious settlement of Ceará came about.[94] These events take second place to the central drama of the novel, although the tension between war and alliance and the initial failure to establish a colony in the region are clearly vital to the significance of the text.

Losing his way in the interior, the Portuguese soldier Martim Soares comes across a village of the enemy Tobajara but is nevertheless welcomed and falls in love with the shaman's daughter, Iracema. The ensuing intertribal and interracial wars force the couple to take refuge among the Potiguar, and they subsequently set up an idyllic home in the forest, producing a son. However, for reasons that are not immediately obvious, Martim's love for the *índia* fades, and, alone and abandoned, Iracema dies of grief.

Alencar explicitly links the orphanhood and exile of Iracema's son, Moacyr ("child of sorrow"), to his own sense of alienation from his native Ceará, something that, as we have seen, had as much to do with his increasing distance from the family's political traditions as with his geographical separation from his home. The prologue of the novel is the confession of "an absent son, a stranger to many, forgotten perhaps by his few friends and only remembered because of his unceasing disaffection" (OC, III, p. 193). This opening chapter takes the reader straight to the book's ending and to the boat that is drifting in exile on the open sea, in search of a "native rock in the solitudes of the ocean" (OC, III, p. 195). The *mestiço* child of Iracema and Martim, Moacyr is more than simply the first citizen of a remote provincial settlement; he is the symbol of an entire Brazilian people that has been alienated from its *mestiço* identity and divorced from its indigenous roots: "The first native of Ceará, still in his cradle, was emigrating from his homeland. Did the predestination of a race lie therein?" (OC, III, p. 245).

The text of the novel proposes, then, to explain how this child, together with a white-skinned young man and a dog, come to be drifting in this boat and to reveal the true nature of the longing that attaches them to the "land of exile." Thus, the second chapter opens in the forest and finds the Tobajara Indian girl, Iracema, integrated into the harmony of her forest environment. That state of harmony is suddenly shattered by the appearance of Martim, and from that moment a whole series of antagonistic symbolic figures are introduced, defining the two characters and the forces they represent: interior and coast, fertility and death, stability and departure. The alien warrior, perhaps an evil spirit of the forest, carries the mark of death: "He bears on his cheeks the white of the sands that border the sea, in his eyes the sad blue of the deep waters" (OC, III, p. 197). Indeed, when later threatened by his rival Irapuã and told that his possession of Iracema must mean death, he confesses: "The warriors of my blood carry death with them, daughter of the tabajaras. They do not fear it for themselves, they do not spare it for the enemy" (OC, III, p. 205). Paradoxically, though, it is Iracema who commits the first act of aggression, reacting to this intrusion into her world and to the danger this signifies. She shoots an arrow, wounding Martim's cheek, but again, paradoxically, he is the one to show tolerance and restraint, respecting the Christian cult of womanhood but also, we might argue, neutralizing the symbol of male power and indigenous resistance that Iracema has temporarily wielded:

On first impulse, his nimble hand dropped to the cross of his sword; but then he smiled. The young warrior had received his learning from his mother's religion, where woman is the symbol of tenderness and love. (OC, III, p. 197)

Iracema then breaks the arrow of peace, and the first cycle of erotic attraction and conciliation takes over from the initial gesture of conflict. Martim is welcomed into the cabin of Iracema's father, the shaman Araquém, and receives the ritual of hospitality—fire, food, water, and peace pipe.

The incident is falsely reassuring, though, for more profound cultural, racial, and political forces militate against a successful relationship between the couple. One is the barrier of Iracema's tribal role as daughter of the shaman and as keeper of "the secret of the jurema potion and the mystery of dreams," which both demand that she remain a virgin on pain of death. The other is Martim's status as an enemy warrior among the Tobajara and the bonds of loyalty that call him back to his own people; at the center of these affections stands the figure of his white mistress.

As soon becomes apparent, around the straightforward plot of the novel there is woven an ever-tightening web of impossible attractions and inevitable conflicts that can lead only to death. On one hand, the political conditions of Conquest have determined that the white soldier and the Indian woman will be drawn inexorably to each other. But, on the other hand, those same conditions mean that Iracema and Martim approach the relationship on unequal terms and with different expectations, preparing the ground for the betrayal and sacrifice that are bound to follow.

For Iracema it is a first, virgin love, dedicated, selfless, and self-sacrificing; when Martim betrays her in his imagination, dreaming of the girl in his homeland, she expresses not jealousy but regret, remaining concerned only for his happiness. Taking him to the secret grove of the *jurema*, she risks death by violating her vows and invites him to drink the liquor that will allow him to be reunited in his dreams with "the pure angel of his childhood loves." Like Peri, she becomes the white man's protectress, hiding him in the forest from his enemy Irapuã. Risking her life a second time, she goes secretly to meet his Potiguar friend, Poti, giving him the information that he needs to storm the Tobajara camp and rescue Martim. On the fatal night described in Chapter 15, she makes the critical sacrifice; Iracema's father senses that some momentous event is taking place, prefiguring the great sacrifice and betrayal of his entire people in the name of Conquest:

In his dark retreat the old Shaman, plunged into deep contemplation and indifferent to the matters of this world, uttered a mournful groan. Had his heart suspected what his eyes did not see? Or was it some fateful presage for the race of his children, which echoed thus in Araquém's soul? (OC, III, p. 217)

In one act of abandonment, Iracema gives up her virginity to Martim and betrays her duty to the sacred wine of Tupã, knowing all the while that she is only sharing Martim's love with another:

A sad smile stung the lips of Iracema:
—The stranger will always live at the side of the white virgin, never again will his eyes see the daughter of Araquém, yet already he wishes for sleep to close his eyelids and for dreams to carry him to the land of his brothers! (OC, III, p. 218)

As if this were not enough, she then deserts her people in order to follow Martim, seeing them killed in battle by her lover's allies. When her brother Caubi visits her in her new home and generously offers to treat Martim as a brother, she sends him away and so confirms the final and complete break with her origins. Iracema is all self-sacrifice, selfless dedication to the white warrior.

Martim, meanwhile, for all the metaphorical, poetic language of the novel, is essentially the archetypal, promiscuous male colonist, realizing through the submissive Indian woman his fantasies of the exotic and forbidden sexual experience. His exploitative use of the narcotic and aphrodisiac liquor, the *jurema*, translates onto a psychological level the process of colonial oppression and betrayal that, for Alencar, lay at the heart of his country's crisis of identity. On the first occasion, when Iracema freely offers him the *jurema*, Martim's dream represents the Romantic impulse to escape the domestic, conventional world of his European lover, in search of the symbol of nature and sexual freedom:

But why, scarcely has he returned to the cradle of his homeland, does the young warrior once again leave his parents' home and head for the backwoods?
Now he crosses the forests; now he is reaching the meadows of the Ipu. He follows the nimble trail of the wild virgin, casting her sweet name to the breeze amid repeated sighs:
—Iracema! Iracema! (OC, III, p. 203)

Martim is presented with a sexual choice, symbolic of the cultural dilemma faced by the nascent Brazilian nation in its evolution toward maturity, between his distant, absent, white bride and the immediate, seductive presence of the

Indian: "There awaiting him is the blonde virgin of chaste affection; here smil-ing at him is the dark virgin of fervent love" (OC, III, p. 217). On one hand, Martim's loyalty to his European mistress has receded into his conscience to become an abstraction, a focus of guilt; on the other hand, in the "here and now" of the colonial context, his fantasy has suddenly become available as a reality. Like a good Christian, he closes his eyes "and fills his soul with the name and veneration of his God" in an effort to dispel the image of temptation and to postpone the responsibility that this choice entails.

Martim's religious view of the dilemma is important, because it relieves him of this responsibility, placing him in the position of a moral victim at the mercy of conflicting loyalties and temptations. Significantly, however, Alencar inverts the traditional roles of temptress and victim as they appear in the Genesis myth; Iracema is described as the vulnerable "saí bird, mesmerized by the serpent," which is Martim. Iracema attributes the worm of corruption to herself: "The honey of Iracema's lips is like the comb made by the bee in the trunk of the andiroba tree" (OC, III, p. 205); but, as we shall see, she apparently remains guiltless, for Martim, instead of openly assuming the responsibility that the politics of colonialism have imposed upon him, searches for a means of avoid-ing the guilt of betrayal while enjoying the fulfillment of his exotic sexual fan-tasy. In wishing to have his cake and eat it, too, Martim betrays both women and produces a son who is bereft of both a mother and a homeland.

In a fit of inspiration, he asks—or, rather, orders—Iracema to violate her vows for a second time, on this occasion against her will, and to bring him the potion once again. Snatching the liquor from her hands, he intends to savor the illusion of sexual possession, albeit a frustrated one, without assuming its real consequences. In a hypocritical act of rationalization, Martim projects his own fears of corruption onto Iracema, whom he believes to be sparing from the guilt that the sexual act would entail:

> Now he could live with Iracema and gather from her lips the kiss that was blooming amid smiles like the fruit in the corolla of the flower. He could love her and imbibe from that love the honey and fragrance, without leaving any poison in the virgin's breast.
>
> The pleasure was life, for he felt it most strongly and intensely; the wrongdoing was a dream and illusion, for he was possessing the image of the virgin, nothing more.
>
> Iracema withdrew oppressed and sighing. (OC, III, p. 218)

Ironically, however, Iracema forces the reality upon Martim, obliging him to accept the responsibility he thought to escape by means of the *jurema*. As he dreams, reaching out and calling her name, she naturally responds and goes to him, "as the juruti goes to its nest at the call of its companion." Consummating the union that Martim believes to be only a fantasy but that Conquest has made inevitable, Iracema nevertheless remains the innocent, frail bird uncorrupted by the sexual act; the body washed by the river on the following morning is still "the chaste body of the recent bride." Paradoxically, though, while innocent, Iracema, too, bears the responsibility for this momentous transgression of the boundary between colonial fantasy and actual possession, for it is she who takes the decision to realize Martim's dream, voluntarily yielding to her own erotic impulse to fall into his arms.

However, what leads to the eventual tragedy of Iracema's abandonment and death is Martim's refusal to acknowledge the implication of this act of possession and confirm the break with his white mistress, his refusal to acknowledge that in waking to discover Iracema in his arms, he is simply waking to reality. Instead, he continues to shelter behind the guilt of his betrayal of the other woman and to treat Iracema as his seductress and corruptress, poisoning the relationship from its inception:

> The warriors' war-cry, thundering through the valley, wrenched him out of his sweet deception; he realized that he was no longer dreaming, but was living. His cruel hand wiped from the virgin's lips the kiss that was trembling there.
> —Iracema's kisses are sweet in dreams; the white warrior filled his soul with them. In life, the lips of Tupã's virgin turn bitter and wound like the thorn of the jurema. (OC, III, p. 218)

The couple's idyllic home in the forest, isolated both from the Tobajara village that they have abandoned and from the camp of Martim's Potiguar allies, appears to provide the hope for the colonial marriage; it resembles the mythical paradise that Peri and Ceci discover, a place where Eden may be redeemed, and a new society may begin. The hope is illusory, however, for even before they arrive there, during their journey to the coast, Martim reaffirms his ties with his former home in a symbolic act of communion:

> The white warrior's eyes cast across the vast reaches; his breast gave a sigh. That sea also kissed the white seas of Potengi, the cradle of his birth, where he had seen the light of America. He flung himself into the waves and believed himself to be bathing his body in the waters of his fatherland, as he had bathed his soul in his longing for it. (OC, III, p. 226)

Similarly, the place where they eventually settle is chosen by Martim for military reasons; having gained the friendship of all the Potiguar tribes on the east-west coast, he considers this inlet an ideal refuge for Portuguese ships on their way to fight the French and the Tobajara Indians. The historical significance of the settlement for the future of the Indian is revealed by the ancient chief Maranguab, whose words to Martim, Poti, and Iracema are explained in a note to the text as a prediction of the colonial destruction of his people: "Tupã wanted these eyes, before their light fades away, to see the white hawk beside the narceja" (OC, III, p. 229). Despite the alliances and friendships and the apparent renewal of Martim's love for Iracema, the embryonic colony is overshadowed by the image of the white bird of prey standing next to its victim. The alienation that is already gnawing at the relationship between Martim and Iracema symbolizes the broader, fundamental alienation of white and Indian. In both cases, the Indian is the faithful, conciliatory partner offering friendship and love, and in both cases the Indian is sacrificed and betrayed. Iracema and her people are victims of a masculinist, militarist, colonial mentality that has a morbid impulse to confront love with death. In the language of Romanticism, it discovers its ideal and, somehow knowing it to be impossible, feels compelled to destroy it.

Interestingly, fraternal love seems to present an alternative to the tragic sexual relationship between Martim and Iracema; Caubi's offer of friendship as a brother to Martim represents the basis of peace and alliance between two warring peoples. But the friendship between Martim and Poti stands as the strongest example of reconciliation between white and Indian, and, as Iracema fears, it proves more durable than her own marriage to Martim:

> The two brothers stood brow to brow and breast to breast, to express that they both had one head and one heart alone.
> —Poti is happy because he sees his brother, whom the evil spirit of the forest snatched away from his eyes.
> —Happy is the warrior who has beside him a friend like the brave Poti; all the warriors will envy him.
> Iracema sighed, thinking how the pitiguara's affection was enough for the foreigner's happiness. (OC, III, p. 220)

Indeed, Martim does seem to prefer the male company of Poti, who is the pretext, if not the active cause, of the white man's prolonged absences at war and of his reluctance to return to Iracema. Poti lives with the couple in the forest to form an unusual emotional triangle; on being separated from Martim, he hears words of regret that rival the affection shown by Iracema for her husband:

> —Poti's hut will be left abandoned and sad.
> —Your brother's heart will be deserted and sad, far from you. (OC, III, p. 226)

While the birth of Moacyr momentarily revives the ties of affection between Martim and Iracema, the *india* is increasingly compelled to compete with Poti for her husband's loyalty. The expressions of love offered by the two Indians demonstrate how the relationships differ: between the men there is a bond of equality, whereas Iracema's attachment is one of "clinging" dedication and self-denial:

> Poti sang:
> —Like the snake that has two heads on a single body, so is the friendship of Coatiabo [Martim] and Poti.
> Iracema came forward:
> —Like the oyster that does not leave the rock, even after it has died, so is Iracema beside her husband. (OC, III, p. 233)

These songs, like the ceremonial painting of his body by the two Indians, are intended to celebrate Martim's ritual assimilation as an Indian, a "son of Tupã," and his acceptance of his new "fatherland." Again, the qualities they each invoke represent the contrasting values that define their respective relationships to the European. Poti asks that Martim should have the strength and speed of the warrior, while Iracema wishes that her husband's courage be tempered with "sweetness." However, it is the masculine, warrior fraternity that ultimately gains possession of Martim. Iracema dies not so much because Martim continues to long for the "white virgin" but because he deserts her to accompany the "inseparable one," Poti, in his distant wars against her tribespeople. Confirming this, Martim does not abandon his new homeland definitively, even though Iracema tells him, before the birth of the child, that with her death all the ties keeping him in the country will be severed:

> When your son leaves Iracema's bosom, she will die, like the maize-flower after it has given up its fruit. Then the white warrior will have no one left to keep him in this foreign land. (OC, III, p. 239)

In fact, she is proved wrong, for Martim does eventually return, to found a colony based on the brotherhood of Indian and white man, sanctioned by God:

> Poti was the first to kneel at the foot of the holy cross; he would not allow anything to separate him ever again from his white brother. They must both have a single God, as they had a single heart. (OC, III, p. 246)

This exclusive, all-male bond between Indian and white is reminiscent of the North American myth of the "Good Companions in the Wilderness," which Leslie Fiedler discusses in relation to Fenimore Cooper's *Leatherstocking* novels.[95] Natty Bumppo's friendship with the Mohicans Uncas and Chingachgook constitutes what Fiedler considers a basically antiheterosexual, "homoerotic" relationship, a flight from the dominant woman of white bourgeois society. It is interesting to note, then, that for Martim, his relationship with Poti represents a flight not from his white mistress but from the Indian Iracema. This difference must be explained by the divergent historical experience of race relations in the two colonial situations, North American and Brazilian. In the former, the white community's social and sexual hostility to the Indian leaves it freer to fantasize about a mythical new American native in the ideal world of the forest. Alencar, on the other hand, recognizes that he cannot formulate his version of the new Brazilian national without confronting the historical reality of miscegenation. The myth of Indian-white brotherhood, based as it apparently is on a notion of equality, may act as a distraction from the sexual violence and oppression of Conquest. But Indians such as the "loyal" Poti, who voluntarily betrays the long-term interests of his people and fights his fellow Indians, were a minority, if not exceptions, in the history of the colony.

The myth of fraternal military alliance as the basis for the colony is, in any case, ultimately unsustainable because it is an essentially sterile "marriage." Martim and Poti may live happily ever after as blood brothers sharing battles, war paint and a common god, but they cannot produce a new *mestiço* generation, the new "race" of Brazilians conscious of their independent, American identity. As Alencar's novel aims to demonstrate, the sources of that postcolonial identity can be sought only within the sexual politics of the relationship between Martim and Iracema, in the history of white betrayal and Indian sacrifice, and in the character of their offspring, the rootless, motherless Moacyr, "child of pain." As the embryonic heart of the infant nation, it is left to Moacyr to grow to adulthood and in the process reconcile himself with his history. But the collusion of both parents, Indian and European, in Alencar's mythical re-reading of the colonial seduction, can leave no room for recrimination, anxiety, or guilt in the postcolonial order. The anticipation, personified in Moacyr, that this tragic birth will give way to hope and to a guiltless future recalls another biblical figure, the son of Jacob and Rachel. Like Moacyr, he was first baptized Ben-Oni, "son of my sorrow," but was later renamed Benjamin, "son of the right hand or son of good omen."[96] As the bearer of this optimism, emerging from the birth pangs of the colonial era, all that remains for Moacyr, rather like the mulatto son of the slave woman Joana in Alencar's play *Mother*, is to remember his mother's sacrifice, to take his place in modern society, and to make his own history. The non-European, Indian or African, has played her part and can be safely and reassuringly consigned to a mythical past, mourned but never avenged.

But if *Iracema* at least takes the tragic narrative of sacrifice and betrayal as its starting point, at an aesthetic level the language and style of the novel appear to offer a less ambiguous celebration of the cultural legacy of miscegenation. In fact, the majority of critical attention has been concerned not with the mythical content of the novel as earlier examined but with its stylistic qualities, its status as a "prose poem." On its first publication, *Iracema* was greeted with the outraged reaction of the academic establishment, such as that of Antônio Henriques Leal in his "Questão Filológica." As the criticisms of Leal and others indicate quite manifestly, their objections to the novel's unorthodox syntax, phraseology, and vocabulary represented a basic resistance to the point Alencar was consciously attempting to make, that the existence of a peculiarly "Brazilian" language must be acknowledged as proof of the nation's distinctive cultural identity. It was precisely against this that Leal and others were protesting: "I cannot, however, cease to revolt against the false doctrine that the language is different in Brazil and that it should be transformed so as to make it independent."[97]

In a number of statements Alencar made it clear that *Iracema* was, to a large extent, intended as a vehicle for these radical new ideas concerning the place of language in the consolidation of an independent culture: "In it you will see realized my ideas regarding the national literature; and you will find in it a wholly Brazilian poetry, absorbed from the language of the savages."[98] The country's unique experience of contact and interaction between the Portuguese colonist and the indigenous landscape and its people required not just new myths and vocabulary but whole new structures and means of expression:

[I]f those peoples live in different continents, under different climates, not only are political ties broken, there also occurs a separation of ideas, feelings, customs and therefore language, which is the expression of those moral and social facts.[99]

While the language, style, and syntax of *Iracema* are unquestionably artificial, bearing little relation to any real Brazilian vernacular, they, nevertheless, constitute a remarkable rhetorical achievement, suggesting a unique mythical and psychological world ordered not by conventional measures of time but by the cycles of nature. The narrator speaks the same metaphorical language as his characters, as if the story were being told from within the indigenous world by one of its members. The historical background to the novel's events is disposed of in a preliminary synopsis, eliminating the notion of suspense and allowing a lyrical, rather than narrative, structure to predominate. Chapters closely resemble poetic stanzas, rarely extending beyond a couple of pages, and they mark self-contained episodes that end not in anticipation or revelation but in closure. This is frequently suggested by the image of departure, resignation or nightfall, for example: "The cauã falcon hooted way off at the far end of the valley. Night was falling" (Chapter 3); "The old man sat in his hammock again. The virgin left, closing the door of the hut" (Chapter 12); "Martim withdrew so as not to bring shame to Iracema's sadness" (Chapter 18); "The Christian encircled the beautiful Indian girl's waist and drew her close to his breast. His lips laid upon the lips of his wife a kiss, but one that was brusque and cool" (Chapter 28).

Through a constant flow of metaphorical images, the central, psychological drama of the novel appears to unfold not as a consequence of external social or historical forces but within the natural cycle of life and death in the forest. Familiarity with this world is assumed, and present and imperfect tenses remove events from an objective, historical past into the reader's subjective present:

—Can your eyes not see the beautiful jacaranda over there, rising up into the clouds? At its foot still lies the dry root of the leafy myrtle, which every winter becomes covered with foliage and red berries and embraces its brother trunk. If it did not die, the jacaranda would have no sunlight to grow so tall. Iracema is the dark leaf that casts a shadow over your soul: she must fall, so that joy can light up your heart. (OC, III, p. 239)

This is the real substance of the novel, the accumulation of pseudoindigenous, poetic imagery that its characters live and speak, defining them as the inhabitants of a special, mythical universe, a primitive, "Brazilian" world. Its function, beyond Alencar's rhetorical argument about the status of Brazilian Portuguese, is to suggest that the novel's mythohistorical narrative is somehow absorbed into a larger, timeless order of things, in other words, that the social, political, and sexual history of human individuals has become naturalized; Iracema's death, like that of her people, appears as natural and inevitable as the falling away of the myrtle leaf from the jacaranda tree. As the novel's closing words put it:

A jandaia cantava ainda no olho do coqueiro; mas não repetia já o mavioso nome de Iracema.
Tudo passa sobre a terra.

(The *jandaia* still sang in the eye of the coconut-palm; but it no longer repeated the tender name of Iracema./ Everything passes from the face of the earth.)

Iracema became the target of a new current of criticism in the 1870s, beginning with Távora and Castilho and their *Letters to Cincinato* and *Issues of the Day*.[100] Questioning the validity of the Indianist theme as an appropriate means of exploring contemporary Brazilian society, they signaled the rise of new scientific, philosophical, and literary developments—sociology, positivism and realism— that were to lead to an enormous reassessment of the contribution of tribal society to the national culture. But well before these currents of thought began to be manifested in the next generation of Indianist writing, the tensions and contradictions that had been contained within Alencar's conciliatory interpretation of miscegenation were becoming exposed in the fiction of his immediate successors.

As early as 1857, the year in which *The Guarani Indian* was published, the issue of tribal integration was explored in rather less mythical terms by the Amazonian writer Lourenço da Silva Araújo Amazonas in his novel *Simá*. The work of a military officer stationed in Amazonas, like Wilkens's *A Muhraida* a century earlier, *Simá* was not rooted organically within the national Indianist tradition but was instead a distinctly Amazonian product of very specific local experiences and conditions. Consequently, it does not figure in nineteenth-century histories of Brazilian literature and has only recently been examined in critical studies of Brazilian Indianism.[101] Nevertheless, its theme—the rebellion of the Manau Indians two years after Pombal's 1755 Laws of Liberty—went to the heart of the movement's ideological concerns, that is to say, the notion of Indian assimilation into white society as a model and stimulus for the integration of the nation-state.

The novel's innovation lay in its critique of the eighteenth-century *diretoria* system for its failure to address the continuing ethnic monopoly of resources and property by a white, European-born elite. Only a policy of genuine mesticization, offsetting the traditional dominance of the Portuguese by incorporating both the indigenous communities and a new immigrant population into Amazonian society, could guarantee the future social and economic well-being of the region. That Araújo Amazonas also had in mind the more recent post-independence history of the Regency period is clear from the book's opening pages. Here we find a description of a ruined settlement similar to that which is to provide the focus for the novel's tragic events. However, its immediate purpose is to recall the devastation caused by the Mura Indians during the 1835 Cabanagem "Revolution," which raised the specter of sociopolitical chaos and disintegration early in the life of the Empire.

The other major point of interest is that the book's protagonists are a detribalized *tapuio* settler, Marcos, and his bastard granddaughter Simá, whose mother was raped by an evil *regatão* or river trader, Regis. Regis determines to prevent Simá's marriage to the Manau Indian Domingos, who is one of the few tribespeople to favor the new mission system. When it is rumored that father, granddaughter, and Domingos alike are reverting to tribal ways, the three are drawn inexorably and fatally into the Manau rebellion that is already beginning to destroy the Portuguese settlements and butcher their inhabitants.

Thus, the introduction of the secular directorate system is seen as a tragically wasted opportunity to incorporate the region's social and ethnic forces into a single community, the embryo of a future nation-state. The year 1755 forms a vital chronological fulcrum in the book, marking the beginning of Marcos's attempt to start a new life with his granddaughter under a different name and Regis's new assumed role as a mission director. Extended discussions among the book's characters focus on the significance of the Pombaline Laws of Liberty, seriously questioning their value for the Indians themselves and anticipating the outcome of the novel.

Araújo Amazonas rightly insinuates that the enlightened, humanitarian policy of "emancipation," in fact, concealed as its underlying purpose the opening up of the newly ratified territories of the Amazon to systematic agricultural exploitation on a grand capitalist scale. Through his characterization of Regis, the author exposes as highly ingenuous the spokesmen for Pombal's policy who believed in the philanthropic motives of the new mission directors. Regis abandons his occupation as *regatão* to join the flood of opportunistic settlers who poured into the region following the announcement of the new legislation, in expectation of more lucrative forms of activity created by an accessible pool of indigenous manpower. As well as exploiting their labor more intensively than before, these *arrivistas* were now also competing with the Indians for possession of their land and women; local missions experienced a serious decline because their young women were "disappearing" in increasing numbers.

Years later, speaking sometime after Pombal's laws have begun to take effect, Jarumá, the leader of the Manau revolt, exposes the promise of emancipation for the sham that it is. The open slavery of the mission Indian has been replaced by the slavery of the wage laborer; equality of opportunity is meaningless in a society that has retained all the old racial prejudices, all the traditional economic relationships between master and slave:

How sincerely can the Indian aspire, like any other Portuguese subject, to honors and employment by virtue of his abilities and merits! what a mockery! what sarcasm! for what qualification can have been acquired by an individual for social distinctions who has been raised in slavery and brutalized by it? Go in the midst of that Society that is supposed to belong to us fraternally today: what will you observe? The Portuguese in the drawing-room, and the Indian in the kitchen! the Portuguese educated, and the Indian ignorant! the Portuguese rich, and the Indian poor! and in short the Portuguese with his whip across the Indian's back! with indignation forever in his heart, and insults in the mouth of the Portuguese, and feelings in the Indian's heart, and tears in the Indian's eyes! . . . oh what freedom, what generosity, what concessions!!![102]

In the light of this powerful indictment of the congenital failure of Pombal's policy of integration, how does Marcos justify his initial opposition to the Manau rebellion and his continued efforts to succeed as a prosperous farmer within the white-dominated colonial society of Amazonas? Because, for Marcos and the author, whatever the iniquities of both the Jesuit mission system and the *diretoria* administration, in the last resort the material and social progress of the Indians is inextricable from that of the nation as a whole. This identity of Indian and national interests clearly has a more substantial political and economic rationale than the token use of the theme during the first phase of the movement. The narrator compares the "patriotic enthusiasm" of Marcos and his daughter with that of those celebrated Indians, such as Antônio Filipe Camarão and

Tibiriçá, who fought alongside the Portuguese to preserve the Brazilian territory against the threats to its integrity by Dutch and French incursions. For Domingos, also initially opposed to the rebellion, it is the responsibility of the integrated *tapuio* to contribute all his energies to the construction and consolidation of an independent national economy, free from the control of foreign interests:

—Who can deny the desirability and importance of Independence? but I do not believe that one should be Independent only to return to the old savagery. Once a certain degree of civilization has been achieved, I think it should be cultivated and passed on to those who will come after us, with the recommendation that it be applied opportunely and advisedly to the benefit of the Country, so that a true Independence can then be announced, through which they will not continue (as we should, today, if we were to do so) to be slaves in their own Country, which will irremediably occur if hastily and inexpertly they are so senseless as to lend their names to the inauguration of an order of things whose benefits are monopolized by the clever and greedy foreigner.[103]

The hope for this independent, *mestiço* nation lies with *tapuios* such as Domingos and Simá, who have acquired the best, "natural" qualities of a Rousseauian, tribal childhood "but adapted to civilization as taught to them by the Carmelite missionaries on the Upper Amazon."[104]

Simá was therefore a critical examination of the real social and economic implications of the integrationist policies of the 1850s that had informed the Indianist movement during this central phase and the fictional mythologies of Alencar, in particular. Following more closely in the wake of the tradition established by Alencar was his younger relative Tristão de Alencar Araripe Júnior, who, in two short stories from the collection *Contos Brazileiros* (1868), written under the pseudonym Oscar Jagoanharo, reproduced the familiar dramas of sacrifice, alliance, and conflict between the forces of love and war, with characters closely resembling Peri and Iracema. However, although Araripe Júnior continued to explore the integrationist mythology of military-political alliances and miscegenation, his fiction increasingly confronted the knowledge that the "social contract" on which the postcolonial order was based imposed an inordinate burden of sacrifice on one of the parties, the Indian.

The Tobajara chief of his short story "Tabyra" (1868), for example, is clearly modeled on Alencar's Peri, "a fantastic being, or a mysterious genie of the forests" who, in loyalty to the governor of Pernambuco, leads his warriors into battle against the murderous, bestial Caeté. But the story's closing scene, a fraternal embrace between the two allies, cannot completely dispel Tabyra's sense of regret and guilt for his part in a war against fellow Indians, which leaves him permanently scarred: "All that could be found there, like the traces of an extinct volcano, were the relics of a hero wounded by misfortune and overwhelmed by the contingencies of perishable matter."[105]

In Araripe Júnior's novella *Jacina, a Marabá* (1870), meanwhile, the *mestiça* has ceased to provide a potential point of convergence between races, cultures, and antagonistic political forces and is instead the expression of marginalization and prejudice, as in Teixeira e Sousa's *The Three Days of a Marriage*. The historical setting is once more the sixteenth-century Tamoios war, examined this time from the perspective of the Portuguese alliance with the Guaianaz Indians, the enemies of the Tamoios. While the tribal *morubixaba* or chief, Inimbó, has long since been cowed by colonial rule, and his son has succumbed to the influence of the Jesuits, the strongest defender of independence and tribal tradition is ironically Jacina, an Amazon-like figure who, unknown to herself, is a *marabá* or *mestiça*. In an unspoken warning to Jacina, Inimbó predicts that this irony will be her downfall: "Jacina! The hatred that the daughter holds for the white men will perhaps one day turn against her own blood."[106]

Indeed, the independence that she advocates for the tribe also echoes her own social and sexual isolation, as well as her tragic fate at the end of the story. The young warrior Urutágua has returned to lead joint Indian and white forces against the Tamoios but is distracted from this responsibility by his love for Jacina. She, however, despises him because he remains fascinated by the white god, Abaruna. Under her influence, the traditional values of the tribe begin to recover their ascendancy, and the shaman regains his spiritual control from the missionary. Against the background of this reawakening of tribal nationalism, Jacina's unusually pale complexion is suspiciously denounced as being that of a *marabá*; like the evil French spy, Morangarana, who earlier infiltrated the Guaianaz camp in order prepare the way for a Tamoio attack, Jacina is now singled out as an intolerable and dangerous presence:

And Morangarana, who is mixing the blood spilt from Jacina's veins with that of the tribe, will be the chief of the Guaianases. Do they not see how the virgin's cheeks do not match those of her brothers in their colour?[107]

Urutágua risks the defeat of his people by attempting to save Jacina from execution, in the face even of her own ironic accusations: "Urutágua has died!/ Why did the bravest Guaianás warrior leave the verdant forests that witnessed his birth?"[108] He ends the book about to plunge to his death, with Jacina's corpse in his canoe, in a final, futile attempt to destroy Morangarana and those of his race.

As we shall see in the next chapter, Araripe Júnior's Indianist novella heralded a new phase in the movement in which the myth of Conciliation was discredited and in which the processes of miscegenation and detribalization were expressive not of racial democracy or sociopolitical integration but of the fragmentation and dividedness of postcolonial society. In a sense, then, the movement returned during those last two decades of Empire to its beginnings; but at the same time, by following through the consequences of this transformation of tribal society in its contact with the colonizer, it inevitably anticipated the end of the tradition of mythical, nationalist Indianism and the emergence of a new literary genre—regionalism—inhabited by a different version of the indigenous primitive, the *caboclo*.

NOTES

1. Cited by Hélio Vianna, *História do Brasil* (São Paulo: Melhoramentos/USP, 1975), p. 468, in Tania Rebelo Costa Serra, *Joaquim Manuel de Macedo ou Os Dois Macedos: A Luneta Mágica do II Reinado* (Rio de Janeiro: Fundação Biblioteca Nacional/Departamento Nacional do Livro, 1994), p. 63.

2. Serra, *Joaquim Manuel de Macedo*, p. 64.

3. José Honório Rodrigues, *Conciliação e Reforma no Brasil: um desafio histórico-cultural* (Rio de Janeiro: Nova Fronteira, 1982), pp. 57-58.

4. José Murilo de Carvalho, *Teatro de sombras: a política imperial* (São Paulo: Vértice, 1988), p. 17.

5. Ibid., pp. 17-18.

6. Rodrigues, *Conciliação e Reforma no Brasil*, p. 62.

7. Ibid., p. 64.

8. Ibid., p. 63.

9. R. Magalhães Júnior, *Três Panfletários do Segundo Reinado* (São Paulo: Companhia Editora Nacional, 1956), pp. 218-19.

10. José Joaquim Machado de Oliveira, "Noticia raciocinada sobre as aldeias de indios da provincia de S. Paulo, desde o seu começo até à actualidade," *Revista do Instituto Histórico e Geográfico Brasileiro* 8 (1846), p. 205.

11. Manuela Carneiro da Cunha, "Política indigenista no século XIX," in *História dos Índios do Brasil* (São Paulo: Companhia das Letras/Secretaria Municipal de Cultura/FAPESP, 1992), p. 139.

12. Carlos de Araújo Moreira Neto, "A Política Indigenista Brasileira Durante o século XIX" (mimeo.) (Doctoral thesis, Faculdade de Filosofia, Ciências e Letras de Rio Claro, São Paulo, 1971), pp. 68-69.

13. *Guanabara: revista mensal artistica, scientifica e litteraria* (Rio de Janeiro: Typ. Guanabarense de L.A.F. de Menezes, 1849-55), vol. 1, pp. 396-97.

14. Marques Rebêlo, *Vida e obra de Manuel Antônio de Almeida* (Rio de Janeiro: Instituto Nacional do Livro, 1943), pp. 25-34.

15. Manuel Antônio de Almeida, "Civilização dos indígenas: Duas palavras ao autor do 'Memorial Orgânico,'" *Obra Dispersa* (Rio de Janeiro: Graphia, 1991), pp. 7-13.

16. *Revista do Instituto Histórico e Geográfico Brasileiro* 17, 3d series, no. 14 (1854), p. 229.

17. *Guanabara*, vol. 2, pp. 191-92.

18. Ibid., pp. 194-95.

19. Francisco Adolfo de Varnhagen, *História Geral do Brasil antes da sua separação e independência de Portugal*, 2 vols. (São Paulo: Melhoramentos, 1959), vol. 1, pp. 52-53.

20. Varnhagen, *História Geral do Brasil*, vol. 1, p. 56.

21. Heitor Lyra, *História de Dom Pedro II: 1825-1891*, 3 vols. (Belo Horizonte: Itatiaia, 1977), vol. 2, p. 122.

22. José Honório Rodrigues, *Independência: Revolução e Contra-revolução*, 4 vols. (Rio de Janeiro: Francisco Alves, 1975), vol. 2, p. 105.

23. Francisco Adolfo de Varnhagen, "O matrimônio de um Bisavô ou O Caramuru (Romance historico braziliero)," *Florilégio da Poesia Brazileira*, 3 vols. (Rio de Janeiro: Publicações da Academia Brasileira, 1946), vol. 3, pp. 225-38; Francisco Adolfo de Varnhagen, *O Caramuru: romance histórico brasileiro* (Rio de Janeiro: Typografia de Pinto de Sousa, 1861); see also Varnhagen's historical study of the legend: Francisco Adolpho de Varnhagen, "O Caramurú perante a historia," *Revista do Instituto Histórico e Geográfico Brasileiro* 3, no. 10 (2d trimester of 1848), pp. 129-52; David Treece,

"Caramuru the Myth: Conquest and Conciliation," *Ibero-Amerikanisches Archiv* 10, no. 2 (1984), pp. 139-73.

24. Emília Viotti da Costa, *Da Monarquia à república: momentos decisivos* (São Paulo: Grijalbo, 1977), pp. 88-97.

25. Francisco Adolfo de Varnhagen, *Sumé: lenda mytho-religiosa americana, recolhida em outras eras por um Indio Moranduçara; agora traduzida e dada á luz com algumas notas por Um Paulista de Sorocaba* (Madrid: Imp. da V. de Dominguez, 1855), pp. 23-27.

26. Varnhagen, *Sumé: lenda mytho-religiosa americana*, pp. 35-36.

27. J. S. McClelland (ed.), *The French Right (From de Maistre to Maurras)* (London: Jonathan Cape, 1970), p. 52.

28. João Francisco Lisboa, *Crônica do Brasil Colonial (Apontamentos para a História do Maranhão)* (Petrópolis: Vozes, 1976), p. 174.

29. Ibid., pp. 158-59.

30. Ibid., p. 159.

31. Ibid., p. 188.

32. Cited in ibid., p. 187.

33. Ibid., pp. 175-76.

34. Paulo Pinheiro Chagas, *Teófilo Ottoni, Ministro do Povo* (Belo Horizonte: Itatiaia, 1978), p. 157.

35. Cited in ibid., p. 163.

36. Ibid., p. 179.

37. *Report to the President of Minas Gerais*, 1854, in ibid., p. 184.

38. Chagas, *Teófilo Ottoni, Ministro do Povo*, p. 194.

39. Ibid., p. 192.

40. Leônidas Lorentz, *Teófilo Otoni no tribunal da história* (Rio de Janeiro: Author, 1981), pp. 71-74.

41. Chagas, *Teófilo Ottoni, Ministro do Povo*, p. 245.

42. José Honório Rodrigues, *História da História do Brasil*, vol. 2, tome 1: *A Historiografia Conservadora* (São Paulo: Editora Nacional, 1988), p. 27.

43. See Flora Süssekind's critical Introduction, "*As vítimas-algozes* e o imaginário do medo," Joaquim Manuel de Macedo, *As Vítimas-Algozes: quadros da escravidão* (São Paulo: Scipione/Fundação Casa de Rui Barbosa, 1991), pp. xxi-xxxviii.

44. Joaquim Manuel de Macedo, *Cobé, Teatro Completo*, vol. 2 (Rio de Janeiro: Serviço Nacional de Teatro, 1979), pp. 25-26.

45. Ibid., pp. 53-54.

46. Ibid., p. 58.

47. Lyra, *História de Dom Pedro II*, vol. 2, p. 14. See also Lilia Moritz Schwarcz, *As Barbas do Imperador: D. Pedro II, um monarca nos trópicos* (São Paulo: Companhia das Letras, 1998), p. 134.

48. Nelson Werneck Sodré, *História da literatura brasileira: Seus Fundamentos Econômicos* (Rio de Janeiro: Civilização Brasileira, 1969), p. 209; Antonio Candido, *Formação da literatura brasileira (Momentos decisivos)*, 2 vols. (São Paulo: Martins, 1962), vol. 1, p. 300.

49. Domingos José Gonçalves de Magalhães, *A Confederação dos Tamoios* (Rio de Janeiro: Dous de Dezembro, 1856), note 311.

50. Magalhães, *A Confederação dos Tamoios*, p. 181.

51. Alexandre Herculano, "Carta a D. Pedro II, sobre 'A Confederação dos Tamoios,'" *Brasilia* 10 (1958), p. 314.

52. Magalhães, *A Confederação dos Tamoios*, pp. 114-15.

53. In José Aderaldo Castello (ed.), *A Polêmica sôbre "A Confederação dos Tamoios"*: *Críticas de José de Alencar, Manuel de Araújo Porto-Alegre, D. Pedro II e outros* . . . (São Paulo: Faculdade de Filosofia, Ciências e Letras da Universidade de São Paulo, 1953), p. 5.

54. Afrânio Coutinho, *A Tradição Afortunada (O Espírito de Nacionalidade na Crítica Brasileira)* (Rio de Janeiro: José Olympio, 1968), p. 93.

55. José de Alencar, "Benção Paterna," *Sonhos d'Ouro* (São Paulo: Ática, 1981), p. 10.

56. Doris Sommer, *Foundational Fictions: The National Romances of Latin America* (Berkeley: University of California Press, 1993), pp. 151-52. See also Salgado Guimarães, "Nação e civilização nos trópicos . . .," cited by Sommer.

57. Pierre Albouy, *La Création Mythologique chez Victor Hugo* (Paris: José Corte, 1968), p. 89.

58. Josué Montello, "A 'Comédia Humana' de José de Alencar," *Clã*, no. 21 (December 1965), pp. 11-12.

59. Pierre Barberis, *Mythes Balzaciens* (Paris: Armand Colin, 1972), p. 37.

60. Barberis, *Mythes Balzaciens*, p. 37.

61. Pierre Barberis, *Balzac: une mythologie réaliste* (Paris: Libraire Larousse, 1971), p. 112.

62. H. Levin, *The Gates of Horn: A Study of Five French Realists* (New York: Oxford University Press, 1966), p. 212.

63. Ibid., p. 211; see also John Cruickshank (ed.), *French Literature and Its Background*, 6 vols. (London, Oxford, New York: Oxford University Press, 1969), vol. 4: *The Early Nineteenth Century*, p. 118.

64. Honoré de Balzac, *Les Chouans (Une passion dans le désert) ou La Bretagne en 1799* (Paris: Calmann Lévy, 1898), pp. 19-20.

65. Ibid., p. 131.

66. Barberis, *Balzac: une mythologie réaliste*, p. 112.

67. Sir Walter Scott, *Ivanhoe* (London: Dean and Son, n.d.), p. 217.

68. Ibid., p. 219.

69. Georg Lukács, *The Historical Novel* (London: Merlin Press, 1989), p. 36.

70. Benedict Anderson, *Imagined Communities: Reflections on the Origin and Spread of Nationalism* (London: Verso, 1991).

71. José de Alencar, *Obra Completa*, 4 vols. (Rio de Janeiro: Aguilar, 1965), vol. 4, p. 691; all quotations are taken from this edition unless otherwise indicated. References begin with the abbreviation OC, followed by the volume and page number.

72. Rodrigues, *Conciliação e Reforma no Brasil*, pp. 57-58.

73. Schwarcz, *As Barbas do Imperador*, pp. 134-35.

74. Luís Viana Filho, *A Vida de José de Alencar* (Rio de Janeiro: Instituto Nacional do Livro, 1979), p. 228; this and the following works are the sources for the biographical details given here: R. Magalhães Júnior, *José de Alencar e sua época* (Rio de Janeiro: Civilização Brasileira, 1977); José de Alencar, "Como e Porque sou romancista," *O Guarani, Obras Completas* (Rio de Janeiro: Letras e Artes, 1967), pp. 9-29; Brito Broca, "Alencar: Vida, Obra e Milagre," *Ensaios da mão canhestra* (São Paulo: Polis, 1981), pp. 155-76; Raimundo de Menezes, *José de Alencar: literato e político* (São Paulo: Martins, 1965) and *Cartas e Documentos de José de Alencar* (São Paulo: Hucitec, 1977).

75. Magalhães Júnior, *José de Alencar e sua época*, p. 279. For a study of master-slave-relations as represented in Alencar's fiction after the Law of the Free Womb was passed, see Cláudia Pazos Alonso, "The Uses and Implications of the Master/Slave Im-

age in Alencar's Novel *Senhora,*" *Ipotesi. Revista de Estudos Literários* 1, no. 1 (July/December 1997), pp. 25-36.

76. João Roberto Faria, *José de Alencar e o teatro* (São Paulo: Perspectiva/EDUSP, 1987), pp. 38-46, 99-100.

77. Ibid., pp. 107-8.

78. Ibid., pp. 41-44.

79. Ibid., p. 105.

80. Ibid., p. 98.

81. Richard Graham, *Patronage and Politics in Nineteenth-Century Brazil* (Stanford, Calif.: Stanford University Press, 1990), pp. 26-27.

82. See Emília Viotti da Costa, *The Brazilian Empire: Myths and Histories* (Chicago and London: University of Chicago Press, 1985), Chapter 9: "The Myth of Racial Democracy: A Legacy of the Empire," pp. 234-46; Michael George Hanchard, *Orpheus and Power: The* Movimento Negro *of Rio de Janeiro and São Paulo, Brazil, 1945-1988* (Princeton, N.J.: Princeton University Press, 1994), Chapter 3, "Racial Democracy: Hegemony, Brazilian Style," pp. 43-74, for critical accounts of this tradition.

83. João Camillo de Oliveira Torres, *A Democracia Coroada: Teoria Política do Império do Brasil* (Petrópolis: Vozes, 1964), p. 37.

84. Gilberto Freyre, *Sobrados e Mucambos: Decadência do Patriarcado Rural e Desenvolvimento do Urbano* 3 vols. (Rio de Janeiro: José Olympio, 1951), vol. 2, p. 640.

85. Ibid., pp. 637-38.

86. Alencar, "Os 'Sonhos d'Ouro,'" *Sonhos d'Ouro*, p. 160.

87. Scalvini, *Il Guarany: Opera-Ballo in Quattro Atti (libretto)* (Milano: Coi. Tipi do Francesco Lucca, 1870); Anon., *Guarany ou O Amor no deserto* (Lisbon: Typ. 62, Rua do Crucifixo 66, 1875); *O Guarany: folha illustrada litteraria, artistica, noticiosa, critica*, year 1, no. 1 (January 1871). See also Cleusa Aparecida Valin, "Escritores Brasileiros: Filmografia," *Filme Cultura* 20 (May-June 1972), p. 42.

88. See, for example, the extract from Alencar's biography of Antônio Filipe Camarão of 1849, cited in Magalhães Júnior, *José de Alencar*, pp. 36-37. Alencar's main source for the novel is Balthazar da Silva Lisboa, *Annaes do Rio de Janeiro*, 7 vols. (Rio de Janeiro: Na Typ. Imp. e const. de Seignot-Plancher e Cia., 1834), vol. 1.

89. Silviano Santiago's otherwise excellent essay on the novel, "Liderança e Hierarquia em Alencar," *Vale Quanto Pesa (Ensaios sobre questões político-culturais)* (Rio de Janeiro: Paz e Terra, 1982), pp. 89-116, fails to make this distinction.

90. Ibid., p. 101, cited in Sommer, *Foundational Fictions*, p. 145.

91. Afonso Romano de Sant'Anna, "O Guarani," *Análise Estrutural de Romances Brasileiros* (Petrópolis: Vozes, 1973), pp. 54-83.

92. Candido, *Formação da literatura brasileira*, vol. 2, p. 265. See also Edgard Cavalheiro, *Fagundes Varela* (São Paulo: Martins, 1953), pp. 235-36.

93. Fagundes Varela, *Anchieta ou O Evangelho nas selvas, Poesias Completas* (São Paulo: Saraiva, 1956), pp. 619-922, canto X, stanza viii.

94. John Hemming, *Red Gold: The Conquest of the Brazilian Indians* (London: Macmillan, 1978), pp. 207-10, 294-98, 304 ff.

95. Leslie A. Fiedler, *The Return of the Vanishing American* (London: Paladin, 1972).

96. My thanks to Anne Burke for this suggestion.

97. Antônio Henriques Leal, "A Literatura Brasileira Contemporânea," *Locubrações* (São Luiz: Magalhães & cia, 1874), p. 213; see also Pinheiro Chagas, "Literatura Brasileira—José de Alencar," *Novos Ensaios Críticos* (V. M. Porto, em casa da viuva More Editora/Praça de D. Pedro, 1869), p. 198.

212   •   *Exiles, Allies, Rebels*

98. Alencar, "Carta ao Dr. Jaguaribe," OC, III, p. 255.

99. Alencar, "Pós-escrito (à 2ª ed.)," OC, III, p. 260.

100. See, for example, Franklin Távora (Semprônio), "Carta III," in Chagas, *Novos Ensaios Críticos*.

101. Only regional studies of Amazonian culture, such as Mário Ypiranga Monteiro's *Fases da literatura amazonense* vol. 1 (Manaus: Imprensa Oficial, 1977) and Márcio Souza's *A Expressão Amazonense: do colonialismo ao neocolonialismo* (São Paulo: Alfa Omega, 1978), have made known the existence of the novel. My thanks to Neide Gondim de Freitas Pinto of Manaus for bringing *Simá* to my attention and for providing me with a copy of her study of the novel, "A Representação da conquista da Amazônia em *Simá, Beiradão,* e *Galvez, Imperador do Acre*" (mimeo.) (Masters Dissertation: PUC do Rio Grande do Sul, 1982). See also David Brookshaw's discussion of the novel in *Paradise Betrayed: Brazilian Literature of the Indian* (Amsterdam: CEDLA, 1988), pp. 129-34.

102. Lourenço da Silva Araújo Amazonas, *Simá: romance historico do Alto Amazonas* (Pernambuco: Typ. de F.C. de Lemos e Silva, 1857), pp. 64-65.

103. Ibid., p. 68.

104. Ibid., p. 109.

105. Oscar Jagoanharo (pseud.), *Contos Brazileiros* (Recife: Typ. do Correio Penambucano, 1868), p. 87.

106. Tristão de Alencar Araripe Júnior, *Jacina, a Marabá* (Rio de Janeiro: Três, 1973), p. 34.

107. Ibid., p. 152.

108. Ibid., pp. 179-80.

4

The Savage Strikes Back

SHATTERING THE INDIANIST DREAM

As we have seen, the regeneration of the Indianist movement during the 1850s and 1860s was due principally to the special character of Alencar's work, its success in capturing the mood of political conciliation and providing it with a mythical foundation. Over the next few years Alencar continued to explore and rework the basic narrative formulas and structure of *The Guarani Indian* in three regionalist novels. The changes introduced in these texts, in particular, the degeneration of the archetypal patriarchal community of the rural interior, suggest that Alencar's faith in the mythology of Conciliation was becoming increasingly eroded as the political consensus of Empire began to collapse. Whereas *The Guarani Indian* was largely structured around the Flood myth, a myth of purification and renewal, the regionalist novels tend to be increasingly dominated by the burden of the past, by the legacies of crime and retribution, and by the image of a guilty, repressed society.

In the latest of the three texts, *O Sertanejo* (The Backwoodsman, 1876), for example, gone is the chivalric nobility of Dom Antônio de Mariz. In its place is the crude authoritarianism of the northeastern land barons, which acquires tyrannical, despotic proportions:

They exercised the supreme right of life and death, *jus vitae et necis*, over their vassals, who numbered all those embraced by their strong arm in the enormity of that hinterland. They were the sole dispensers of justice in their dominions, and they acted instantly, summarily, without appeal or exemption, at any of the three levels of their jurisdiction, the lower, middle and upper. They had no need of courts for this, nor ministers or judges; their will was at one and the same time the law and sentence; all that was required was the executor.

Such potentates, born and raised in the enjoyment and exercise of an unbridled despotism, accustomed to seeing every head bowed at a sign from them, and to receiving displays of timorous deference, which went beyond mere vassalage to the extent of superstition, were incapable, as can easily be understood, of living in peace except in isolation and so distant from one another, that the arrogance of one would not offend the other.[1]

The novel opens with a false accusation of arson, which sets the rancher Campelo and his daughter Dona Flor at odds with the cowhand Arnaldo, and, despite their eventual reconciliation, the young couple is denied the ideal marriage that concluded Alencar's first novel. Arnaldo's more intransigent alter ego in the novel, Aleixo Vargas, also unjustly suffers humiliation and punishment at the hands of the "Captain-Major." Intent on exacting his revenge, Aleixo offers his services to a rival and is instrumental in bringing about the near abduction of Dona Flor. Significantly, Arnaldo, the "good," ultimately loyal rebel, intervenes to save the day with the help of the local Jucá Indians, forcing Campelo to acknowledge the injustice of his regime.

The abuse of patriarchal authority is represented rather less simplistically in *O Tronco do Ipê* (The Trunk of the Ipê, 1871). Here the rancher Joaquim Freitas has come into possession of the Nossa Senhora do Boqueirão estate through a criminal act of cowardice, whose consequences are now to be revisited upon him. The rightful heir, Joaquim's childhood companion José, the son of his protector and benefactor, had drowned in the Boqueirão whirlpool after Joaquim, stretching out his hand to save him, withdrew it rather than risk his own life. José's own dispossessed son Mário takes the part of the embittered "marginal," a dependent in the Freitas household until his suspicions lead him to the truth, and the Baron is forced to beg for his forgiveness. Interestingly, Mário shares this role of marginality with Benedito, an old black slave who, although long since freed, has remained voluntarily with his wife on the fringes of the farm in loyalty to Mário and to his father's memory. Alencar's myth of voluntary servitude thus finds here its most overt manifestation.

But the most interesting variation on the formula set out in *The Guarani Indian* is *Til* (1871-72), whose curious cast of characters is a far cry from the ideal, archetypal figures who inhabit Alencar's first historical novel. As before, the role of conciliator is played by an adolescent female, Berta, who ends the novel refusing a new life in the city, instead preferring to devote the remainder of her existence to the sick animals and degenerate human inhabitants of the forest: the mad slave Zana, the retarded young epileptic Brás, and the violent *caboclo* descendant of Caiapó Indians, Jão Fera (Wild Man Johnny). She is the only person able to communicate with Brás, and her "mysterious, supernatural influence" pacifies the violent impulses of Jão Fera.

Ironically, though, Berta is also the focus for the conflict between the novel's oppressive, patriarchal figure, the rancher Luís Galvão, and the marginal Jão Fera. The orphaned, bastard offspring of Luís's rape of his former lover, Besita, Berta is raised by a humble family on the margins of the *fazenda*. Jão Fera, meanwhile, is the modern, degenerate counterpart to Peri, more interesting and complex than his ideal model; for he draws out the contradictions that are rendered unproblematic in the Guarani hero, combining both the destructive and creative principles, the Indian as primitive monster and Noble Savage.

Jão's initial devotion to the patriarch, Luís Galvão, is violently betrayed when he witnesses the rape of Berta's mother and her subsequent murder by another man. This turns him into the twisted, embittered *capanga*, the hired killer known as "o Bugre," the pejorative epithet applied to the Indian in the Brazilian interior. Ironically, the only person to defend his character is the guilt-ridden *fazendeiro*, Luís Galvão, who cannot afford to provoke the witness to his crimes. Revealing this knowledge to no one, Jão Fera dedicates himself to Berta's protection, seeing in her the living image of her mother. Indeed, only by her special influence is he restrained for so long from killing the two men who destroyed Besita and left her daughter an orphan.

However, stirred one day by a premonition that Berta is in danger, he discovers her mother's murderer, Ribeiro, about to lay his hands on the girl as she lies asleep. Dragging him into the forest, he then tears him apart with his bare hands. But on hearing the truth about her origins, Berta will not accept Luís as her father; instead she turns to Jão, redeeming him from his embittered, alienated condition and rewarding the sacrifice that was betrayed so cruelly:

—No! no! . . . she exclaimed. You are my father, you who gathered me from my mother's arms as she uttered her last sigh. It is you, who worshipped her like a saint; and when she departed this world, you had no other feeling in your heart but hatred for everyone but me, who reminded you of her. Oh! I understand now, Jão, what made you bad! . . . But I was left in this world, in her place, to make you good! (OC, III, p. 850-51)

The novel is therefore a disturbing parody of *The Guarani Indian* and the ideal world of conciliation it represents; for Jão Fera, a disfigured travesty of the Guarani hero, Peri, there is no just society worth defending but the poor Berta, the offspring of a double crime of violence. While the patriarchal regime continues, guilty and decaying, its victims also live on in the world of the suffering, an adoptive father and daughter consoling each other in their loss and remorse, without hope for the future. Conflict is not resolved openly, in a dynamic equilibrium between equally opposed forces; rather it is suffocated, suppressed onto a level of unconfessed crime, oppressive guilt, and frustrated revenge whose outcome is only further resentment and violence. Alencar's myth of Conciliation has given way to the reality of the Second Reign, a reality that, as the author himself feared, was merely concealed by the superficial politics of party compromise and unanimity.

The works examined so far take us to the beginning of the 1870s, a decade when the political and economic foundations of the Imperial order were being seriously undermined. The appointment of the 1868 Itaboraí government, effectively an Imperial coup, had upset the balance of power shared by Crown and Parliament until then. Pedro II's support of the 1871 Free Womb bill, the first step toward the abolition of slavery, divided Conservatives, creating a new radical group representing those planters who felt a threat to their independence and property rights and who, like Alencar, warned of the economic and social chaos that they believed would ensue. The year 1870 also marked the first serious challenge to the centralization of power under the Second Reign and the emergence of a provincial opposition based on real contact with the local electorate.[2] Liberal abolitionists such as Joaquim Nabuco, meanwhile, criticized the limited range of the reforms being passed and defended the free labor market as a guarantee of economic progress.

Nabuco's role at this stage of the Indianist movement is worth examining in more detail, for he provides a clear focus for the links between abolitionism, the new theories of race, and the anti-indigenist shift within Brazilian culture. The public debate between Nabuco and Alencar, which occupied the Sunday and Thursday editions of the Rio newspaper *O Globo* over several weeks in 1875, suggests at first that Indianism was simply a casualty of the historical triumph of Realism over Romanticism. The Indianists' mythical treatment of their theme, the recourse to early colonial images of primitive man and their elevation into an ideal symbol of liberal and nationalist values, certainly marked out the movement as essentially Romantic in character. Nabuco, recently returned from Europe, attacked Alencar's works from an apparently straightforward, Realist standpoint, criticizing their idealization of events and situations, their lack of verisimilitude, Peri's capture of the lynx in *The Guarani Indian*, for instance, his heroic suicide and miraculous resuscitation from the poison:

He is an effeminate Indian who gives up everything for a woman he worships; who possesses not a single one of the sentiments of his race; who seems to enjoy his slavery, denying his indigenous traditions; in a word, he is a comic-opera savage.[3]

Nabuco's aggressively anti-Indianist stance clearly sprang out of the environmentalist and broadly empirical approaches that positivism was now bringing to bear upon cultural criticism: "Anyone who reads Sr. J. de Alencar's novels will see that he has never left his study and has never taken off his spectacles. The man he depicts for us is never in communication with the environment he inhabits."[4]

However, closer examination of some of Nabuco's remarks reveals that his hostility to Alencar's Indianism was rooted in more than a mere disagreement about novelistic technique and descriptive authenticity. In the first place, his notion of the "authentic" Indian rested on an extremely self-conscious sense of the cultural distance separating modern Western civilization and the primitivism of tribal man:

The Indians in *Iracema*, *Ubirajara* and *The Guarani Indian* are not true savages. Humanity, in order to move from the state in which our savages from the interior still exist to that of our modern civilization has crossed thousands of years. Sr J. de Alencar suppresses that long period and makes out of his savage a man many times superior to that of our race. His Indians think and feel as we do, and speak better, as if they were all poets. Where does this race exist?[5]

Second, in reasserting that cultural gulf that Alencar's work had sought to close up, Nabuco was effectively turning his back on the indigenous world of the rural interior as a possible source of cultural identity, in favor of an unapologetically Eurocentric conception of the civilization to which Brazilian society must aspire:

This Indian literature has pretensions to become the Brazilian literature. Certainly anyone who studies the savage dialects, the crude religion, the confused myths, the coarse customs of our Indians, is lending a service to science, and even to art. What, however, is impossible, is to wish to make of the savages the race to whose civilization our literature must be the monument.[6]

Afrânio Coutinho, who brought together the material of the Alencar-Nabuco debate, rightly reassesses the roles of the two figures, not in terms of the Romantic-Realist paradigm but as representative of two philosophies of Brazilian civilization: one "brasilista" current, which, though not ignoring its European ancestry, addressed a new and peculiarly Brazilian reality born from the fusion of various racial, cultural, social, linguistic, literary, and historical elements; the other, "ocidentalista" perspective expressing a continued identification with the country's European roots, promoting the interests of the descendants of the traditionally dominant class of white Portuguese.[7]

As we shall see, critical and sociological thinking during the last years of Empire and the beginning of the First Republic was essentially polarized in terms of those two viewpoints. On one hand, there were those, such as Capistrano de Abreu, Araripe Júnior, and Couto de Magalhães, who, although modifying the traditional image of the Indian in the light of immigration and the evidence of contact with white society, remained essentially loyal to Alencar's notion of indigenist, *mestiço* nationalism. On the other hand, Sílvio Romero and José Veríssimo took up the concept of miscegenation as an ongoing eugenic process, whose inevitable outcome would be the assimilation or submergence of the inferior Indian and African races and the rise of a new, white European-dominated national type.

Meanwhile, Nabuco's anti-indigenism was not merely confined to the sphere of literature and culture. As Carlos Moreira has observed, it may be of some surprise to learn that Nabuco, one of the leading liberal campaigners for the abolition of slavery, was also the author of an official government document prescribing Indian policy for the first years of the Republic, a policy whose language and ideas are unmistakably based on those of Varnhagen, the apologist for extermination half a century earlier.[8]

During a border dispute between Brazil and Britain over the latter's Guyanese colony, European public opinion was largely influenced by British propaganda that reported cases of Brazilian cruelty and forced labor among the Indians of the Upper Negro and Branco Rivers. Nabuco was Brazil's special envoy in the negotiations, and in his "Final Exposition" he defended his country's policy with the argument that, under Brazilian law, the Indian was not recognized as owning any political sovereignty; as a result, he could possess no legal title to the land he occupied and no rights or control over the transfer of such a title to the colonizing nation. Imperial documents dating from the middle of the century were cited to reaffirm this lack of political status and the consequent freedom of the postcolonial power in disposing of the territories and their inhabitants:

It is not a question of independent Indians, but of rights over the territory. These wandering hordes do not constitute sovereign, independent nations according to the right of peoples. They are subject to the jurisdiction and authority of the civilized nations and regular, recognized governments, to which the territory occupied by those hordes belongs.[9]

The most eminent representative of the opposing view during the same period, the "conciliatory" policy of humane pacification and integration of the Indian into the national society, was General José Vieira Couto de Magalhães (1837-98). A polymath, explorer, entrepreneur, statesman, and author of the linguistic and ethnographic study *O Selvagem* (The Savage), Couto de Magalhães made significant contributions not only to the evolution of indigenist policy but also to the emerging cultural debate on the question of nationality and primitivism. Indeed, he provided the intellectual community of the First Republic, particularly the Modernist movement, with its single most important source of ethnographic material and tribal myths.

While still a relatively young man, during the 1860s Couto de Magalhães occupied the presidencies of Goiás, Pará, and Mato Grosso, where he knew the novelist Bernardo Guimarães, and distinguished himself as a hero of the Paraguayan War in the post of commander-in-chief of the army. But, a loyal monarchist, he renounced his office as president of São Paulo when the Republic was proclaimed, suffering imprisonment under the government of Floriano Peixoto. Commissioned by Pedro II for the Universal Exhibition of the Centenary of the United States in Philadelphia, *The Savage* was the fruit of a number of expeditions to the river Araguaia in Mato Grosso and was first presented in 1874 to the Historical and Geographical Institute before its publication in 1876. Indeed, Magalhães had been granted membership of the Institute in 1862 at the age of just twenty-five, and he remained the Emperor's chief interlocutor on indigenist matters during the latter years of the Second Reign.[10] He had also been a youthful contributor to literary Indianism, with his 1860 novella *Os Guayanazes*; betraying a considerable debt to Alencar's *The Guarani Indian*, the work is considered by David Brookshaw to be essentially a discourse on the contrast between the authentic values of nature and the materialism of modern urban civilization.[11]

The Savage is a very different intellectual and political enterprise altogether. Alongside its history of the preconquest migrations, its firsthand account of the Tupi culture and zoological myths, and its course in the tupi-nheengatu language, which was at that time still widely spoken in the Amazon region, *The Savage* contains Magalhães's views concerning the economic development of the Brazilian interior and the role to be played by indigenous labor. As much as any of the contributors to the debate, Magalhães accepted unquestioningly the legitimacy of his society's wish to exploit the resources, both material and human, of the Brazilian interior. As the following extract from his chapter entitled "The Savage as an Economic Element" shows, he envisaged the incorporation of two elements into that economy, the immigrant settler and the Indian population, with its specialized knowledge of the ecology of the rain forest:

To populate Brazil means:
(1) Importing settlers from Europe to cultivate the lands already opened up in the populated centers, or close to them.
(2) Making use, for the national population, of the still virgin lands where the savage is an obstacle; these lands represent almost two thirds of the territory of the Empire. Making productive a population that is today unproductive is at least as important as bringing in new manpower.
(3) Using the approximately million savages we have, and who are those who can offer the best services in these two thirds of our territory, because the extractive industries, the only viable ones in these regions (as long as there are no roads), have only been and can only be exploited by the savage.[12]

However, what made Magalhães's views so modern and progressive in relation to what had gone before was not simply his understanding of the crucial role of the Indian in any economic project for the region, not only his recognition that alien forms of plantation agriculture could not be imposed upon a forest environment whose delicate ecological balance depended on the prudent extraction of its renewable, indigenous resources. His belief, too, in the cultural potential of the Indian represented an important advance on the somewhat abstract notions of "integration" and "civilization" that had been held by the Romantic Indianists until now. In addition, the methods he proposed for the assimilation of the tribal communities into national society were equally novel and progressive. In the chapter of *The Savage* entitled "Assimilation of the Savage by Means of the Interpreter," we find one of the first explicit statements of the positivist faith in the perfectibility of primitive cultures through contact with higher civilizations, a faith that was to lead to the founding in 1910 of the first official indigenist agency, the Serviço de Proteção ao Índio (Indian Protection Service):

The experience of all peoples and of our own teaches that at the moment when it comes about that a barbarous nationality understands the language of the Christian nationality that is in contact with it, the former will be assimilated into the latter.
The law of human perfectibility is as inflexible as the physical law of the gravitation of bodies.
As soon as the savage possesses, through the intelligence of language, the possibility of understanding what civilization is, he absorbs it as necessarily as a sponge absorbs the liquid that is put in contact with it.
Those men, ferocious and fearful as long as they do not understand our language, have an almost childlike meekness as soon as they understand what we are saying to them.[13]

Having rejected the policy of military subjugation and extermination espoused by Varnhagen and his successors, Couto de Magalhães nevertheless remained equally opposed to the system of villagization that many of the Indianists had advocated, that is, the gathering of whole tribes into large settlements for the purposes of teaching them white methods of farming and Christian morality. Instead, he recommended pacifying hostile tribes in their own territory by means of three institutions: the military settlement, as an outpost of colonization and the first line of contact; the interpreter, who should form part of a trained, organized body of professionals; and the missionary, who would complete the process of assimilation.[14]

Indeed, the propositions raised by Couto de Magalhães were the subject of an intense debate in political and intellectual circles during the first twenty years of the Republic. The main protagonist of that debate, the legendary Cândido Rondon, was, like Magalhães, a soldier, a scientist committed to, and profoundly involved in, the process of economic penetration into the Indian territories of the western interior. Taking up Magalhães's principle of systematic, but humane, "pacification" through the medium of the Indians' own languages, he ushered in a new era in the relationship between Brazilian society and the indigenous populations.

As at previous moments in Imperial history, this new discussion of official indigenist policy was inseparable from the broader cultural debate on nationalism. The renewed interest in the economic potential of Indian labor, together with the acceptance of European immigration as an inevitability, clearly reflected the perceived labor shortage (in reality a shortage of compliant and cheap manpower) that had been imminent since the 1850 ban on the external trade in African slaves. These preoccupations also reflected the dramatic shift in racial composition that Brazilian society underwent during this period. At the beginning of Empire a third of the population had consisted of slaves, while a further 10-15 % were colored freemen; by the end of the Second Reign well over half of the total population was colored.[15] In contrast to this, by the end of the First Republic (1930) 80 % of the plantation slave labor had been replaced by immigrant workers from Italy, Portugal, Spain, and Germany, 2.7 million of whom had entered the country by 1914.

The ruling elite's acute awareness of the impact of immigration on the ethnic and cultural composition of the nation is evident from the series of decrees prohibiting the entry of Asians and Africans in 1850 and 1890 and imposing further limitations in 1921 and 1924. To complicate matters, in the midst of this convergence of African and European elements there remained a considerable marginalized population of Indians, caipiras, matutos, and caboclos—largely indigenous in origin, therefore—which in 1890 stood at 1 million, a twelfth of the total population.[16] The imminence of abolition therefore precipitated a crisis of racial and cultural identity, which was also reflected in the discussions of the new pseudoscientific and materialist theories of social development recently imported from Europe and being applied to the Brazilian situation.

Two "schools" in the northeast of the country were responsible for disseminating these theories. The first was the so-called Recife school, led by Tobias Barreto and Sílvio Romero. With the interest in Germanic ideas following the Franco-Prussian War, Barreto began to publish his studies of German philosophy, while Romero was to apply the determinist theories of the French and

Germans, such as Haeckel, to literature. Another, parallel movement espousing the evolutionist, historical, and environmentalist theories of Spencer, Buckle, and Taine, respectively, appeared in Ceará at about the same time (1874); the Academia Francesa and the Escola Popular were founded, bringing together Araripe Júnior, Capistrano de Abreu, Rocha Lima, and Tomás Pompeu.[17] Along with the more independent critic José Veríssimo, Romero, Araripe Júnior, and Capistrano constituted the most influential body of critical opinion for the period linking the Empire and the Republic, and all recorded significant observations regarding Romantic Indianism and the future place of the Indian in Brazilian society and culture.

Like Nabuco, Romero abhorred the nostalgic idealism of Alencar and his followers, their inability to understand the contemporary social picture, and their insistence on privileging the role of the nonwhite races in shaping the future character of the nation.[18] As he put it in his best-known work, the *História da Literatura Brasileira* (1888), published in abolition year: "It is not a definitive ethnic group; for it is the rather indeterminate result of three different races, which are still separated into different camps alongside one another."[19] Although the *mestiço*, in its fusion of the three principal races, represented "Brazil's genuine historical formation," it, too, was only a transitional stage in the inexorable evolution of the nation in its upward progress toward "whiteness." Having absorbed, to a large degree, the pure African and Indian, the *mestiço* would, in its turn, be assimilated through sheer strength of numbers by the white Aryan.

By contrast, for the historian Capistrano de Abreu, not race but geography was the most influential factor in shaping the character of the Brazilian people. Following the environmentalist theories of Buckle and Ratzel, he was one of the first scholars to attempt a serious evaluation of the popular culture of the Brazilian interior, the *sertão*. In the essay "Contemporary Brazilian Literature" (1875), after defining the physical and cultural laws governing Brazil's evolution, he concluded: "Indolent and excitable, melancholic and nervous, this is the Brazilian people such as the forces and aspects of Nature have made it. . . . The proof of this lies in the study of the Indians."[20] Primitive man's special sensibility to the natural world was the barrier obstructing the emergence of a cohesive political structure in tribal society.

At the same time, though, this indigenous sensibility contained all that was authentically "Brazilian" in the national character, for it expressed the nationalist resistance of the nation's popular culture to the oppressive colonial influence of Portugal. Brazilian folktales, argued Abreu, were invariably "inspired by a contempt for the oppressor," giving the lie to the notion of an inferiority complex with respect to the colonizing power. On that basis he made the rather implausible claim that the Romantic Indianist movement had its roots in popular literature.

More significant than this, though, was the fact that Abreu located the most fertile source of nationalist culture in the folk literature of the *caboclo*, the contemporary "semicivilized Indian" of the *sertão*. He, therefore, gave the first impulse to the emergent regionalist tendencies of *sertanismo* and *caboclismo* that were developing out of Brazilian Romanticism.

Another critic who participated actively in those developments was Araripe Júnior, whose own early Indianist writings were examined in the previous chapter. The close similarities that have been observed between several of Alencar's regionalist works and *The Guarani Indian* indicated the direction that Romantic Indianism might take. Indeed, in the essay "O Nosso Cancioneiro," Alencar invited his colleagues to explore the possibilities of the folk literature of the *sertão*. Araripe Júnior took up this suggestion in two letters published in 1875 in *O Globo* under the title "A Poesia Sertaneja." Here, discussing the work of the early *sertanista*, Juvenal Galeno, he acknowledged the need to turn away from the mythical, semidivine heroes of Romantic Indianism and to recognize the existence of a real race of *mestiço sertanejos*. Araripe Júnior's most valuable observation was his understanding that the heroic, epic world of the Romantic Indianists was a fiction that could no longer be sustained; a history of persecution, servitude, and marginalization had produced a new kind of antihero, the *caboclo*:

Out of this century, when the backwoodsman or the cowhand was no longer the product of that indomitable aspiration to all that was unknown and threatening, when most of the lands had been opened up, when Brazil was no longer that enchanted, mysterious country, into which one's spirit would descend as if into an unfathomable abyss, when, finally, that semi-aboriginal race, through the gradual transformation of causes, found itself enslaved by the rich masters and notable farmers who subjugated the lands granted to them by the king by way of inheritance, who ravaged the fields where the centaurs once bounded fearlessly, as free as the savage in olden times; out of this century, I repeat, since the backwoodsman has been placed in the terrible dilemma of serving or being crushed, what poetry could possibly spring forth? What heroic feeling could be found in individuals who, disparaged in their noble aspirations, living like slaves, oppressed, were obliged to roam the fields in pursuit of some stray head of cattle, not like the man fighting out of a feeling for his own life, but out of an obligation and duty?[21]

The Indianist writing of the final years of Empire offered two responses to Araripe Júnior's question. One current assimilated the sociological perspective of the regionalists, exploring the condition of the contemporary, detribalized *caboclo* as a new kind of social marginal or as the product of elemental biological and environmental forces. At the same time, though, there seems to have been something of a harking back to the tragic Indianism of the first Romantic phase, as represented by Gonçalves Dias. It is almost as if, in revisiting once again the genocidal history of the colonial years, this last generation were, in its own way, exposing the conservative idealism of Alencar's mythology of Conciliation that had helped sustain the self-image and legitimacy of Empire. The term "selvagem" appears with insistent regularity in the vocabulary of both these new currents of Indianism—consider the titles of Couto de Magalhães's *O Selvagem*, Gomes de Amorim's *Os Selvagens*, and Melo Moraes Filho's *Pátria Selvagem*—as somehow symptomatic of the collapse of the idealism that lay at the heart of the Romantic image of the Indian.

This sense of an impasse, of the impossibility any longer of writing a heroic, epic Indianism celebrating some sort of continuity in Brazil's social and political formation is no more dramatically represented than in Luís Delfino dos Santos's *A Epopéia Americana* (The American Epic, 1865-75). Considered by the Parnassianist generation in 1885 to be "Brazil's greatest poet," Delfino dos Santos was an abolitionist writer who played host to the rising literary trends of his time, including symbolism, but who sank from popularity himself shortly after his death in 1910. Unpublished until 1940 and unearthed more recently by David Haberly, only a fragment of *The American Epic* survives. The 127 stanzas are interrupted by what amounts to an admission of a loss of faith in the Indianist illusion:

Agora morre, agora lento e lento
A negra noite horrendo a mente avança,
E da descrença o formidável espectro
A alma me assalta, e me espedaça o plectro.[22]

(Now she is dying, now slowly, slowly/ The awful dark night bears my thoughts onwards,/ And the formidable specter of disbelief/ Assaults my soul, and shatters my plectrum.)

This crisis of disillusionment is the culmination of a tragic narrative in which an Indian girl is drowned in a tidal wave and is subsequently mourned by her people. The narrator accompanies the witness to these events, an old man whose mission, it becomes clear, is to "Chorar na cova de uma raça inteira" (Weep on the grave of an entire race). The old man's contemplation of the girl's corpse, inspired perhaps by Victor Meirelles de Lima's painting *Moema* (1866), is strangely charged with a voyeuristic, erotic fascination, as if it were struggling against the evidence of mortality and finality. If the deaths of individuals undermine the organized world of human relationships, the poem seems to ask, does not genocide, the destruction of a whole people, defy the capacity of memory to redeem it from oblivion? "Tudo acabará então? Já não havia/Amigos e inimigos sobre a terra?"[23] (Must everything end, then? Were there no more/ Friends and enemies left upon the earth?). In echoing the sentiment of despair, the poet declares his inability to collude any longer in the deception of a historical continuity between indigenous and national identities, which the Romantic Indianist mythology had sustained for forty years.

THE RETURN OF THE REBEL

The clearest illustration of how the Indianist movement absorbed the developments previously outlined can be found in the evolution of the writing of Bernardo Guimarães. On one hand, his use of the biblical formulas of martyrdom and redemption in the early work, together with his examination of the relationship between authority, the community, and the rebel, immediately aligns him with Alencar. On the other hand, his interest in the Indian as a more contemporary phenomenon, transformed by contact with white society, and his uninhibited treatment of sexuality and violence in the rural setting indicate that he had assimilated certain of the Realist and regionalist tendencies that emerged during the 1870s.

Guimarães was, like Fagundes Varela, a member of the bohemian Sociedade Epicuréia, giving him a taste for hard drink and nightlife that frequently left him in a state of poverty, drunkenness, and squalor, as Couto de Magalhães was to witness when he visited him in Goiás. In contrast to Varela, though, he possessed a radical, independent streak even as a youth, when he reputedly ran away from school in Ouro Preto to join the 1842 Minas and São Paulo liberal revolution. His unorthodox views during his legal and administrative career in Goiás led him to quarrel with the president of the province and with the magistrate of the district, and on one occasion he freed the prisoners at a trial, allegedly out of sympathy for their plight. This dissenting attitude extended into his literary activities on the Rio newspaper *Atualidade*, where, according to one biographer, "he readily got stuck into Junqueira Freire and Joaquim Manuel de Macedo,"[24] by now two of the most eminent representatives of Brazilian Romanticism. His own early experiments with Indianist writing, meanwhile, such as the poem "O ermo" (The Wilderness) from *Cantos da solidão* (Songs of Solitude, 1852), with its nostalgic regret for an extinct indigenous world and its hopes of future progress, give few clues as to the subsequent evolution of his work.

However, Guimarães's growing dissatisfaction with the Romanticism that shaped his early artistic career can be detected in his first short novel, *O Ermitão de Muquém* (The Hermit of Muquém), which was published in 1858, just a year after *The Guarani Indian*. The story concerns Gonçalo, a local bully and layabout who, after flirting with his friend's girl at a country dance, slips off with her. The friend follows and is found butchered the next day. Gonçalo emerges in the next part of the book, having taken refuge with a group of Coroado Indians during his flight from the law. Upon leaving the Coroados, having acquired many of their skills and habits, he is attacked by a more hostile tribe, the Xavantes, but after impressing them with his courage and abilities, he is accepted as one of their own and is nursed back to health from his wounds by the girl Guaraciaba. Mellowed by his experiences, by the solitude of the landscape, and by his life among these people, Gonçalo, now named Itajiba, experiences for the first time in his life a deep and genuine passion, and he falls in love with Guaraciaba.

However, after gaining a prestigious reputation by his attacks on the *bandeiras* sent to take reprisals against the Xavantes, his hopes of marrying Guaraciaba and assuming the leadership of the tribe are dashed. A rival warrior stages an incident in which Guaraciaba appears to betray Itajiba; the latter's jealous reaction is to kill the couple, and when the innocent nature of the episode is revealed, his enemy challenges him to a duel. Now wishing only to die, Itajiba/Gonçalo is miraculously saved from death by the image of the Virgin that he wears at his throat and that deflects his rival's arrow. He then drifts aimlessly in his canoe, having cast himself out from his own society and having destroyed the community that had accepted him. Realizing that he must pay a penance for his crimes in order to find spiritual rest, he returns to white society as a hermit, living off charity and converting Indians to Christianity. Among those who visit him at the chapel and sanctuary that he sets up at Muquém is none other than his first conquest Maria, sent mad by Gonçalo's murder of her fiancée at the outset of the story. Hearing Gonçalo's story, she forgives him and recovers her sanity.

Reduced to its essential elements, then, the somewhat tortuous and melodramatic plot of *The Hermit of Muquém* illustrates the Christian principles of sin and redemption through faith and works. There are precedents for the story in the European tradition of Robert le Diable, the offspring of a sterile mother and the devil, who leads a life of wickedness until his repentance in old age. The legend still circulates in Portugal and the Brazilian northeast, where it exists as a popular ballad called "Roberto do Diabo."[25] The religious overtones are certainly in evidence in Guimarães's text; the *romaria*, or pilgrimage, provides the novel's structure, for it is recounted to travelers on their way to Muquém and concludes at the end of the pilgrim's journey, with man's rediscovery of his God.

Of particular interest are the central sections of the novel, in which Gonçalo renounces his identity as a *civilizado* and enters Indian society. Parallel to the lesson of Christian salvation and redemption, the return of the Prodigal Son to the moral and spiritual fold, is another, social dimension. The sinner is also the outlaw, the rebel against authority, who must suffer absolute isolation, exclusion, and humiliation in order that he will submit to, and be reconciled with, the laws and codes of civil society. At the beginning of the novel, Gonçalo's abuse of his energy and strength is rendered symbolic of all that is antisocial, the antithesis of Peri's selfless dedication to the white community:

But instead of putting his great strength and courage at the service of the fatherland and of liberty, like that hero, Gonçalo, naturally and compulsively rough and disorderly, flung himself body and soul into a career of debauchery and became an utter idler, a notorious troublemaker.[26]

The society of the Xavante Indians, equally inimical and threatening to the dominant, civilized order, is the natural refuge for Gonçalo after his archetypally antisocial act of murder. More than that, though, it offers him a possible means of resolving his status as outcast and pariah without any act of submission. His meteoric rise to power within the tribe, his extreme popularity, and the expectation of his marriage to Guaraciaba suggest that he might build a rival empire within the Indian world, civilizing the tribes under his influence and negotiating political and economic terms with the state authorities of Goiás on an equal footing. In Gonçalo's rebel empire tribal integration into the state economy becomes an instrument of political influence. His dream is the despotic feudal power of the *fazendeiro* as Alencar was to see him in *The Backwoodsman*:

By becoming in this way the supreme chief of a huge active, industrious and warlike population, he would become fearsome to the weak governments of Goiás, he could deal with them as one power to another, and would impose his conditions on them. With this kind of conversion and organization of the Indian tribes not only would he acquire great power and prestige in those parts, but would also lend the State an eminent service, for which he would reserve for himself the right to fix the price and remuneration.[27]

However, Gonçalo's white parentage, his disruptive influence on the Xavante community, and his eventual expulsion from the tribe suggest that this defiance of the dominant social and political order is ultimately untenable. The emotional triangle formed by Itajiba/Gonçalo, Guaraciaba, and the rival warrior Inimá reproduces the same triangle of relationships with which the novel began, just as Gonçalo's murder of the two Indians repeats the initial crime of his first life. Only by being cast out for a second time by the society that he sought to dominate does he come to recognize his error. Only by suffering the humiliation and alienation of a marginal life dependent on charity, hearing his name insulted as a criminal, can he come to terms with his subordinate place in the social hierarchy and accept his forgiveness.

Although overlaid with Christian morality and ultimately resolved by appealing to the same conservative, conformist values defended by Alencar, Guimarães's exploration of crime and rebellion in the Indianist context of *The Hermit of Muquém* clearly anticipates his later fiction, where his confidence in conventional notions of justice and sociopolitical order appears to break down. At the same time, his increasingly critical view of the classical Indianist tradition led him to foreground the sexuality and violence that had until now appeared only in an either sanitized or caricatured form. Guimarães's treatment of these two closely allied themes abandons the mythical, epic mode of Alencar's work for a sensationalist approach, emphasizing, like Gonçalves Dias before him, the radical alterity of the primitive and the social and cultural distance separating him from the country's growing urban population.

The eponymous protagonist of the short story "Jupira" (1872) represents an intermediate stage in this development, for she is a grotesque version of the tragically marginalized *mestiça* figure, a modern Marabá or Miry'ba. Jupira's first act, at the tender age of fourteen, is to shoot arrows at an overzealous admirer and then smash his skull with an oar. Armed with a knife and her awesome reputation, she is pursued by Quirino, the son of a rich farmer, who proposes to capture her body through marriage and thereafter conquer her soul in the manner of a Jesuit missionary: "Once married to her it would be easier to catechize her and win over her heart and will."[28] However, Jupira successfully repels his advances by threatening to repeat her first act of violence, and she falls in love instead with Carlito, a white boy of her own age and her equal in agility and rebelliousness. In a scene of uninhibited erotic appeal, Carlito spies on Jupira while she is bathing, surprises her, and, following her invitation to chase her, he disappears with her to be seduced in the depths of the forest.

Their idyllic happiness is short-lived, though, for Carlito tires of his lover and defies her threats by pursuing an infatuation with Rosalia, "a beautiful blonde, white girl." The abandoned *mestiça* Jupira enlists the help of Quirino, who is still obsessed with her, and persuades him with a passionate kiss to kill Carlito. Awed by the magnitude of his imminent crime, Quirino invites Carlito on a fishing trip, and, watched by Jupira, he raises his knife to his rival, striking him three times to see him collapse, vomiting in his own blood. To his consternation and surprise, however, Jupira covers the corpse with kisses, and, inviting Quirino to embrace her, she pierces his heart with a knife, cursing him with the words: "Die, too, vile murderer! I do not love you."[29] She disappears, and her skeleton is later found hanging from a tree by a liana cord.

Guimarães's tragic heroine is exceptional in committing acts of murder and so actively avenging her mistreatment by both Indian and white society, rather than suffering her fate as a passive victim. But what is more remarkable and innovative about the story are the lengths to which the author goes in exploring this attitude of intransigent rebellion against an oppressive world. In his indictment of the integrationist policy of the Empire, Guimarães locates this attitude of resistance within a broader social critique that far surpasses any previous Indianist work in its sociological insight. The opening pages of the text describe the failure of the missionaries from the seminary of Nossa Senhora Mãe dos Homens, in southwest Minas, to exert any effective control over the tribes of the region; the latter retained their independence and became disenchanted with the "benefits" offered by white civilization:

Attracted by the desire to obtain a few clothes, tools, weapons and adornments, they would come to the seminary from time to time; but after one or two months when they had become rather tired of the work, they gave themselves up to their natural indolence and, if pressure was put on them, they would vanish back into the forests of the Rio Grande, resuming their nomadic, jungle life.[30]

The two dramatic examples of the Indians' success in resisting the pressure to assimilate are Jupira and her mother Jurema. Jurema is "catechized" by the white settler José Luís and bears him a daughter, who is baptized with the name Maria. However, she soon leaves José Luís to rejoin her people, returning two years later with her daughter, who now answers to the name of Jupira, and a second child by an Indian husband.

Despite her father's attempts to civilize her in the ways of his society, Jupira prefers the company of the Indians, quickly becoming the rebellious darling of the community. But the contact with white society and the white blood within her have left their mark; despite her "natural" temperament, her love of the nomadic freedom of tribal life, she possesses an unusual tenderness to which the physical advances of her first admirer and victim, the Indian Baguari, are repulsive.

From this point onward, though, following her murder of Baguari, her relationships with men assume a sinister intensity, a fatal, egotistic passion that transforms Jupira suddenly from a gentle, vulnerable creature into a grotesque psychopath. The unnatural personality of the femme fatale takes precedence over the question of her racial isolation, so that rather than being reducible to sociological causes, the final, gruesome tragedy is confused with, or attributable to, a perverted feminine psyche. As Carlito's initially spontaneous love for her begins to wane, her own feelings for him intensify, to the point where she threatens him with death should he ever cease to love her. When she actually discovers his infidelity, she confronts him and bites his arm, drawing blood, a foretaste of the violence to come:

In fact, for a first tiff, a bite like that wasn't a bad start, and it promised for the next one a broken arm, and a stabbing for the third. . . . her eyes blazed with bloodshot flashes; she was foaming at the mouth, and her lips and nostrils were trembling convulsively. An imperious, wild and frightening air reigned over her entire being.[31]

Resisting the impulse to take her immediate revenge on the couple and fearing some lapse into feminine weakness, rather implausibly, considering the existing exploits to her credit, she enlists the aid of Quirino. The image of diabolical purpose and obsession is completed as she invites him to receive his reward: not, as he expects, her love but a knife thrust into his heart:

—Bravo! bravo! . . . excellent! cried the *cabocla*, with a smile of hellish irony. —Now hurry to take your reward! [32]

By contrast to *The Hermit of Muquém*, then, the problem of the protagonist's social maladjustment is not resolved by a reconciliation but, instead, leads only to further disruption and death. The uncompromising passion that is typical of the Indian heroes of the Indianist movement thus far has ceased, in Guimarães's story, to be turned to the service of the white community. Instead, it has become a destructive, consuming force, alien to any notion of social conformity or political order; Jupira, the rebellious *cabocla*, is transformed out of all recognition into a pathological monster.

In Guimarães's last Indianist novella, *O Índio Afonso* (Afonso the Indian, 1873), this exploration of the condition of marginality and the acculturation of Indian society reaches its mature culmination. The ultra-Romantic drama of Jupira gives way to a more naturalistic, although nonetheless sensationalist, account of rural life.

Afonso the Indian first appeared in serialized form in the newspaper *A Reforma* in January 1872. Its protagonist is a new kind of Indianist hero, both in terms of his individual stature and by virtue of his relation to the dominant moral values and laws of white society. A modern, detribalized Indian, or *caboclo*, he lives with his sister Caluta, her husband, and children, providing them with food through his skill as a cattle rustler. While the men are away one day, Toruna, a local bandit, attacks and attempts to rape Caluta, apparently causing her to commit suicide by jumping into the torrent of a river. Caluta later reappears, having swum to safety, but her two sons have meanwhile told Afonso of the occurrence, and he sets about avenging his sister. Tracking Toruna down, he castrates and mutilates him, cutting off his lips, nose, and ears; but despite being repeatedly pursued and several times captured by the agents of the law, he always defies them, escaping into the refuge of the forest or the waters of the river that seem to protect him, transforming him into a local legend.

As the text progresses, a shift in taste from the sentimentalism of the earlier Romantic Indianists, to a new, brutal sensationalism is increasingly detectable, as is the move away from the noble, epic motives of Alencar's characters to the more material desires and ambitions of those of Guimarães. In the opening pages of the story, the narrator's mock concern teases the sensibility of his female readers, warning them that the company of "a gang of nearly savage caboclos" may not be altogether pleasant but, nevertheless, inviting them to board his fantastic carriage and to accompany him into the wildest depths of the forest. The Preface, "To the Reader," meanwhile, pretends to establish the documentary credentials of the story, at the same time disclaiming any suggestion that it is an apology for a common criminal:

> As can be seen, Afonso the Indian is a real and still living figure. His appearance, habits, manner, tone of voice, way of life, are just as I have described them, for I have had the opportunity to see him and converse with him. . . .
>
> It is true that when I was in the province of Goiás in 1860 and 1861, I heard stories of the renowned *caboclo*'s various exploits; but when it occurred to me, more or less a year ago, to write this novel, all that I retained of them was a vague reminiscence, and it is therefore possible that in one or other of them there may be some trace of truthfulness.
>
> In order to draw his character I based myself on what I heard everyone say in Catalão. They all depicted him with the character and habits that I attribute to him, and it was the general opinion that he had only committed one murder, and that to defend or avenge a friend of his or a member of the family. . . .
>
> That is what is real about my novel. If, however, Afonso the Indian is a common bandit, a wild and villainous criminal like so many others, it matters little to me.
>
> The Indian Afonso of my novel is not the criminal of Goiás; he is a pure creature of my fantasy.[33]

Whatever the factual authenticity or otherwise of his protagonist, and Guimarães clearly aims deliberately to blur the boundary between fact and fiction, what matters most is his declaration at the beginning of the text, his identification with the special, but real, world of the *sertão*: "My muse is essentially of the *sertão*, *sertaneja* by birth, *sertaneja* out of habit, *sertaneja* by inclination."[34]

Thus, while Afonso still resembles the Romantic superman whose skill and courage surpass those of twenty ordinary men, he is no longer an aristocratic tribal chief but one of "that race of *mestiço* Indians who live a semi-nomadic and semi-barbaric life along the banks of the great rivers of the interior, subsisting almost exclusively from hunting and fishing."[35] Similarly, his punishment of Toruna forms an ironic contrast to the Herculean struggles that take place between the Indian warriors of Romantic narratives from Gonçalves Dias onward. Afonso jumps onto the shoulders of Toruna, who is crouching at a stream, and forces his face into the mud; he drags him out and ties him to a branch of a tree, forcing him to beg pitifully for mercy and to invoke the five wounds of Christ. In response, Afonso then performs what the narrator describes with relentless attention to detail as "the barbaric revenge," making his five amputations in utterly cold blood.

But if the descriptive level of the narrative has been brought down from an epic, heroic register to one of mundane sensationalism, a mythical element remains, and that is Afonso's eternal defiance of the law. Having first fled from the area with his family, he then becomes homesick, above all for his river; the magical relationship with the river is the correlative of his permanent state of rebellion and autonomy:

"I am desperate to wash my body in the waters of the Parnaíba; only there am I a real human being. The bossman in Goiás must have forgotten about me by now; and besides, if I am standing at the edge of my river, who can possibly lay a hand on me? If I fall into the waters of the Parnaíba, as you well know, it's the same as falling into the arms of my father or my mother."[36]

Just as he says, the Parnaíba protects him as a son. During one arrest he is hand-cuffed to two soldiers, and, as he is taken on board a makeshift trimaran, he blesses himself with the water of the river. A storm breaks, and a huge tree trunk is thrust against the boat, distracting his captors and enabling him to drift away into freedom, like "the genie of the river on his floating throne, governing the restless and turbulent waves with a gesture and his gaze."[37]

The final pages of the story, though, offer an interpretation of the character's actions that would have been unimaginable in the traditional Indianist novel, where the Indian is either a loyal defender of white codes of morality and justice or a savage rebel alien to the social pact. Guimarães's view of the Indian mar-ginal is an important advance, a rejection of the Romantics' compulsion to transform the tribal primitive into an honorary citizen of their own society or into a projection of stereotypical notions of primitive Otherness. Afonso com-bines, instead, acts of the cruelest violence with displays of loyalty, tenderness, and even religious veneration. Narrating from within the world of the *caboclo* rather than from outside it, Guimarães depicts a physical and moral environment that is divorced from the civil institutions and laws of white society, where natu-ral justice prevails, and the freedom of the marginal is respected. Just as the local farmers tolerate his cattle-rustling activities as the normal order of the *sertão*, so the police of Goiás eventually give up their pursuit of Afonso, recog-nizing the inappropriateness of "social justice" in judging crimes of passion and brotherly devotion.

It is a view that must have appealed to the author's unorthodox sense of legal and political responsibility, which seems to have made his career in the rural interior of Goiás such an interesting one. It also leads one to question the judg-ment of Nelson Werneck Sodré and Afrânio Coutinho, for whom Guimarães's was simply a Romantic regionalism, idealizing and artificializing the pictur-esque qualities of local life, "at the same time that it sought to disguise it, attrib-uting to it qualities, feelings, values that do not belong to it, but to the culture that is being superimposed on it."[38] Rather, Guimarães's departure from the tra-ditional portrayal of rural culture lies precisely in his insistence on seeing the social order and human condition as lived in the rural interior as fundamentally irreducible to the ethical framework of urban, bourgeois society:

The readers will have gathered from this true story of mine that the Indian Afonso is not a criminal, but rather a good man, full of fine qualities and generous sentiments, but living in an almost natural state in the heart of the forest, struggling at once with the bandits and criminals who surround him, with the natural world of the jungle and the wild beasts of the sertão, and with the police who are pursuing him. It is this primitive, restless life that has developed in him to an extraordinary degree the cunning, the bravery and the strength that are peculiar to his nature.

In those deserts, in the depths of those immense forests, where the action of social justice is almost nil, man, however inoffensive his nature may be, often finds himself forced to defend himself against his kind, like someone defending himself against the lynxes and snakes.[39]

If Bernardo Guimarães's Indianist fiction, especially "Jupira" and *Afonso the Indian*, expressed a growing aversion to the Romantics' mythical formulas and their epic mood, then the poem "Elixir do Pagé" ("The Shaman's Elixir") was an outright satire on the movement in its traditional form. I referred earlier to Guimarães's attacks on the Romantics Junqueira Freire and Macedo in the paper *Atualidade*. In his biographical sketch of Gonçalves Dias,[40] Manuel Bandeira notes that in the same publication Guimarães also wrote a series of articles criticizing the poet's unfinished epic *Os Timbiras*, which had only recently received the praise of Macedo, Francisco Otaviano, and Franklin Távora. Basílio de Magalhães has suggested that the pentasyllabic stanzas of "The Shaman's Elixir" are intended to parody sections of *Os Timbiras*. Whether this is the case or whether, as seems more likely, the target of the parody is, in fact, "The Warrior's Chant," Guimarães's text taken as a whole is certainly a merciless satire on the kind of heroic Indianism for which Gonçalves Dias was best known.

Moving on from the sensationalist sex and violence of "Jupira" and *Afonso the Indian*, to a theme of explicit obscenity, the poem evidently struck a chord with the reading public, suggesting that the plausibility of traditional Indianism was now on its last legs. According to Artur Azevedo, the only contemporary to have condemned Bernardo Guimarães's obscene poetry, "The Shaman's Elixir" was the most popular of his poems, despite not having an official printing, much to the publisher Garnier's despair: "It is rare to find a resident of Minas Gerais who does not know it by heart. There are countless numbers of this good-for-nothing, mischievous poem scattered about the province"; despite censorship there were apparently several clandestine printings after the first edition of 7 May 1875.[41] As an indication of its continuing appeal, two editions were produced in the 1950s, sale of the illustrated 1958 Piraquê edition being prohibited, with 500 copies exclusively reserved for "bibliophiles." Adding to its amusement value, an anonymous Preface, "To the Reader," claims to redeem it from any pornographic intention, describing it as "erotic-comic," while the poem is prefaced by a quotation from Boileau—"D'un pinceau délicat l'artifice agréable/ du plus hideux object fait un object aimable." It is said that, having signed the poem simply with his initials, B. G., Guimarães escaped the charge of obscenity; denying authorship, he protested that not he, but a local priest, "o beato Gregório," was responsible![42]

The poem recounts the legendary, indigenous origin of an elixir renowned as a cure for male sexual impotence; the speaker addresses his unresponsive, flaccid organ and laments its decline, with appropriately colorful imagery and anthropomorphic metaphors. Hope is not lost, though, because he has obtained a miracle remedy, concocted from magical herbs in a distant land by an Indian shaman and fellow sufferer. At this point the initial decasyllables of the poem turn to pentasyllables as the narrator describes the prodigious return of the sha- man's sexual proficiency and vigor. As a comparison with stanzas from Gon- çalves Dias's "The Warrior's Chant" makes clear, Guimarães reproduced both the rhythmic pattern and even the syntactic structures of the earlier poem in a scurrilous sexual parody of the Indianist martial theme:

"The Warrior's Chant"	"The Shaman's Elixir"
Valente na guerra	"Mas neste trabalho,
Quem há, como eu sou?	dizei, minha gente,
Quem vibra o tacape	quem é mais valente,
Com mais valentia?	mais forte quem é?
Quem golpes daria	Quem vibra o marzapo
Fatais, como eu dou?	com mais valentia?
—Guerreiros, ouvi-me;	
—Quem há, como eu sou? . . .	Quem conas enfia
	com tanta destreza?
	Quem fura cabaços
	com mais gentileza?" . . .
Se as matas estrujo	Se a inúbia soando
Co'os sons do Boré,	por vales e outeiros,
Mil arcos se encurvam,	à deusa sagrada
Mil setas lá voam,	chamava os guerreiros,
Eis surgem, respondem	o velho pagé
Aos sons do Boré!	que sempre fodia
—Quem é mais valente,	na taba ou na brenha,
—Mais forte quem é?	no macho ou na fêmea,
	deitado ou de pé,
	e o duro marzapo,
	que sempre fodia,
	qual rijo tacape
	a nada cedia![43]

("The Warrior's Chant": Courageous in war/ Who can compare to me?/ Who wields his club/ With greater valor?/ Who could deal such/ Lethal blows as I do?/ —Warri- ors, hear me;/ —who can compare to me?. . .// If I thunder through the forests/ With the sounds of the horn,/ A thousand bows flex/ A thousand arrows fly/ A thousand cries echo,/ A thousand men appear/ Before me, in response/ To the sound of the horn!/ —Who is braver than I,/ —Who is stronger than I?

"The Shaman's Elixir": "But in this work,/ tell me, my people,/ who is braver than I,/ who is stronger than I?/ Who wields his prick/ with greater valor?// Who pokes cunts/ with such skill?/ Who cracks cherries/ more nicely than I?". . .// If the horn thundered/ through hills and vales/ calling the warriors/ to the sacred goddess,/ by night or by day,/ no one would ever see/ the old medicine-man/ who went on and on fucking/ in the village or the wood/ with female or male,/ lying down, standing up/ and his stiff prick,/ that went on and on fucking/ just like a stout club/ gave way to nothing!)

Continuing in the same vein, the story of the shaman inspires the narrator's own "marzapo" with the hope that he may one day be elected "rei dos caralhos" (king-cock).

Consisting of little more than this simple episode and a succession of comic euphemisms for the act of copulation, the poem, for all its satirical intent, is strangely enough faithful to the chauvinistically masculine spirit of Gonçalves Dias's Indianism. Just as women are rarely permitted to enter the male, bellicose environment of the "Poesias Americanas" other than as abandoned objects of the warriors' arbitrary will, so the "donzelas e putas" (damsels and bitches) of Guimarães's poem figure merely as a host of passive, faceless victims of his militaristic campaign of sexual conquest.

As the logical conclusion of Guimarães's fascination with the Indian as a symbolic repository of "primitive," elemental forces, sex and violence in their purest form, the poem marks a clear rejection of the mythical idealism of the Romantic Indianists. This shift also reflects the growth of interest during the 1870s in materialist, scientific theories of individual and social behavior, whose role in the crisis of Romantic Indianism has already been noted. One manifestation of such developments was the rise of ethnography as a systematic methodology for the study of non-Western cultures, including those of the Indians.

Whereas the Romantic and earlier myths regarding tribal peoples had a fantastic or idealized character, the new accounts of indigenous man pursued with the confidence of pseudoscientific respectability their theories of race and crossbreeding. One of the first examples of the new scholarship in Brazil was Couto de Magalhães's *The Savage*, which has already been discussed. In his account of the indigenous races of Brazil, Magalhães referred to "a variety that is so distinguished by the exaggerated development of the penis that the savages themselves characterize it by reference to this feature."[44] Whether or not Magalhães had already passed on this story to his friend and colleague, Bernardo Guimarães, before the publication of "The Shaman's Elixir" (1875) and *The Savage* (1876), such tales of the Indians' prodigious sexual powers were evidently now beginning to replace the Romantic myths of loyalty and devotion that had been the staple diet of Indianism for forty years.

Certainly, for Couto de Magalhães, one of the most influential pro-indigenist figures of the period, the relationship between sex, sexuality, and the Indian ran very deep. While resident in London from 1880 to 1881, during the negotiations for a concession to build the Sul-Mineiro railway, Magalhães kept a diary, recently edited under the title *Diário Íntimo*.[45] Here, alongside his more mundane business dealings and financial accounts, he recorded the vicissitudes of his private life, including his sexual fantasies and dreams. Fascinatingly, the most intimate references to bodily functions, the genitals and fantasies or dreams of sexual intercourse, both heterosexual and homosexual, are distinguished from the rest of the text by the fact that they are recorded in the Tupi language. Was this recourse to Tupi simply a code of secrecy, or did it represent, at a personal level, the kind of "primitivist" association found in the literature of the period between the most deep-seated, instinctual urges, the psychic subconscious of modern man, and the "savage" being of the Indian? For Maria Helena P. T. Machado,

[The Indians] emerge, on the one hand, as an extension of the exotic and barbaric language of tupi-nheengatu, in short the bodies on which this sensual language is inscribed are themselves, too, savage and free, organically linked to nature. On the other hand, the same narrative that situates them as sensual beings, does so through the projection onto the other of that which is sealed off in the subject-author; thus, what is inscribed thereon is the sensuality of the narrator and his fantasies, imprisoning in a web of passivity and depersonalization bodies which do not actually constitute beings.[46]

One cannot help but be reminded here of the construction of the indigenous "blank slate" in Pero Vaz de Caminha's *Letter* of 1500 to Dom Manuel I, discussed in Chapter 1, in particular, the processes of linguistic representation by which he both manifests the disturbed European's voyeuristic fascination with the sexuality of the Indians and at the same time disempowers and empties them as autonomous cultural beings.

At a more sociological and ideological level, Machado also sees Magalhães's expression of his sexual life in these "indigenized" terms as symptomatic of how the Brazilian elite was responding, at the end of Empire and in the late nineteenth century, to the pressures of a changing world, reconfiguring their sense of individuality in relation to an entire cultural-historical landscape—that of the colonial and postcolonial world—that was rapidly disappearing.[47] Magalhães, with his commitment to Indianist scholarship, as a loyal monarchist, the defender of a humanitarian, liberal indigenist policy, but also as an entrepreneur dedicated to a modernizing project for the nation, directly involved in the building of a transport infrastructure for the country's interior, which would have a profound impact on the Indian communities themselves, personified those tensions between the colonially oriented historicism of the Romantic Indianists and the more modern materialist perspective of the regionalists and naturalists.

If, for Bernardo Guimarães, the new sensationalist naturalism, with its emphasis on sex and violence, was linked to a sense of rebellious dissatisfaction with the conservative mythology of Romantic Indianism, others drew more reactionary conclusions from the same correlation. Francisco Gomes de Amorim's *Os Selvagens* (1875) (The Savages) combined sentimentalism, grotesque melodrama, and bathos to convey a hysterical horror of popular revolt, in the form of the Cabanagem, the rebellion of black, *mestiço*, and Indian laborers that shook the province of Pará in 1835.

A Portuguese-born poet, novelist, and playwright, born in 1827, Gomes de Amorim came to Brazil as a young man, traveling in the interior of Pará and working as a river trader and oarsman. As well as publishing *Versos* (1866), and *Cantos Matutinos* (1866) he was known in the region for a celebrated poem, "A Tapuia." *The Savages* is essentially an apology for Ambrósio Ayres, or Bararoá, as he was better known, the man responsible for the eventual repression of the Cabanagem, which included horrific massacres of the rebel captives and their supporters among the Mundurucu, Mauê, and Mura Indians.[48] The first meeting between the Mundurucus and the missionary Félix is typical of Amorim's crudely caricatural approach:

—A white man— said Cashew Flower. —He's the first one I've seen!
—A priest! informed a warrior, who had seen a lot of the world.
—A missionary!— added a second, more knowledgeable than the first.
—Good to eat?— asked a third.
—Hough!— answered all the others, licking their lips.
—Old!— observed one with displeasure.
—But he's white! countered some, who perhaps had pleasant memories of the taste of the flesh of unfortunate priests.[49]

What follows is the author's first description of the revolutionaries, which attaches to them the same savage caricature first reserved for the Indians. They all, *tapuios*, mulattos, *mamelucos*, *cafuzas*, and blacks alike, share an indiscriminately bestial appearance, naked or clothed in rags, barefoot, with man-elike, tangled hair, resembling "bands of monkeys in carnival dress, or uncaged lunatics who had rifled through the old wardrobes of ten provincial theatres."[50] Far from being an explosion of anger and revolt against years of ethnic and economic oppression, the uprising, in Amorim's distorted account, was a primitive conspiracy of ambitious, jealous, and xenophobic outlaws against civilization itself:

The hard core of the gang, which later would call itself political, in an attempt thus to cleanse itself of the ignominy with which the whites associated with their vileness and atrocities were covered, had not consisted only of colored men without any education or social rank. Hatred of the Portuguese, jealousy, envy, unchecked ambition, avarice, spite, contempt for social laws, the ferocious inclinations of people whom civilization had not been able to raise morally to the social level at which it had placed them, all the evil passions, in short, which stir up the souls of beings depraved by a thirst for pleasure, or brutalized by vices, contributed to the alliance of those criminals.[51]

THE "SAVAGE HIERARCHY" OF EMPIRE

While writers as diverse as Guimarães and Amorim were assaulting the Romantics' idealist conception of the Indian as a mythical repository of values such as self-sacrifice, conciliation, or loyalty, others were shedding a new, critical light on the Empire's social and political structures by means of allegorical readings of tribal society as a whole. This was a trend initiated by Alencar's fellow *cearense*, Franklin Távora, who, in his *Letters to Cincinato* of 1871, berated the author of *Iracema* for the lack of sociological and historical rigor of his Indianist narratives. Távora's own contribution to the movement, *Os índios do Jaguaribe*, probably published for the first time in 1870 but then lost until the mid-1980s, is described by David Brookshaw as a "thesis" novel, a vehicle for his republican and regionalist politics.[52] Certainly, its depiction of the rivalry between two tribal warriors, Jaguari and Jurupari, as symbolic of the struggle between absolutism and liberalism, between the Imperial center of power and the provincial periphery, clearly situates Távora at a crucial turning point in the evolution of the Indianist imaginary and its interpretation of Empire:

Jurupari fought for the predominance of merit which he, perhaps without being conscious of it, and only as an instrument of providence, dreamt of and wanted to establish in his country; Jaguari, on the other hand, defended the predominance of arbitrary and strident authority, fortified by anachronistic traditions and supported by the medicine man. It was the struggle of a nascent democracy against deep rooted absolutism.[53]

Whether or not Alencar was persuaded directly by Távora's example, his last Indianist novel, *Ubirajara* (1874), does suggest that he was moving in the same direction. For this work he chose a precolonial setting to explore themes familiar from his previous novels: the dialectic between a masculine, patriarchal principle of militarism and alienation and a feminine, matriarchal principle of love and reconciliation; and its resolution through the medium of alliance and marriage. The copious notes that accompany the text, detailing the documented historical evidence on which the novel was based, suggest that Alencar was anxious to refute the criticisms that his work lacked authenticity and to defend the "realist" credentials of his Indianism (something he had begun to attempt in the notes to *Iracema*). At the same time, in so doing he was reaffirming the indigenist nationalism that lay at the center of Romantic Indianist writing, rehabilitating the negative image of tribal society as it had been handed down by the colonial chroniclers. Thus, he has notes asserting the symbolic, ritual nature of Indian cannibalism, its similarity to the Christian Eucharist, and other observations of tribal customs and traditions that he cites as evidence of their advanced level of civilization.

But the chief interest of what is otherwise an unremarkable work lies in the peculiar nature of three of the notes that accompany the text, notes 20 to 22. Here Alencar attempts an exercise that Machado de Assis was to repeat just a year later in his own *Americanas*: to describe the structure of indigenous society in terms that clearly mirror the Imperial hierarchy of the Second Reign. Within the "savage hierarchy" he distinguishes between "a civil society and a political society," the latter represented by the *taba* "village" and based on the family unit.[54] His portrayal of the microcosmic patriarchal order, governed independently by the head of each tribal household, immediately brings to mind the self-styled authoritarian "kingdoms" of Dom Antônio or the *fazendeiros* of the regionalist novels:

The master of the house, or literally, he who made the house, *moacara*, was the perfect image of the patriarch. He governed his people; and he formed an independent society in the bosom of the great political society, of which he was a member and to whose defense he contributed not only out of self-interest, but also for the honor of the nation. (OC, III, p. 323)

The struggle for overall, national power within the parliamentary "council of *moacaras*," meanwhile, resembles the dispute between Conservative and Liberal

Parties: ideally a vigorous, dynamic process, "essentially democratic" but also, as Gonçalves Dias had feared, potentially self-destructive:

> The boldest and strongest imposed himself: both the duration and extent of his authority depended upon the respect that he could instill in his warriors.
> As soon as another ambitious individual emerged to contest his power, the latter became the prize of the most valiant. What then took place was that the loser, together with his followers, would rise up in revolt; hence the frequent civil wars, which annihilated the Indian race, perhaps even more than the cruelty of the Europeans. (OC, III, p. 324)

Finally, the unmistakable influence of Alencar's critical views on the function of monarchy, absolutism in government, and the misuse of "personal power" is brought to bear upon his description of the often stormy relationship between the warrior chief of the tribe and the representative council of family heads:

> Between the warrior chief (executive power) and the council of *moacaras* (legislative power) conflicts were inevitable. There would be *morubixabas*, like the celebrated Cunhambebe, who were real despots. The club of many a Tupi hero must have governed as absolutely as the sword of Caesar or Napoleon. (OC, III, p. 324)

While Alencar was most concerned with power relations at the top of the "savage hierarchy," his future successor as the country's leading novelist, Machado de Assis, was turning his attention to the dynamic of social relations *between* the classes. Machado had already paid his critical respects to the Romantic Indianist legacy in two essays, "A tradição indígena na obra de Alencar" (The Indian Tradition in the Work of Alencar, 1866) and "Instinto de Nacionalidade" (Instinct of Nationality, 1873). Indeed, some years after the Empire had fallen, in 1895, he reiterated this homage to the Indianist tradition in the poem "Lindoya," commemorating the centenary of the death of Basílio da Gama with a roll call of the female Indianist heroines who succeeded da Gama's Lindóia.[55] Published in 1875, the same year as Guimarães's "The Shaman's Elixir," Machado's *Americanas* was the second of three books of poetry written during his "Romantic" phase, before the period of the great fictional masterpieces. Like Guimarães, though, Machado was already drawing on ethnographic insights into tribal culture to depict a society of recognizable human individuals rather than a mythical world of semigods. Machado's Indians act out a series of dramatic conflicts in which Christian morality is no longer the agency of reconciliation and social order but rather serves to highlight division, alienation, sexual weariness, infidelity, and jealousy.

On occasions, such as in the poem "Lua Nova" (New Moon), with its direct reference to the tribal fertility cults described in Couto de Magalhães's *The Savage*, the indigenous world inspired a faith in love, peace, and salvation. More typical of the collection, though, is the poem "Niâni," which is informed by Francisco Rodrigues do Prado's *History of the Horseman Indians or the Guaicuru Nation*, written in 1795 and published in 1839 in the first edition of the Historical and Geographical Institute's journal. As well as its description of the Guaicurus' monogamous marriage system and simple divorce procedure, the

book gave an account of the tribe's caste structure that clearly offered suggestive material for an Indianist allegory of social relations in modern Brazil:

> The Guaicuru nation is divided into three parts: the first is that of the *nobles*, whom they
> call captains, and the wives of the latter, *conas*, a title that their daughters also have; a
> second they call *soldiers*, who obey from the parents through to the sons and daughters;
> and the third, which is most substantial, is that of the *captives*, as they call all those they
> take in war and their descendants, whom they treat with great love, without obliging
> them to do any work. There is, however, the circumstance that it is deemed unworthy to
> marry a slave, to the extent that the son will have contempt for the mother who has mar-
> ried a slave.[56]

This description must have appealed to Machado's sensitivity to the class
character of Imperial society as he would scrutinize it in his fiction. "Niâni," in
some senses, anticipates the contemporary world of the novels in its concern
with the interference of discrimination in personal relations. It is based on Rodrigues do Prado's story of the lovers Panenioxe and Nanine, whose fathers are
both "captains," or Guaicurú chiefs. Despite all her protests, Panenioxe deserts
Nanine, "[a] woman of noble countenance," in favor of "a girl of lower rank"
and "common blood."[57] Before dying of grief, Nanine avenges the insult by
freeing a captive on condition that he take her former lover's name, so leaving a
permanent and humiliating reminder of his act of betrayal, identifying him with
the lowest element of the social hierarchy. A note to the text makes quite clear
Machado's intentions as regards the analogy between the semifictional tribal
society of the Guaicurús and its modern Imperial counterpart composed of "nobles, plebes and captives."

The iniquity of slavery past and present, Indian and African, was denounced
in more outraged tones by the Bahian abolitionist Alexandre José de Mello
Moraes Filho (b. 1843), in *Os Escravos Vermelhos* (The Red Slaves). The text
forms part of a collection entitled *Pátria Selvagem* (Savage Fatherland), which
also includes *Os Escravos Negros* (The Black Slaves) and *Ciganos* (Gypsies)
and was probably written between 1882 and the early 1900s, when his other
works were published. It returns to the familiar territory of the sixteenth-century
war against the French and the Tamoio confederation, which provided the material for Gonçalves de Magalhães's epic poem. In Mello Moraes Filho's version,
however, the traditional Imperial foundation myth is revised in order to accommodate the forgotten facts of Indian slavery and thereby to denounce the legacy
of social injustice that underpinned Empire. In his opening dedication Mello
Moraes Filho explicitly links the two causes of Indian and African slavery:

> Beneath this soil two enslaved races lie in rest.
> Parading their bloodstained flanks in the arena of slavery, two wild beasts are still
> gorging themselves on the corpses of the Indian and the black.
> The Fatherland, in its intoxicating corruption, watches this spectacle out of a Roman
> amphitheater; and while the king sits gloating, it forgets its greatest men.
> But one day you will lift the stone away from your tomb with your arm and will melt
> away the night that has formed around your name.[58]

The text is not fiction as such, then, rather a half-lyrical, half-documentary essay that, by drawing attention to the institutionalized crimes of the past, sought to denounce those of the present. The traditional, official heroes of the country's colonial history, such as the soldier Mem de Sá and the Jesuit priest Antônio Vieira, were no longer to be revered but condemned as the precursors of a trade in human beings that had become the shameful foundation of Brazil's wealth:

From captaincy to captaincy, the missionaries of death examine the Indian slaves, choosing those which would fall to the Order, stipulating the price of each article to their settler cronies, dealing out among the soldiers and the poor the excess from the forays into the interior.

As this criminal trade enriched itself, what would the loss of liberty matter, what would the tortured agony of so many murdered, imprisoned nations matter?[59]

In the tradition of Gonçalves Dias's *Meditation*, the final words of the book are spoken by an apocalyptic voice, the spirit of the river Negro lamenting in biblical cadences the bondage of its children:

"I was Guriguacurú.
But one day the foreigner betrayed my waves and my forests, my climes and lonely wastes. . . . And I saw my tribes file past enslaved with their warriors, their women and their shamans of Tupã.
The Jesuit poisoned my air with bondage and the cross of redemption was the gallows for three million slaves!
And my forests were taken with sadness, they gathered on my banks and asked:
'Guriguacurú, what have you done with your children?'"[60]

DAYBREAK IN COLOMBIA, NIGHTFALL ACROSS THE AMERICAS

The end of Empire produced, then, a brief echo of the tragic, outraged Indianism of the early Romantics, as abolitionists and republicans again struggled to break with the colonial inheritance that the Empire had preserved. The last, most extraordinary contribution to that tradition was Joaquim de Sousândrade's *O Guesa* (The Wanderer), a hybrid work that combined the epic theme of exile with a precociously modernistic vision of a contemporary world beset by crisis and chaos. *The Wanderer* was a final, ambitious attempt to resuscitate the Romantic, Rousseauian dream of a natural model of moral and social order and to confront this critically with the nightmare of the capitalist transformation of the New World.

One of the most important literary influences on Sousândrade was his fellow *maranhense* Gonçalves Dias, with whom he had many friends and experiences in common, including the familiar sight of Indians during their rural upbringing. Sousândrade was born Joaquim de Sousa Andrade, the son of a rich farming family in Alcântara, Maranhão, in 1832. Unlike his contemporaries, he studied in Paris, rather than Coimbra, and took up an unfashionable subject, engineering. On his return he became involved in the *Semanário Maranhense*, which, during the mid-1860s, was the most prestigious literary journal in Maranhão, and it was here that Sousândrade began to publish parts of *The Wanderer*. Moving with his daughter to New York in 1871, he continued to work on the poem, an incomplete version of which was published in 1888, and he wrote articles for the New York-based paper *O Novo Mundo*. As a young man, he had pointedly refused the financial patronage of Pedro II, and when the Emperor visited the headquarters of *O Novo Mundo* in New York, Sousândrade was conspicuous by his absence.[61]

While Gonçalves Dias's Romantic indigenist sensibility typified the cultural and economic conditions of his provincial origins, Sousândrade's experience of North American society and of the expanding northern port of São Luís afforded him an unusually broad perspective on his society and age. The originality of his language was due, according to Luís Costa Lima, to the frustration of this perspective within what amounted to a cultural straitjacket, "the vacuum of a nation that saw itself through borrowed spectacles";[62] he resorted to a kind of stylistic violence in order not to succumb to the traditional grandiloquence and sentimentalism of the period, something that also explains the fragmented structure of *The Wanderer*.

It was doubtless Sousândrade's concern with broadly American themes that led him to choose a myth derived from the culture of the Muyscas, one of the indigenous races of Colombia, as the structural thread of the poem. It is a myth of human sacrifice, in which the *guesa*, a "wanderer" or "exile," is raised from childhood in the temple until his coming-of-age, when he is taken along the divine path, or *suna*, toward his death.[63] The narrator or poet is often indistinguishable from the character of this sacrificial victim during the course of the poem, identifying in him his personal experience of physical exile and ideological isolation as a political dissident in Imperial Brazil.

Throughout his historical and geographical journey of enlightenment across the continent in thirteen cantos, Sousândrade sets this contemporary experience against an ideal golden age, the lost Eden of Brazil's indigenous prehistory. In the second canto, he enters an Indian *festa* and witnesses the sad degeneration of the tribal communities. This episode, known as the Tatuturema, along with the later "Wall Street Inferno" of canto X, constitutes the principal example of the poem's stylistic originality. It is an orgy of mythical and historical figures that subverts the conventional interpretation of Brazilian history as a coherent succession of heroic achievements culminating in the Second Reign of Pedro II— precisely that providential view of history that Gonçalves de Magalhães, one of the chief intellectual apologists of Empire, took as the basis of his own Indianist epic.

For Sousândrade, the sacrifice of the Indian was not a necessary, purposeful martyrdom heralding the salvation of God's chosen people but a kind of original sin, the primal crime whose legacy was a modern world of exploitation and corruption; it embraced even the society of the United States, from which his republican ideals took much of their political inspiration:

O povo infante
O coração ao estupro abre ignorante
Qual às leis dos Christãos as mais formosas.
Mas, o egoismo, a indifferença, estendem
As éras do gentio; e dos passados
Perdendo a origem chara este coitados,
Restos de um mundo, os dias tristes rendem. . . .

Raiou Colombia! anoiteceu Americas,
Quando lhe foste a maldição primeira!
"Quando o primeiro Indio à escravidão
Viu-se por tuas proprias mãos vendido
E foi, desde esse instante denegrido,
No mundo novo a morte e a confusão!"[64]

(The infant people/ Laid its unwitting heart open to the rape/ As it did to the most beautiful of the Christians' laws./ But egotism, indifference, prolong/ The ages left for the heathen to live; and these poor people,/ Bereft of their dear ancestors' parentage,/ Yield up their sad days, remains of a world. . . .// Day broke over Colombia! night fell over the Americas,/ When you were their first curse!/ "When the first Indian found himself/ Sold by your own hands into slavery/ And was from that moment denigrated,/ Death and confusion reigned in the new world!")

As the poet's hopes of recovering his lost Eden are progressively disillusioned by the urban societies he encounters, the spirit of the Indian gradually recedes into an inaccessible utopia:

Além da Serra,
E nos seios azues da natureza,
Nas chammas dos volcões, do Sul nos grandes
Mares, ao occidente, além dos Andes,
Que irá na glória descansar o Guesa![65]

(Beyond the Mountains,/ And in the azure bosom of nature,/ In the flames of the volcanoes, in the great Seas of the South, to the West, beyond the Andes,/ The Wanderer will rest in glory!)

NOTES

1. José de Alencar, *Obra Completa*, 4 vols. (Rio de Janeiro: Aguilar, 1965), vol. 3, p. 980; all quotations are taken from this edition unless otherwise indicated. References begin with the abbreviation OC, followed by the volume and page number.
2. Raymundo Faoro, *Machado de Assis: a pirâmide e o trapézio* (São Paulo: Companhia Editora Nacional, 1974), p. 103.
3. Afrânio Coutinho (ed.), *A Polêmica Alencar-Nabuco* (Rio de Janeiro: Tempo Brasileiro, 1965), p. 90.
4. Ibid., p. 209.
5. Ibid., p. 189.
6. Ibid., p. 180.
7. Ibid., pp. 7-8.

8. Carlos de Araújo Moreira Neto, "A Política Indigenista Brasileira Durante o século XIX" (mimeo., doctoral thesis, Faculdade de Filosofia, Ciências e Letras de Rio Claro, São Paulo, 1971), p. xiv.

9. Ibid., p. xvii.

10. For a useful summary of Magalhães's life and career, see Maria Helena P. T. Machado's Introduction to José Vieira Couto de Magalhães, *Diário Íntimo* (São Paulo: Companhia das Letras, 1998), especially pp. 9-19.

11. David Brookshaw, *Paradise Betrayed: Brazilian Literature of the Indian* (Amsterdam: CEDLA, 1988), pp. 86-89.

12. General Couto de Magalhães, *O Selvagem* (São Paulo: Itatiaia, 1975), pp. 22-23.

13. Ibid., p. 227.

14. Ibid., p. 16.

15. Thomas Skidmore, *Black into White: Race and Nationality in Brazilian Thought* (New York: Oxford University Press, 1974), p. 41.

16. Ibid., pp. 137, 142, 144; Edgard Carone, *A República Velha: (Instituições e Classes Sociais)* (São Paulo: Difusão Européia do Livro, 1970), pp. 14, 146-48.

17. See Ivan Lins, *História do Positivismo no Brasil* (São Paulo: Companhia Editora Nacional, 1967).

18. See Sílvio Romero, *Ethnologia Selvagem: estudo sobre a memoria "Região e raças selvagens do Brasil" do Dr Couto de Magalhães* (Recife: Typ. da Província, 1875), pp. 9-10; *A Literatura Brazileira e a crítica moderna* (Rio de Janeiro: Imprensa Industrial de João Paulo Ferreira Dias, 1880), pp. 43-45, 134.

19. Sílvio Romero, *História da Literatura Brasileira*, 5 vols. (Rio de Janeiro: José Olympio, 1943), vol. 1, p. 84.

20. J. Capistrano de Abreu, *Ensaios e Estudos (Crítica e História)*, 1st series (Rio de Janeiro: Briguiet, 1931), p. 68.

21. Tristão de Alencar Araripe Júnior, *Obra Crítica de Araripe Júnior*, 5 vols. (Rio de Janeiro: Casa de Rui Barbosa, 1958), vol. 1, p. 101.

22. David T. Haberly, "Uma desconhecida Epopéia Indianista," *Revista do Instituto de Estudos Brasileiros*, no. 12 (1972), p. 107.

23. Ibid., p. 103.

24. Antônio de Alcântara Machado, "O Fabuloso Bernardo Guimarães," *Cavaquinho e Saxafone (Solos) 1926-1935* (Rio de Janeiro: José Olympio, 1940), p. 224.

25. Luís da Câmara Cascudo, *Dicionário do folclore brasileiro* (Rio de Janeiro: Edições de Ouro, 1972), pp. 783-84.

26. Bernardo Guimarães, *O Ermitão de Muquém* (Rio de Janeiro: Edições de Ouro, 1966), p. 3.

27. Ibid., p. 164.

28. Bernardo Guimarães, *História e Tradições da Província de Minas Gerais* (Rio de Janeiro: Civilização Brasileira, 1976), p. 164.

29. Ibid., p. 192.

30. Ibid., pp. 144-45.

31 Ibid., pp. 177-78.

32. Ibid., p. 192.

33. Bernardo Guimarães, *Quatro Romances* (São Paulo: Martins, 1944), pp. 361-62.

34. Ibid., p. 364.

35. Ibid., p. 366.

36. Ibid., p. 387.

37. Ibid., p. 391.

38. Nelson Werneck Sodré, *História da Literatura Brasileira: Seus Fundamentos Econômicos* (Rio de Janeiro: Civilização Brasileira, 1969), pp. 403-4, quoting Afrânio

Coutinho (ed.), *A Literatura no Brasil*, 5 vols. (Rio de Janeiro: Sul Americana, 1968), vol. 2, pp. 145-46.

39. Guimarães, *Quatro Romances*, p. 402.

40. Manuel Bandeira, *Poesia e Prosa*, 2 vols. (Rio de Janeiro: Aguilar, 1958), vol. 2, p. 731.

41. Basílio de Magalhães, *Bernardo Guimarães (Esboço Biographico e critico)* (Rio de Janeiro: Typ. do Annuario do Brasil, 1926), p. 113.

42. My thanks to Olímpio Matos of Rio de Janeiro for this anecdote.

43. Bernardo Guimarães, *Elixir do Pagé* (Belo Horizonte: Movimento Editorial Panorama, 1951), pp. 27-33. My thanks to Dr. Plínio Doyle of Rio de Janeiro for kindly allowing me to consult his copies of this and other editions of the poem.

44. Magalhães, *O Selvagem*, p. 62.

45. José Vieira Couto de Magalhães, *Diário Íntimo* (São Paulo: Companhia das Letras, 1998).

46. Ibid., p. 38.

47. Ibid., p. 42.

48. See Moreira Neto, *A Política Indigenista*, pp. 20-21.

49. Francisco Gomes de Amorim, *Os Selvagens* (Lisbon: Matos Moreira e Cia., 1875), p. 28. My thanks to Neide Gondim de Freitas Pinto of Manaus for kindly allowing me to consult her copy of this edition.

50. Ibid., p. 204.

51. Ibid., pp. 209-10.

52. Brookshaw, *Paradise Betrayed*, pp. 106-14.

53. Franklin Távora, *Os índios do Jaguaribe* (Fortaleza: Secretaria de Cultura e Desporto, 1984), p. 88, cited in Brookshaw, *Paradise Betrayed*, pp. 109-10.

54. For some idea of the extent to which Alencar has reinterpreted the character of the tribal social structure, see Florestan Fernandes, *Organização Social dos Tupinambás* (São Paulo: Difusão Européia do Livro, 1963).

55. Ivan Teixeira, "Epopéia e modernidade em Basílio da Gama," *Obras Poéticas de Basílio da Gama* (São Paulo: EDUSP, 1996), pp. 29-30.

56. Gen. Raúl Silveira de Mello, *Para além dos bandeirantes* (Rio de Janeiro: Biblioteca do Exército, 1968), p. 122.

57. Joaquim Maria Machado de Assis, *Obra Completa* (Rio de Janeiro: José Aguilar, 1973), vol. 3 , pp. 108, 109.

58. Mello Moraes Filho, *Pátria Selvagem: Os Escravos Vermelhos* (Rio de Janeiro: Faro e Lino, n.d.), p. i.

59. Ibid., p. 83.

60. Ibid., pp. 153-54.

61. Frederick G. Williams, *Sousândrade: Vida e Obra* (São Luís: SIOGE, 1976).

62. Luis Costa Lima, "O Campo Visual de uma experiência antecipadora," in Augusto e Haroldo de Campos, *ReVisão de Sousândrade* (Rio de Janeiro: Nova Fronteira, 1982) , p. 422.

63. Alexandre de Humboldt, *Vues des cordillères et Monumens* [*sic*] *des peuples indigènes de l'Amérique*, 2 vols. (Paris: J. Smith, Libraire Grecque-Latine-Allemande, 1816), vol. 2, p. 244, Sousândrade's declared source for his poem.

64. Joaquim de Sousândrade, *O Guesa* (São Luís: SIOGE, 1979), pp. 21, 61.

65. Ibid., p. 208.

Epilogue: The Indianist Legacy

Sousândrade's *The Wanderer* suggested that Brazil's inexorable integration into a modern, capitalist American continent had finally marked the death of the Romantic Indianist utopia. For the elite of the new Republic (declared in 1889), anxious to emulate the metropolitan centers of modern, urban civilization, the Indian might remain acceptable as an exotic figure in some picturesque tableau, as would be the case in some of the genteel, Parnassianist poems of Olavo Bilac. More often, though, as in Bilac's "Guerreira" (Warrior), "Anchieta," or "O Caçador de esmeraldas" (The Emerald Hunter), he would come to be identified with the still-threatening presence of barbaric social and cultural forces clamoring at the gates of the republican fortress of civilization.

The "return of the savage" to literary reflections on the Indianist theme in the last two decades of Empire set the tone for the continuing debates around ethnicity and cultural identity during the First Republic, as pathological explanations were sought for the country's economic and social backwardness in the language of scientific racism. The defense of Indian culture or of the indigenous cause by prominent philanthropists such as Leolinda Daltro, the founder of the Association for the Protection and Assistance of Brazil's Forest Dwellers, now became the subject of journalistic and fictional ridicule. An article of 1919, "O Nosso Caboclismo," by the novelist Lima Barreto, attacked both Dona Leolinda and the more celebrated indigenist pioneer, Cândido Rondon, for what he considered their bourgeois, romantic obsession with *caboclo* ancestry: "My city has long since ceased to be an Indian *taba*; and I, in spite of everything, am not a savage."[1] Indeed, Lima Barreto had chosen as the protagonist of his most successful novel, *Triste Fim de Policarpo Quaresma* (The Sad End of Policarpo Quaresma, 1911), a misguidedly naive patriot whose tragic downfall begins when he innocently proposes that Tupi should be adopted as Brazil's official language (an idea ridiculed half a century before by João Francisco Lisboa, as we saw in Chapter 3). Like his other gestures of indigenist zeal (he is met with stunned incomprehension when he offers his friends the traditional Indian greeting of tears and nearly suffocates after donning a tribal mask), this is derided by the author, not so much for its patriotic motives but for its Romantic impracticality and remoteness from the more urgent social concerns of the population.

Likewise, in 1914 the São Paulo writer Monteiro Lobato launched a controversy with his article "Urupês," which denounced the contemporary "mania" of *caboclismo*, exemplified by the poet Cornélio Pires, for folklorizing the peasant just as the Romantics had idealized their Indians:

Fortunately for us—and for Dom Antônio de Mariz—Alencar never saw them [the Indians]; he dreamed them up like Rousseau. Otherwise there we'd have the son of Araré roasting the lovely young girl on a nice brazil-wood barbecue, instead of accompanying her adoringly through the jungles, like the benevolent Ariel of the Paquequer.[2]

The "new" trend was, Monteiro Lobato argued, nothing but Romantic Indianism by another name, and its *caboclo* subjects were simply tribesmen in disguise:

The parrot-feather headdress has given way to a straw hat pushed back from the forehead; the village clearing has turned into a thatched barn; the club has got thinner, sprouted a trigger, acquired a breech and is today a twist-barrel shotgun; the *boré* horn has degenerated pitifully into the hoot of the *inhambú* bird; the loincloth has moved upwards to become an open-necked shirt.[3]

If, in appearance, the *caboclo* Jéca Tatú was nothing more than a modern caricature of the Romantic Indian, Lobato also found little to recommend him morally; viewed through the prism of the new scientific racism, with its insistence on the innate slothfulness of the Indian, Jéca Tatú was the epitome not of the traditional Indianist qualities of independence and heroism but rather of all that was backward, ignorant, and conformist in the national character. The *caboclo*'s resignation, indolence, listlessness, and indifference to the urgent political and economic issues of the day were summed up in his catchphrase "Não paga a pena" (It's not worth the trouble):

All of the *caboclo*'s unconscious philosophizing can be heard in this mumbled word that is shot through with fatalism and lethargy. Nothing is worth the trouble. Neither cultivation, nor conveniences. You can live in any old way.[4]

However, in shattering the mythical aura of Romantic Indianism, the materialist, antitraditionalist critique of the movement in the last quarter of the century had also helped opened up the way for alternative theories of Brazil's postcolonial development, in which the idea of cultural difference and diversity would be counterposed to the homogenizing, assimilationist ideology of nineteenth-century nationalism. Indeed, the Modernist movement of the 1920s was ideologically divided down the middle by those two rival interpretations of the indigenous cultural legacy, pitting the revolutionary "cannibalists" against the neo-Indianist *mestiço* nationalists, the so-called *verdeamarelistas* (Greenandyellowists).

The latter, in their *Manifesto Nhengaçu Verde Amarelo* (Nhengaçu Green and Yellow Manifesto, 1929), held up the Tupi Indian as the spiritual common denominator of an emergent "cosmic race" and thus unashamedly took over as their own a key plank of colonial and postcolonial discourse, namely, the paradigmatic dual stereotype that had counterposed the conciliatory, civilizing "race" of Tupi Indians to the intractable, savage Tapuia. By contrast to the "suicidal" intransigence of the Tapuias, the Tupis' putative lack of resistance and consequent defeat at the hands of the colonizers were paradoxically the condition of their subjective "survival" within the consciousness of the *mestiço* Brazilian. Thus, they personified the renunciation of difference, of identity, whether ethnic, political, or ideological, in favor of a quietist attitude of passive surrender to the corporate identity of the nation. As such, the Greenandyellowist movement represented an extreme, protofascist expression of the integrationist nationalism first encountered in Alencar's Indianist mythology of miscegenation, self-sacrifice, and alliance.[5]

Diametrically opposed to the project of the *verdeamarelistas* was the Movimento Antropofágico, or Cannibalist movement, led by Oswald de Andrade. Rather than the mythology of surrender and conciliation, this movement explored the subversive possibilities suggested by fresh readings of indigenous culture as informed by the European avant-gardes, modern anthropology and Freudian thinking. In his *Anthropophagous Manifesto* of 1928 Andrade advocated the principle of cannibalism—the very concept that had, in colonial discourse, most defined the Latin American "Other" as primitive and barbaric—as a revolutionary strategy for reformulating the dynamic of cultural relations in order to liberate those popular, indigenous, and non-European identities that had been suffocated under the weight of colonialism and imperialism. Through a critical act of "devouring," the new culture could move toward a dialectical synthesis of contradictory forces; by selectively "digesting" or assimilating those that offered most nutritional value, it could preserve their energy but neutralize any oppressive power they might previously have exerted.[6]

The transgressive, subversive power of cannibalism was also a central theme of Mário de Andrade's "rhapsody" *Macunaíma* (1928), which explored the complex potential offered by the magical mentality of the "primitive" in the face of capitalist modernization. If, on the hand, the antihero Macunaíma's "characterless" indolence and irresponsibility seemed to reinforce the contemporary positivist stereotypes of pathological racial degeneracy, by the same token his mercurial, chameleon-like shiftiness, his immunity to logic, moral codes, and to the structures of organized labor marked him out as an eternal rebel, irrepressibly exposing and subverting the alienating, oppressive modernity that the positivist Republic had sought to impose under the banner of "Order and Progress!"[7]

The Modernists, therefore, followed through to its extreme consequences the dualism that had always underpinned colonial and postcolonial discourse: the Indian as Tupi or as Tapuia; as self-sacrificing ally and loyal servant or as dangerous, intractable savage; as mother or protector of the postcolonial Brazilian family or as rebel and outlaw, alien to the social pact; as the symbol of a conciliation of interests, social, political, and cultural or as the vengeful, marginalized victim of an oppressive colonialism.

The Indianist movement's own internal evolution was driven, as we have seen, by this fundamental dialectic between the radical alterity posed by indigenous society and the compulsion to tame and neutralize its more disturbing aspects; between the defense of the liberal idea of individual autonomy and its subordination to the dominant interests of the Imperial slave-owning, planter class; between the Indianist mythology of shared ancestral origins and a common anti-colonial cause, and the presence of the country's surviving Indians as an ongoing reminder of an unfinished history of interethnic and class conflicts. While the language of negotiation, of social pacts and alliances exercised the imagination of Indianists such as Alencar during the central years of the movement, as it had done in the eighteenth century, the promise of freedom, equality, and citizenship for the Indian within a postcolonial Brazil was, in reality, never anything more than liberal rhetoric or Romantic mythology. Nineteenth-century Indianism was incapable of imagining any alternative to the stark choice between absolute exclusion from the social pact, exile, or extermination, on one hand, and voluntary servility and self-effacement, on the other. The Indianist imaginary could only ever manufacture Imperial subjects, never citizens.

The imperative of national integration, which lay at the heart of the Imperial project of state-building, was projected symbolically and literally onto the figure of the Indian, whose irreducible "otherness" represented its most extreme challenge. That imperative remained central to the development strategies of successive regimes, whether Getúlio Vargas's New State or the post-1964 military dictatorship.[8] Even the humanitarian vision of the legendary Cândido Mariano da Silva Rondon, the positivist founder of the Indian Protection Service, a descendant of Terena, Bororo, and Guaná Indians, and the pioneering defender of pacifist methods of contact under the maxim "Morrer se preciso for, matar nunca" (Die if necessary, but never kill), could not escape it. In 1900 Rondon wrote:

> If the Republic is the incorporation of the proletariat into modern society, the special mission of the Brazilian Government must reside in the incorporation of the savages into our society.
> Brazil will not have fulfilled its political mission, until it has achieved that incorporation.[9]

At the end of the twentieth century, the consequences of that project of national integration were still being visited in the most terrible ways upon the country's indigenous population. But as successive generations have rediscovered, indigenous culture itself has always offered alternative models for thinking the relationship between individual and community, self and other, for imagining forms of social interaction and coexistence in which difference and identification, autonomy and integration, collective self-realization and the realization of the individual might be compatible, rather than mutually exclusive. The most disturbing and provocative such model of social incorporation and integration remains, of course, the ritual practice of cannibalism. While it is true that the Modernists of the 1920s were the first systematically to elaborate a theory of cannibalism as a positive symbol of transgression, cultural resistance, and subversion of the colonizing process, we should not forget that it was actually a Romantic poet, Gonçalves Dias, who, first and uniquely within the history of Brazilian Indianism, reclaimed the significance of this practice from centuries of misrepresentation and who, in his poem "I-Juca Pirama," grasped something of its power as the expression of an alternative, utopian vision of social integration and self-realization.

NOTES

1. Afonso Henriques de Lima Barreto, "O Nosso Caboclismo," *Marginália: Artigos e Crônicas, Obras* (São Paulo: Brasiliense, 1961), vol. 12, p. 70.

2. José Bento Monteiro Lobato, *Obras Completas* 13 vols. (São Paulo: Brasiliense, 1956), vol. 1, p. 277.

3. Ibid., p. 278.

4. Ibid., p. 284.

5. See R. Johnson, "Notes on a Conservative Vanguard: The Case of Verde-Amarelo/Anta," *Hispanic Studies* 4 (1989), pp. 31-42.

6. See J. R. Johnson, "Tupy or Not Tupy: Cannibalism and Nationalism in Contemporary Brazilian Literature and Culture," J. King (ed.), *Modern Latin American Fiction: A Survey* (London: Faber and Faber, 1987), pp. 41-59.

7. See Randall Johnson, "Macunaíma as Brazilian Hero," *Latin American Literary Review* (1978), pp. 38-44, for a brief overview of the book.

8. See Seth Garfield, "'The Roots of a Plant that Today is Brazil': Indians and the Nation-State under the Brazilian Estado Novo," *Journal of Latin American Studies* 29, part 3 (October 1997), pp. 747-68; David Treece, "Indigenous Peoples in Brazilian Amazonia and the Expansion of the Economic Frontier," in David Goodman and Anthony Hall (eds.), *The Future of Amazonia: Destruction or Sustainable Development?* (London: Macmillan, 1990), pp. 264-87.

9. Letter to D. Leolinda Daltro, 16 August 1900, in Leolinda Daltro, *Da Catequese dos Índios no Brasil (1896-1911)* (Rio de Janeiro: Typ. da Escola Orsina da Fonseca, 1920), p. 322.

Select Bibliography

The bibliography is divided into four sections for the sake of convenience: Primary Sources; Secondary Sources on Indianist Writing; Sources for the History of Indigenist Policy and Anthropology; General Works on History, Literature, and Culture.

PRIMARY SOURCES

d'Abbeville, Claude. *História da missão dos Padres Capuchinhos na Ilha do Maranhão e terras circunvizinhas em que se trata das singularidades admiráveis e dos costumes estranhos dos índios habitantes do país* (trans. Sérgio Milliet). São Paulo: Martins, 1945.

Abreu, J. Capistrano de. *Ensaios e Estudos (Crítica e História)*, 1st series. Rio de Janeiro: Briguiet, 1931.

Alencar, José de. "Benção Paterna." *Sonhos d'Ouro*. São Paulo: Ática, 1981, pp. 7-12.

Alencar, José de. *Como e Porque Sou Romancista*. Rio de Janeiro: Academia Brasileira de Letras, 1987.

Alencar, José de. "Como e porque sou romancista." *Obra Completa*. Rio de Janeiro: Aguilar, 1965, pp. 101-21.

Alencar, José de. *Iracema* (ed. do Centenário). Rio de Janeiro: José Olympio, 1965.

Alencar, José de. *Obra Completa*. 4 vols. Rio de Janeiro: Aguilar, 1965.

Alencar, José de. *Obras de Ficção de José de Alencar*. 16 vols. Rio de Janeiro: José Olympio, 1955.

Almeida, Manuel Antônio de. "Civilização dos indígenas: Duas palavras ao autor do 'Memorial Orgânico.'" *Obra Dispersa*. Rio de Janeiro: Graphia, 1991, pp. 7-13.

Amazonas, Lourenço da Silva Araújo. *Simá: romance historico do Alto Amazonas*. Pernambuco: Typ. de F.C. de Lemos e Silva, 1857.

Amorim, Francisco Gomes de. *Os Selvagens*. Lisbon: Matos Moreira e Cia., 1875.

Anchieta, José de. *Poesias*. São Paulo: Museu Paulista, Boletim IV, Documentação Lingüística, 4, Years IV-VI, 1954.

Andrade, Mário de. *Macunaíma: o herói sem nenhum caráter* (ed. crítica de Telê Porto Ancona Lopez). São Paulo: SCCT, 1978.

Andrade, Oswald de. *Do Pau-Brasil à Antropofagia e às Utopias: manifestos, teses de concursos e ensaios.* 2d ed. Rio de Janeiro: Civilização Brasileira, 1978.

Anon. *Guarany ou O Amor no deserto.* Lisbon: Typ. 62, Rua do Crucifixo 66, 1875.

Anon. "Carta do Compadre do Rio de S. Francisco do Norte, ao filho do compadre do Rio de Janeiro, na qual se lhe queixa do parallelo, que faz dos indios com os cavallos, de não conceder aos homens pretos maior dignidade, que a de reis do rozario, e de asseverar, que o Brazil ainda agora está engatinhando; E crê provar o contrario de tudo isso, por J.J. do C.M." Rio de Janeiro: na Impressão Nacional, 1821.

Anon. "Justa Retribuição dada ao compadre de Lisboa em desagravo dos brasileiros offendidios por varias asserções, que escreveo na sua carta em resposta ao compadre de Belem, pelo filho do Compadre de Rio de Janeiro, que offerece, e dedica aos seus patricios." Rio de Janeiro: na Typographia Regia, 1821.

Araripe Júnior, Tristão de Alencar. *Jacina, a Marabá.* Rio de Janeiro: Três, 1973.

Assis, Joaquim Maria Machado de. "Americanas." *Obra Completa.* 3 vols. Rio de Janeiro: José Aguilar, 1973, vol. 3.

Ataíde, João Martins de. *Iracema* (folheto). Gé Bernardo, de Juázeiro do Padre Cícero, n.d.

d'Ávila, Arthur Lobo. *Os Caramurús: Romance histórico da descoberta e independencia do Brazil.* Lisbon: João Romano Torres, 1900.

Balzac, Honoré de. *Les Chouans (Une passion dans le désert) ou La Bretagne en 1799.* Paris: Calmann Lévy, 1898.

Barreto, Afonso Henriques de Lima. "O Nosso Caboclismo." *Marginália: Artigos e Crônicas, Obras.* Vol. 12. São Paulo: Brasiliense, 1961, pp. 69-70.

Barreto, Afonso Henriques de Lima. *Triste Fim de Policarpo Quaresma.* Rio de Janeiro: Edições de Ouro, n.d.

Basílio da Gama. *See* Gama, José Basílio da

Bilac, Olavo. *Poesias.* Rio de Janeiro: Francisco Alves, 1942.

Bonifácio, José. *See* Silva, José Bonifácio de Andrada e

Caldas, Antônio Pereira de Souza. *Poesias Sacras e Profanas.* 2 vols. Paris: P. N. Rougeron, 1821.

Caminha, Pero Vaz de. *A Carta de Pero Vaz de Camina.* Rio de Janeiro: Livros de Portugal, n.d.

Cardim, Fernão. *Tratados da Terra e Gente do Brasil.* São Paulo: Companhia Editora Nacional, 1939.

Chateaubriand, François-René de. *Oeuvres romanesques et voyages.* Tours: Gallimard, 1969.

Cooper, James Fenimore. *The Works of James Fenimore Cooper.* 9 vols. New York: Greenwood Press, 1969.

Cortesão, Jaime (ed.). *A Carta de Pêro Vaz de Caminha, Obras Completas de Jaime Cortesão.* Vol. 13. Lisbon: Portugalia, n.d.

Debret, Jean Baptiste. *Viagem pitoresca e histórica ao Brasil* (trans.). 2 vols. São Paulo: Círculo do livro, n.d.

Denis, Jean Ferdinand. *Brésil, par M. Ferdinand Denis, L'Univers, ou Histoire et Description de tous les peuples, de leurs religions, moeurs, coutumes etc.* Paris: Firmin Didot Frères, 1837.

Denis, Jean Ferdinand. *Résumé de l'histoire littéraire du Portugal suivie du Résumé de l'histoire littéraire du Brésil.* Paris: Lecointe et Durey, 1826.

Dias, Antônio Gonçalves. *Poesia completa e prosa escolhida.* Rio de Janeiro: José Aguilar, 1959.

Dias, Antônio Gonçalves. *Brazil e Oceania: estudo ethnographico.* Rio de Janeiro: Felix Ferreira, 1879.

Dias, Antônio Gonçalves. *Obras Posthumas.* 3 vols. São Luiz: Typographia de B. de Mattos, 1867/8.

Durão, José de Santa Rita. *Caramuru: poema épico do descobrimento da Bahia.* (ed. Hernâni Cidade). Rio de Janeiro: Agir, 1961.

Durão, José de Santa Rita. *Caramurú, poema epico do descubrimento da Bahia.* Lisbon: Na Regia Officina Typografica, 1781.

Erasmo (pseudonym). *Diatribe contra a Timonice do Jornal de Timon Maranhense acerca da Historia do Brazil do Senhor Varnhagen.* Lisbon: Typ. de José da Costa, 1859.

França, Ernesto Ferreira. *Lindoya: tragedia lyrica em quatro actos.* Leipzig: Brockhaus, 1859.

Gama, José Basílio da. *Obras poéticas de Basílio da Gama* (ed. Ivan Teixeira). São Paulo: EDUSP, 1996.

Gama, José Basílio da. *The Uruguay (a Historical Romance of South America)* (Translation of *O Uraguai* by Richard F. Burton). Berkeley and Los Angeles: University of California Press, 1982.

Gama, José Basílio da. *O Uraguai* (ed. Mário Camarinha da Silva). Rio de Janeiro: Agir, 1964.

Gama, José Basílio da. *Obras Poéticas.* Rio de Janeiro: Garnier, 1921.

Gavet, D., and Boucher, P. *Jakaré-Ouassou, ou les Tupinambás: Chronique Brésilienne.* Paris: Timothée de Hay, 1830.

Gonçalves de Magalhães. *See* Magalhães, Domingos José Gonçalves de

Gonçalves Dias. *See* Dias, Antônio Gonçalves

Gonzaga, Tomás Antônio. *Obras Completas.* Rio de Janeiro: Instituto Nacional do Livro, 1957.

Guanabara: revista mensal artistica, scientifica e litteraria, redigida por uma associação de litteratos e dirigida por Manuel de Araujo Porto-Alegre, Antônio Gonçalves Dias, Joaquim Manuel de Macedo. Rio de Janeiro: Typ. Guanabarense de L.A.F. de Menezes, 1849-55.

Guerra, Gregório de Matos e. *Poemas Escolhidos.* São Paulo: Cultrix, 1976.

Guimarães, Bernardo. *História e Tradições da Província de Minas Gerais.* Rio de Janeiro: Civilização Brasileira, 1976.

Guimarães, Bernardo. *O Ermitão de Muquém.* Rio de Janeiro: Edições de Ouro, 1966.

Guimarães, Bernardo. *O Elixir do Pagé.* Rio de Janeiro: Edições Piraquê, 1958.

Guimarães, Bernardo. *Elixir do Pagé.* Belo Horizonte: Movimento Editorial Panorama, 1951.

Guimarães, Bernardo. *Quatro Romances.* São Paulo: Martins, 1944.

Guimarães Júnior, Luiz. *Sonetos e Rimas.* 4th ed. Lisbon: Clássica, 1925.

Helliot, João Henrique. "Aricó e Caocochee ou Uma Voz no deserto." *Guanabara: revista mensal artistica, scientifica e litteraria.* Rio de Janeiro: Typ. Guanabarense de L.A.F. de Menezes, 1850, vol. 1, pp. 158-73.

Jagoanharo, Oscar (pseudonym of Tristão de Alencar Araripe Júnior). *Contos Brazileiros.* Recife: Typ. do Correio Pernambucano, 1868.

Jaguaribe Filho, Domingos José Nogueira. *Os Herdeiros de Caramuru: romance historico.* São Paulo: Jorge Seckler, 1880.

Kaulen, Padre Lourenço. "Refutação das calumnias contra os Jesuitas contidos no poema 'Uruguay' de José Basilio da Gama." *Revista do Instituto Histórico e Geográfico Brasileiro* 68, part 1 (1907), pp. 93-224.

Léry, Jean de. *Histoire d'un voyage fait en la terre du Brésil, autrement dit Amérique.* Lausanne: Bibliotèque Romande, 1972.

Lima Barreto. *See* Barreto, Afonso Henriques Lima

Lisboa, Balthazar da Silva. *Annaes do Rio de Janeiro.* 7 vols. Rio de Janeiro: Na Typ. Imp. e const. de Seignot-Plancher e Cia., 1834, vol. 1.

Lisboa, João Francisco. *Crônica do Brasil Colonial (Apontamentos para a História do Maranhão).* Petrópolis: Vozes, 1976.

Lobato, José Bento Monteiro. *Idéias de Jéca Tatú, Obras Completas.* 1st series. 13 vols. São Paulo: Brasiliense, 1964, vol. 4.

Lobato, José Bento Monteiro. "Urupês." *Obras Completas.* 1st series. 13 vols. São Paulo: Brasiliense, 1956, vol. 1.

Macedo, Joaquim Manuel de. *Cobé, Teatro completo.* Vol. 2. Rio de Janeiro: Serviço Nacional de Teatro, 1979, pp. 9-80.

Machado de Assis. *See* Assis, Joaquim Maria Machado de

Magalhães, Domingos José Gonçalves de. "Discurso sobre a historia da literatura do Brasil." *Obras*, vol. 8: *Opusculos historicos e litterarios.* Rio de Janeiro: Garnier, 1865, pp. 241-71.

Magalhães, Domingos José Gonçalves de. *A Confederação dos Tamoyos.* Rio de Janeiro: Dous de Dezembro, 1856.

Magalhães, Domingos José Gonçalves de. "Os Indígenas do Brasil perante a História." *Revista do Instituto Histórico e Geográfico Brasileiro* 23 (1860), pp. 3-66.

Magalhães, General Couto de. *O Selvagem.* São Paulo: Itatiaia, 1975.

Magalhães, José Vieira Couto de. *Diário Íntimo,* ed.. Maria Helena P. T. Machado. São Paulo: Companhia das Letras, 1998.

Mello, Sebastião José de Carvalho e (Marquês de Pombal). *Relação Abreviada da Republica, que os Religiosos Jesuitas das Provincias de Portugal, e Hespanha, estabeleceram nos Dominios Ultramarinos das duas Monarchias . . .* In *Recueil de pièces.* Paris: n.p., 1758.

Montaigne, Michel de. "Des Cannibales." *Oeuvres Complètes*, vol. 2. Paris: Conard, 1924, pp. 233-66.

Monteiro Lobato. *See* Lobato, José Bento Monteiro

Moraes Filho, Mello. *Pátria Selvagem: Os Escravos Vermelhos.* Rio de Janeiro: Faro e Lino, n.d.

Navarrete, D. Martín Fernandez. *Colección de los viajes y Descobrimientos que hicieron por Mar los Españoles.* 5 vols. Madrid, 1825-37.

Nóbrega, P. Manuel da. *Cartas do Brasil e mais escritos.* Coimbra: Acta Universitatis Conimbrigensis, 1955.

Nóbrega, P. Manuel da. *Diálogo sobre a conversão do gentio.* Lisbon: União Gráfica, 1954.

Norberto, Joaquim. *See* Silva, Joaquim Norberto de Souza

O Guarany: folha illustrada litteraria, artistica, noticiosa, critica, year 1, no. 1 (January 1871).

Obry, Olga. *Catherine du Brésil: Filleule de Saint-Malo.* Paris: Nouvelles Editions Latines, 1953.

Oliveira, José Joaquim Machado de. "Notícia raciocinada sobre as aldeas de indios da provincia de S. Paulo, desde o seu começo até à actualidade." *Revista do Instituto Histórico e Geográfico Brasileiro* 8 (1846), pp. 204-50.

Peixoto, Inácio José de Alvarenga. *Obras Poéticas de Inácio José de Alvarenga Peixoto.* São Paulo: Clube de Poesia, 1956.

Pires, Cornélio. *Scenas e Paizagens da minha terra (Musa caipira).* São Paulo: Revista do Brasil, Monteiro Lobato e Cia., 1921.

Pitta, Sebastião da Rocha. *História da America Portugueza desde o anno de mil e quinhentos de seu descobrimento até o de mil e setecentos e vinte e quatro.* 2d ed. Lisbon: Francisco Arthur da Silva, 1880.

Rendon, José Arouche de Toledo. "Memoria sobre as aldeias de indios da Provincia de S. Paulo, segundo as observações feitas no anno de 1798—Opinião do auctor sobre a sua civilisação." *Revista do Instituto Histórico e Geográfico Brasileiro* 4 (1842), pp. 295-317.

Rohan, Henrique de Beaurepaire. "Considerações acerca da conquista, catechese e civilisação dos selvagens no Brasil." *Guanabara*, vol. 2. Rio de Janeiro: Typ. Guanabarense de L.A.F. de Menezes, 1854, pp. 191-208.

Romero, Sílvio. *História da Literatura Brasileira.* 5 vols. 3d ed. Rio de Janeiro: José Olympio, 1943.

Romero, Sílvio. *A Literatura Brazileira e a crítica moderna.* Rio de Janeiro: Imprensa Industrial de João Paulo Ferreira Dias, 1880.

Romero, Sílvio. *Ethnologia Selvagem: estudo sobre a memoria "Região e raças selvagens do Brasil" do Dr. Couto de Magalhães.* Recife: Typ. da Província, 1875.

Rousseau, Jean-Jacques. "A Discourse on the Origin of Inequality." *The Social Contract and Discourses.* London, Melbourne, and Toronto: Dent, 1973.

Salgado, Plínio. "O Brasil e o Romantismo." *Despertemos a nação!, Obras Completas*, vol. 10. São Paulo: Ed. das Américas, 1955, pp. 59-68.

Salvador, Frei Vicente do. *História do Brasil 1500-1627.* São Paulo: Edições Melhoramentos, 1965.

Santos, Joaquim Felício dos. *Acayaca: Romance Indígena. 1729.* Ouro Preto: Typ. do Estado de Minas, 1895.

Scalvini, A. *Il Guarany: Opera-Ballo in Quattro Atti (libretto).* Milan: Coi. Tipi di Francesco Lucca, 1870.

Scott, Sir Walter. *Ivanhoe.* London: Dean and Son, n.d.

Silva, Firmino Rodrigues. "Nenia, ao meu bom amigo O Dr. Francisco Bernardino Ribeiro." *Minerva Brasiliense* 2, no. 18 (15 July 1844), pp. 558-60.

Silva, Joaquim Norberto de Souza. *Cantos Epicos.* Rio de Janeiro: Typographia Universal de Laemmert, 1861.

Silva, Joaquim Norberto de Souza."Memoria historica e documentada das aldeias de indios da Provincia do Rio de Janeiro." *Revista do Instituto Histórico e Geográfico Brasileiro* 17, 3d series, no. 14 (1854), pp. 71-271.

Silva, José Bonifácio de Andrada e. *Projetos para o Brasil* (org. Miriam Dolhnikoff). São Paulo: Companhia das Letras, 1998.

Silva, José Bonifácio de Andrada e. "Apontamentos para a civilisação dos Índios Bravos do Império do Brasil." *Obras Científicas, políticas e sociais de José Bonifácio de Andrada e Silva* (ed. Edgard de Cerqueira Falcão). 3 vols. São Paulo: Empresa Gráfica da Revista dos Tribunais, 1963, vol. 2, pp. 103-14.

Silva, José Bonifácio de Andrada e. *Poesias de Américo Elísio, Obras de José Bonifácio de Andrada e Silva.* Vol. 1. Rio de Janeiro: Imprensa Nacional, 1946.

Sousa, Antônio Gonçalves Teixeira e. *As Tardes de um Pintor ou As Intrigas de um Jesuita.* Rio de Janeiro: Três, 1973.

Sousa, Antônio Gonçalves Teixeira e. *Os Três Dias de um Noivado.* Rio de Janeiro: Typ. Imparcial de Paula Brito, 1844.

Sousa, Gabriel Soares de. *Notícia do Brasil.* Vol. 1. São Paulo: Martins, 1949.

Sousândrade, Joaquim de. *O Guesa.* São Luís: SIOGE, 1979.

Távora, Franklin. *Os índios do Jaguaribe.* Fortaleza: Secretaria de Cultura e Desporto, 1984.

Távora, Franklin (Semprônio). "Carta II." In Pinheiro Chagas. *Novos Ensaios Críticos.* Praça de D. Pedro: V.M. Porto, em casa da viuva More Editora, 1868, pp. 202-11.

Teixeira e Sousa. *See* Sousa, Antônio Gonçalves Teixeira e

Teles, Gilberto Mendonça. *Vanguarda Européia e Modernismo Brasileiro: apresentação e crítica dos principais manifestos vanguardistas.* Petrópolis: Vozes, 1972.
Titara, Ladislau dos Santos. *Obras Poéticas.* Bahia: Typographia do Diario,1835.
Varela, Fagundes. *Anchieta ou O Evangelho na selvas, Poesias Completas.* São Paulo: Saraiva, 1956, pp. 619-922.
Varnhagen, Francisco Adolfo de. *História Geral do Brasil antes da sua separação e independência de Portugal.* 7th ed., 2 vols. São Paulo: Melhoramentos, 1959.
Varnhagen, Francisco Adolfo de. "O matrimônio de um Bisavô ou O Caramuru (Romance historico brasileiro)." *Florilégio da Poesia Brasileira,* 3 vols. Rio de Janeiro: Publicações da Academia Brasileira, 1946, vol. 3, pp. 225-38.
Varnhagen, F. A. de. *Os Indios Bravos e O Sr. Lisboa, Timon.* Lima: Na Imprensa Liberal, 1867.
Varnhagen, F. A. de. *O Caramuru: romance histórico brasileiro.* Rio de Janeiro: Typografia de Pinto de Sousa, 1861.
Varnhagen, Francisco Adolfo de. *Sumé: lenda mytho-religiosa americana, recolhida em outras eras por um Indio Moranduçara; agora traduzida e dada á luz com algumas notas por Um Paulista de Sorocaba.* Madrid: Imp. da V. de Dominguez, 1855.
Vasconcellos, Simão de. *Chronica da Companhia de Jesu do Estado do Brasil.* Officina de Henrique Valente de Oliveira Impressor del Rey N.S., 1663.
Veríssimo, José. *Estudos Brazileiros.* 2d series (1889-93). Rio de Janeiro: Laemmert e Cia., 1894.
Vieira, P. Antônio. *Obras Escolhidas.* Vol. 5: *Obras Várias* (III). Lisbon: Sá da Costa, 1951.
Voltaire. *Candide and Other Stories.* Oxford: Oxford University Press, 1990.
Wilkens, Henrique João. *A Muhraida . . .* (facsimile of 1785 manuscript and 1819 edition with accompanying studies). *Anais da Biblioteca Nacional.* Vol. 109 (1989). Rio de Janeiro: A Biblioteca, 1993.
Wilkens, Henrique João. *A Muhraida, Senhor ou A conversão, e reconciliação do Gentio Muhra* (ed. P. Cypriano Pereira Alho). Lisbon: Na Imprensa Regia, 1819.
Wilkens, Henrique João. *Muhraida ou O Triumfo da Fé, Na bem fundada Esperança da enteira Converção, e reconciliação da grande, e feróz Nação do Gentio Muhúra, Poema Heroico . . .* Manuscript, Torre do Tombo, Lisbon, 1785.

SECONDARY SOURCES ON INDIANIST WRITING

Ackermann, Fritz. *A Obra Poética de Antônio Gonçalves Dias.* São Paulo: Conselho Estadual de Cultura, 1964.
Alencar, Heron de. "José de Alencar e a Ficção Romântica." Afrânio Coutinho (ed.), *A Literatura no Brasil.* 2d ed., 4 vols. Rio de Janeiro: Sul Americana, 1969, vol. 2, pp. 217-300.
Amaral, Amadeu. "Gonçalves Dias." *O Elogio da Mediocridade (Estudos e notas de literatura).* São Paulo: Nova Era, 1924.
Andrade, Carlos Drummond de. "O sorriso de Gonçalves Dias." *Confissões de Minas, Obra Completa.* Rio de Janeiro: Aguilar, 1964, pp. 517-21.
Andrews, J. R. Norwood. "A Modern Classification of Bernardo Guimarães' Prose Narratives." *Luso-Brazilian Review* 3, no. 2 (December 1966), pp. 59-82.
Araripe Júnior, Tristão de Alencar. *Obra Crítica de Araripe Júnior,* 5 vols. Rio de Janeiro: Casa de Rui Barbosa, 1958.
Araripe Júnior, Tristão de Alencar. *José de Alencar (Perfil Litterario).* Rio de Janeiro: Fauchon & cia., 1894.

Assis, Joaquim Maria Machado de. "A tradição indígena na obra de Alencar." *Obra Completa.* 3 vols. Rio de Janeiro: José Aguilar, 1973, vol. 3, pp. 848-52.

Azevedo Filho, Leodegário A. de. *Anchieta, a Idade Média e o Barroco.* Rio de Janeiro: Gernasa, 1966.

Bandeira, Manuel. "Gonçalves Dias: Esboço biográfico." *Poesia e Prosa.* 2 vols. Rio de Janeiro: Aguilar, 1958, vol. 2, pp. 617-804.

Bandeira, Manuel. "A poética de Gonçalves Dias." *Academia Brasileira de Letras: Conferências* (1948), pp. 111-37.

Blake, Augusto Victorio Alves Sacramento. *Diccionario Bibliographico Brazileiro.* 6 vols. Rio de Janeiro: Imprensa Nacional, 1899.

Bosi, Alfredo. "Anchieta ou as flechas opostas do sagrado." *Dialética da colonização.* São Paulo: Companhia das Letras, 1992, pp. 64-93.

Bosi, Alfredo. "Um mito sacrificial: o indianismo de Alencar." *Dialética da colonização.* São Paulo: Companhia das Letras, 1992, pp. 176-93.

Bourdon, Léon. "Lettres Familières et fragment du Journal intime *Mes sottises quotidiennes* de Ferdinand Denis à Bahia (1816-1819)." *Brasilia* 10 (1958), pp. 143-286.

Broca, Brito. "Alencar: Vida, Obra e Milagre." *Ensaios da mão canhestra.* São Paulo: Polis, 1981, pp. 155-76.

Broca, Brito. *Românticos. Pré-Românticos. Ultra-Românticos: Vida Literária e Romantismo Brasileiro.* São Paulo: Polis, 1978.

Brookshaw, David. *Paradise Betrayed: Brazilian Literature of the Indian.* Amsterdam: CEDLA, 1988.

Campos, Augusto de, and Campos, Haroldo de. *ReVisão de Sousândrade.* Rio de Janeiro: Nova Fronteira, 1982.

Candido, Antonio. "A dois séculos d'*O Uraguai*." *Vários Escritos.* São Paulo: Duas Cidades, 1970, pp. 161-82.

Candido, Antonio. "Estrutura literária e função histórica." *Literatura e sociedade.* São Paulo: Companhia Editora Nacional, 1967, pp. 193-220.

Candido, Antonio. *Formação da Literatura Brasileira (Momentos decisivos).* 2 vols. 2d ed. São Paulo: Martins, 1962.

Carpeaux, Otto Maria. *Pequena Bibliografia Crítica da Literatura Brasileira.* 4th ed. Rio de Janeiro: Edições de Ouro, 1967.

Casa, Maria Luisa Garzón de la. *La Sombra de Cooper sobre el americanismo de Alencar.* Mexico City: Publicación del Instituto Hispánico en los Estados Unidos, 1944.

Cascudo, Luís da Câmara. "O folclore na obra de José de Alencar." *Obras de ficção de José de Alencar.* 16 vols. Rio de Janeiro: José Olympio, 1955, vol. 11, pp. 13-20.

Castello, José Aderaldo. "Os Pródromos do Romantismo." In Afrânio Coutinho (ed.), *A Literatura no Brasil,* 2d ed., 5 vols. Rio de Janeiro: Sul Americana, 1969, vol. 2, pp. 33-63.

Castello, José Aderaldo. "Iracema e o Indianismo de Alencar." José de Alencar, *Iracema.* Rio de Janeiro: José Olympio, 1965, pp. 270-80.

Castello, José Aderaldo (ed.). *A Polêmica sobre "A Confederação dos Tamoios": Críticas de José de Alencar, Manuel de Araújo Porto-Alegre, D. Pedro II e outros . . .* São Paulo: Faculdade de Filosofia, Ciências e Letras da Universidade de São Paulo, 1953.

Cavalheiro, Edgard. *Fagundes Varela.* 3d ed. São Paulo: Martins, 1953.

Chagas, Pinheiro. "Literatura Brasileira—José de Alencar." *Novos Ensaios Críticos.* Praça de D. Pedro: V. M. Porto, em casa da viuva More Editora, 1869, pp. 212-24.

Chaves, Vania Pinheiro. "A glorificação do Tratado de Madrid, forma original da brasilidade de *O Uraguay*." In Basílio da Gama, *Obras Poéticas de Basílio da Gama.* São Paulo: EDUSP, 1996, pp. 452-55.

Chinard, Gilbert. *L'Amérique et le rêve exotique dans la littérature française au XVIIe et au XVIIIe siècle.* Paris: E. Droz, 1934.

Chinard, Gilbert. *L'éxotisme américain dans l'oeuvre de Chateaubriand.* Paris: Hachette et Cie., 1918.

Coutinho, Afrânio. *A Tradição Afortunada (O Espírito de Nacionalidade na Crítica Brasileira).* Rio de Janeiro: José Olympio, 1968.

Coutinho, Afrânio. "Araripe Júnior e o nacionalismo literário." *Euclides, Capistrano e Araripe.* Rio de Janeiro: Ministério da Educação e Cultura, 1959, pp. 77-149.

Coutinho, Afrânio (ed.). *A Literatura no Brasil.* 5 vols. 2d ed. Rio de Janeiro: Sul Americana, 1968.

Coutinho, Afrânio (ed.). *A Polêmica Alencar-Nabuco.* Rio de Janeiro: Tempo Brasileiro, 1965.

Driver, David Miller. *The Indian in Brazilian Literature.* New York: Hispanic Institute in the United States, 1942.

Faria, João Roberto. *José de Alencar e o teatro.* São Paulo: Perspectiva/EDUSP, 1987.

Fernández, Oscar. "José de Anchieta and Early Theatre Activity in Brazil." *Luso-Brazilian Review* 15, no. 1 (Summer 1978), pp. 26-43.

Fiedler, Leslie A. *The Return of the Vanishing American.* London: Paladin, 1972.

Franco, Afonso Arinos de Melo. *O Índio Brasileiro e a revolução francesa: as origens brasileiras da teoria da bondade natural.* Rio de Janeiro: José Olympio, 1976.

Freixeiro, Fábio. "Romantismo e Romantismo no Brasil — caracteres e pontos marcantes." *Minas Gerais, Suplemento Literário,* no. 721 (26 July 1980).

Freixeiro, Fábio. "Iracema, a terra." *Da razão à emoção II: Ensaios Rosianos: Outros ensaios e Documentos.* Rio de Janeiro: Tempo Brasileiro, 1971, pp. 13-24.

Freyre, Gilberto. *José de Alencar.* Rio de Janeiro: Ministério de Educação e Saúde, 1952.

Fróes, Leonardo. *Um outro. Varella.* Rio de Janeiro: Rocco, 1990.

Galvão, Walnice Nogueira. "Indianismo Revisitado." In Afonso Arinos et al., *Esboço de figura: homenagem a Antonio Candido.* São Paulo: Duas Cidades, 1979, pp. 379-91.

Gonçalves, Augusto de Freitas Lopes. *Dicionário Histórico e literário do teatro no Brasil.* Rio de Janeiro: Cátedra, 1979.

Gonçalves, Maria da Conceição Osório Dias. "O índio do Brasil na literatura portuguesa dos séculos XVI, XVII e XVIII." *Brasília* 11 (1961), pp. 97-209.

Gondim, Neide. *A Invenção da Amazônia.* São Paulo: Marco Zero, 1994.

Haberly, David. *Three Sad Races: Racial Identity and National Consciousness in Brazilian Literature.* New York: Cambridge University Press, 1983.

Haberly, David T. "Uma desconhecida Epopéia Indianista." *Revista do Instituto de Estudos Brasileiros,* no. 12 (1972), pp. 81-107.

Hazard, Paul. "De l'Ancien au Nouveau Monde: les Origines du Romantisme au Brésil." *Revue de Littérature Comparée* (1972), pp. 111-28.

Herculano, Alexandre. "Carta a D. Pedro II, sobre 'A Confederação dos Tamoios.'" *Brasília* 10 (1958), pp. 309-22.

Hessel, Lothar, and Raeders, Georges. *O Teatro Jesuítico no Brasil.* Porto Alegre: Ed. da Universidade do Rio Grande do Sul, 1972.

Holanda, Sérgio Buarque de. *Visão do Paraíso: os motivos edênicos no descobrimento e colonização do Brasil.* São Paulo: Companhia Editora Nacional, 1969.

Holanda, Sérgio Buarque de. "Prefácio Literário." *Obras Completas de D.J.G. de Magalhães,* vol. 2. Rio de Janeiro: Serviço Gráfico do Ministério da Educação, 1939, pp. ix-xxxi.

Ishimatsu, Lorie Chieko. "The Poetry of Machado de Assis." Doctoral thesis, Indiana University, 1982 (mimeo.).

Johnson, J. R. "Tupy or Not Tupy: Cannibalism and Nationalism in Contemporary Brazilian Literature and Culture." In J. King (ed.), *Modern Latin American Fiction: A Survey.* London: Faber and Faber, 1987, pp. 41-59.

Johnson, R. "Notes on a Conservative Vanguard: The Case of Verde-Amarelo/Anta." *Hispanic Studies* 4 (1989), pp. 31-42.

Johnson, Randall. "Macunaíma as Brazilian Hero." *Latin American Literary Review* (1978), pp. 38-44.

Jorge, Miguel. *Couto de Magalhães: A Vida de um homem.* Goiânia: Dep. Estadual de Cultura, 1970.

Jucá Filho, Cândido. "Uma obra clássica brasileira." In José de Alencar, *Iracema.* Rio de Janeiro: José Olympio, 1965, pp. 329-402.

Leal, Antônio Henriques. "A Literatura Brasileira Contemporânea." *Locubrações.* São Luiz: Magalhães & cia., 1874.

Leal, Antônio Henriques. *Gonçalves Dias.* Lisbon: Imprensa Nacional, 1874.

Leite, Serafim Soares. "O tratado do Paraíso na América e o ufanismo brasileiro." *Novas Páginas de História do Brasil.* Lisbon: Civilização Brasileira, 1963, pp. 379-82.

Lemaire, Ria. "Re-Reading *Iracema*: The Problem of the Representation of Women in the Construction of a National Brazilian Identity." *Luso-Brazilian Review* 26, no. 2 (1989), pp. 59-75.

Machado, Antônio de Alcântara. "O Fabuloso Bernardo Guimarães." *Cavaquinho e Saxafone (Solos) 1926-1935.* Rio de Janeiro: José Olympio, 1940, pp. 215-24.

Machado de Assis. See Assis, Joaquim Maria Machado de

Magaldi, Sábato. *Panorama do Teatro Brasileiro.* São Paulo: Difusão Européia do Livro, 1962.

Magalhães, Basílio de. *Francisco Adolpho de Varnhagen.* Rio de Janeiro: Imprensa Nacional, 1928.

Magalhães, Basílio de. *Bernardo Guimarães (Esboço Biographico e critico).* Rio de Janeiro: Typ. do Annuario do Brasil, 1926.

Magalhães Júnior, R. *José de Alencar e sua época.* 2d ed. Rio de Janeiro: Civilização Brasileira, 1977.

Martins, Wilson. *História da inteligência brasileira.* 6 vols. São Paulo: Cultrix, 1978.

Massa, Jean-Michel. *A Juventude de Machado de Assis (1839-1870): ensaio de biografia intelectual.* Rio de Janeiro: Civilização Brasileira, 1971.

Matos, Cláudia Neiva de. *Gentis guerreiros: o indianismo de Gonçalves Dias.* São Paulo: Atual, 1988.

Meirelles, Cecília. "Iracema, a Virgem dos lábios de mel." *O Jornal* (1 May 1929).

Meléndez, Concha. *La Novela indianista en Hispanoamérica (1832-1889).* Rio Piedras: Universidad de Puerto Rico, 1961.

Mello, Antônio Joaquim de. *Biografias de Alguns Poetas, e homens illustres da Provincia de Pernambuco.* 3 vols. Recife: Typographia Universal, 1858.

Menezes, Raimundo de. *Cartas e Documentos de José de Alencar.* 2d ed. São Paulo: Hucitec, 1977.

Menezes, Raimundo de. *José de Alencar: literato e político.* São Paulo: Martins, 1965.

Merquior, José Guilherme. *De Anchieta a Euclides: breve história da literatura brasileira - 1.* Rio de Janeiro: José Olympio, 1977.

Meyer, Augusto. "Alencar." *A Chave e a Máscara.* Rio de Janeiro: O Cruzeiro, 1964, pp. 145-58.

Meyer, Marlyse. "Chateaubriand et l''Indianismo' brésilien." *La Bretagne, le Portugal, le Brésil.* Rennes: Université de Haute Bretagne, 1974, pp. 293-313.

Meyer, Marlyse. "Para brindar Iracema . . ." *Pireneus, Caiçaras . . .* São Paulo: Conselho Estadual de Cultura, 1967, pp. 75-85.

Miguel-Pereira, Lúcia. *Prosa de Ficção (De 1870 a 1920)*, Álvaro Lins (ed.). *História da literatura brasileira*, vol.12. Rio de Janeiro: José Olympio, 1950.

Miguel-Pereira, Lúcia. *A Vida de Gonçalves Dias*. Rio de Janeiro: José Olympio, 1943.

Monteiro, Mário Ypiranga. *Fases da literatura amazonense*. Vol. 1. Manaus: Imprensa Oficial, 1977.

Monteiro, Mário Ypiranga. "A Muhraida." *Jornal de Letras*, nos. 193/194 (May 1966).

Montello, Josué. "A 'Comédia Humana' de José de Alencar." *Clã*, no. 21 (December 1965), pp. 5-18.

Moraes, Eugénio Vilhena de. "Segundo Centenário do Nascimento de Frei José de Santa Rita Durão." *Revista do Instituto Histórico e Geográfico Brasileiro*. Tome 99, vol. 153 (1926), pp. 185-218.

Norberto, Joaquim. See Silva, Joaquim Norberto de Souza

Nunes, Cassiano. "Gonçalves Dias e a Estética do Indianismo." *Luso-Brazilian Review* 4, no. 1 (June 1967), pp. 35-49.

Pinto, Neide Gondim de Freitas. *A Representação da conquista da Amazônia em Simá, Beiradão, e Galvez, Imperador do Acre* (mimeo.). Dissertação de Mestrado: PUC do Rio Grande do Sul, 1982.

Polar, Antonio Cornejo. *La novela indigenista*. Lima: Editorial Lasontay, 1980.

Preto-Rodas, Richard A. "Anchieta and Vieira: Drama as Sermon, Sermon as Drama." *Luso-Brazilian Review* 7, no. 2 (December 1970), pp. 96-103.

Proença, M. Cavalcanti. *José de Alencar na literatura brasileira*. Rio de Janeiro: Civilização Brasileira, 1966.

Proença, M. Cavalcanti. "Transforma-se o amador na coisa amada." In José de Alencar, *Iracema* (ed. do centenário). Rio de Janeiro: José Olympio, 1965, pp. 281-328.

Queiroz, Rachel de. "José de Alencar." In José de Alencar, *Iracema* (ed. do centenário). Rio de Janeiro: José Olympio, 1965, pp. 251-53.

Ramos, Frederico José da Silva (ed.). *Grandes Poetas Românticos do Brasil*. São Paulo: Edições Lep Ltda., 1949.

Ramos, Péricles Eugênio da Silva. "Uma Nenia formosa." *Estado de S. Paulo, Suplemento Literário* (12 September 1964).

Rebelo, Marques. *Vida e obra de Manuel Antônio de Almeida*. Rio de Janeiro: Instituto Nacional do livro, 1943.

Reis, Roberto. "Alencar Revisitado." *Minas Gerais, Suplemento Literário* 8, no. 15 (22 September 1979).

Reis, V. Paula. *A Filosofia de José de Alencar*. Rio de Janeiro: Estado de Guanabara, 1964.

Ribeiro, Luis Filipe. *Mulheres de Papel: um estudo do imaginário em José de Alencar e Machado de Assis*. Rio de Janeiro: EDUFF, 1996.

Ricardo, Cassiano. "Gonçalves Dias e o Indianismo." In Afrânio Coutinho (ed.), *A Literatura no Brasil*, 5 vols., 2d ed. Rio de Janeiro: Sul Americana, 1968, vol. 2, pp. 70-107.

Sant'Anna, Affonso Romano de. "O Guarani." *Análise Estrutural de Romances Brasileiros*. Petrópolis: Vozes, 1973, pp. 54-83.

Santiago, Silviano. "Liderança e Hierarquia em Alencar." *Vale Quanto Pesa (Ensaios sobre questões político-culturais)*. Rio de Janeiro: Paz e Terra, 1982, pp. 89-116.

Santiago, Silviano. "Roteiro para uma leitura intertextual de Ubirajara." In José de Alencar, *Ubirajara*, 4th ed. São Paulo: Ática, 1976, pp. 5-9.

Schwarz, Roberto. *Ao Vencedor as Batatas: forma literária e processo social nos inícios do romance brasileiro*. São Paulo: Duas Cidades, 1977.

Silva, Joaquim Norberto de Souza. "Noticia sobre Antonio Gonçalves Teixeira e Sousa e suas obras." *Revista do Instituto Histórico e Geográfico Brasileiro* 39, 1st part (1876), pp. 197-216.

Silva, M. Nogueira da. "Gonçalves Dias e sua influencia na poesia brasileira." *Jornal do Comércio* (13 January 1935), pp. 6-7.

Silva, Odete B. "'I Juca Pirama': o Indianismo de Gonçalves Dias." *Brotéria* 97, no. 11 (November 1973), pp. 403-15.

Sodré, Nelson Werneck. *História da Literatura Brasileira: Seus Fundamentos Econômicos.* 5th ed. Rio de Janeiro: Civilização Brasileira, 1969.

Sommer, Doris. *Foundational Fictions: The National Romances of Latin America.* Berkeley: University of California Press, 1993.

Sousa, J. Galante de. *O Teatro no Brasil.* 2 vols. Rio de Janeiro: Instituto Nacional do Livro, 1960.

Souza, Márcio. *A Expressão Amazonense: do colonialismo ao neocolonialismo.* São Paulo: Alfa Omega, 1978.

Teixeira, Ivan. "Bibliografia ilustrada de *O Uraguay.*" In José Basílio da Gama, *Obras Poéticas de Basílio da Gama.* São Paulo: EDUSP, 1996, pp. 134-40.

Teixeira, Ivan. "Epopéia e modernidade em Basílio da Gama." In José Basílio da Gama. *Obras Poéticas de Basílio da Gama.* São Paulo: EDUSP, 1996, pp. 23-25.

Teixeira, Ivan. "História e ideologia em *O Uraguay.*" In José Basílio da Gama. *Obras poéticas de Basílio da Gama.* São Paulo: EDUSP, 1996, pp. 45-98.

Treece, David. "Introdução crítica à *Muhraida.*" *Anais da Biblioteca Nacional* 109 (1989), pp. 205-25.

Treece, David. "The Indian in Brazilian Literature and Ideas (1500-1945)." Doctoral thesis, University of Liverpool, 1987.

Treece, David H. "Victims, Allies, Rebels: Towards a New History of Nineteenth-Century Indianism in Brazil." *Portuguese Studies* 1 (1985-86), pp. 56-98.

Treece, David. "Caramuru the Myth: Conquest and Conciliation." *Ibero-Amerikanisches Archiv* 10, no. 2 (1984), pp. 139-73.

Varnhagen, Francisco Adolpho de. "Ensaio Histórico sobre as lettras no Brazil." *Florilégio da Poesia Brazileira*, vol. 1. Rio de Janeiro: Academia Brasileira, 1946.

Varnhagen, Francisco Adolpho de. "O Caramurú perante a história." *Revista do Instituto Histórico e Geográfico Brasileiro* 3, no. 10 (2d trimester 1848), pp. 129-52.

Vasconcellos, João Marques de. "Santa Rita Durão, Vítima de Parâmetros Literários." *Minas Gerais, Suplemento Literário*, nos. 719, 720 (12 & 19 July 1980).

Veríssimo, José. "Duas Epopéas Brazileiras." *Estudos de Litteratura Brazileira.* 2d series. Rio de Janeiro: Garnier, 1901, pp. 89-129.

Vianna Filho, Luís. *A Vida de José de Alencar.* Rio de Janeiro: Instituto Nacional do Livro, 1979.

Viegas, Arthur. *O Poeta Santa Rita Durão: revelações históricas da sua vida e do seu século.* Brussels: L'editions d'Art Gaudio, 1914.

Wasserman, Renata R. Mautner. "The Red and the White: The 'Indian' Novels of José de Alencar." *PMLA* 98, no. 5 (October 1983), pp. 815-27.

Williams, Frederick G. *Sousândrade: Vida e Obra.* São Luís: SIOGE, 1976.

Wolf, Ferdinand. *O Brasil literário (história da literatura brasileira)* (trans.). São Paulo: Companhia Editora Nacional, 1955.

Zilberman, Regina. "Natureza e Mulher—uma visão do Brasil no romance romântico." *Modern Language Studies* 19, no. 2 (1989), pp. 50-64.

Zilberman, Regina. "Myth and Brazilian Literature." In Fernando Poyatos (ed.), *Literary Anthropology: A New Interdisciplinary Approach to People, Signs and Literature.* Amsterdam: John Benjamins, 1988, pp. 141-59.

262 • Select Bibliography

Zilberman, Regina. *Do Mito ao Romance: tipologia da ficção brasileira contemporânea.* Porto Alegre: Universidade do Rio Grande do Sul, 1977.

SOURCES FOR THE HISTORY OF INDIGENIST POLICY AND ANTHROPOLOGY

Amazonas, Lourenço da Silva Araújo. *Diccionario topographico, historico, descriptivo da Comarca do Alto Amazonas.* Recife: Meira Henriques, 1852.
Arens, W. *The Man-Eating Myth: Anthropology and Anthropophagy.* New York: Oxford University Press, 1979.
Barber, Francis, and Hulme, Peter (eds.). *Cannibalism and the Colonial World.* Cambridge: Cambridge University Press, 1998.
Beltrão, Luiz. *O Índio, um Mito Brasileiro.* Rio de Janeiro: Vozes, 1977.
Beozzo, José Oscar. *Leis e Regimentos das Missões: política indigenista no Brasil.* São Paulo: Loyola, 1983.
Boxer, C. R. *Race Relations in the Portuguese Colonial Empire 1415-1825.* Vol. 3: *Brazil and the Maranhão.* Oxford: Oxford University Press, 1963.
Chagas, Paulo Pinheiro. *Teófilo Ottoni, Ministro do Povo.* 3d ed. Belo Horizonte: Itatiaia, 1978.
Coutinho, Antonio Carlos da Fonseca. "Noticias da voluntaria reducção de paz e amizade da feroz nação do gentio Mura nos annos de 1784, 1785 e 1786, do Furriel Commandante do destacamento do lugar de Santo Antonio do Maripi, no Rio Jupurá." *Revista do Instituto Histórico e Geográfico Brasileiro* 36, 1st part (1873), pp. 323-92.
Cunha, Capitão Jacinto Rodrigues da. "Diário da expedição de Gomes Freire de Andrada às Missões do Uruguay." *Revista do Instituto Histórico e Geográfico Brasileiro,* 3d series, 16, no. 10 (1853), pp. 137-321.
Cunha, Manuela Carneiro da. "Política indigenista no século XIX." In Manuela Carneiro da Cunha (ed.), *História dos Índios do Brasil.* São Paulo: Companhia das Letras/Secretaria Municipal de Cultura/ FAPESP, 1992, pp. 133-54.
Fernandes, Florestan. *Organização Social dos Tupinambá.* 2d ed. São Paulo: Difusão Européia do Livro, 1963.
Ferreira, Alexandre Rodrigues. *Viagem filosófica pelas capitanias do Grão Pará, Rio Negro, Mato Grosso e Cuiabá.* Conselho Federal de Cultura, Departamento da Imprensa Nacional, 1974.
Gambini, Roberto. *O Espelho Índio: os jesuítas e a destruição da alma indígena.* São Paulo: Espaço e Tempo, 1988.
Garfield, Seth. "'The Roots of a Plant That Today Is Brazil': Indians and the Nation-State under the Brazilian Estado Novo." *Journal of Latin American Studies* 29, part 3 (October 1997), pp. 747-68.
Greenblatt, Stephen J. *Marvelous Possessions: The Wonder of the New World.* Oxford: Clarendon Press, 1991.
Gregório, Irmão José. *Contribuição Indígena ao Brasil.* 3 vols. Belo Horizonte: União Brasileira de Educação e Ensino, 1980.
Grupioni, Luís Donisete Benzi (ed.). *Índios no Brasil.* São Paulo: Secretaria Municipal de Cultura, 1992.
Hanke, Lewis. *Aristotle and the American Indians: A Study in Race Prejudice in the Modern World.* Ontario: Hollis and Carter, 1959.
Hecht, Susanna, and Cockburn, Alexander. *The Fate of the Forest: Developers, Destroyers and Defenders of the Amazon.* London: Penguin, 1990.

Hemming, John. *Amazon Frontier: The Defeat of the Brazilian Indians.* London: Macmillan, 1987.

Hemming, John. *Red Gold: The Conquest of the Brazilian Indians.* London: Macmillan, 1978.

Hulme, Peter. "Caribs and Arawaks." *Colonial Encounters: Europe and the Native Caribbean, 1492-1797.* London and New York: Methuen, 1986.

Humboldt, Alexandre de. *Vues des cordillères et Monumens [sic] des peuples indigènes de l'Amérique.* 2 vols. Paris: J. Smith, Libraire Grecque-Latine-Allemande, 1816.

Hvalkof, Søren, and Aaby, Peter (eds.). *Is God an American? An Anthropological Perspective on the Missionary Work of the Summer Institute of Linguistics (SIL).* Copenhagen and London: International Work Group for Indigenous Affairs and Survival International, 1981.

Kieman, Mathias C. *The Indian Policy of Portugal in the Amazon Region, 1614-1693.* Washington, D.C.: The Catholic University of America Press, 1954.

Lestringant, Frank. *Cannibals: The Discovery and Representation of the Cannibal from Columbus to Jules Verne.* Cambridge: Polity Press, 1997.

Lorentz, Leônidas. *Teófilo Otoni no tribunal da história.* Rio de Janeiro: Author, 1981.

Lugon, Clovis. *A República "Comunista" Cristã dos Guaranis 1610-1768.* 3d ed. Rio de Janeiro: Paz e Terra, 1977.

MacLachlan, Colin M. "The Indian Labor Structure in the Portuguese Amazon, 1700-1800." In Dauril Alden (ed.), *Colonial Roots of Modern Brazil.* Berkeley, Los Angeles, and London: University of California Press, 1973, pp. 199-230.

Marchant, Alexandre. *Do escambo à escravidão: as relações econômicas de portugueses e índios na colonização do Brasil 1500-1580.* São Paulo: Cia. Editora Nacional, 1943.

Martins, Edilson. *Nossos Índios Nossos Mortos.* 4th ed. Rio de Janeiro: Codecri, 1982.

Mello, Gen. Raúl Silveira de. *Para além dos bandeirantes.* Rio de Janeiro: Biblioteca do Exército, 1968.

Moreira Neto, Carlos de Araújo. "A Política Indigenista Brasileira Durante o século XIX" (mimeo.). Doctoral thesis, Faculdade de Filosofia, Ciências e Letras de Rio Claro, São Paulo, 1971.

Nimuendajú, Curt. "As Tribos do Alto Madeira." *Jornal de la Société des Américanistes de Paris*, no. 17 (1925), pp. 137-72.

Pagden, Anthony. *The Fall of Natural Man: The American Indian and the Origins of Comparative Ethnology.* Cambridge: Cambridge University Press, 1982.

Paiva, Mário Garcia de. *A Grande Aventura de Rondon.* Rio de Janeiro: Instituto Nacional do Livro, 1971.

Pinto, Estevão. "Introdução à história da antropologia indígena no Brasil (século XVI)." *América Indígena* 17, no. 4 (October 1957), pp. 341-85, and 18, no. 1 (January 1958), pp. 17-49.

Ribeiro, Darcy. *Os Índios e a Civilização.* 4th ed. Petrópolis: Vozes, 1982.

Spix, J. B. von, and Martius, C.F.P. von. *Viagem pelo Brasil* (trans.). Rio de Janeiro: Imprensa Nacional, 1938.

Steward, Julian H. *Handbook of South American Indians.* Washington, D.C.: U.S. Government Printing Office, 1948.

Sweet, David "Native Resistance in 18th-Century Amazonia: The 'Abominable Muras' in War and Peace." *Radical History Review* 53 (1992).

Treece, David. "Indigenous Peoples in Brazilian Amazonia and the Expansion of the Economic Frontier." In David Goodman and Anthony Hall (eds.), *The Future of Amazonia: Destruction or Sustainable Development?* London: Macmillan, 1990, pp. 264-87.

Treece, David. *Bound in Misery and Iron: The Impact of the Grande Carajás Programme on the Indians of Brazil.* London: Survival International, 1987.

Williams, Suzanne. "Land Rights and the Manipulation of Identity: Official Indian Policy in Brazil." *Journal of Latin American Studies* 15, part 1 (May 1983), pp. 137-61.

GENERAL WORKS ON HISTORY, LITERATURE, AND CULTURE

Albouy, Pierre. *La Création Mythologique chez Victor Hugo.* Paris: José Corte, 1968.

Alden, Dauril (ed.). *Colonial Roots of Modern Brazil.* Berkeley, Los Angeles; London: University of California Press, 1973.

Alonso, Cláudia Pazos. "The Uses and Implications of the Master/Slave Image in Alencar's Novel *Senhora.*" *Ipotesi. Revista de Estudos Literários* 1, no. 1 (July/December 1997), pp. 25-36.

Anderson, Benedict. *Imagined Communities: Reflections on the Origin and Spread of Nationalism.* London: Verso, 1991.

Arinos, Afonso, et al. *Esboço de figura: homenagem a Antonio Candido.* São Paulo: Duas Cidades, 1979.

Auerbach, Erich. *Mimesis: The Representation of Reality in Western Literature.* Princeton: Princeton University Press, 1953.

Barberis, Pierre. *Mythes Balzaciens.* Paris: Armand Colin, 1972.

Barberis, Pierre. *Balzac: une mythologie réaliste.* Libraire Larousse, 1971.

Barman, Roderick J. *Brazil: The Forging of a Nation, 1798-1852.* Stanford, Calif.: Stanford University Press, 1988.

Bell, Michael. *Primitivism.* London: Methuen, 1972.

Berger, John. *Ways of Seeing.* London: BBC/Penguin, 1972.

Boas, George. *Essays on Primitivism and Related Ideas in the Middle Ages.* Baltimore: Johns Hopkins University Press, 1948.

Calmon, Pedro. *História do Brasil.* Rio de Janeiro: José Olympio, 1959.

Carone, Edgard. *A República Velha (Evolução Política).* São Paulo: Difusão Européia do Livro, 1971.

Carone, Edgard. *A República Velha (Instituições e Classes Sociais).* São Paulo: Difusão Européia do Livro, 1970.

Carvalho, José Murilo de. *Teatro de sombras: A política imperial.* São Paulo: Vértice, 1988.

Cascudo, Luís da Câmara. *Dicionário do Folclore Brasileiro.* Rio de Janeiro: Edições de Ouro, 1972.

Costa, Emília Viotti da. *The Brazilian Empire: Myths and Histories.* Chicago and London: University of Chicago Press, 1985.

Costa, Emília Viotti da. *Da Monarquia à república: Momentos decisivos.* São Paulo: Grijalbo, 1977.

Cruickshank, John (ed.). *French Literature and Its Background.* 6 vols. London, Oxford, and New York: Oxford University Press, 1969; vol. 4: *The Early Nineteenth Century.*

Cunha, Euclides da. *Rebellion in the Backlands (Os Sertões).* London: Picador, 1995.

Dudley, Edward, and Novak, Maximillian E. (eds.). *The Wild Man Within: An Image in Western Thought from the Renaissance to Romanticism.* Pittsburgh: University of Pittsburgh Press, 1972.

Faoro, Raymundo. *Os Donos do Poder: Formação do Patronato Político Brasileiro.* 2 vols. 5th ed. Porto Alegre: Globo, 1979.

Ferreira, Aurélio Buarque de Holanda. *Novo Dicionário da Língua Portuguesa.* Rio de Janeiro: Nova Fronteira, 1975.

Franco, Jean. *Spanish American Literature since Independence.* London: Ernest Benn, 1973.

Franco, Maria Sylvia de Carvalho. *Homens livres na ordem escravocrata.* São Paulo: Instituto de Estudos Brasileiros, 1969.

Freyre, Gilberto. *Sobrados e Mucambos: Decadência do Patriarcado Rural e Desenvolvimento do Urbano.* 2d ed., 3 vols. Rio de Janeiro: José Olympio, 1951.

Frye, Northrop. *Anatomy of Criticism: Four Essays.* Princeton: Princeton University Press, 1957.

Graham, Richard. *Patronage and Politics in Nineteenth-Century Brazil.* Stanford, Calif.: Stanford University Press, 1990.

Guimarães, Manoel Luís Salgado. "Nação e civilização nos trópicos: O Instituto Histórico e Geográfico Brasileiro e o projeto de uma história nacional." *Estudos Históricos* 1 (1988), pp. 5-27.

Holanda, Sérgio Buarque de (ed.). *História Geral da Civilização Brasileira.* 7 vols. São Paulo: Difusão Européia do Livro, 1964.

Hugo, Victor. *Oeuvres Complètes.* Paris: Nelson, 1952.

Jobim, Anísio. *A Intellectualidade no extremo norte.* Manaus: Clássica, 1934.

Levin, H. *The Gates of Horn: A Study of Five French Realists.* New York: Oxford University Press, 1966.

Lins, Ivan. *História do Positivismo no Brasil.* 2d ed. São Paulo: Companhia Editora Nacional, 1967.

Ludmer, Josefina. *El género gauchesco: un tratado sobre la patria.* Buenos Aires: Sudamericana, 1988.

Lukács, Georg. *The Historical Novel.* London: Merlin Press, 1989.

Lyra, Heitor. *História de Dom Pedro II: 1825-1891.* 3 vols. Belo Horizonte: Itatiaia, 1977.

Magalhães Júnior, R. *Três Panfletários do Segundo Reinado.* São Paulo: Companhia Editora Nacional, 1956.

McClelland, J. S. (ed.). *The French Right (From de Maistre to Maurras).* London: Jonathan Cape, 1970.

Mercadente, Paulo. *A Consciência Conservadora no Brasil: contribuição ao Estudo da Formação Brasileira.* 3d ed. Rio de Janeiro: Nova Fronteira, 1980.

Morison, Samuel Eliot. *The European Disocovery of America: The Southern Voyages 1492-1616.* New York: Oxford University Press, 1974), pp. 210-35.

Mota, Carlos Guilherme. *Ideia de Revolução no Brasil (1789-1801): estudo das formas de pensamento.* 3d ed. São Paulo: Cortez, 1989.

Mota, Carlos Guilherme. *Ideologia da cultura brasileira (1933-1974): (Pontos de partida para uma revisão histórica).* 4th ed. São Paulo: Ática, 1978.

Ortiz, Renato. *Cultura brasileira e identidade nacional.* São Paulo: Brasiliense, 1986.

Rodrigues, José Honório. *História da História do Brasil*, vol. 2, tome 1: *A Historiografia Conservadora.* São Paulo: Editora Nacional, 1988.

Rodrigues, José Honório. *Conciliação e reforma no Brasil: um desafio histórico-cultural.* 2d ed. Rio de Janeiro: Nova Fronteira, 1982.

Rodrigues, José Honório. *Independência: Revolução e Contra-revolução* 4 vols. Rio de Janeiro: Francisco Alves, 1975, vol. 2.

Schwarcz, Lilia Moritz. *As Barbas do Imperador: D. Pedro II, um monarca nos trópicos.* São Paulo: Companhia das Letras, 1998.

Schwarz, Roberto. *Misplaced Ideas: Essays on Brazilian Culture.* London: Verso, 1992.

Sevcenko, Nicolau. *Literatura como missão: tensões sociais e criação cultural na Primeira República.* São Paulo: Brasiliense, 1983.

Shumway, Nicolas. *The Invention of Argentina*. Berkeley, Calif.; Oxford: University of Carolina Press, 1991.

Skidmore, Thomas. *Black into White: Race and Nationality in Brazilian Thought*. New York: Oxford University Press, 1974.

Sousa, Octávio Tarquínio de. *História dos Fundadores do Império do Brasil*. 2d ed., 7 vols. Rio de Janeiro: José Olympio, 1957, vol. 6.

Torres, João Camillo de Oliveira. *A Democracia Coroada: Teoria Política do Império do Brasil*. 2d ed. Petrópolis: Vozes, 1964.

Valin, Cleusa Aparecida. "Escritores Brasileiros: Filmografia." *Filme Cultura* 20 (May-June 1972).

Weinstein, Barbara. *The Amazon Rubber Boom: 1850-1920*. Stanford, Calif.: Stanford University Press, 1983.

Index

About the Author

DAVID TREECE is Reader in Brazilian Studies and Director of the Centre for the Study of Brazilian Culture and Society, King's College London, where he has lectured since 1987. He has worked with a number of Latin America–related NGOs, including the human rights organization Survival for Tribal Peoples. He is a translator of Brazilian fiction and poetry; he teaches and researches on Brazilian popular music, poetry, literature and other aspects of Brazilian culture. He is also an editor of the international *Journal of Latin American Cultural Studies*.

ISBN 0-313-31125-0

EAN

9 780313 311253

90000>

HARDCOVER BAR CODE